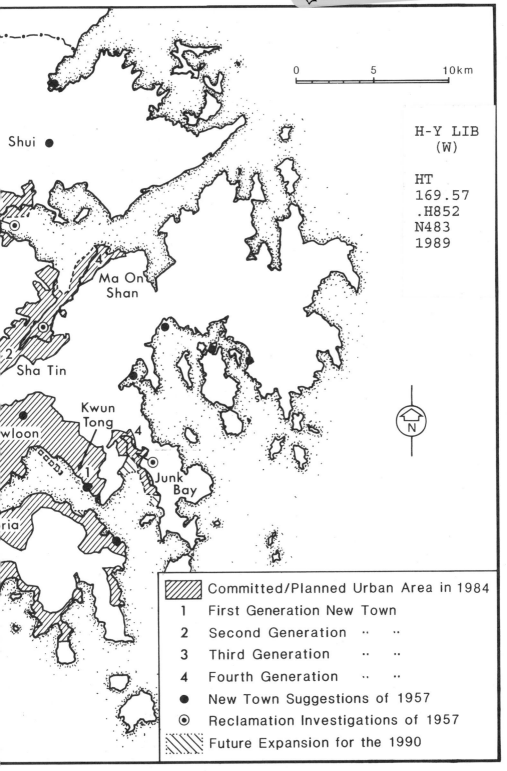

0   5   10km

Shui ●

Ma On
Shan

Sha Tin

Kwun
Tong

wloon

4

1

Junk
Bay

ria

N

▨▨▨ Committed/Planned Urban Area in 1984
1   First Generation New Town
2   Second Generation ··   ··
3   Third Generation   ··   ··
4   Fourth Generation   ··   ··
●   New Town Suggestions of 1957
⊙   Reclamation Investigations of 1957
▨▨   Future Expansion for the 1990

HONG KONG'S NEW TOWNS
A SELECTIVE REVIEW

HONG KONG'S
NEW TOWNS

A Selective Review

ROGER BRISTOW

HONG KONG
OXFORD UNIVERSITY PRESS
OXFORD   NEW YORK
1989

Oxford University Press

Oxford New York Toronto
Petaling Jaya Singapore Hong Kong Tokyo
Delhi Bombay Calcutta Madras Karachi
Nairobi Dar es Salaam Cape Town
Melbourne Auckland

and associated companies in
Berlin Ibadan

© Oxford University Press 1989

'Oxford' is a trade mark of Oxford University Press

First published 1989
Published in the United States
by Oxford University Press, Inc., New York

Library of Congress Cataloging-in-Publication Data
Bristow, Roger 1938–
Hong Kong's new towns: a selective review/
Roger Bristow. p.   cm.
Bibliography: p.
Includes Index.
ISBN 0-19-584210-3: $29.95 (U.S.: est.)
1. New towns—Hong Kong—History.
2. City planning—Hong Kong—History. I. Title.
HT169.57.H85B75   1989
307.7'68'095125—dc20
89-8761
CIP

British Library Cataloguing in Publication Data
Bristow, M. R. (Michael Roger), 1938–
Hong Kong's new towns: a selective review.
1. Hong Kong. New towns
I. Title
307.7'68'095125
ISBN 0-19-584210-3

Printed in Hong Kong by Calay Printing Co.
Published by Oxford University Press, Warwick House, Hong Kong

Preface

MANY visitors to Hong Kong and China, when travelling by the modern international trains between Kowloon and Guangzhou and passing through the mountain barrier to the north of the harbour area, become quite amazed by the extent of high-density urbanized development that now occupies much of their overland route through the New Territories to the Chinese frontier. Although many do not realize it, what they are witnessing is a major part of the current Hong Kong new-town programme, for today three of Hong Kong's eight new towns lie along that transportation corridor, and over two million people live there on land which less than two decades ago was either uninhabited, rural, or remained as sea-bed in the shallow inlets of the South China Sea.

The new towns of Hong Kong, therefore, are a major achievement by world standards — to aim to relocate three and one half million people over some thirty years requires a major programme of commitment and public and private investment. Here is a story which deserves to be known. The Hong Kong new-town programme can easily take its place alongside others in the rest of the world. Those in Britain, France, the United States, Israel, or Singapore are better known and more publicized programmes. Up till now, only academic papers, short articles, and official publications have appeared on the subject of Hong Kong's new towns, and no detailed or major study has yet been done. It is as a contribution to filling this void that this book has been researched and written.

While the new-town story in Hong Kong is quite properly thought of as an achievement of the past two decades, its origins, in fact, go back much further. Hong Kong is, after all, a major international city. It should, therefore, come as no surprise that foreign influences on urban development have affected the Territory, since the planners, both Chinese and expatriate, have until recently been without exception trained overseas. The fundamental reasons for new-town development in Hong Kong are accordingly much the same as elsewhere; decongestion of the urban core and the building of better social, living, and working environments are basic requirements, and well-worn concepts like self-containment and balanced development are adopted as basic tenets of new-town design. Discovering why these have not necessarily been achieved is among the fascinating aspects of investigating the fortunes of new-town planning in Hong Kong.

It may, however, come as a surprise to some to learn that new-town planning in Hong Kong has even older and more honourable antecedents. The global garden-city movement of the early years of this century, for example, out of which it is commonly agreed the new-town concept developed, in fact, has its echoes in Hong Kong in the 1920s development of Kowloon Tong. Also, Sir Patrick Abercrombie, of London new-towns fame, made his own contributions to the planning history of the

Territory and its new-town development as a planning consultant in 1948. Thus the global waves of successive planning fashions have swept into Hong Kong's planning and development processes for many decades, and so form part of the background to its current new-town story.

But it would be wrong to treat Hong Kong's new towns as mere derivatives of some overall global conceptual model. The interest of and the value behind Hong Kong's story lies in the way that the global ideas have been imported, adopted, modified, or even rejected in order to produce the new towns of today, in an attempt to match these ideas to the built-form representation of contemporary Hong Kong life-style with its peculiarities of the oriental, high-density, and intensely urban mode. Ultimately, the Hong Kong new towns are but a reinterpretation of all these factors. This unique result can be examined in all kinds of ways, whether in terms of overall concept, design, plan, administration, financing, or any other of the thousand and one ways in which the development of new settlements and communities becomes interesting and informative. It is hoped that at least some of the more important of these investigations have been attempted here.

It is also appropriate at this stage to comment a little on the structure of this book. Its strength might be said to lie in its treatment of the administrative and procedural history of the Hong Kong new towns. Design and the development of the new social communities are touched on; but they are not the focus, which lies instead in the area of planning methodologies. The book does not claim to be fully comprehensive; for reasons of space, and the complexity and amount of source material available, a complete and detailed examination of all eight Hong Kong new towns would not be practicable.

Therefore, this book is deliberately selective. The overall conceptualization of the new-town programme is examined at length and detailed analysis of individual towns and of specific topics has been undertaken illustratively rather than comprehensively. Thus, earlier phases of new-town development, after initial experiments at Luen Wo Market and Kwun Tong, are represented by analysis of Sha Tin and Tuen Mun (Castle Peak) new towns in some detail, with a sideways glance at Tsuen Wan. Later phases are covered by reviews of Junk Bay and Tin Shui Wai, the last two of the Hong Kong new towns to be designated. This effectively leaves out the so-called expanded market towns of Tai Po, Sheung Shui/Fanling, and Yuen Long, which were begun in the early 1970s and finally incorporated into the new-town programme in 1978/9. It also omits the many smaller-scale developments associated with some of the rural townships and island centres in the Territory. In both of these cases it is suggested here that their status as new towns *per se* is not entirely valid, though this is arguable; and that in any event, their planning histories are repetitions of their big brothers' elsewhere, and hence can safely be put to one side, at least in terms of the requirements of this book.

How, then, would one sum up the Hong Kong new-town story? Certainly it is a major one — homes for three and one half million people over three decades at a cost of some HK$78 billion is a major public investment by any standards. Indeed, the provision of homes has proved to be a main driving force, together with the periodic provision of industrial land. Many commentators have already noted that the construction of the Hong Kong new towns has been basically motivated by this need for public housing. Their sites have been made available as a part of successive Territory-wide searches for yet more housing land, and their every shift and change has been at the whim of the public housing programme. Thus, as with many other new-town programmes elsewhere in the world, there has been a dominant purpose in mind, and the planning processes have, therefore, become predominantly reactive in nature. Within any overall strategies for developing Hong Kong, or as prescriptive possibilities as prototypes and tools of urban design or for social development, their role in any proactive sense has proved to be much more problematical, open to debate, and certainly subservient to their major purpose; indeed, there are contributions to this debate to be found in this text.

Nevertheless, whatever the current debates about the present form and content of Hong Kong's eight new towns, and whatever the outcome of current discussions on the future strategic development of Hong Kong into the twenty-first century, to which parts of the new-town programme may well be required to contribute, the story at the end of the 1980s is sufficiently advanced to deserve telling. For all its blemishes, it is a story of which the present Hong Kong government deserves to be proud; and the openness and frankness with which the government's professionals and others have welcomed the research upon which this text is based has enabled at least this academic review to be made and is worthy of commendation. In presenting this interpretation of the story, I hope that others will now be able to make their own assessment of the place of Hong Kong's achievements within the global new-town movement, and to learn something more of the reasons and justifications behind any assessment and appreciation of the value of Hong Kong's efforts.

Manchester and Hong Kong   ROGER BRISTOW
September 1988

Contents

Tables

Figures

Plates

Acknowledgements

THE author and publisher wish to make grateful acknowledgement to the following for permission to reproduce copyright material: Brian Clouston and Partners Hong Kong Limited, Cumbernauld Development Corporation, Mansell Publishing, the Singapore Housing Authority, Sun Hung Kai Properties Limited, and Wong & Ouyang (HK) Limited. Additional assistance on various technical matters is also acknowledged from Maunsell Consultants Asia and Scott Wilson Kirkpatrick & Partners. Transcripts, translations, and reproductions of Crown copyright materials published in the United Kingdom appear by kind permission of the Controller of Her Majesty's Stationery Office in London. Transcripts, translations, and reproductions of Crown copyright materials held in the Public Records Office, Hong Kong, the Town Planning Office, and the Survey and Mapping Office of the Buildings and Lands Department, the Territory Development Department, the Housing Department, and the Lands and Works Branch of the Secretariat, together with the quotation of extracts from Hong Kong Hansard and other government reports, and photographs from the Hong Kong Government Information Services and the Hong Kong Housing Authority all appear by kind permission of the Hong Kong government. Readers should note that references in the Notes for each Chapter which refer to Hong Kong government departments refer to titles before the reorganization of 1989–90, which introduced a new environmental branch and Planning Department to the government's organization.

The author would also like to thank personally the many officials and professional officers in the various branches of the Hong Kong government who made the whole research enterprise possible by their willing assistance and advice. Special thanks must go however to just two — Michael Wigglesworth and Peter Pun, then in the Town Planning Office and Territory Development Department respectively, without whom the telling of the Hong Kong new-town story would not have proved possible.

The author's personal gratitude is also due for the continued support that has been given over the years by colleagues in the University of Manchester, both from the Department of Planning and Landscape, and the Department of Geography, whose cartographer Graham Bowden made such an excellent job of many of the figures for this book. The research, too, would not have been possible without the generosity of the British Academy, the Nuffield Foundation, and the University of Manchester, all of whom provided research funding to allow the various periods of necessary field research to take place.

Finally, any acknowledgements would not be complete without reference to those friends who have helped in a more personal way to get an author's efforts under way. Firstly, thanks must go to those university colleagues in the two institutions in Hong Kong who have always made the overseas visitor feel so very welcome — with special thanks to both Bruce Taylor and Anthony Yeh with whom over the years many ideas and opinions have been swapped. Thanks are also due to those old Manchester planning graduates in Hong Kong who have both tolerated and encouraged the seemingly endless intrusions of their old tutor, and especially to Stanley Yip, who so often provided that critical creative spark for further ponderings on the workings of planning in Hong Kong.

As always, however, the bringing to fruition of academic endeavour depends mostly on motivation, and for that one returns again to thank those personal friends in both Hong Kong and Manchester without whom the ability and atmosphere to undertake personal academic research would remain untapped.

1. The New-town Idea

THERE is always a certain difficulty when discussing the subject of new towns, whether or not in Hong Kong, and that concerns the matter of definition. It is very necessary to be quite precise about just what kind of new settlement or development justifies the label 'new town', for any examination of the literature about the subject betrays a wide variety of ideas. To be pedantic for a moment, it can be pointed out quite legitimately that all urban places at some time in their lives have justified the label 'new', just as Hong Kong itself did as the city of Victoria in the early years after the foundation of the colony in 1841. In terms of this book a more promising start might be to look back at local usages of the term to see if there are any common characteristics that might be discerned about how and why the term was used and understood. New towns are therefore treated here from the Hong Kong point of view; but it must be said immediately that these views originated elsewhere, and it is to the origins and their influences upon ideas and practices in Hong Kong that we must turn.

Perhaps one of the first points to note in any Hong Kong context is an ambiguity arising from language. The local Cantonese term for 'new town' is written as 新市鎮, which in common parlance is taken to mean a new settlement of almost any size, contrary to the Western understanding that a certain minimum size of settlement is to be expected. Thus, when coming across references to new towns in Hong Kong, especially when the source has been translated from a Chinese original, the reality may well not be what a Westerner would normally assume. Good examples of this are the early references to the new agricultural settlement of Luen Wo Market, founded in the years immediately after the Second World War. While referred to variously at the time as a model village, townlet, or new market town, in reality, it consisted of approximately one hundred houses grouped around a single market building, all built by a single developer (see Fig. 2.1). Thus, while it was also referred to sometimes as a new town in government official publications, it was, and is, vastly different in scale and concept to the large cities that now form the major building blocks of Hong Kong's current new-town programme, and which form the basis of contemporary Hong Kongers' conceptions of the realities of modern new-town development.

There is, however, another point about the terminology currently being applied to the new-town programme of present-day Hong Kong, which again concerns the precision of the definitions being used under the general term 'new town'. Although virtually all the current major urban development taking place in Hong Kong's New Territories is now subsumed within the general term 'the new-town programme', more careful examination of the urban development processes actually being implemented suggests that more precise definitions can be usefully applied, for as in many other countries the nature of the development activity does vary from location to location. Thus, the development of new towns in Hong Kong concerns the development of major new cities (in the population range of 200 to 800,000) on virtually virgin undeveloped sites, or the complex problem of transforming an existing major settlement into a major city which at the same time is becoming absorbed into the main urban area (the situation for the Tsuen Wan/Kwai Chung/Tsing Yi complex which will have grown from 80,000 to almost a million on completion). Yet again, as a further contrast, since the mid-1970s, the programme has also included a series of quite major rural settlement expansion programmes which have embraced three of the former rural market towns in the New Territories. Thus, the current term 'new town' in Hong Kong covers some variety of planning and design solutions, even though their origins in terms of policy have often been the same. Partly to devote enough attention in detail to the programme while remaining within manageable size, more attention here has deliberately been paid to what might be termed the 'purer' form of new-town development in Hong Kong — that is, the development of the major cities on 'virgin' sites, rather than expansions of existing substantial settlements. But the various groupings should not be thought of separately, since the whole programme of urban expansion into the New Territories has always been conceived of as one by the Hong Kong government, and its different manifestations have been developed and set out within a continuous process of learning, design, and implementation.

There is also one further point of clarification that it is useful to sort out here at the beginning. This concerns the more common nomenclature used elsewhere with regard to the cycles of new-town development in Hong Kong. A quick glance at the endpapers in this book shows that it is suggested here that there have been four successive major cycles of new-town development in Hong Kong. The first, at Kwun Tong, was certainly thought of at the time of its commencement in the late 1950s as new-town development, even though now many would argue that in design and concept terms it was not. The second saw the commencement of schemes at Tsuen Wan, Sha Tin, and Castle Peak (now Tuen Mun), which were looked at jointly in a reclamation study at the end of the 1950s; followed in the mid-1970s by the decisions to expand the major rural townships. Finally, the 1980s saw the initiation of a fourth cycle of new development associated with the go-aheads for Junk Bay and Tin Shui Wai, together with major further expansions of Sha Tin at Ma On Shan. Yet common usage in Hong Kong and elsewhere often refers to only first- and second-generation new towns; the first being associated with the major public housing expansion programme of the early 1970s and taken as the big three of Tsuen Wan, Sha Tin, and Tuen Mun and sometimes including the market towns, while the subsequent development of the 1980s is collectively termed as the second generation. However, for reasons of accuracy and more detailed explanation, we shall not generally use this simplified concept.

Although we can now say that we have settled some possible problems on the term 'new town' as used in Hong Kong, we have yet to agree on a more general definition of the idea implicit in the term. Just what is a new town? Galantay has suggested that:

New towns are planned communities consciously created in response to clearly stated objectives. Town creation as an act of will presupposes the existence of an authority or organisation sufficiently effective to secure the site, marshal resources for its development, and exercise continued control until the town reaches viable size.[1]

The beauty of Galantay's definition is that it is both simple and general. The purpose of the town may be quite various — Golany in his typology of new towns lists 16 examples,[2] but all are characterized by the common conscious decision, whether by public authority or private capital, to initiate new urban development on a major scale on a site not yet urbanized. Often, new-town building is triggered by deeper and more fundamental changes in the structure of the society whose needs they are partially designed to meet. Moreover, it is not accidental that new urban forms emerged out of the industrialization of the nineteenth century, or the impact of technology upon the development of twentieth-century towns and cities. In this, the new towns have pointed the way as prototypes for the subsequent more general remodelling and reshaping of our existing urban stock, and have been utilized as laboratories to test out the sometimes theoretical notions of the planners and architects that society has entrusted with their development. It is in the nature of things that such experiments have not always quite worked as expected!

Such comments lead to the consideration of motives — after all, the main point of Galantay's comment is that a major act of will is involved, an act that often has both short-term and long-term antecedents. Thus before we can realistically look in detail at how and why new towns came to be seen in Hong Kong as an answer to strategic planning and social development questions, it is necessary to ask from where the then policy-makers derived their ideas and objectives. In other words, Hong Kong necessarily fitted into a wider network of international planning thinking of the day, and perhaps not surprisingly, given the Territory's place as a crossroads of international travel and ideas together with the influence of Britain as the colonial power, it can be readily demonstrated that much of the basis of the early new-town thinking on Hong Kong came from overseas. As we shall see, while it is true to state that by far the dominant ideal proved to be the British new-town programme of the post-war years, this rapidly came to be blended with more local notions that derive from a longer history of urban development in the colony, which in turn contained some earlier echoes of ideas imported from overseas.

Reviews of the history of modern town planning have suggested that 'the idea of town planning was something that presented itself as an answer to a group of problems that had arisen in contemporary urban life',[3] and that through the reform of the physical environment, aspects of the varied social evils of the time that were recognized might be alleviated or removed. In nineteenth-century Britain that desire was partially articulated through the search for new urban utopias, either the portrayal of imaginary schemes or the building of experimental projects like Saltaire, Bourneville, or Port Sunlight, which flourished under the influences of the few philanthropic manufacturers who wished to provide improved living conditions for their captive work-forces.

Once the factory system had become thoroughly established, new model towns appeared mostly in the realms of theory rather than practice, but there were occasional individual attempts to create new industrial settlements; and, eventually, as the deficiencies of existing towns became more widely realised, resettlement of industry and population on new sites, at any rate on a small scale, became recognised as one practical contribution to urban improvement. The possibility of such resettlement was never quite forgotten in the nineteenth century, though it was not prominent, and there was a body of thought, writing and practice which makes a clear and unbroken, though tenuous chain, linking the new towns begun after the Second World War with some of the small, carefully-regulated settlements of the early factory system.[4]

The late nineteenth century also saw the parallel development, particularly in London, of the 'salubrious suburb' as a reaction to the by-law street that had so monotonously covered large tracts of the later Victorian industrial cities of Britain. Bedford Park, at Turnham Green in west London, is but one pioneering example of how the suburban estate developer attempted to generate a sense of 'village', community, and intimacy by the placing of individualized buildings and a street layout which emphasized the incorporation of the garden into the town through conscious landscaping. Yet such environments initially remained only the privilege of the few, against the regulated terraces and the grid-iron street patterns of the Victorian industrial town.[5]

Thus, even before Ebenezer Howard set out the ideas in *Tomorrow: A Peaceful Path to Real Reform*[6] which are often regarded as the real foundation stone for the subsequent new-town planning movement, for the evolution of a new urban form that he termed 'the garden city', there was already an attempt under way in Britain to devise new means of better integrating the best features of town and country into a single urban form. It was the 'garden' suburb of the early nineteenth century that led the way. Even Howard's name 'the garden city' was not new, for it is now known to have been used in the United States as early as 1869.[7] Howard's real significance, however, was not that he was able to disseminate his ideas widely in print, but that his writing led to the founding of the Garden Cities Association in 1899, within which he was able slowly to gain sufficient support to translate his dreams into realities. The reality began with the creation of Letchworth Garden City, set in the Hertfordshire countryside to the north of London, and started in 1903. The designs were by two of Howard's disciples, Barry Parker and Raymond Unwin,[8] major pioneers of early British town planning, who took on the basic form:

a garden city is a town designed for healthy living and industry; of a size that makes possible a full measure of social life, but not larger; surrounded by a rural belt; the whole of the land being in public ownership or held in trust for the community[9]

and turned it into the living prototype for all subsequent British new-town experiments.

But if 'Letchworth was brought into being as an idealistic community to demonstrate just what could be achieved by the application of Howard's principles to a nascent community',[10] two more new towns were to be created in inter-war Britain which had even more decisive influences upon subsequent post-war new-town planning history.

The first of these was the second effort of Howard's disciples, begun in 1919 at Welwyn Garden City, also in Hertfordshire on one of the main railway routes north out of London.

In Welwyn the purpose was to create a new town independent of London but with the intention of solving the housing problem of that city ... Welwyn marked the beginnings of the subsequent 'new towns' policy,[11]

to be formulated first in the war-time plans of Sir Patrick Abercrombie for the reconstruction of London.

The object of the company will be to build an entirely new and self-dependent industrial town, on a site twenty-one miles from London, as an illustration of the right way to provide for the expansion of industries and population of a great city. Though not the first enterprise of the kind (the main idea having already been exemplified at Letchworth), the present project strikes a new note by addressing itself to the problems of a particular city.[12]

From the tone of the wording there is a certain arrogance about the righteousness of the authors, yet there is little doubt that, were they to know it, they were indeed building the prototype for the post-war British new town.

Despite all the mistakes and obstacles, the towns were built, and because they were built, they provided an enduring three-dimensional expression of the general ideas for all the world to see. In the process of development, the towns also pioneered some significant planning innovations, including use and density zoning, a form of ward and neighbourhood planning, employment of an agricultural green belt to control urban size containment, and unified land ownership for the purpose of capturing rising land values for the benefit of the residents.[13]

Welwyn Garden City, and Letchworth before it, provided a valuable set of insights into at least some of the problems of designing and building for a major new urban community from scratch. But Welwyn, in particular, has to be looked at in the specific context of 1930s Britain. It was a town built by private capital through the vicissitudes of the world economic slump of that period. As such it was not, in fact, notably successful (by 1946 it still only had a resident population of 18,000), and acted as a warning for the new post-war British planners against expecting the private enterprise development model to prove capable of initiating and sustaining a large-scale new-town programme for the post-war years. These difficulties were, in fact, also replicated elsewhere, particularly in the United States, where again private enterprise development of major new settlements had a very chequered history of successes and failures in the years between the two World Wars of the first half of this century.

The second major British inter-war experiment concerned the development of the satellite town of Wythenshawe, begun as a municipal enterprise by the City of Manchester under the guidance of Barry Parker in 1919, but not finally completed until well after the end of the Second World War. Parker's town is noteworthy not only for its housing designs which set new standards for English municipal housing, but perhaps more importantly for setting out an alternative development mechanism and urban growth strategy to that demonstrated concurrently by Howard and his followers. Not only did it show some of the possibilities of public enterprise, but strategically it represented a compromise, for to work it had to be placed close to the parent city (about ten miles centre to centre) for it was neither envisaged nor designed as an independent entity. There was no need to embed it within its rural surroundings, but rather it was to look towards the parent city to which it was bound by improved transport links that twentieth-century technology now provided — in Wythenshawe's case this was first a reserved-track tramway, to be replaced later by the express bus and the motor car.

The new town could now remain dependent upon the viability of the parent city to support it, and as such became an integral part of a new and wider metropolitan region. Wythenshawe also represented a triumph for British municipal enterprise, and its success led to later pressures from Manchester City Council to be allowed to build a new town of their own in the post-war new-town building programme.

The concepts of the new town and the satellite town in fact proved to be fairly slow ideas to gain planning currency in inter-war Britain. Yet support for them grew, alongside a slow recognition of the need to consider congestion and controlled decentralization as plausible and required planning policies for the largest cities.

The view was gaining increasing influence that individual towns could not be planned in isolation and the principle of decentralisation was studied in relation not only to the diffusion of the town among suburbs, but also to regional and even national planning. . . Emphasis was passing from the design of residential estates to the more general problem of the allocation of land among various uses. Planning was beginning to be seen less in terms merely of visual appearance, health and amenity, and more in terms of social and economic function.[14]

These views were minority ones in inter-war Britain, but their growth and their more general acceptance as the 1930s passed proved to be of major significance in the development of a recognizable national town-planning policy in Britain, which was to come to the fore in the war years in the Barlow and Scott reports.[15]

But in early twentieth-century Britain the development of completely new towns was rare, and something of a luxury. The chief importance of the garden-city movement lay in the translation of the Victorian suburb into the garden suburb so beloved of the British inter-war speculators. Once again it was Parker and Unwin who began the process by designing 'what can fairly be the aesthetic culmination of that movement',[16] the Hampstead Garden Suburb of 1905 in north London. But it was the fact that electric traction and the motor car made it possible for all but the poorest workers to have a house in a garden some miles from the workplace that ultimately proved more important.

Suburbia ceased to be the prerogative of the few...or who happened to be employed by a philanthropic industrialist, and the garden suburb, not the garden city, became the typical housing pattern of the twentieth century.[17]

Howard's city in a garden had become transformed into a city of gardens, however maligned or belaboured the concept often turned out to be in the speculators' literature of the 1930s.

In terms of relevance to Hong Kong however, perhaps the best illustration of the importance of Howard's influences lies in the rapid dissemination and copying of his ideas overseas. Nearby in Europe, *die gartenstadt* in Germany, *la cité-jardins* in France, and the *cuidad-jardin* of Spain were just three derivations of the ideas brought from England; while further afield, the United States,[18] Australia,[19] and Japan[20] all boast examples of developments copied and translated into their own cultural idioms of the day. In fact, Hong Kong too was influenced by the planning fashion, and the use of the garden-city model in the building boom of the 1920s represents one of the first major manifestations of overseas' design influences in the planning of Hong Kong.

The Garden City Movement in Hong Kong

As pointed out elsewhere,[21] the first real attempt at imposing rigorous standards for building in Hong Kong arose out of public health concerns. In Britain, too, various attempts had been made to combat the worst effects of slums in Victorian times:

Sanitarians like Chadwick [who also came to Hong Kong] sought to improve conditions by such measures as providing proper sewerage and water supplies, fixing minimum standards for street-widths and construction of dwellings, and appointing medical officers of health.[22]

Identical measures were suggested for Hong Kong in Chadwick's own reports of 1882 and 1902 on sanitary conditions in the Territory, but in the main the laying out and building of Hong Kong followed the traditions of the British colonial city and the Chinese tenement shop-house, rather than any direct allegiance to the more innovative planning practices gradually evolving in Britain and elsewhere. The one major exception to this generalization, however, was the garden suburb as a concept of suburban living, which arrived in Hong Kong in the 1920s.

One of the first developments of this kind to gain a mention was a small scheme at Ho Man Tin in 1921, where the Kowloon–Canton Railway opened a small railway halt 'handy to their district for the Garden City residents',[23] but most attention came to be focused upon the Kowloon Tong scheme first promoted by a Mr. Ede in 1920, and finally completed, with government assistance, over a decade later in the early 1930s.

Papers sent to London in 1930 (when financial assistance was being sought to help the promoters to complete the scheme) tell us that the scheme's object was:

to build houses for persons of small means ... and to enable such persons to reside in their own houses or homes in more healthy and pleasant surroundings ... The scheme contemplated a small community living in detached or semi-detached houses with small gardens, and enjoying a common recreation ground.[24]

Associated with the newly formed Kowloon Resident's Association, initial attempts were made to get government to allow the erection of cheap detached houses, 'particularly wooden houses as elsewhere in the Far East'[25] on the colonial bungalow model. But by October 1921 the matter had been finalized in that:

it has been decided that the best method of carrying the scheme into effect is for the Government to do the work of levelling and draining the area and to sell the land to a company, which under certain restrictions, will arrange for the building of houses[26]

designed on conventional British lines (see Plate 1a).

Fuller details of the scheme were given in a special report, 'Homes for the People: Garden City Scheme, A Hundred Applications Already', (*China Mail*, August 1921). It stated:

there is good news for the man of moderate means who, hankering after a home of his own with a bit of garden attached, can't afford to buy one outright. Since last October a committee upon which some of Hong Kong's soundest financiers are represented has been pushing along towards maturity a project for transforming 62 acres [25 hectares] of waste land at Kowloon Tong into a garden city where comfortable houses may be acquired under a system of provident purchase. Negotiations with the Government are not quite complete but it is hoped that the scheme will be under way next month. In the majority of instances not more than four houses will be built upon each acre [10 per hectare] so that there will be plenty of elbow room and ample space for the activities of the suburban gardener. Standard designs for the dwellings are being prepared but it will not be impossible, under certain conditions, to modify these to fit in with the individual taste of the applicant. It is expected that the houses will cost between $8,000 and $12,000, and a scale of payments has been worked out which will make it possible for the applicant to become the owner of his home within a reasonable period of years. The site is handy to the railway at Kowloon Tong and there will be communication with Kowloon itself by both train and road. There is a good deal of surveying and levelling to be done before the building operations are begun and probably it will be twelve months before the first house stands erected. In the meantime a company is to be floated to provide the capital necessary to put the scheme into execution and the public will be invited to subscribe. The fact that the heads of the Hong Kong and Shanghai Bank, Messrs. Jardine Matheson & Co., and the Union Insurance Society of Canton are members of the building committee warrants the financial soundness of the proposition and the circumstance that about a hundred applications for houses have been received already indicate that the venture will be warmly welcomed by those it is especially designed to assist.[27]

In fact the initial success of the scheme (see Fig. 1.1 and Plates 1a and 1b) prompted others to suggest similar schemes to government in the conditions of the property boom of the early 1920s. Schemes for Ma Tau Wai, Kai Tak, and Kowloon Tsai were outlined, again on the basis of European-style dwellings at 10 to the hectare, by both Chinese and European promoters; but two events caused them to fail. Firstly, the downturn in the property market of the mid-1920s put an end to successful property speculation, and secondly, the implementation by government in 1922 of a Town Planning Scheme for the development of the whole of the Kowloon peninsula, which in general frowned upon the land-extensive garden suburb in favour of the more traditional colonial city grid-iron layout lined with the traditional Chinese shop-house, caused government to turn down the promoters' suburban schemes in favour of its more conventional layout plans. In fact density arguments and the maximum utilization of valuable land were already beginning to influence the planning thinking of government in Hong Kong; a theme that dominated all subsequent planning in the Territory.

Examination of Kowloon Tong, which, because of lease controls and its location beneath the present airport flight path, remains largely intact today, reveals nothing especially revolutionary in contemporary planning terms. Indeed, the layout of crescents and avenues (see Fig. 1.1), with its nostalgic English place-names to remind their original inhabitants of home, is perfectly derivative on a small scale of the layouts pioneered by Raymond Unwin in Letchworth and Hampstead Garden Suburb and set down for all to see and copy in the British government's *Housing Manual* of 1919.[28] Yet for Hong Kong, the introduction of the detached two-storey residence set in its own individual garden, with the adjacent communal open space in the tradition of the English village green, was as revolutionary as it was inappropriate. It was an experiment that was not to be repeated, except perhaps in the bastardized forms of the speculative housing estates built in the New Territories during the building boom of the early 1980s. Yet, as a proposal only, the idea reappeared again briefly after the Second World War when textile interests proposed a small garden-suburb scheme on a site adjacent to Sha Tin station in the early 1950s. Although this scheme remained as a proposal only, it proved to be the

Fig. 1.1 Plan of Kowloon Tong Garden Suburb in 1983. The layout of the
original scheme lies between Norfolk Road, Waterloo Road, Boundary
Street, and the railway. It was later extended northwards.

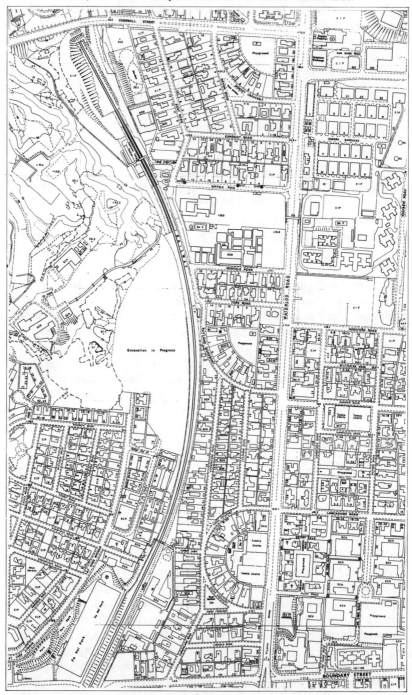

Source: Plan Sheets 11-NW-B4 and 11-NW-D2, Survey Division, Buildings and Lands
Department, Hong Kong government. Crown copyright reserved.

initial spark that set off the interest in Sha Tin as a possible new-town site for post-war Hong Kong.

Other Formative Influences

It would be wrong to assume that the British garden-city movement was the only and major influence upon twentieth-century international new-town building. There were also other important agents at work in the years between the wars. Le Corbusier, for instance, in his ideas for rebuilding French cities, published as *La Ville Radieuse* in 1933,[29] challenged the whole ethos of low-density development for urban areas which dominated twentieth-century British planning. He preferred his own concept of the vertical city with densities of up to 1,000 people to the hectare, placing his super-blocks on stilts to maximize the air, space, and greenery that were meant to surround them. Later, this particular concept of urban living was to exert great influence through its adherence to the rigid segregation of functional areas, vehicular–pedestrian separation, and the hierarchical ordering of the traffic system based on the speed of movement. Not only was it to be demonstrated in his later work on the capital of the Punjab in India, Chandrigah, but the spacing of high-rise towers in a surrounding parkland proved influential in British post-war city planning, and generated urban forms which were to give rise to a whole new debate about the appropriateness of high-rise living in the city.[30] These urban forms greatly influenced later Hong Kong planning.

In North America, the garden suburb rapidly evolved in the 1920s into a unique derivative of its own, which in turn was to travel back across the Atlantic to reinfluence later British urban planning ideas after the war. Sunnyside Gardens in Queens, New York, designed by Clarence Stein and Henry Wright in 1924 was:

a uniquely successful demonstration of how the garden suburb idea can be adapted to the grid typical of most American cities. At Sunnyside the unit of development was the block rather than the house ... thus containing the germ of the development pattern that was to reach fuller expression at Radburn [in 1928] where the super-block was the basic unit of development.[31]

Radburn was conceived of as a town for the motor age and became famous as the first proponent of full vehicle/pedestrian segregation.

Radburn's professional acceptance lies in its combination of ideas derived from the Garden Suburb tradition with new strategies developed to deal with the potentially disruptive pressure that the automobile brings to cities.[32]

To achieve this the houses were grouped around culs-de-sac which gave the vehicular access, but their main frontages were reversed, so that they looked out on to the central green spaces which contained the foot- and cycle-path networks interconnecting the various parts of the suburb, rather than traditionally overlooking the road frontages. In 1929, Clarence Perry, working in New York, went one step further and advocated the formation of self-contained neighbourhoods of 5,000 people with a community centre, schools, and other institutions at its centre — within four minutes walk of any building,[33] thus creating the pedestrian neighbourhood concept, unfettered and undisturbed by the competition of the motor car. This was to form a cornerstone of all subsequent new-town planning.

These ideas came together collectively in the Suburban Resettlement Program of Roosevelt's New Deal in the United States of the 1930s. Perhaps the best examples were to be found in the layouts of the new settlements of Greenbelt, Maryland, and Greenhills, Ohio. These government-sponsored towns were the first experiments in the combined development of the three basic ideas of modern community planning, from which Hong Kong's new towns also derive, namely, the garden city, the Radburn principle of segregation, and the clustering of the neighbourhood unit. As such, they also proved to be influential on British designers when their new-town planning programmes began in earnest in the years immediately after the Second World War.

The British New Towns

By including a section which describes in some depth the development of the British new towns in a book about new-town development in Hong Kong, one needs first of all to offer some words of explanation. These can, in fact, be provided by Pierre Merlin, writing in 1969 prior to the promotion of a new-town policy for France:

England is often quoted as an example by town planners in many countries, some of its plans — such as the Abercrombie Plan — and its new towns being world famous. The new towns, conceived as part of a national policy of land development (the Barlow Report of 1940) and a regional town planning policy deriving from this (the Abercrombie Plan of 1944), comprise one of the most remarkable achievements in town planning in the last twenty years.[34]

In short, because of the magnitude of the new-town programme in Britain and its timing just after the Second World War, as well as its long planning pedigree, it rapidly became in the immediate post-war decades an object of international admiration, and professionally generated a considerable number of visits from overseas planners wishing to adapt British expertise to their own requirements. Planners and engineers from Hong Kong were a few of those visitors during the 1940s and 1950s,[35] although their concerns were more precise than general questions about new-town planning as a whole. Mostly they were required to examine specific questions of interest to Hong Kong at that time, such as the mechanisms for compulsory purchase of land or the design of factory industrial estates (needed for the development of Kwun Tong, see Fig. 2.3).

A more subtle point, but one of importance in influencing Hong Kong's own new-town programme, was the involvement at the time of the British professional planning schools in the new-town design process. The necessity to produce a number of simultaneous master plans led to the development of major new British consultancy partnerships, many of which evolved around the professors of the various university planning schools. Thus, there was a direct link between education, professional training, and the new innovations in practice, which allowed the planning students of the day to be involved at the grassroots of the new urban planning and thinking in Britain. Not only were the ideas to spread from Britain, but as the students themselves became professionals and many moved overseas, so they took the new ideals and utilized them as their overseas careers developed. This diffusion process affected Hong Kong as much as elsewhere, both through the influence of expatriate British planners, and through the training in Britain of Hong Kong's Chinese professionals. So, developments in Britain can be represented as the post-war foundation of the idea of instituting and implementing new towns as a conscious and effective part of a national urbanization strategy. For Britain, that conscious effort began in 1940. Barlow's commission[36] had then proposed the creation of a central planning agency:

to facilitate redevelopment of congested urban areas, to decentralize or disperse both industries and industrial population from such areas, and to encourage a reasonable balance and diversification of industrial development throughout the various regions of Great Britain. Among the methods advocated in pursuing these objectives were garden cities or garden suburbs, satellite towns, trading estates, and further development of existing small towns or regional centres.[37]

Abercrombie's eight new towns proposed in 1945 and set in the Outer Country Ring around Greater London were the first to give expression to that general national strategy, and formed the prototype for similar decentralization proposals in other British wartime reconstruction plans such as those for Manchester and Clydeside.

Abercrombie's *Greater London Plan* rested upon five basic assumptions:[38] that no new industry would be admitted to London and the Home Counties except in special cases; that decentralization of persons and industry from the congested centre should take place; that the total population of the whole area would not increase; that the port would remain; and that new planning powers would become available. All except the fourth were relevant to the new-town idea. The new towns which Abercrombie argued for as an essential part of his overall concept for the planning of London were to be placed in the outer of four concentric rings of development, beyond the containment ring of the Green Belt.

Finally, beyond the Green Belt Ring, and extending to the boundary of the area, is the Outer Country Ring containing distinct communities situated in land which is open in character and in prevailing farming use. While this general character will be preserved, it is intended to allow in this ring a more generous expansion of existing centres and also to provide the sites for new satellites: both expansion of old and new growths will be occasioned by the decentralised population and industry from inner London.[39]

As Abercrombie reported in his preamble:

the choosing of sites for new communities is always an exhilerating side of the planner's work: it is impossible to escape from the sequel that opportunity is to be offered for the creation of a town which will embody the latest ideas of civic design. The London Region is fortunate in possessing two such new communities, Letchworth and Welwyn, both due to the genius of the late Ebenezer Howard.[40]

The legacy was now to be drawn upon by a new generation of town designers in the pursuit of building new communities out of the despair of the destruction of Britain's wartime cities.

Abercrombie did however include in his plan, 'some sample studies, as an indication of what is meant by the general proposals when they are worked out in detail',[41] and one of these was for the new satellite-town concept. This concept was illustrated by a case-study design for the proposed new town at Chipping Ongar in Essex some 21 miles east of Central London (see Plate 2a). The study[42] suggested a pattern of six neighbourhood communities of about 10,000 each (based on the school requirements laid down by the Ministry of Education) surrounding a town centre, and set out at a net residential density of 75 persons to the hectare. Each neighbourhood also contained 70 to 100 shops, and was broken down into smaller housing areas by green wedges or park strips. The road system was also hierarchical, consisting of main traffic routes with looped distributors into each neighbourhood, off which were set the residential roads to serve the houses. Public transport was to serve the main distributor loops. It was suggested that the main centre should be pedestrianized and contain the town's shopping and business buildings and the civic centre. The new shops were to be planned around paved courtyards planted with flowers and shrubs as a pedestrian precinct. The service roads and car parks were situated behind the shops. The open-space plan was based on the existing river and stream system on the site and formed an organic network of green into which the neighbourhoods were set, of which playgrounds and playing fields (set at 3.6 hectares per 1,000 population) were considered important elements. Finally, industrial employment was allowed for in a trading estate set in a valley on its own to the north-east of the town site, so that any smoke or other pollution might be carried away from the town by the prevailing wind. Chipping Ongar was, in fact, never built (the proposal was abandoned on cost grounds in 1946), but its ideas formed a precursor for the design of Stevenage, the first of the London first-generation new towns, which began construction in December 1946 following a blueprint originally prepared in the new Ministry of Town and Country Planning, and finalized in the master plan of 1946.[43]

But before any new town could actually be built in the new post-war Britain, legislation was required to set up appropriate mechanisms for implementing the schemes. The New Towns Act of 1946 was the result of that requirement, and it rapidly followed the setting up and reporting of the New Towns Committee chaired by Lord Reith,[44] which had been asked:

to consider the general questions of the establishment, development, organization and administration that will arise in the promotion of New Towns in furtherance of a policy of planned decentralisation from congested urban areas; and in accordance therewith to suggest guiding principles on which towns should be established and developed as self-contained and balanced communities for work and living.[45]

The legislation articulated a new principle for urban development in Britain. Whereas before, the key features of British cities were largely the outcome of a multitude of private development decisions by private individuals, companies, and public enterprises operating broadly within a free market system of land and property, with only marginal changes implemented from time to time by the planners: new towns were now to operate differently. Factors such as the essential character and make-up of the area were now to be decided theoretically in advance, thus setting an ideal framework for urbanization within which the private market was expected to operate. That framework was in turn related to overall social goals, which derived from the roles that each new town was expected to perform in the planning strategy that had been determined by government for the wider metropolitan region of which each was designed to form a part.

The primary purpose of the new legislation was, of course, to translate the theoretical framework into a manageable administrative machine capable of transforming policy and plan into reality.

To build new towns, machinery had to be created for organizing, planning, and decision making, for financing, site acquisition, building, and management. This instrument had to be responsive to policies of the central government, yet able to serve local and regional needs and at the same time cope with all the traditional entrepreneurial problems on a vaster scale.[46]

It needed to be planner, financier, developer, and manager all rolled into one. The chosen vehicle proved to be the public development corporation, independent of both local and central government, but effectively controlled in practice by its purse-strings, which were held by the Treasury — it being funded principally by public loans authorized by them.

New Town Design

While many aspects of the post-war British new towns proved influential, it is fair to state that it was in matters of design that their significance was felt upon subsequent events in Hong Kong. It is therefore appropriate to say something here of that evolving story both before and during the period of the development of the Hong Kong towns.

We should perhaps first recapitulate by reminding ourselves that in meeting the decongestion objective, which in 1945 was undoubtedly uppermost in the thinking of the United Kingdom government, a number of possible urban development strategies could have been utilized. Galantay lists these as four in his book about new towns:

the development of alternative growth regions; the creation of a parallel, or twin, city; independent new towns; or, satellite towns.[47]

Here, in this book, we are primarily concerned with the last two:

Independent new towns are deliberately located as far from the metropolis as to discourage commuting to its centre. Consequently, such new towns must offer a complete range of urban activities and services. Job provision must correspond to the number of potential job seekers. Social and cultural equipment must be of sufficient variety to entice migration from the metropolis. This implies above all a large and lively town centre. Satellite towns are comprehensively planned new communities within the metropolitan area which maintain strong functional ties with the centre city. Good communications are vital and commuting time to the centre should not exceed 30 to 45 minutes. Job provision need not be balanced, since the satellite profits from the job market of the metropolis. It also remains dependent on the central city for higher level services, speciality shops, cultural and entertainment facilities.[48]

The problem for Hong Kong, as we shall see, was that its planners tried to implement its new-town programme on the basis of the first criteria, when reality in most instances forced the second to operate.

From these two definitions it can be seen that new-town location crucially determines the way in which the town might be expected to function relative to the parent city. Simply, it is unwise to expect a new town to operate as an independent self-contained centre when it is geographically located near to the main urban core. To compete in such a location the new must be able to rival the old from a position of near equality — in strategic planning terms one has moved towards the twin-city concept rather than towards that of the parent city and the independent or satellite new town. Nevertheless, as we have seen, with some exceptions, Britain's new towns were largely designated as part of a wider metropolitan planning process to control the form and character of the wider city region. The core city was to be decongested, and balanced new towns were to be created around the periphery to aid that process. To perform that task an altogether higher purpose was set than just that of providing a better environment by urban design.

Our responsibility ... is rather to conduct an essay in civilisation, by seizing an opportunity to design, solve and carry into execution for the benefit of coming generations the means for a happy and gracious way of life.[49]

These broader aims were reflected in the design features which the towns shared in common:

moderate size; relatively low density; gross unmixed land uses; unified public land ownership; fairly rapid comprehensive development; and an emphasis on more open space.[50]

But the use of some of the best of Britain's professional planning talent meant that in detail the design of the new towns brought into reality a series of explorations of new urban forms and designs for community living which were both varied and exciting, as new methods of urban development and social engineering came to be tested out in the British countryside.

The concept of the new town in the British context was now clear. As expressed by the Minister (Silkin) concerned with setting up the programme in 1946,

by satellite towns I mean self-contained, balanced communities for both work and living. Steps are being taken to ensure that by careful organization and concerted action, and with the powerful assistance of governmental influences, this object is secured; and that, although they will remain within the sphere of influence of the metropolis for certain specialised and major purposes, e.g. university life or theatreland, these towns will not repeat the mistake of the dormitory suburbs. They will be built beyond the green belt in pleasant surroundings and on inexpensive land; and be of a size to provide homes, industry, shopping and recreation ready to hand and under attractively planned conditions. They will recreate the type of town that has form and develops a character of its own.[51]

It represented the epitome of a new life-style now that the war was over. It was now up to the planners to determine the reality of what that new life-style should be.

Houghton-Evans[52] has pointed out that the form of the British new towns evolved quite rapidly from the initial ideas set out in Abercrombie's prototype of 1944, and that a number of quite radical experiments in urban form came to be tried out in the later generations of British new towns (see Figs. 1.2 and 1.3). In the first-generation new towns the schematic form that emerged for the town as a whole consisted of a hierarchy of spaces which,

starting with a basic dwelling cluster, combine with a primary school and a few shops to form a neighbourhood. Neighbourhoods with district shopping [and higher order facilities such as the secondary school and the branch library] combine into a district. Districts together with central and industrial areas unite to form a town. To this hierarchy of spaces is married a hierarchy of routes; foot and cycle ways at the lowest level penetrating close to the heart of localities; principal roads at the highest level routed between built-up areas, through the 'green wedges' which kept them apart.[53]

There are however limits to such a form. Given that overall densities are set by the requirements of the two-storey house with its own garden (the first-generation new towns averaged out at 85 persons to the hectare), the association of each primary school within a child's walking distance of home meant that neighbourhoods were limited to about 5,000 people

Fig. 1.2 New-town conceptual forms: (a) grid iron, as in parts of 1920s Hong
        Kong, and the Singapore Prototype Model of 1982 (see Fig. 1.3); (b)
        radial with neighbourhoods, as with most early UK new towns (see Plate
        2a); (c) rectangular, as with Cumbernauld, UK (see Plate 2b), Sha Tin
        (see Plate 5b), and Tuen Mun (see Plate 6b); (d) figure-of-eight linear,
        as Runcorn, UK; (e) poly-nuclear, similar to Milton Keynes, UK
        (see Fig. 1.3).

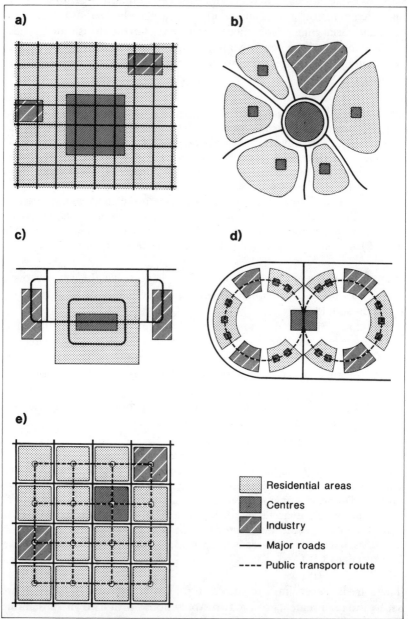

Source: Based partly on Fig. 5.21 in W. Houghton-Evans, 'Schemata in British Town
        Planning' in G.E. Cherry (ed.), *Shaping an Urban World: Planning in the Twentieth
        Century* (London, Mansell, 1980), p. 116.

Fig. 1.3 Overseas influences on new-town planning in Hong Kong: (a) Cumbernauld, UK, 1956 (see Plate 2b); (b) Milton Keynes, UK, 1970; (c) Singapore prototype new town, structural model, 1982.

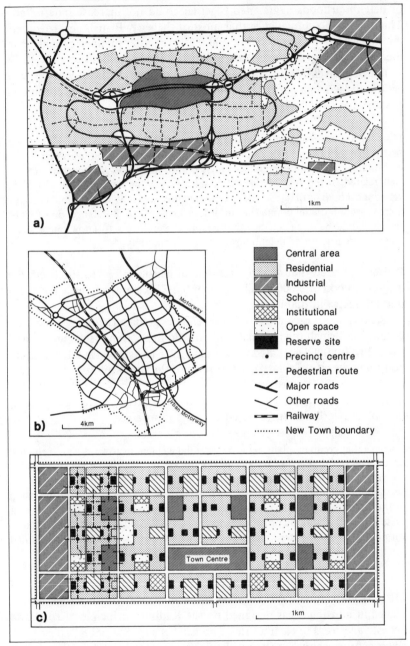

Sources: Based on figures from W. Houghton-Evans, 'Schemata in British Town Planning' in G.E. Cherry (ed.), *Shaping an Urban World: Planning in the Twentieth Century* (London, Mansell, 1980), Figs. 5.14 and 5.26, pp. 111 and 120; and K.J. Tan, C.T. Loh, S.A. Tan, W.C. Lau, and K. Kwok, 'Physical Planning and Design' in A.K. Wong and S.H.K. Yeh (eds.), *Housing a Nation: Twenty Five Years of Public Housing in Singapore* (Singapore, Maruzen Asia, 1985), Plate 8, p. 103.

only, or with careful design could be integrated into two-school/10,000 person units. These constraints in turn meant that within reasonable limits the optimal size of the town as a whole was also limited, since the number of neighbourhoods aggregated together could not increase indefinitely. Thus, it was no coincidence that most of the early British new towns remained with populations below 100,000, even after planned expansion in the 1960s over and above their original design populations.

The objectives of this initial approach to structuring the new towns were set out in 1951 in a paper by Anthony Minoprio, who was the consultant planner for Crawley New Town in West Sussex.

How far are we in agreement about neighbourhood planning? We might agree, firstly, that the ideal neighbourhood should be beautifully laid out, with well designed buildings and landscaping; secondly, that it should be convenient, safe and well related to the rest of the town; thirdly, that its development should be economical both in first cost and in maintenance; fourthly, that it should contain a cross section of the population in order to ensure social balance; and fifthly, that it should be of such a size that people can easily get to know one another and acquire a sense of neighbourliness and community.[54]

It was suggested that at a net residential density of 85 to the hectare a neighbourhood of 5,000 should cover about 77 hectares and measure about one kilometre in diameter.

The one major exception to this general design pattern amongst the first-generation British towns was Cumbernauld in Scotland (see Fig. 1.3 and Plate 2b); finally designated in February 1956 to assist with relieving congestion in the city of Glasgow. The form of the site, a hill top with a gross area of only 376 hectares, with its clearly defined limits, led Hugh Wilson to conceive of the town as a compact urban centre containing a population of only 50,000, surrounded by recreation areas.

I believe that compact planning is an essential element of town design if the full advantages of urban living and the maximum contrast between town and country are to be obtained. A compact plan can well result in the discarding of the neighbourhood unit concept. In saying this I am not arguing against the provision of [facilities] related to the needs of the various groups of people, but rather that these facilities should be provided where they are needed and not in accordance with any system of pattern making ... In other words the facilities are provided for the people and not the people arranged to make use of the facilities.[55]

In Wilson's final design, the average net residential density utilized was 210 persons to the hectare (or over twice the density of the other towns), placed in housing areas designed on the Radburn principle of road and pedestrian access to each house or housing group. Shopping, apart from single 'corner shops' in the residential areas, was centralized in a single linear centre along the hill ridge (see Plate 2b), with a pedestrianized area above road access and car parking on the lower levels below. The town's road system was also designed hierarchically, consisting of local development roads to provide access to buildings, feeder roads but with no frontage development, main town roads as radials, and trunk roads linked at grade-separated junctions. The practice of not providing footpaths alongside the principal roads, in fact, was to cause problems later, as people tended to try to walk in the roads, despite the provision of a separate pedestrian network, especially where their routing was more direct. Industry and open space were also integrated into the design scheme. The town design did not however prove wholly successful, and when it was expanded in the 1970s its original design concepts were modified in favour of more traditional neighbourhood-based development patterns.[56]

The ideas set out at Cumbernauld were carried further in the theoretical design produced by the London County Council in 1961 for their proposed new town at Hook in north-east Hampshire, and in Buchanan's analytical schemes for the better integration of high-intensity transport networks and urban form produced for the Ministry of Transport under the title *Traffic in Towns* and published by the government in 1963.[57] They later were to influence early Hong Kong planning, particularly in Tuen Mun. Wilson, meanwhile, continued his exploration of the unified town in his 1966 design for Skelmersdale in central Lancashire. In this scheme, the main residential area consisted of a rectangular block some four by one and a half kilometres, accommodating about 61,000 people at a net density of between 100 and 175 persons to the hectare. To the west and south-east were placed subsidiary settlements for 14,000 and 5,000 respectively.

Perhaps the most fully developed example of this urban form, however, came with Tom Hancock's 1970 design for the major expansion of the city of Peterborough, as one of the final sequence of London new towns planned in the 1970s.[58] Here, the designated area was divided into four townships, each being developed for a population of between twenty and thirty thousand. Each of these had its own centre, and was in turn divided into residential neighbourhoods with district facilities provided. In the centre, stretching for nearly 16 kilometres was set a linear park:

the first attempt to create what Ebenezer Howard, the original advocate of new towns, conceived as their ultimate form — the Social City, consisting of a cluster of separate townships or 'garden cities' in a green setting, each largely self-sufficient but all closely linked with one another and with a somewhat larger 'central city' [the old original town in the Peterborough case], the whole sustaining a regional centre of big-city calibre.[59]

The final expression of urban clustering at this macro-scale can be found in Matthew, Johnson-Marshall and Partners' scheme for Central Lancashire New Town, produced in 1974. The essential structure of the new development consisted of villages of about 3,000, combined to make districts of about 20,000, which again were combined to make five townships, each with ultimate populations of between 52,000 and 130,000; the whole city having an ultimate design population of nearly half a million. The lowest size units were derived from an attempt to find a block that was identifiable both physically and socially, yet large enough to be viable as a base for local facilities. However, a much better choice of facilities was argued to become available at the 20,000 threshold, which was why the district requirement was built into the design. The form of the townships on the other hand was largely dictated by the large amount of existing settlement already on the site, including the major town of Preston, and the wish to keep green-belt separations in being between the major proposed township elements. Regrettably perhaps, the changing population trends for the north-west of England in the 1980s have meant that this final expression of the hierarchical urban design system is now most unlikely to see full implementation in its designed form. But it can still be noted that new-town design itself moved a long way in Britain in the 30 years since Chipping Ongar, and by the mid-1970s the hierarchical breakdown of town form had fully matured into a comprehensive expression of urban functions through the location and layout of the built form.

However, the second generation of the British new towns in the late 1960s was also important for another design reason. Following Buchanan's transport planning ideas of 1963, the towns were used as laboratories in the new search for satisfactory design relationships between the increasing traffic requirements of the day and an appropriate urban form. While many now look back on this era as one dominated by the transport modellers and the comprehensive land-use transportation model, and later by the subsequent reaction and the growth of interest in public transport integration in the town, the new towns again were utilized to explore in the real world some of the theoretical design relationships that were developing between transport networks and related urban forms. Thus, a renewed search for better and more efficient urban layouts once again had the British new-town planners in the vanguard.

The central design problem, which was well recognized, was how to relate the cellular structure of the town neighbourhoods or the Radburn traffic-free housing areas with the linear requirements essential to the organization and operation of efficient public transport and road networks. The key to the puzzle, whatever the technology of the transport system proposed, came to be seen through the functions, locations, and spacing of the pick-up or entry points on the transport network, for it was there that the interchange between the transportation system and the walking-based or parking structures of the town's components cells had to take place. This puzzle gave rise over the next decade to a number of practical and theoretical design solutions.[60]

Perhaps the best known, and partly because it proved to be unique, was that employed in the Runcorn master plan of 1967 by Arthur Ling[61] (see Fig. 1.2d). While the principle of neighbourhoods was still followed in the basic layout of the town, each of about 8,000 persons at 175 to the hectare, they were distributed rather like beads on a string, the string being formed by a dedicated busway arranged in the form of a figure of eight, with an enclosed air-conditioned multi-level town centre forming the focus at the centre of the two loops. Local centres were then distributed at about half-mile intervals, and all houses within each of the communities were arranged within five-minute's walk of the central transit stop. The important innovation was that the reserved-track public transport system was routed centrally through the heart of each neighbourhood, and the layout of each area was consciously designed around the central transfer point. Access for the car, and the normal road network were seen as peripheral to this overriding design principle. Thus, while an urban motorway system was also included to surround the town, with a central link tangential to the town centre to service it, the housing layouts — many in the form of inward-looking courtyards, focusing upon the segregated public transport layout — were all designed to shift the more usual modal split in transport usage in the town away from the use of the car for urban journeys towards the use of the bus, in order to produce an almost equal modal split for the town. For the first time, the structures of the 'walking' or 'motoring' town were rejected in favour of a planned balance between the use of the private car and public transport, which provided the central theme of the plan around which all the functions of the town were centred. In particular, by the routing of the busway through the centre of each neighbourhood cell, the layout encouraged a new intimacy between the walking network at the local level and the transport system for the whole town at the higher level; a link which was designed to exclude the car, and which has proved durable in the subsequent history of the functioning of the town after completion.

Sir Hugh Wilson took the 'beads-on-a-string' principle further in his own subsequent designs for further British new towns. His first attempt, in 1965, was for a theoretical study for a city in the area that was eventually to be chosen as the site for the new city of Milton Keynes in Bedfordshire, north of London.[62] Here, the idea of urban cells nucleated around the public transport stop was also tried, but with private transport gaining access tangentially from each side of the individual cells in order to avoid level junction conflicts with the public transport routeway. This was developed in practice in the Radburn-style residential cells that he included in his later 'bead' design for Redditch (near Birmingham),[63] where the social facilities became associated with the transport stops rather than the neighbourhood centres of earlier plans. The concept was taken still further in linear form in Wilson's plans for the new town of Irvine in Scotland.[64]

Wilson and Wolmersley likened the concept to a necklace, the beads of varying shape and size representing the districts and the string the public transport system. In the Redditch case, the public transport network formed a variant of the figure-of-eight pattern used in Runcorn (although not all of it on exclusive right-of-way), whereas Irvine utilized a central spine concept whereby the neighbourhoods were distributed lineally at differing locations along a single multi-purpose routeway. This latter idea was later modified into the 'community route' and residential unit concept of the Irvine 1971 plan revision which the consultants also influenced. Wilson emphasized:

the dynamic potential of his scheme, arguing that development may commence along an all-purpose route ... Later, everything other than public transport may be diverted onto new tangential routes alongside, thus allowing the original road to continue as the community route linking the urban cells [which may be residential, industrial, or multi-purpose]. The 'triple strand' [i.e., the parallel routeways] may also be developed eventually to provide a 'tartan grid' [of routeways at right angles to each other] of alternating routes capable of infinite extension by 'finite' modular stages.[65]

This was an adaption of the basic grid pattern as a means of distributing traffic over a finite but extendable space. In fact, by accident rather than design, there have been echoes of this sequential change in the recent development of Hong Kong's Tuen Mun.

Mention of the grid-iron as a pattern of providing a network of communication for a town introduces a third area of innovation that was explored in the designs of the later British new towns and allied studies. In *Traffic in Towns*, Buchanan had suggested that an orthogonal grid might best distribute the inevitable heavy flows of metropolitan traffic in a city.

The underlying assumption was that the best device for distributing traffic evenly over an area was a uniform grid ... High local concentrations are avoided and there is always an alternative path.[66]

The design problem, of course, is about the spacing of the grid. The conventional 'block' of the North American or colonial city, as found in parts of Hong Kong, is far too closely spaced if traffic segregation principles are to be applied within each cell. A further question raised by the grid principle in design terms is the location and use required for each of the cells. The idea of the grid suggests or even attempts to impose uniformity; the uniqueness or dominance of certain locations is lessened rather than intensified. This raises questions about the distribution and locations of the various centralized facilities about the town.

While Buchanan was to develop his initial thoughts further in his South Hampshire Plan of 1966 at the strategic level,[67] Livingston new town in Scotland was the first to explore this revised grid pattern as an urban form, and it was further developed, from 1967, in Washington new town, County Durham.[68] Daniel's plan for Livingston[69] represented a variant on the neighbourhood principle within a rectangular grid of roads. Each major cell was then served by an internal distributor road from which access to culs-de-sac or internal courtyards was provided to service the housing units. In Washington, the idea was taken further by Llewellyn-Davies in that the initial idea of a one-kilometre spacing for the grid was increased in practice to 1.6 kilometres — each larger cell therefore containing four separate communities linked to the surrounding road network. Traffic generators were also spread in an attempt to prevent the local build-up of vehicular traffic on the road network.

The plan consists of eighteen neighbourhoods or villages, as they are called, each with a population of about 4,500, and occupying an area of approximately half a square mile [64 hectares]. Each village is planned round a centre containing some shops for daily needs, the primary school, a village social centre, and a public house, similar to the neighbourhood centres of the older new towns but with more pedestrian precincts. The villages are grouped within the grid of primary roads that form approximately one-mile squares [2.6 square kilometres]. In the interim plan the road network was based on a half-mile [kilometre] grid, each square enclosing one village. Such a road network consisted of one level of road only which it was hoped could carry the predicted peak traffic effectively. This was found not to be the case, so in the master plan the grid is changed to one-mile [1.61 kilometre] squares with two, three or four villages in each, with a system of secondary roads feeding the primary road network at specified points ... In addition to the road system there is a comprehensive pedestrian network, mainly of straight footpaths, termed village walkways, based on a half-mile [kilometre] grid. These walkways link the residential areas with each village centre.[70]

The same designers were later involved in the planning of Milton Keynes from 1970, which represented the last major design of a new town in Britain for an almost virgin site (see Fig. 1.3b). This freedom allowed them to refine further their use of the grid principle as a basic urban form. It was also, for Britain, a large scheme — for a design population of 250,000 on some 8,865 hectares. Once again consideration of the transportation requirements for the city dominated the thinking behind the urban form. This time Llewellyn-Davies reverted to their original Washington new-town thinking in that they set themselves a one-kilometre road grid as the basic pattern for the town (see Fig. 1.3b) even though at the detailed level the focal point of the 'activity centre' in each of the land-use cells represented yet another variant of the transit-stop and neighbourhood-centre principles of earlier plans.

A system of pedestrian routes traverses the whole city crossing the primary roads roughly in the middle of the sides of the squares and at the corners by over or under-passes. At the former points are the 'activity centres' with major bus stops, and a concentration of residential facilities like shops, first schools, pubs, places of worship and other requirements. There will be about sixty of these centres with different groupings at each ... A person could comfortably walk to his nearest centre ... or if he is wanting a service provided in another centre ... he can either use the frequent bus service or go by car ... It will be seen that the residential areas are not planned as inward looking neighbourhoods, as in the first generation of new towns, but rather as outward looking to a transport route that links rapidly with other parts of the city. Following the principle of giving the maximum possible freedom of choice to future residents, the plan aims to give scope for the 'free use of the car unconstrained by congestion' while at the same time providing 'a high quality public transport system from the beginning'.[71]

Soon after the plan was published, however, it became obvious that the urban form chosen could not fulfil the goals set for it. Its very dispersed, low-density structure was shown to be incapable of supporting the good public transport service demanded by the goals of [its] design. It was hoped that small minibuses might help resolve this problem, but given the structure of Milton Keynes, the cost of running such a system was prohibitive [at least until after bus deregulation in 1986] ... By giving priority to the convenience of car travellers [the reality of designing the city on the basis of a grid of multi-purpose roads] the efficiency of conventional public transport is diminished ... Pedestrian and cycle movement, although safe, is deterred physically and psychologically [by the low densities], and facilities are so dispersed that there is no option but to use motorized means of transport, with their consequent expense and social costs.[72]

Milton Keynes can thus be regarded as an experiment which created a problem. Unrestricted urban movement with individually controlled personal transport for every user had not yet proved to be attainable in British society, and as a consequence personal mobility for everyone in Milton Keynes has proved to be an expensive planning goal to achieve effectively.

To sum up therefore, the 30 years of British new-town design represent a consistent story of continuous experiment and design formulation as planning teams reacted to the various demands being made upon them by their clients, the Development Corporations, and by their own learning processes as new-town development and the explorations of new urban forms progressed. 'Yet, there persists the notion of a city sub-divided into separate spaces. Fundamental in this regard is the notion of the land-use zone, and especially the separation of "living" from "working" areas';[73] though mixed-use zoning and the integration of land uses have again become a recent planning issue under the challenges of such people as the American, Jane Jacobs, and others concerned with the possible social damage of compartmentalizing life through the separation of activity locations because of planning requirements. Nevertheless, the development of concepts of urban form through the medium of the British new-town programme represents one of the few structured and consistent analyses of the functioning and optimal form of the contemporary city, and as such present a whole series of theoretical and working models to be copied, applied, and adapted elsewhere in the world. One such location was, of course, Hong Kong.

New-town Objectives

We have already seen that in the British case the origins and dominant objective for the new towns' locations and wider regional purposes were most often to do with decongestion of the central city. That is a role that has been widely emulated elsewhere. The French new towns around Paris, or the early Malaysian and Singaporean new towns are just two widely separated examples of direct derivatives of this British principle, and it is the one that has dominated the Hong Kong case too. Other development requirements must however also be mentioned. For example, in the case of some of the non-London British new towns, and more importantly in their use in developing countries, such centres have often been built more as development centres or 'growth poles' as a part of regional economic development programmes. Examples of these can be found in Israel or again in Malaysia. Thus, one of the more important questions that has to be answered about any new-town development programme is the role that the new settlements are expected to play within the existing or planned settlement network for the area; this is a specialized question within more general processes of strategic land-use planning that are undertaken as a part of the wider economic and other planning goals of the nation state. New-town programmes are thus often determined as an integral part of wider urban strategies, rather than more limited objectives.

Additional to these external objectives, internal goals are also commonly set for each town to meet. Two of the best known of these are epitomized by the terms 'balance' and 'self-containment', objectives set early on and long argued about in the context of the development history of the British new-town programme, and often transferred along with the new-town idea itself to new-town development programmes elsewhere, including Hong Kong.

The creation of socially balanced communities was the most pervasive of these ... The major function of the new towns was to help to solve the housing problems of the major cities. The prime purpose was to accommodate members of relatively low-income groups who were inadequately housed in the slum areas of the city, but another aim was to avoid the one class nature of the earlier public housing estates.[74]

For some the aim was ideological or sociological — a conscious plan to mix social groupings for a whole variety of explicit or ulterior motives, while others wished to replicate the community mix of the fully developed city, or argued that by encouraging certain community groups to come to the new towns, the establishment and growth of the cultural and community life of the new neighbourhoods, and hence the town, would be speeded up and somehow enhanced. Whatever the varied motives, it did become generally accepted in Britain that the new towns, through their housing and letting policies, should attempt to attract a representative cross-section of the population of the parent city, especially where decentralization was the primary planning objective. Equally, it can be said that for many who have instigated new-town programmes, the opportunity to create new communities has led them to attempt to replicate what to them seems an ideal of what such a new community should be; in short, it has provided them with an opportunity to indulge in a little bit of social engineering in order to provide the society of their day with a new demonstration of its social ideals.

It has also been suggested that the general success of Britain's new towns in social terms has been through their employment policies.

To avoid the problems of economic fluctuations associated with towns dependent upon a single firm or a single industry [associated in the planners' minds with the unemployment problems of the pre-war years in Britain], the development corporations have sought to obtain a variety of different industries and employers. This variety in employment composition within the town has generated a corresponding variety in the town's social composition.[75]

If successful at all, and British statistics suggest that by and large in this case it was, it is of course only related to the economically active portion of the town's population.

More controversial has proved to be the ability of the new towns to take a proportion of the more deprived or disadvantaged groups in society, the elderly, the handicapped, racial minorities, and so forth. Criticism on these grounds was part of the argument used for the shift in government resources that occurred in Britain from 1977 away from the new towns and into inner-city problem relief. The implication is that only by instituting specific targeting policies, particularly in housing and employment, can such mismatches amongst the new immigrants be combated during the early days of new-town growth. Nevertheless, the question remains, and has to be addressed, of what the ideal balance in the community should be and how it should be arrived at; a reflection of quite fundamental questions about the social structures of a society within which new towns are expected to play a part.

Mismatches of another kind are symptoms of problems with the other design objective that is often set within new-town development programmes, that of self-containment. This concept can take two forms — the development within the town itself, and/or the overall position of the town within the wider settlement system, particularly in terms of job and labour markets.

Mismatches between the demand for facilities and their provision are the 'bread-and-butter' of residents' complaints during the early development of almost any new town, ranging from comments about inadequate provision of the multitude of urban goods and services to the absence of elements of the town design like infrastructure, public transport facilities, and employment choice. The fundamental problem is that even for services not subject to commercial requirements of equating demand against provision, providing facilities in almost any field in advance of the designed population (demand) is both expensive and likely to be uneconomic. Only as the new town approaches maturity in population terms can it reasonably be expected to function and have the full range of facilities as designed. Yet people still have to live in the partly completed settlement for many years before that end-state is reached, and thus suffer the attendant deficiencies, unless there is active intervention on their behalf by the development authorities. Perhaps the most difficult balance of all in these terms to arrive at artificially is that between the provision of housing and the availability of employment opportunity.

This last question also of course relates long term to the role and place of the town in its region. In the British case, there has been a consistent attempt to make the new towns balance in terms of the numbers of houses provided and the numbers of jobs brought in to meet the demands of the residents of those houses. In other words, self-containment in the provision of jobs has been allied to the concept of self-containment in travel patterns. In the early years of the British towns this was largely achieved through the operation over many years of a 'homes-with-job' policy for the new immigrants to the towns (that is, as firms brought essential workers with them, so they took up specific housing allocations). As time passed however, and people have changed both homes and jobs, these initial controls have of course weakened, and in more recent years the new-town populations have gradually become integrated within their local and regional labour markets. This is of course only to be expected.

The employment role of the new towns thus depends ultimately on their relative competitiveness within the region in terms of job opportunities — in other words it is again an aspect of the town's location and placing within the urban hierarchy and structure of their region. Since so many new towns are placed within the ambit of the regional influence of their parent metropolitan city, we should not be at all surprised that within the general limitations generated by their success as vibrant new economic community, most of the British new towns have continued to remain a part of the wider metropolitan labour market within which they were located. Yet, they can still reasonably be pointed to as exemplary examples of Blumenfeld's good city-planning maxim, that they should 'minimize the need for commuting and maximise the opportunity'.[76]

One has to look elsewhere than Britain however to find wider goals for new-town development set out explicitly. In France, their Sixth National Plan of the mid-1970s set out the following as the goals for their new towns within a national strategy for development:

To restructure the suburbs by organising new concentrations of employment, housing and services; to reduce the amount of commuting and ease the transport problems in the particular urban regions; to create truly self-contained cities, as measured by a balance between jobs and housing, variety of different jobs and housing, provision of housing and supporting services at the same time and place, the rapid creation of urban centres, and concern for recreational facilities and environmental protection; to serve as laboratories for experiments in urban planning and design.[77]

Perhaps it is only the French who would care to make the fourth objective so explicit as a part of new-town policy, yet it is, as we have seen, as true implicitly of the past 30 years of British new-town development. In assessing the real importance in the world of the British experience, it is, in fact, this position of performing the role of the prototype that gives away the real significance of British new towns in the development of contemporary urban forms elsewhere in the modern world. To demonstrate this further it is instructive, in the Hong Kong case, to turn to an examination of British new-town policies applied in the Far East after the Second World War, and to those places which preceded and therefore influenced subsequent developments in Hong Kong.

The New-town Concept in the British Far East

While the rest of this book is concerned with the detailed story of the adoption of what is essentially the British model of new-town development in

Hong Kong, it is useful to remember that the new-town model was first exported to various of the other British Far Eastern dependencies in the years immediately following the Second World War, and that these examples to a degree influenced later experiences in Hong Kong. In terms of immediate impact on Hong Kong those developed early on in the Malay peninsula proved predominant.

As in Britain, the first examples were developed essentially as overspill developments for the largest local metropolitan areas. In 1952 a proposal was made to the colonial government in Malaya to allow development to take place on an area of old rubber plantation land some eight miles to the west of Kuala Lumpur, at Petaling Jaya, on a large site of some 486 hectares.[78] This new-town proposal was essentially seen as relieving the existing development pressures in the capital, particularly to address a problem which was exemplified by the massive increase in urban squatting immediately following the war, and also to allow for a major expansion for local industry — identical, in fact, to Kwun Tong, Hong Kong's first new town, also of the 1950s. In the new town, apart from control over the layout and land sales, development was largely left in the hands of private developers. Nevertheless, in the first two years, over 3,000 houses had been completed and 26 industrial firms were located on the 121 hectares of industrial land provided in the plan.

Over the years a town centre of traditional two-storey Chinese-style shop-houses developed on a grid-iron layout, surrounded by residential streets lined with wooden one- and two-storeyed houses set in neighbourhoods on the British new-town model. As in the home country, the industrial users were kept separate in their own trading estate. Today, Petaling Jaya has far outgrown its original plan — the old town centre, for example, has become submerged as a subsidiary suburb of a modern larger town, while new neighbourhoods and industrial areas have been added to the original site. Now the town is a major element of metropolitan Kuala Lumpur, to which it is physically joined, and it has become the dominant manufacturing centre for the whole of Malaysia. Nevertheless, the remnants of the original genteel, colonial, satellite town still remain, to remind us of its former importance as the first implantation of the British new town in the Far East.

Of much greater significance as precursors for the Hong Kong model were the subsequent developments in Singapore, which built upon the initial experience outside Kuala Lumpur. However, development in Singapore also leant upon earlier work begun with the founding of the Singapore Improvement Trust in 1927 (modelled on the Indian prototypes) to promote urban renewal and the improvement of sanitary conditions in the city. In 1936 the Trust began Singapore's first satellite housing development at Tiong Bahru, but it was not until 1954 that Singapore saw the beginnings of a proper new-town programme at Queenstown, on the western outskirts of the central city.

In January 1952 Sir George Pepler [author of the early investigation into British new towns in 1944] brought a team of experts to Singapore to do a major survey of the island's planning needs. The reports of their findings were published in 1955 under the title of the *Master Plan* ... An immediate result of the report (and of the work of the Housing Committee) was the beginning in 1954 of Queenstown — a completely planned satellite town containing public housing, schools, factories, and recreational facilities.[79]

The site was a former military base, combined with a former low-lying, wet area which had to be reclaimed. The plan formed a part of a wider scheme set out in the master plan,[80] which aimed at controlling public development through zoning and land reservations.

Major proposals included a green belt to arrest the further expansion of the central area, together with inducements to reduce its population in order to overcome congestion in the downtown area. Three self-contained new towns were to be built under a decentralisation policy of urbanisation to absorb future urban population growth.[81]

But actual implementation was slow, and events were overtaken by political changes and the formation of the Housing Development Board in 1960. One of the first effects of this was the introduction of an accelerated housing programme built at much greater densities, and the search for suitable housing sites on almost every available area of vacant land. The significance of these early events to Hong Kong proved to be twofold; the upholding of Singapore and the Singapore Improvement Trust model as an example by the Hong Kong government in the early years after the war, and the transfer in the late 1950s of key personnel to Hong Kong from Singapore, with a resultant transfer, too, of their relevant experience of Singapore developments and methods, which proved to be somewhat unpopular in the different conditions of 1950s Hong Kong.

In Singapore, however, a fully fledged new-town programme had to await the second phase of comprehensive territory-wide planning introduced in the Singapore Concept Plan of 1970,[82] following a visit to the city by Charles Abrams, Otto Koenigsberger, and Sususme Kobe as a United Nations team in 1963,[83] and a further follow-up UN team in the years 1967–71. The new plan suggested four corridors of urbanized development radiating from the central area.

The future new towns, which are also concentration points of population, will be sited along these corridors ... They will serve not only the people in the low-cost housing, but also those in the surrounding districts. Moreover, the more self-sufficient these new towns are, the stronger will be their drawing power and fewer people will be attracted to the central city.[84]

In planning principles the Singapore new towns thus followed strategically the international model, though the actual design parameters developed over the years turned out to be rather different. As in Hong Kong, density quickly became a primary concern. Thus, it is not surprising that Singapore is now so often used as a point of comparison for the new towns of Hong Kong, for only in the Lion city does one find one of the few new-town programmes in the world where planning parameters have some similarity to those currently in operation in Hong Kong.

In Singapore, overall population targets are set at around 200,000 for each town, at densities of between 295 and 495 persons to the hectare, thus making the centre of each town accessible to the whole population on a walking basis. Nevertheless, the neighbourhoods of 10,000 or more are now divided into high-rise precincts with sub-centre facilities, utilizing standards of about 2,000 units on 10 hectares maximum density; the overall spatial structure and its facilities being conceptualized on the basis of predetermined convenience standards.[85] Experience has shown there to be advantages in reducing the precinct sizes still further to about 400 to 800 units only in later versions of the Singapore new-town model (see Fig. 1.3c). By 1985, 16 new towns had been either completed or planned in Singapore. Initial site design in the early Singapore new towns like Queenstown or Toa Payoh was largely concerned with maximizing the coverage of the confined sites with standardized multi-storey housing blocks, as in Hong Kong. In practice, Queenstown:

is considered from the planning point of view to be a conglomeration of small public housing estates with the town centre added to it later on ... The second stage ... can be identified with Toa Payoh New Town, commenced in 1965 — the first to have been conceived with a target population (180,000 persons), a town centre and a range of complementary facilities. With Toa Payoh, we see pedestrianisation of the town centre mall, segregated from vehicular traffic, put to practice for the first time.[86]

Later new towns gradually lowered their densities as improved facilities, standards, and increasing numbers of larger flat units were incorporated in each further new-town design.

By the 1980s, evolution of the Singapore derivative had led to the development of a new prototype, the theoretical structural model, which formed a basic conceptual framework upon which all future Singaporean new towns could be planned (see Fig. 1.3c). This model incorporates current planning principles and environmental design criteria within a set of land-use distribution maxims first developed in the 1970s. The precinct has now become the basic building block of the Singapore new town.

It is a cluster of apartment blocks with well-defined spaces and facilities for the 400 to 800 dwelling units that constitute the precinct ... It repeats itself in clusters of 4 hectares or sometimes half this size ... As structural elements in the overall town plan, the precincts can be interlocked and combined to create rhythms along the different categories of roads. Together they circumscribe sites for facilities in the manner of courtyards, essentially relieving the high-rise, high-density precincts with the low-rise structures of the neighbourhood centres, the schools, the institutions and the sports fields and open spaces; the so-called checker-board principle of new town development.[87]

Associated with this system of blocks is the development of a pedestrian-linkage system which has become an important environmental element at the human scale within each overall scheme. This need to accentuate what the Singaporean planners term as 'identity' has been more recently reflected by attempts to provide within individual estate layouts specific design features and architectural additions to the basic standard designs which are intended to make each place become unique.

The emphasis is on enhancing the liveability of the high-rise, high-density environment, with the introduction of the precinct — the neighbourhood of community — and its accompanying precinct garden, games courts, playgrounds, precinct shops and landscaping with its profusion of human scale indicators. In new town planning, special attention is placed on character and identity: to orchestrate the larger architectural and urban design elements as well as the natural and topographical features to achieve character and individuality for the new town, and to counteract the basically stereotype nature of the standardised public housing development.[88]

In the words of the contemporary Singapore planners there can be detected yet another variation in the way in which a society views its new-towns programme as a part of its wider aspirations and desires.

Some Conclusions

The Singapore case represents a major translation of the cellular design of British and other western new-town models to the high-rise, high-density requirements of the land-hungry city. As such, it has always invited comparison with the new-town programme in Hong Kong, and as mentioned before, it was to Singapore that those in Hong Kong who wished to see their urban development better planned and managed in the early days after the Second World War tended to look for inspiration and emulation. From Fraser's early paper to the British Town Planning Summer School in 1960[89] to more recent reciprocal visits by the professionals of the Hong Kong and Singapore Institutes of Planners, that sense of learning and later rivalry has continued, and, in considering the story of the Hong Kong new towns in the rest of this book, it is a theme that will reappear from time to time.

Nevertheless, in the Far East the debt for giving the initial impetus and thinking remains with those British and Commonwealth planners who began the new-town programmes in the 1950s, and who had learned their trade from the earlier years of the British new-towns programme. It is that direct historical legacy, and the direct transfer of professional experience, that represents the true link between the Hong Kong new towns of today and the British examples of the early post-war years. While direct design comparisons have sometimes proved less than useful, there is no doubt that concepts of neighbourhood, land-use separation and distribution, segregated transport networks, balance, and self-containment all originated in the British model, and were absorbed, applied, and sometimes modified for the Hong Kong context.

But, before we develop an understanding of how these details were applied, first we have to ask the question why the new towns came to Hong Kong at all; and for that we need to develop an understanding of the perceived roles of the new towns in the early development and planning history of post-war Hong Kong.

Notes

1. E.Y. Galantay, *New Towns: Antiquity to the Present* (New York, George Braziller, 1975), p. 1.

2. G. Golany, *New Town Planning: Principles and Practice* (New York, John Wiley, 1976), pp. 22–5.

3. W. Ashworth, *The Genesis of Modern British Town Planning: A Study in Economic and Social History of the Nineteenth and Twentieth Centuries* (London, Routledge and Kegan Paul, 1954), p. 2.

4. Ashworth (1954), see note 3 above, p. 119. A fuller discussion of the evolution of planning thought relevant to this book can be found in Chapter 5 of Ashworth, 'The Creation of New Model Villages and Towns'; and in S. Bayley, *History of Architecture and Design 1890–1939, Unit 23: The Garden City* (Milton Keynes, Open University Press, 1975). See also, G.E. Cherry, *Cities and Plans: The Shaping of Urban Britain in the Nineteenth and Twentieth Centuries* (London, Arnold, 1988).

5. A full analysis of how suburbia originated in the British context can be found in H.M. Edwards, *The Design of Suburbia: A Critical Study in Environmental History* (London, Pembridge Press, 1981); while a comparable study of the parallel development of suburbia in Britain and the United States is available in R.A.M. Stern (ed.), with J.M. Messenga, *The Anglo-American Suburb* (London, Architectural Design, 1981).

6. E. Howard, *Tomorrow: A Peaceful Path to Real Reform* (London, Swan Sonnartschein, 1898). Currently available under its 1902 title of *Garden Cities of Tomorrow* (Eastbourne, Attic Books, 1985).

7. A term used by A.T. Stewart to describe a model estate laid out on Long Island, New York in 1869; and to which the name 'garden city' was given.

8. An invaluable contemporary analysis of new-town planning at this period is available in C.B. Purdom, *The Building of Satellite Towns* (London, Dent, 1925); while Unwin's own ideas were presented in R. Unwin, *Town Planning in Practice* (London, T. Fisher Unwin, 1909).

9. Purdom (1925), see note 8 above, p. 32.

10. Bayley (1975), see note 4 above, p. 40.

11. Bayley (1975), see note 4 above, p. 40.

12. Purdom (1925), see note 8 above, p. 173.

13. L. Rodwin, *The British New Towns Policy: Problems and Implications* (Cambridge, Mass., Harvard University Press, 1965), p. 15.

14. Ashworth (1954), see note 3 above, pp. 201–2.

15. M. Barlow, *Report of the Royal Commission on the Distribution of the Industrial Population*, Command 6153 (London, His Majesty's Stationery Office, 1940); and L.F. Scott, *Report of the Committee on Land Utilisation and Rural Areas*, Command 6837 (London, His Majesty's Stationery Office, 1942).

16. Bayley (1975), see note 4 above, p. 36.

17. Edwards (1981), see note 5 above, p. 84.

18. See J. Bailey (ed.), *New Towns in America: The Design and Development Process* (New York, Wiley, 1973); and W.L. Creese, *Search for Environment: The Garden City, Before and After* (New Haven, Yale University Press, 1966).

19. See Cities Commission, *Report to the Australian Government: A Recommended New Cities Programme for the period 1973–1978* (Canberra, Australian Government Publishing Services, 1973); and R. Freestone, 'The Conditions of the Cities and the Response: Early Garden City Concepts and Practice', in I. Burnley and J. Forrest (eds.), *Living in Cities: Urbanism and Society in Metropolitan Australia* (Sydney, Allen and Unwin, 1986), pp. 13–27.

20. A Japanese example, built between 1918 and 1928 near Tokyo, is described in Shun-Ichi J. Watanabe, 'Garden City Japanese Style: The Case of Den-en Toshi Company Ltd., 1918–28'; Chapter 6 in G.E. Cherry (ed.), *Shaping an Urban World: Planning in the Twentieth Century* (London, Maunsell, 1980), pp. 129–43.

21. Roger Bristow, *Land-use Planning in Hong Kong: History, Policies and Procedures* (Hong Kong, Oxford University Press, 1984), pp. 31–7.

22. Edwards (1981), see note 5 above, pp. 51–2.

23. *China Mail*, Thursday 12 September 1921, p. 10.

24. *Report of the Committee Appointed to Advise the Governor of Hong Kong as to whether Any and if so What Relief or Monetary Assistance should be granted to the Kowloon Tong and New Territories Development Co. Ltd. or to the Subscribers to the Kowloon Tong Scheme* (Hong Kong, Government Printer, 1929), p. 1. Copy with Despatch of 16 June 1930 (London, Public Record Office, CO 129/520).

25. *China Mail*, Tuesday 5 October 1920, p. 8.

26. *China Mail*, Thursday 27 October 1921, p. 8. 'Report on the Governor's Budget Speech'.

27. *China Mail*, Wednesday 10 August 1921, p. 3.

28. Local Government Board, *Housing Manual on the Preparation of State-Aided Housing Schemes* (London, His Majesty's Stationery Office, 1919).

29. Le Corbusier, *The Radiant City* (New York, Orion Press, 1964, English translation); see also Le Corbusier, *The City of Tomorrow* (London, Architectural Press, 1929).

30. An excellent overview of some of these issues, including papers on Hong Kong, can be found in Singapore Professional Centre Convention, *High Rise, High-Density Living: Selected Papers* (Singapore, Singapore Professional Centre, 1984).

31. Stern (1981), see note 5 above, p. 46.

32. Stern (1981), see note 5 above, p. 84.

33. C. Perry, 'The Neighborhood Unit', in *Regional Plan of New York and its Environs: Vol. VII, Neighborhood and Community Planning — Regional Survey* (New York, Committee on the Regional Plan of New York and Its Environs, 1929), pp. 34–5.

34. P. Merlin, *Les Villes Nouvelles* (Paris, Presses Universitaires de France, 1969); translated into English as P. Merlin, *New Towns* (London, Methuen, 1971), p. 3.

35. Crawley new town seems to have been a particular magnet for Hong Kong visitors, and particular issues examined in reports submitted by them to the Hong Kong government were on 'compulsory purchase and leases', and 'matters of compensation and betterment'. See files BL4/5282/53, *Visit of Mr. A.R. Giles, Land Surveyor, to London New Towns, August 1953*, and BL7/3/5282/51, *Correspondence with Crawley Development Corporation*; both in the Public Records Office, Hong Kong.

36. Barlow (1940), see note 15 above.

37. Rodwin (1956), see note 13 above, p. 18.

38. P. Abercrombie, *Greater London Plan 1944* (London, His Majesty's Stationery Office, 1945), p. 5.

39. Abercrombie (1945), see note 38 above, p. 8.

40. Abercrombie (1945), see note 38 above, p. 14.

41. Abercrombie (1945), see note 38 above, p. 168.

42. Abercrombie (1945), see note 38 above, pp. 169–71.

43. Ministry of Town and Country Planning Technical Team, *1946 Technical Report, Stevenage New Town — Provisional Development Proposals* (London, Ministry of Town and Country Planning, 1946).

44. How the planning proposals for new towns in Britain might be implemented by the government was largely detailed in three reports issued in 1946: New Towns Committee, *Interim Report*, Command 6759; *Second Interim Report*, Command 6794; and *Final Report*, Command 6876, all (London, His Majesty's Stationery Office, 1946). These reports in turn had been preceded by the internal *Report of the Interdepartmental Group on Administrative and Legislative Arrangements Needed for the Development of Satellite or New Towns* (London, Ministry of Town and Country Planning, 1944) — the Pepler Report. A full version of this report can be found as *Appendix E* of J.B. Cullingworth, *Environmental Planning 1939–1969: Volume III, New Towns Policy* (London, Her Majesty's Stationery Office, 1979), pp. 592–602.

45. New Towns Committee (1946), see note 44 above, Command 6759, p. 3.

46. Rodwin (1956), see note 13 above, pp. 39–40.

47. Galantay (1975), see note 1 above, p. 53.

48. Galantay (1975), see note 1 above, pp. 53–4.

49. New Towns Committee (1946), see note 44 above, Command 6759, p. 4.

50. Rodwin (1956), see note 13 above, p. 55.

51. Extract from a paper prepared by John Silkin, Minister of Town and Country Planning, and submitted to the Lord President's Committee on 23 November 1945. Quoted in Cullingworth (1979), see note 44 above, p. 20.

52. W. Houghton-Evans, 'Schemata in British New Town Planning', in G.E. Cherry (1980), see note 20 above, pp. 101–28.

53. Houghton-Evans (1980), see note 52 above, p. 109.

54. A. Minoprio, 'Some Design Problems and Trends in the Planning of Towns', *Town and Country Planning Summer School: Report of Proceedings, Oxford University 1951* (London, Town Planning Institute, 1951), pp. 21–2.

55. L.H. Wilson, 'Cumbernauld — The Design of a High Density New Town', *Town and Country Planning Summer School: Report of Proceedings, St. Andrews 1960* (London, Town Planning Institute, 1960), p. 59.

56. M. Hillman and S. Potter, 'Movement Systems for New Towns' in G. Golany (ed.), *International Urban Growth Policies: New Town Contributions* (New York, John Wiley, 1978), pp. 38–41.

57. C.D. Buchanan, *Traffic in Towns: A Study of the Long Term Problems of Traffic in Urban Areas — Report of the Working Group* (London, Her Majesty's Stationery Office, 1963).

58. Peterborough Development Corporation, *Greater Peterborough Master Plan* (Peterborough, Peterborough Development Corporation, 1970).

59. Peterborough Development Corporation (1970), see note 58 above, p. 12.

60. A full description of the various design concepts used in the British new towns programme over the full 20 years of its development can be found in Part 2 of F.J. Osborn and A. Whittick, *New Towns: Their Origins, Achievements and Progress* (London, Leonard Hill, 1977), pp. 117–453; while transport solutions specifically are discussed in H. Dupree, *Urban Transportation: The New Town Solution* (Aldershot, Gower, 1987).

61. A. Ling, *Runcorn New Town: Master Plan* (Runcorn, Runcorn Development Corporation, 1967).

62. Ministry of Housing and Local Government, *Northampton, Bedford and North Buckinghamshire Study* (London, Her Majesty's Stationery Office, 1965).

63. L.H. Wilson and L. Wolmersley, *Redditch New Town — Report on Planning Proposals* (Redditch, Redditch Development Corporation, 1966).

64. L.H. Wilson and L. Wolmersley, *Irvine New Town Planning Proposals* (London, Her Majesty's Stationery Office, 1967).

65. Houghton-Evans (1980), see note 52 above, pp. 116–8.

66. Houghton-Evans (1980), see note 52 above, p. 119.

67. Colin Buchanan & Partners, *South Hampshire Study: Report on the Feasibility of Major Urban Growth* (London, Her Majesty's Stationery Office, 1966).

68. R. Llewellyn-Davies, J. Weeks, and Partners, *Washington New Town Master Plan* (Washington, Co. Durham, Washington Development Corporation, 1966).

69. Livingston Development Corporation, *Livingston Plan* (Livingston, Livingston Development Corporation, 1979).

70. Osborn and Whittick (1977), see note 60 above, p. 285.

71. Osborn and Whittick (1977), see note 60 above, p. 238.

72. Hillman and Potter (1978), see note 56 above, pp. 44–6.

73. Houghton-Evans (1980), see note 52 above, p. 125.

74. R. Thomas, 'Britain's New-Town Demonstration Project', in Golany (1978), see note 56 above, p. 26.

75. Thomas (1978), see note 74 above, p. 27.

76. H. Blumenfeld, 'Transportation in the Modern Metropolis' in P.D.I. Spreiringen (ed.), *The Modern Metropolis: Selected Essays by Hans Blumenfeld* (Cambridge, Mass., MIT Press, 1971), p. 123.

77. J. Rubenstein, 'French New-Town Policy' in Golany (1978), see note 56 above, p. 83.

78. H.K. Lim, *The Evolution of the Urban System in Malaya* (Kuala Lumpur, Penerbit, Universiti Kebansan, Malaysia 1978), pp. 106–8. See also T.A.L. Concannon, 'A New Town in Malaya: Petaling Jaya, Kuala Lumpur', *Malayan Journal of Tropical Geography*, Vol. 5, 1955, pp. 39–43. Further more general information about new towns in Malaysia can be found in B.T. Lee, 'New Towns in Malaysia: Development and Planning Policies', in D.R. Phillips and A.G.O. Yeh (eds.), *New Towns in East and South-east Asia: Planning and Development* (Hong Kong, Oxford University Press, 1987), pp. 153–69.

79. R.E. Gamer, *The Politics of Urban Development in Singapore* (Ithaca, Cornell University Press, 1972), p. 14.

80. Singapore Improvement Trust, *Master Plan: Report of Survey* (Singapore, Government Printing Office, 1955).

81. L. H. Wang and T.H. Tan, 'Singapore' in M. Pacione (ed.), *Problems and Planning in Third World Cities* (Beckenham, Croom Helm, 1981), p. 242. An additional general source is L.H. Wang, 'Residential New Town Development in Singapore: Background, Planning, and Design', in Phillips and Yeh (1987), see note 78 above, pp. 23–40.

82. Singapore State and City Planning Office, *Singapore Long Range Concept Plan* (Singapore, Government Publication Office, 1970).

83. United Nations/C. Abrams, S. Kobe, and O. Koenigsberger, *Growth and Urban Renewal in Singapore: Report prepared for the Government of Singapore* (New York, United Nations Technical Assistance Programme, 1963). See also O.H. Koenigsberger and M. Safie, *Urban Growth and Planning the Development Countries of the Commonwealth — A Review of Experience from the Past 25 Years* (London, United Nations Interregional Seminar on New Towns, June 1973).

84. T.K. Liu, 'Design for Better Living Conditions', in S.H.K. Yeh (ed.), *Public Housing in Singapore: A Multi-Disciplinary Study* (Singapore, Singapore University Press, 1975), pp. 126–9.

85. Liu (1975), see note 84 above, pp. 145–79.

86. K.J. Tan, C.T. Loh, S.A. Tan, W.C. Lau, and K. Kwok, 'Physical Planning and Design', in A.K. Wong and S.H.K. Yeh (eds.), *Housing a Nation: Twenty Five Years of Public Housing in Singapore* (Singapore, Maruzen Asia, 1985), pp. 92–3.

87. Tan et al. (1985), see note 86 above, pp. 105–6.

88. Tan et al. (1985), see note 86 above, p. 111.

89. J.M. Fraser, 'Planning and Housing at High Densities in Two Crowded Tropical Cities', *Town and Country Planning Summer School: Report of Proceedings, St. Andrews, 1960* (London, Town Planning Institute, 1960), pp. 104–16.

2. Birth of a Strategy

First Thoughts

It seems that the first mention of the possibility of new-town development as an option for public policy in Hong Kong was made by W.H. Owen in his memorandum to the 1935 Housing Commission report, published in 1938. *

> The clearance of slums involves the settlement of the dispossessed surplus elsewhere. Sites for new settlements must be found and planned. There are several possible sites in the New Territories such as Shatin, Tsuen Wan, Un Long, Taipo and Fanling, but before development can be commenced the questions of water supply, communications, flood protection, drainage and sewage disposal, and in some cases, reclamation must be given serious consideration.[1]

Although the Hong Kong government's consideration of the Commission's recommendations did lead to the rapid introduction of town-planning legislation in Hong Kong (the Town Planning Ordinance, No.20 of 1939), more comprehensive change, particularly for development and housing, was overtaken by the more pressing matters caused by the requirements of the oncoming war. Radical policy changes had to await the ending of hostilities.

The disruption caused by the Japanese occupation from 1941 to 1945, and the administrative effort required to reimpose British control after the war, meant that town planning took a relatively minor role in the deliberations of the early post-war administrations in Hong Kong. Nevertheless, the influx of refugees, and the problems of housing rehabilitation, meant that the longer-term development of Hong Kong could not be shelved indefinitely as a policy question. Moreover, the welfare intentions of the newly-elected Labour government in Britain, and more specifically their passing of the 1945 Colonial Development and Welfare Act, meant that the Hong Kong authorities were under some pressure to respond in terms of setting out objectives for a longer-term (ten-year) programme of economic and social development for the Territory.

Although one of the six sub-committees set up in July 1946 to consider draft development schemes as a part of this programme was made specifically responsible for housing and town-planning matters, it rapidly became apparent to the government that targeting and utilizing such funds effectively on projects within the urban area was not easy without some broad idea of where and how Hong Kong was to change in development terms. This doubt was reinforced in a letter to the Governor by the then Port Administration Inquiry Committee (which had been set up to study Sir David Owen's earlier recommendations of 1941 on the future development of the harbour).[2]

In a Colony where a chronic land hunger gives rise to conflict between the need for land for housing purposes and a need for areas close to the water front for storage and other port requirements, it is obvious that port development cannot be planned either by Government or by private enterprise except as an integral part of a comprehensive plan for the development of the Colony as a whole. Accordingly we decided to submit interim representations to Your Excellency that it was our considered opinion that the lack of an agreed and comprehensive plan was now retarding further rehabilitation and that we felt that it was a matter of great urgency that such a plan should be prepared and agreed as speedily as possible.[3]

It was this policy conundrum that led to the Governor's request of November 1946 for an adviser on planning and development to be sent out from London, and thus to the appointment of Sir Patrick Abercrombie in August 1947 'to advise. . . on the lines and principles to be followed in planning the future development of the port and urban area of the Colony'.[4]

Given Abercrombie's fame as the creator of the first-generation London new towns,[5] it is not surprising that he should also be thought of as the originator of the idea in Hong Kong.[6] But careful reading of his report to the colonial government makes it clear that, while new towns were indeed in his mind as a possible part of his solution to Hong Kong's problems, they were not an immediate policy option with which he was seriously concerned. He clearly stated that 'it has been assumed throughout this Report that the major urban activities should be confined to Hong Kong Island and Kowloon'.[7]

Central to his recommendations, in fact, were decisions about population targets and densities:

the question of an ultimate housing density will affect the area in Kowloon required for rehousing the decentralised population. Finally and perhaps most important of all, a target figure of maximum population should be decided upon.[8]

It was only in relation to these targets that the possible utilization of the new-town concept actually gained a mention.

It was decided to find out what was the maximum additional population that could be accommodated in and near Kowloon ... this would, therefore, give a grand total of two million inhabitants for the Colony as a whole ... There are two factors which would vary this figure. Firstly, if a lower density standard were adopted ... The other varying factor, operating in the opposite direction, allows the urban population to pass beyond the mountain barrier into the New Territories. A new town of 100,000 could be developed with its own industrial trading estate, and increased road and rail connection with the harbour.[9]

Thus, while Abercrombie foresaw the possibility of a policy to expand urban development beyond the mountain barrier into the New Territories, in 1948 his recommended solutions for the immediate development of

Hong Kong centred on new expansions and reclamations in the areas immediately around the harbour.[10]

Abercrombie's development ideas formed the basis for the growth of Hong Kong over the next decade or so, even though his population calculations were rapidly overtaken by events. It was not really until pressures for housing, in part generated by the huge influx of refugees, required a further look at long-term development requirements in the mid-1950s that his ideas were effectively superceded. Moreover, it is interesting to note that, as he himself acknowledged,[11] his report was largely a considered compilation of the development ideas of others. For example, in a report of September 1945 to the Military Administration,[12] Mr Nicol, the pre-war Port Engineer, noted that the Tsuen Wan and Central reclamations had been considered pre-war, as had investigations into a cross-harbour tunnel, and removal of the railway alongside Chatham Road and the provision of freight branches to the Hong Kong and Kowloon Wharf and Godown Company off Canton Road and to the Kwun Tong reclamation. This reclamation in turn had been begun in the 1930s as the main urban area refuse tip. Not least of these pre-war ideas that reappeared in the years immediately after the Pacific War was the 1939 recommendation to build a new airport at Deep Bay as a replacement for Kai Tak, which in turn led Abercrombie to recommend the old airport site as the main development area for the housing of Kowloon's expected overspill.

However there is no doubt that, despite Abercrombie's proposals, there was little thought in the 1940s of any major urban development scheme in Hong Kong, still less of new towns; at least not in the minds of the Territory's administrators. Much more pressing to them were immediate solutions to the interrelated questions of what to do about population growth, housing demand, and the shortage of resources. As early as 1946 government rejected a recommendation from the Hong Kong Social Welfare Council that temporary housing should be erected for squatters; and following the deliberations of an Interdepartmental Committee on the Squatter Problem in June 1946 there was an initial attempt to return to pre-war squatter policies with a strengthening of legislation on clearances and the introduction of a repatriation scheme.[13] Even as late as December 1950 it was minuted in the Executive Council that there should be 'discouragement of squatters from staying in these areas by a policy of attrition, the aim of which would be to make them as uncomfortable as possible in the hope that they will return to China'.[14]

Early deliberations on how to deal with war-damaged housing were not much more hopeful. In May 1946, the Colonial Secretary was commenting to the new Governor, Sir Mark Young, that the report of the Building Reconstruction Advisory Committee (set up the previous January) was 'disappointing on the whole, tells us little we did not know and is crammed with reasons for doing nothing'.[15] Indeed the Colonial Secretary seemed disenchanted with committees:

during the Military Administration I became convinced that the housing problem would not be solved through the appointment of committees; it seemed to me that the only hope of quick and effective action lay in the appointment of a single officer with very considerable powers, charged with the responsibility of getting on with the job and getting results.[16]

This was a comment which produced the appointment of the Director of Building Rehabilitation in July 1946.

A concern of the Director of Public Works that there was a lack of control over rebuilding which was affecting future land and planning requirements was met by the new Director being given a responsibility:

to define the areas which should be reserved immediately, i.e. the spaces on which rebuilding of demolished houses should be prohibited on the grounds that such spaces are required for street widening, provision of 'lungs', or other public purposes.[17]

While doubtful cases were referred to the Housing and Town Planning Sub-committee of the Colonial Development and Welfare Committee, which also had responsibility for the siting of industrial areas and the clearance of war-damaged properties, more comprehensive consideration of the planning of Hong Kong was, as we have seen, left to await the arrival of the expert who was to prepare 'large and comprehensive plans for town improvement'.[18]

Yet, despite public support for Abercrombie's proposals when they became known,[19] government felt quite incapable of implementing them. As a senior member of the government's secretariat stated:

I am quite certain in my own mind that increasing Defence and Security commitments cannot be met without some curtailment of our normal activities, and Town Planning is a matter which can only be pursued if there is unlimited money available for large-scale resumptions. I know of no successful large-scale re-planning of an already congested city.[20]

My feeling is that Sir Patrick Abercrombie set forth an ideal, and that we must make up our minds that like so many other plans drawn up in the United Kingdom, it must remain an ideal but totally impracticable. Expenditure and finance on the scale proposed is just impossible.[21]

This reluctance to initiate a meaningful town-planning policy in Hong Kong extended to the highest levels of the Hong Kong administration, for the Executive Council itself considered the matter in November 1950 and thought it a waste of time, despite support from the Housing and Town Planning Sub-committee.[22] In fact, on the 8 November 1950, the Governor, Colonial and Financial Secretaries and the Director of Public Works met, and decided not to proceed with the implementation of Abercrombie's recommendation to set up a planning team to produce the recommended Development Plan for Hong Kong.

Were the Unit to come out they will doubtless recommend vast resumptions in the built-up areas which we couldn't afford. Whilst as regards piecemeal resumptions and setting-back street lines, etc., and the planning of new areas, the Public Works Department do this as normal routine.[23]

The result was that it then took a further two years for government to finally make up its mind as to how other aspects of Abercrombie's proposals might be dealt with. In 1952, four objectives were set by the Executive Council for land-use planning in Hong Kong:

(a) limited improvement schemes in the urban area within the bounds of financial and political possibility;

(b) overall planning layouts and development programmes for undeveloped areas;

(c) periodic amendments of the Abercrombie outline to comply with government policy;

(d) and town planning legislation.[24]

The final proposals were sent to London for approval in February 1953.

The Governor's letter to the Secretary of State at the time set out succinctly the reasons for the government's change of policy:

By the time the Report [Abercrombie's] was published in September 1949, emergency conditions already existed as a result of the advance of the Chinese Communist armies to the borders of the Colony. Not only was it necessary to requisition a substantial number of newly completed buildings to accommodate military reinforcements but hundreds of thousands of refugees fleeing across the border created much more severe conditions of overcrowding and land shortage than when Sir Patrick visited Hong Kong. Today large areas of vacant land in or near the urban areas of Kowloon and Victoria are occupied by squatters or required for squatter resettlement areas. As you know, the total population is now estimated at 2¼ million, compared with 1½ million in 1948. Careful consideration has been given to Sir Patrick's recommendation that a definitive development plan should be prepared ... As a result of this consideration I have come to the conclusion, with the advice of Executive Council, that to carry out large-scale town planning schemes will not be practicable until the present congestion of the urban areas is reduced by the temporary or permanent resettlement of squatters in outlying areas or by the end of emergency conditions, which might induce at least some part of the displaced persons now in Hong Kong to return to China.[25]

Such reasoning was not however the whole story, for it is clear that there had been a major debate within government as to what should be done. The initial impetus of setting up the Housing and Town Planning Sub-committee back in 1946, with terms of reference to 'consider and report on the needs of the Colony for improved housing and town planning over a ten-year period and to make recommendations on the action required to meet those needs',[26] had become bogged down in the desire to devise an agreed 'master plan' for the development. The Sub-committee, in fact, never did produce its report, because its chairman (Mr Kenniff, the then Director of Public Works) held that nothing could be done in the urban area until the master plan became available. Thus events had to await the attention of Abercrombie, and by 1950 it was too late. In the same year, the Executive Council chose to reject the Planning Unit proposal (for a special team for four years of six professional staff, and support staff),[27] despite the weight of support from the Colonial Welfare and Development Committee and its sub-committees.

Moreover, the new line was reinforced by the stance of the incoming Director of Public Works. In December 1951 he recommended that:

> no separate large scale town planning unit be established, but that future planning be carried out within the existing organisation already familiar with the problem — i.e. the Crown Lands and Survey Office ... In other words, planning should run in the same channels which at present guide the use of land in the Colony and so fit into an integrated organisation for controlling development. In my opinion only by so doing can it be ensured that theoretical planning will be strictly within the realm of practical possibility.[28]

Town planning in Hong Kong at the beginning of the 1950s was set within strictly limited parameters, and clearly it would require a major policy shift to initiate major change.

Such limitations for the urban area did not however preclude the beginnings of planning for areas in the New Territories. While Bowring, the new Director of Public Works, noted in 1951 that he had no responsibility for town planning in the New Territories, he pointed out that planning was urgently needed, since development was proceeding rapidly and it was an important outlet for the insatiable demand for land in the urban area. In January 1952, the Executive Council responded by suggesting that some recommendations about town planning in the New Territories should be made to it. This suggestion was followed by a Governor's direction under Section Three of the Town Planning Ordinance in 1954 that plans should be prepared for Tsuen Wan and Kwai Chung, Sha Tin, Sai Kung, Yuen Long, Shek Wu Hui, Tai Po Market, and Fanling.[29] However, it was suggested that provided the plans were exhibited and the District Officers followed them in their land dealings, only Tsuen Wan/Kwai Chung would require statutory status. In any case, in terms of the planning workload, only the Tsuen Wan/Kwai Chung plan was given any priority; the others, other than that for Sha Tin, being left bottom of the list of priorities for planning work in the Territory. Nevertheless, this initial recognition of the particular planning needs of Tsuen Wan was the beginning of a concern with urban expansion into the New Territories, the main manifestation of which was to come at the end of the decade; even though the possibilities had been foreseen by Abercrombie in the 1940s.

Consideration of planning in the New Territories does lead us on, however, to the next significant development in the story of new towns in Hong Kong, for it was here in the New Territories that the first new-town initiative began with the initiation of the so-called 'new town' begun at Luen Wo Market (now part of the new expanding town of Sheung Shui/ Fanling), as part of the agricultural development programme funded under the rural section of the Colonial Development and Welfare Fund's ten-year programme, begun after the 1945 British Act.

In origin the proposal was a private one, initiated by the Pang clan of Fanling as a rival scheme to the older established rural market centre of

Fig. 2.1 Luen Wo Market master plan: prepared by a Hong Kong firm of architects in 1947 for the development by private enterprise of a rural market centre near Sheung Shui in the northern New Territories.

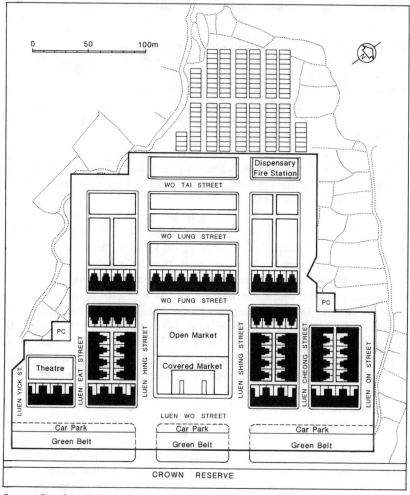

Source: Based on the layout plan by Y.C. Mok for Luen Wo Land Investment Co. Ltd., at 2 in BL 7/3801/48, Buildings and Lands Registry, Hong Kong.

Shek Wu Hui. It was put forward as a co-operative venture of the local villages at the end of 1946, and following discussions with the government's New Territories Administration, the site for the new marketing centre was agreed by the New Territories Sub-committee of the Colonial Development and Welfare Committee in April 1947 as acceptable. This enabled the developers, the Luen Wo Land Investment Company, to issue their prospectus to potential investors in January 1948.

The six-and-a-half-hectare site was to be set out according to a Public Works Department approved plan (see Fig. 2.1), and allowed for the initial construction of 90 houses in two phases, and a private market area. The cost of site preparation and filling was covered by selling the housing plots in advance, and potential owners were also required to pay the development company for the housing construction which was architecturally designed to a common plan. By 1950 the result was that:

you have at Luen Wo the first half of a New Territories townlet of approved layout, on a base built up to approved levels, and with approved drainage, with homogeneous buildings of good type — all an advance on anything yet seen in the New Territories, particularly as to spaciousness and planned provision for future development.[30]

However, by then, undercapitalization of the development company had produced stagnation in the development process, for the company could neither afford to provide the houses with paved streets nor to construct the market building itself from which its long-term income was to be derived. The resultant protracted negotiations with government eventually led to an agreement in 1954 for further development of the then termed 'new town' (at that time 93 houses and the market building had been completed); but eventual failure to comply with the site's lease conditions brought about a full government takeover in 1961, and an end to the project as initially conceived.

The undertaking was of course neither exceptional nor innovative in design terms — after all, although standardized, the buildings were essentially replicas of the usual urban-area six-storey Chinese shop-house. The layout too was based on the conventional grid pattern used elsewhere in Hong Kong from the 1920s, with the addition of the central market square. The originality of the scheme lay in the co-operative nature of the undertaking; its location as a 'model village' in the New Territories ('They are pioneers of the first New Town townlet to be planned from the beginning'[31]); and its place historically as a first attempt by the private sector at comprehensive urbanized development in the New Territories. It was all these things, plus the political wish of the government to support the efforts of the local inhabitants after the war to help themselves, that led government to overlook the irregularities and vicissitudes that beset the project almost from the beginning. Today it still remains as a memorial to Hong Kong's second major attempt at urban development innovation, if Kowloon Tong is regarded as the first. The third, Kwun Tong, had to await another decade, and was to be born out of the problems of the waves of post-war immigrants from China.

Pressures for Housing

There is little doubt that those professionals returning to Hong Kong administration in the early months after the war saw great opportunities to improve living conditions in Hong Kong.

It is quite clear to me that we need a different type of tenement house from the common type existing at present. They may not have been too bad when the Colony was less crowded.[32]

It would be a great pity to miss the present opportunity for planning a really beautiful and healthy Hong Kong ... Our architects and engineers would complete the picture by designing suitable houses for the various classes of the community, apart from our communal needs. With modern methods of construction, new materials, prefabrication, etc., it is to be hoped that real homes can be produced at reasonable costs. A very large percentage of our houses will have to be demolished and no undue hardship should result as long as a reasonable time limit is given. Naturally steps should be taken to get rid of the host of middlemen, who batten on poorer tenants, as well as eliminating our slum landlords.[33]

Yet, despite the idealism, which can be taken as paralleling that expressed in Britain at the time and which was one foundation of its own new-town programme, for Hong Kong the tribulations of founding an effective housing policy were destined to last even longer than the attempts to introduce formal town planning to the Territory that we have just described. Two threads of policy can however be traced — one relating to private sector development, and the other concerned with the search for an acceptable, affordable, and practical programme for public housing in the Territory. It was out of the second that the present Hong Kong new-town programmes were eventually to come.

In 1946, however, the initial problem was the rehabilitation of the Territory's war-damaged existing stock. While unprepared to repair private property at public expense, government did try to offer assistance in other ways. The June 1946 announcement on lease renewal at special terms,[34] for example, led to the building or reconstruction of 38 houses and about 200 flats; while sales of Crown land by private treaty at half the market value, allowed from August 1947, produced a further 299 houses, 148 flats, and 73 four-storey tenements in the two years that it was in force. Such progress even led the authorites to suggest that 'by the early part of 1949, a near sufficiency of the better type of accommodation seemed to be not unlikely'.[35] Yet the more pressing problem remained of how to provide larger numbers of units for the working population. To attempt to meet this need a further concessionary scheme was introduced in October 1948. First offered for two years, and then extended to five, it provided for the private treaty sale of land for large housing schemes initiated by employers or housing societies. But generally the response was poor, and the numbers of units built relatively small.[36] Moreover, politically suspect schemes, such as those put forward by the Kuomintang-backed Trades Union Council, were rejected.

Even without any consideration at all of how to deal with the burgeoning squatter problem, it was very clear early on that private development and the government's assistance schemes were going to be insufficient to meet the demand for normal housing in Hong Kong. The gauntlet first put down for government by the 1935 Housing Commission was going to have to be picked up, if at first rather carefully. Tabling of the Commission's report again in May 1946 induced further consideration within government with regard to the possibilities of introducing a Housing Trust into Hong Kong along the lines of the Singapore Improvement Trust (which had been first founded in 1927). Although there was some distrust, largely on the grounds of the lack of available finance, the 1947 report of the Singapore Housing Committee[37] was studied with great care in Hong Kong, including its proposals for new towns in Singapore.[38] Yet, there was the greatest difficulty in persuading the Executive Council of the merit of such ideas.

As early as August 1947 the Executive Council rejected a proposition that government should give financial support to a public corporation to promote housing construction in Hong Kong. Yet, in December the Director of Public Works put up a proposal to the Secretariat for the setting up of a 'Land Development Office' to provide 'ready-to-build' sites with all services laid on. While support was evident within government, finance, as always, proved to be the obstacle, and on 9 March 1948 the proposal foundered, again in the Executive Council.

This proposal was discussed. In view of the financial risks involved, the cost of extra staff and the anticipated shortage of funds, Council advised and His Excellency ordered that the proposed scheme should be noted for future discussion, but that it should not be put into operation at present.[39]

The supporters of it were sadly disappointed, yet they did not give up. Later in the year,

arising out of an enquiry by Hon. D.P.W. [Director of Public Works] for information as to the way blitzed areas might be taken over and developed by Government, consideration has been given to the desirability of setting up a Housing Improvement Trust here.[40]

By February 1949, the Assistant Colonial Secretary was stating:

I submit that our only justification for deferring the setting up of an Improvement Trust is that the Hong Kong Housing Society, if it eventually expands (or is added to by similar societies) would be a convenient way of carrying out housing improvement.[41]

The realization by the end of 1950 that, although the number of new domestic buildings being erected by private enterprise was considerable, capital was not being attracted for the construction of dwellings affordable by the majority of the population, pushed government further to consider a suitable policy for the provision of public housing. A first step, again with British approval, was a HK $3.75 million grant from the Colonial Development and Welfare Fund for site preparation work for 2,500 low-cost flats. Although draft plans had been prepared by the Public Works Department in August 1949 for a government, four-storey, tenement design,[42] grants were made initially in 1951 to the Model Housing

Society and the Hong Kong Housing Society for pilot schemes in North Point and Sheung Li Uk respectively. It was anticipated that at these two places pilot schemes could be implemented more quickly.

Nevertheless, despite this activity, housing matters were once again before the Executive Council in July 1951, and on the third of that month they finally agreed that a Housing Improvement Trust should be set up in Hong Kong. Given that some HK $15 million were to be set aside for the construction of small flats, it was thought prudent to investigate more thoroughly the Singapore model, and Mr J.T. Wakefield (the Chief Resettlement Officer for the Urban Council) was asked to go there and prepare a report for government.[43] Effectively, his report rejected the Singapore model for Hong Kong. Instead, he proposed the setting up of a Housing Council of independent status with an Unofficial majority 'to prepare proposals for the improvement and extension of housing and other accommodation' and 'to manage and superintend the management of all lands, houses and buildings vested in the Housing Council'.[44]

More importantly, for our purposes here, despite advice from the Secretary of State in London that the housing and planning functions should be combined in Hong Kong, as in Singapore, Wakefield also recommended that:

the Council would not concern itself with planning development, which would remain the responsibility of the Director of Public Works; the Council should, however, be consulted on the suitability of development of any particular locality for housing, industry or otherwise.[45]

This was justified by the then imminent implementation in Singapore of the Hill report on local government reform, which was to result in the abolition of the Singapore Improvement Trust and the reversion of their land-use planning responsibilities to the central administration.

By April 1952, the Executive Council had agreed that a Housing Authority should now be formed, with four sections responsible for administration, architecture, survey, and estate management. But knowledge of the proposals led to strong pressure from the Urban Council, who were already responsible for squatter resettlement, that they be allowed to take on 'the other half of the housing problem'.[46] This pressure led to the amending of the Executive Council decision, and in August 1952 a Housing Authority was formed consisting of the 13 members of the Urban Council plus three additional appointees, with its formal powers divested directly upon the Urban Council.

The decision was announced publicly at the formal opening of the Sheung Li Uk scheme in September, and at the same time the Urban Council was invited to set up a committee to discuss with the Public Works Department the selection of sites to initiate a programme for the production of a thousand public housing units per year. The initial scenario was that government was to grant the sites at one half of the upset price; the Colonial Development and Welfare Fund would pay for the site formation costs; the Public Works Department would plan for and erect the buildings; and the new Housing Authority would accept the finished buildings, select the tenants, and manage the finished estates.

In December 1952, the matter was reviewed again in the Executive Council and opposition arose over the adequacy of the scheme. What was more interesting was that it also echoed and provoked further debate within government. The Financial Secretary attacked the tendency to locate the new sites 'out-of-town', disliked the amounts of subsidy involved, and suggested higher densities by doing away with the height limits then imposed on the buildings. He also stated:

I visualise a 'Development and Housing Corporation': this Corporation should have wide powers to acquire both developed and undeveloped sites, to pull down, build and rebuild, and to resell its redeveloped properties.[47]

This idea in turn brought a rejoinder in the debate from the Chief Building Surveyor: if the population increase were as the Financial Secretary had forecast (the basis for his argument about the necessity of high-density development), then,

it is obvious therefore that a) the rate of building must be increased; b) increased heights must be permitted in view of the scarcity of suitable building land; c) lower standards of accommodation may be necessary; d) the establishment of new towns in the New Territories should be considered; e) ... proposals for slum clearance should be encouraged and supported; f) the operations of the Housing Council should be commenced as soon as possible; g) Government should consider the provision of accommodation for all Government employees; and h) the Landlord and Tenant Ordinance should be amended to permit owners of old property to obtain permission to enable them to rebuild.[48]

It is recorded on the file: 'This is a landslide'; but nevertheless, by mid-1952 new towns in Hong Kong were firmly on the government's policy agenda, besides much else that was to reappear over the next three decades. But the necessity for the first major experiment along these lines by government arose from another strand of government policy-making, and to trace that we must return once again to the years immediately following the Japanese occupation and to address directly the problems brought by the squatters.

The Early Post-war Squatter Problem

It is not necessary here to develop a full discussion of the impact of various squatter policies upon the settlement pattern of early post-war Hong Kong; yet some understanding is necessary as an explanation of the first major urban expansion of the post-war years taking place both where it did, and in the form that it did, in the mid-1950s.[49]

The Hong Kong government's first analysis of the initial wave of population squatting after the war in 1948[50] suggested that there were twenty thousand on Hong Kong Island and ten thousand in Kowloon, located on Crown and War Department land, on the roofs of private dwellings, and on privately owned bomb-damaged sites. While it was recognized at the time that the only long-term solution to the problem was an adequate supply of domestic buildings (the provision of publicly financed four-storey walk-up flats was suggested as a partial solution — hence the Public Works Department designs mentioned previously), the more immediate policy recommendations were the allocation of sites for the controlled building of squatter shacks and the clearance of the urban areas by a policy of gradual attrition.

Gradual clearance has a reasonable chance of success. A single concerted drive on all squatter settlements at once would create political and economic problems of a serious kind.[51]

This policy was endorsed by the Executive Council in July 1948, and preparations began later that year for relocation of squatters on to four sites at Mount Davis, Shau Kei Wan, Ho Man Tin, and Lai Chi Kok, prior to formal inauguration of the clearances following Chinese New Year, 1949. In practice the sites proved unpopular, as few of the squatters met the eligibility rules laid down by the government (only about 14 per cent), for by August 1949 only 35 huts had been erected on all four sites, even though by the end of the year 29 clearance operations had removed eight and a half thousand huts and displaced 45 thousand people, resulting in the colonization of newer but equally illegal squatter areas at the urban fringe. Despite this effort, and although the worst squatter areas were now removed from the built-up areas, the acute problem of housing shortage still remained.

The vast majority of displaced squatters found densely packed colonies in the outskirts where they continue to form a serious health danger and a grave fire risk.[52]

Yet the attitude of the highest levels of government was at worst intolerant, and at best ambivalent. In a confidential letter to the Chairman of the Urban Council in July 1950 from the Colonial Secretary it was noted that government had decided that its long-term objective should be the clearance of all squatters, with a view to eventual dispersal to the New Territories and outlying islands, and that no expenditure on static water tanks, hydrants, water mains or any other measures, except fire-breaks in the large settlements, should be contemplated.[53] As yet, squatters were not viewed as the labour market asset that they were later to become.

But such initial draconian ideas on clearance were soon overwhelmed by further successive influxes of refugees from China, such that by early 1951 estimates of the squatter population were already exceeding 250,000. Government again felt impelled to reinvestigate the problem. The Wakefield Report,[54] completed in April 1951, pointed out that even though squatters had been removed from Hong Kong Island west of the racecourse and from most of urban Kowloon, about 125 hectares of land was cur-

Fig. 2.2 Squatter resettlement in Hong Kong resulting from the Wakefield Report of 1951. It was this dispersion to the urban fringes which led to demands for provision of new employment and the construction of Hong Kong's first new factory town at Kwun Tong.

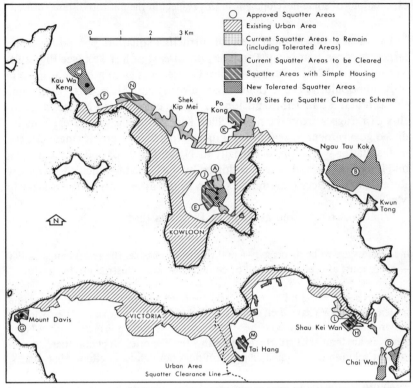

Source: Based on the annotated plan at 4/1 of 1/4 in CR 13/4802/51. Public Records Office, Hong Kong.

rently occupied illegally. To rationalize and attempt to improve the situation the Report suggested that while some further clearances were necessary, resettlement should be encouraged on two bases; one, where small dwellings of standard design would be allowed on government-prepared sites, and the other, in less well-located areas, where self-build would be allowed on agreed layouts. The scheme (the sites for which are shown in Fig. 2.2) went before the Executive Council in July 1951, and appropriate legislation was passed early in 1952.[55] The whole scheme was put under the control of the Urban Council.

Progress on the scheme, particularly in the approved areas, was slow. By April 1954, 46,000 had been resettled in 15 established areas.

It is acknowledged that the progress has been much slower than was hoped. Government has been only too well aware of the slowness of progress, and for this reason has been carefully considering, in the light of experience gained, how to expedite planned resettlement within the limits of our available resources. ... A major dif-

ficulty has proved to be that of decanting, because the areas in which we have
hoped to resettle squatters have of necessity been in the more outlying districts,
and, therefore, regarded by squatters as less accessible; these will be more easily
opened up when industries can be attracted to their neighbourhood, and we have
expectations of some development in this respect in the not too distant future.[56]

   The most problematical area for attracting squatters proved to be the
largest — Area B at Ngau Tau Kok, south-east of Kai Tak (see Fig. 2.2).
Yet by late 1952, the Social Welfare Officer was estimating that in spite
of its unpopularity the settlement was already capable of absorbing some
thirteen and a half thousand jobs, a figure exacerbated by the large influx of refugees from the major Shek Kip Mei fire a year later. This induced government to search for a means to generate employment for the
new squatter work-forces, initially at Ngau Tau Kok and at Chai Wan
on Hong Kong Island, a task endorsed by the Urban Council's Emergency
Resettlement Select Committee set up in the aftermath of the Shek Kip
Mei fire.
   What was recognized as early as 1952 was that,

if squatters are to be dispersed — and this is, in essence, the resettlement policy
— there must also be a dispersal of commercial and industrial establishments.[57]

Squatters squatted on their present sites for economic reasons so that they could
be near money. We have until quite recently been trying to move squatters without
moving the money. Even now the efforts to provide economic attractions at Ngau
Tau Kok are limited to efforts to establish a few factories on permit there. A permanent solution to the squatter problem does not consist in eliminating shacks,
for we cannot do this, but in spreading them out. We cannot even do that unless
we spread out the rest of the town as well. This is not a new argument and although
it may be accepted in principle by Hon. Director of Urban Services its implications are not, I think, accepted by the Public Works Department. 'Why', they
say, 'why should we alter the whole of our town planning technique for the benefit
of squatters?' The answer is that unless we do alter our town planning so as to
provide for people who cannot afford to live in permanent houses the plans are
not realistic and will never be implemented ... I submit that things have become
difficult enough for us to examine the possibility of decentralising commerce and
industry on the mainland — not only as a means of solving the squatter problem
but as a means for planning a City which has a lot of poor people in it.[58]

   Parallel with these internal pressures upon government, there was at
the same time a demand from the Chinese Manufacturers' Union for the
setting-up of a new industrial area. This, and government's own discussions, led to an agreement by the end of 1953 to allow construction of
new standardized, flatted factories on land adjacent to Ngau Tau Kok
and Chai Wan resettlement areas, sites being granted as commented above
by annual permit in the first instance. But by January 1954 the Director
of Public Works, following an investigation he had done into how the
proposed reclamation required at Ngau Tau Kok might proceed, suggested
that a more effective scheme might be to fill parts of Kwun Tong Bay

Fig. 2.3   Kwun Tong new town, 1959 — the development concept for this new town was for the government to form the sites, and then sell them to the private sector for development. Phase 1 of the factory area was zoned and sold by use, but this method of site allocation was rapidly abandoned as unworkable, and sites were subsequently sold by auction in later phases of the development (see also Plates 3a and 3b).

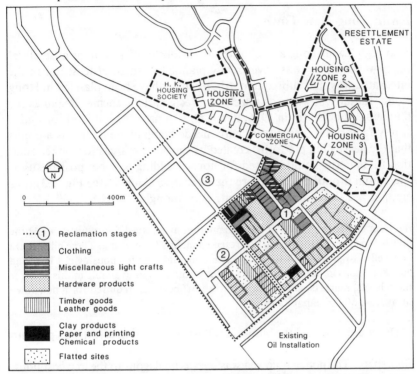

Source: Based on *Kwun Tong New Town Plan* (Hong Kong, Government Printer, 1956), and other plans contained in Files BL 2/5282/53 I–III, Public Records Office, Hong Kong.

with material taken from adjacent borrow areas on the hillsides. This prompted the government to open the whole question again, and to set up a formal inter-departmental committee,

to investigate and report on various proposals which have been made for the leasing of land on favourable terms to industrial interests for the construction of factories, and to advise on long term policy; and to report as a matter of urgency on the desirability and practicability of developing the areas adjoining the resettlement area of Ngau Tau Kok, and possibly certain areas within the present resettlement area, as an industrial site, the factories in which would employ squatters from Ngau Tau Kok for their unskilled labour.[59]

The committee reported in May 1954, and recommended a solution which allowed for a three-staged reclamation of 58 hectares in Kwun Tong Bay (see Fig. 2.3) — about one half of the total area suggested by the

Public Works Department. This was to form part of the site for a new factory town of at least 50,000 people — Kwun Tong New Town as it was called — the first major urban expansion scheme, and the first formally designated new town in Hong Kong.

Kwun Tong New Town

Although Kwun Tong at the time was variously referred to as a 'satellite' or 'new' town,[60] it was never really planned as such, at least not in the integrated way that subsequent urban centres have been planned in Hong Kong. Initially, it was seen purely as a reclamation scheme. Begun as the municipal rubbish tip in 1935, it was now to produce flat land for multi-storey factories to provide urgently needed employment. It was a bonus that the nearby hill platforms created by the borrow areas for the reclamation fill material could be used for house building or other possible uses. The initial proposals put before the Executive Council (see Fig. 2.3) thus emphasized the industrial content, even though:

the Plan shows the whole of the reclamation as reserved for industry while the hills behind the reclamation are ... reserved mainly for housing. These hills would be levelled to provide fill for the reclamation and sites for housing not less than 50,000 persons in multi-storey flats. Sites would also be available in this area for the schools, markets, clinics, Government offices, etc., required for a new town of at least 50,000 inhabitants.[61]

Despite the words, the whole emphasis in planning effort was put into expediting and implementing the rapid development of the industrial floorspace. The policy followed was seen as analagous to the low-cost housing recently introduced under the new Hong Kong Housing Authority — while direct subsidy was not to be allowed, support (particularly to keep down industrialists' costs and to counter overseas accusations of low wage competition from Hong Kong) was given through cheaper land costs. Thus, the costs of land production were monitored carefully, and, for Kwun Tong, sites were made available at HK $5 per square foot (46.5 cents per square metre) payable over a number of years; this income was to reimburse the HK $10 million charged to the Territory's development fund as the loan cost for the new Stage I and II reclamation works. As always, an eventual profit was nevertheless expected.

Approval of the scheme by the Executive Council in July 1954 led to the formation of a further Working Committee to plan and oversee the project, and this met for the first time in September 1954. Its membership is interesting in that it was chaired by the Director of Commerce and Industry, and had only one planner amongst its four members, R.C. Clarke, the Assistant Superintendent of Crown Lands (Planning), who was a surveyor by training. Its first meeting set out a number of fundamentals to be followed in its development policies:

(a) that the industrial layout should be determined by the size demands for sites by the industrialists;

(b) that there should be a special area for flatted factories;

(c) that multi-storey development should generally be insisted upon;

(d) that housing of staff in the industrial area should not be permitted, and that a person buying a site for a factory should normally be expected to buy a site for workers' housing also;

(e) that development should be planned, and this required sales by private treaty rather than by public auction. Control was sought particularly over the distribution of industrial processes in the estate; and,

(f) that sites should be sold by private treaty, zoned by industrial use (as shown in Fig. 2.3). This principle was changed in June 1955 to sales by public auction, and in 1957 in favour of general industrial-user zoning.

That the new urban area was to meet a pent-up need is easily demonstrated. By April 1955, initial applications for industrial sites had reached 458, embracing 17 different industrial groupings requiring almost 900,000 square metres of floorspace.[62] On readvertisement, after the revision of the sale requirements, 993 applications were eventually received for over one and a half million square metres of floorspace; and it was this potential demand that was used as the basis of the planning of the layout of the industrial estate and the allocations of sites to particular industry groupings in the first phase.

By May 1956, the Working Committee's proposals for development were ready,[63] and once again were put before the Executive Council for approval. The essentials of the initial layout were set out on a Key Plan which allocated the 45 hectares of the first three stages of the industrial reclamation into 19 blocks containing 180 sites of varying sizes from 930 to 1,860 square metres, which were recommended to be auctioned as soon as they became available. Additionally, adjacent to the reclamation, the plan allocated areas for residential use in three groupings totalling 34 hectares, including provisions for workers' private housing schemes, government housing (see Fig. 2.5), or private tenements, and an additional area of 15 hectares for new resettlement housing and the central commercial area of 5 hectares (see Fig. 2.4). A number of specific sites were also set aside within the industrial area for flatted factories which were required to have a minimum of five storeys.

The Committee also pointed out that there would have to be certain restrictions imposed, at least initially, on the allocation of the industrial sites, firstly because of limited water supplies, secondly to avoid smoke nuisance affecting the nearby airport, and thirdly to exclude offensive trades. The industrial site arrangements were determined by grouping applicants into appropriate use classes, and then dividing up each available block so as to allow front and rear access to each site. It was also proposed that sites should be sold in some sort of order (decided by the type of industry proposed), which was to be determined in advance by the Committee.[64]

On the housing side it was argued that the probable target population to be catered for was 90,000 in the first five years of the scheme, increasing to 200,000 after ten years. This population was to be housed in five- or six-storey self-contained housing blocks of self-contained units, at an overall density of not less than 3,000 persons to the net hectare. While it was felt that commercial enterprise should be encouraged to provide a large proportion of the housing in the form of traditional tenement housing built on individual sites, it was recognized that a greater variety of available housing was likely to be required than the private sector was willing to provide, which was the reason for the early involvement of both the new Hong Kong Housing Authority, and the designation of a specific site for the Hong Kong Housing Society. In the event the early doubts about the abilities of the private sector to provide proved accurate.

Reclamation of the 33 hectares of Stages I and II of the reclamation (see Plate 3a) was completed in mid-1959, and Stage III was begun in the same year. Even by June 1958, it was reported that 87 sites had been sold, and 42 sets of building plans submitted, but only three factories were complete, with four under construction.

The reluctance to go ahead seems to stem again from the lack of domestic housing, schools and transport facilities in the area.[65]

This was despite the abandonment in May 1957 of the user-allocation system of allocating sites mentioned before. But the problems with the take-up of sites were not the only ones to surface rapidly. Much more important for the longer term were inadequacies in the way that the town had been conceived and developed.

There seems little doubt that the development of Kwun Tong was approached in a manner typical of most other layout schemes in Hong Kong up until that time. Basically, it was seen as a land production exercise designed to produce sites for the private sector of a specific nature (industrial) and at an economic cost to government (profitably). For example, the procedure was such that particular infrastructure services, like water supply, were not guaranteed, or even initially provided. Again, the provision of the housing sites arose largely from the need to utilize profitably the platforms formed on the adjacent hillsides by removing material for the reclamation, rather than from a conscious effort to design the whole development as a comprehensive new self-contained town with a complete range of facilities and services from the beginning.

Thus, it is not surprising that so much of the initial effort on implementation went on the industrial sector, with the result that demands for various other urban facilities from industrialists and, more importantly, their workers in the new factories rapidly outstripped the meagre opportunities provided on what was virtually a virgin building site. In summary, the development of the multitude of back-up services required within a new town was, in Kwun Tong, either entirely absent or fell behind the demands imposed by the incoming workers, and this rapidly became a source of serious and continuous complaint against the government authorities.

An early failure of some consequence was the non-fulfilment of the initial assumption that factory owners would be prepared to invest in housing for their own workers. It quickly became apparent that many of the industrial applicants were not sufficiently capitalized to undertake such schemes anyway, and of those that were, few wished to divert their investment resources away from their primary objective of industrial production. The result was that although by mid-1956 it was apparent that government would have to intervene by providing more housing of its own, the problem was compounded by a shortage of Public Works Department staff, which held up the preparation of the requisite housing sites.

Thus, by the end of that year, it was even being suggested that the sale of the industrial sites should be slowed down in order to allow the completion of sufficient housing. In fact, by mid-1958 the position had so worsened that private sector housing interest in the new town had dwindled to nothing, and it had to be agreed that there was no point in government offering housing lots for auction. While such a policy was a necessity in government land sales terms, it was hardly conducive to effective and 'balanced' development of the town as a working community.

An immediate result of such severe problems was the setting up of yet another investigation by J.T. Wakefield (then Secretary for Chinese Affairs), which duly appeared in May of that year.

This new industrial development is the first occasion since the war in which Government has promoted the birth and growth of a new satellite town; in all other cases new development has been but an extension of the main urban area or of a thriving semi-rural community. Admittedly in a few years time this satellite town of Kwun Tong will become an integral part of the developed urban locality covered by the term 'Kowloon'. In promoting the development of this satellite town something more positive should have been done by Government other than the preparation of land for sale for various uses ... Although over 60 acres [24 hectares] of land has now been sold or surfaced as roads there are still no signs of schools, a clinic, a post office, markets, a police station, Government sub-offices or any other amenities, all of which should have been in the course of erection by the time the first new residents are expected to move in (i.e. November 1958).[66]

At the time of the Report, 400 people were already being employed in the first three factories, and it was expected that there could be a minimum of 3,500 in employment by the end of the year, with an eventual 25,000 for all the lots then sold on the Stage I and II reclamation. On the housing side, one-fifth of a hectare had been sold for tenement shop-houses of five-storey minimum, but the further 1.2 hectares offered in June 1958 failed to attract any buyers. The proposed workers' housing had fared little better, with only just over one hectare under active preparation at that time. However, at least the two-hectare site for the Hong Kong Housing Society was then under development, eventually to provide some 1,090 flat units. The other major scheme which had got under way was the first of the resettlement estates in the Jordan Valley and Kai Liu, which was expecting its first intakes in March 1959 (see Fig. 2.3).

Of the various deficiencies noted in the Report, the most serious proved to be the lack of schools and medical facilities, and within the factory area itself, the almost total absence of daytime eating facilities. The Public Works Department's response to these problems was threefold. Firstly, it pointed out that sites were allocated for most of the public facilities demanded, and that building would commence as soon as funds were made available; secondly, it suggested that development might be speeded up by the introduction of standard designs; and thirdly, that two areas on the reclamation could be set aside for cooked-food stalls, but that these would have to be regarded as temporary pending the provision of adequate restaurant facilities by the private sector.

Clearly, initial moves for improvement proved inadequate, for the situation became sufficiently serious by November 1959 for the Chinese Manufacturers' Association (representing the owners on the reclamation) to complain formally to the government. Four principle areas were specified — the paucity of communications of all kinds, a lack of security (there was still no police or fire station), complaints about poor sanitation, and the difficulty of labour recruitment because of the perceived major lack of residential and commercial facilities for the area.

In reply, government both issued a major press release on how the town was expected to develop, and commented directly on the issues raised. It noted that the new ferry pier was expected by December 1960, while the improved road access to Kowloon would be in place by the end of 1961; while on matters of housing it noted that the take-up of sites on offer was not as good as expected — a case of factory owners complaining, but not being prepared to commit their own resources to alleviate the problem as was required of them. It also stated that by the end of 1960, 7,000 primary school places would be available in four government and private schools, and that the first public services like the police station should be in place by the end of 1961.

Kwun Tong is both an ambitious scheme and something of an experiment in the production of wholly new townships — an experiment which no doubt will be repeated in varying forms in other parts of the Colony in the years to come. The Government is well aware from the experience gained at Kwun Tong that improvements in the processes of making new townships can in future be made, and the lessons learnt in the development of Kwun Tong will be valuable in the future.[67]

It was therefore hopeful for the future, but perhaps of less help in alleviating the immediate problems of the new inhabitants of Kwun Tong.

This imbalance between housing, employment, and community facilities proved to be remarkably persistent, as noted in a much later report on community facilities in Kwun Tong, prepared by the City District Officer for the area in August 1970.[68] By that time, twelve years on, the original estimates for the growth of Kwun Tong had been far outstripped.

Housing for more than 500,000 persons has been built, as have 800 factories, 823 primary school classrooms and an excellent road network. It does appear however that the provision of other community facilities has not kept up with the rapid expansion of the population of the District.[69]

The basic community facilities which decide the quality of life in any community, have generally not been provided at even a minimal rate and this situation could result in serious social upheavals in a young community which is becoming better educated and better paid month by month.[70]

Thus, a spectre of social disorder, to which government felt bound to react, was raised; but by then the major problem in the town had become the lack of suitable vacant sites which could be utilized for the provision of the improvements which were then regarded as necessities.

500,000, in fact, became the planners target for the town — reduced from 650,000 in order to attempt a better match between population and the likely availability of the facilities required to adequately service them on the basis of the then new planning standards promulgated in the Colony Outline Plan (see Table 2.1). The need for the current deficiencies to be made up had been made glaringly obvious (see Table 2.1) in the District Officer's report. Particular concern was also expressed at the time at the large proportion of the population then residing at minimum stand-

Table 2.1 Deficiencies in Planned Community Facilities in Kwun Tong in January 1970

Community Facility	Provision in 1970	Standard Requirement	Planned Provision	Shortfall
Primary classrooms	823	1,100	1,261	—
Secondary schools	3	35	16	19
Polyclinics	—	1	—	1
Hospital beds	20	2,000	379	1,621
Clinics	1	5	2	3
Stadia	—	1	—	1
Hectares of open space	13	61	36	25
Civic centre	—	1	—	1
Markets	—	7	2	5
Cinemas	4	14	5	9
Welfare offices	2	6	5	1
Community centres	1	4	2	2
Refuse collection points	?	21	8	13
Cooked-food stalls	90[1]	180	16	164
Libraries	—	4	—	4

Note: 1. Site required for development.

Source: Based on *Report on the Provision of Community Requirements in Kowloon Planning Area 14* (Hong Kong government, Kwun Tong District Office, 1970) Appendix 1; copy at Float in BL 3/5282/58, Public Records Office, Hong Kong.

ards in the resettlement estates (some 52 per cent of the town's population), and the fact that:

each of the Resettlement Estates in the District contains the population of a fair-sized town and has only the facilities of a village.[71]

Proper consideration of these requirements did lead eventually to some improvement, but the process was slow. Priorities for urban investment were elsewhere in the 1970s, and it was not really until after the setting up of an area management committee within government locally in 1979 (following the model of those created in the new towns on the Tsuen Wan style) that real progress can be demonstrated. Thus the creation of a new multi-purpose town centre, the redevelopment of the resettlement estates, and full integration of the town with the main urban area were all policies only of the 1980s, despite the early recognition of the town's very real inadequacies.

That Kwun Tong really was a prototype from which mistakes had to be learnt was apparent over the years on the industrial side too. For example, a paper prepared for the Secretary of Home Affairs in September 1969[72] noted that there were severe practical problems regarding the loading and unloading of goods in the industrial area, private car parking, the proliferation of illegal hawker food facilities, and the collection of refuse; all of which could be traced back to inadequacies in the original layout design and subsequent management of the area. To a degree, these same problems continued into the 1980s — Kwun Tong became a victim of its own success.

While few would argue now that Kwun Tong has any particular merit in town-planning terms, it does deserve consideration on two particular grounds. Firstly, it clearly demonstrated to government the inadequacies of its traditional approaches to urban development, and in particular the necessity of finding and developing new administrative arrangements for effectively planning and implementing new-town development schemes. Secondly, while much of the development was carried out on conventional layout planning lines, for the time, there was also some innovative work carried out in Kwun Tong.[73] Within this area two particular schemes are worthy of examination here: the designs for the Kwun Tong commercial centre and that for the Hong Kong Housing Authority's first housing estate in the town — the first estate specifically designed for a new town in Hong Kong.

The plan for the commercial centre (see Fig. 2.4), first produced at the end of 1960, is interesting, not only because it was the first produced in Hong Kong for a new major urban centre, but because it very much replicated contemporary British new-town designs of the period for their own neighbourhood shopping centres. Thus, the landscaped internal service courtyards and associated car parks for shoppers and residents, with pedestrianized shopping squares, seem more reminiscent of their British models than relevant to the realities of Hong Kong life. Most important

Fig. 2.4   Kwun Tong Commercial Centre, 1960 (Plan LK 14/15A) — the design
is typical of British new-town neighbourhood shopping precincts of the
day, with a pedestrian mall lined with shops, and servicing and car
parking at the rear.

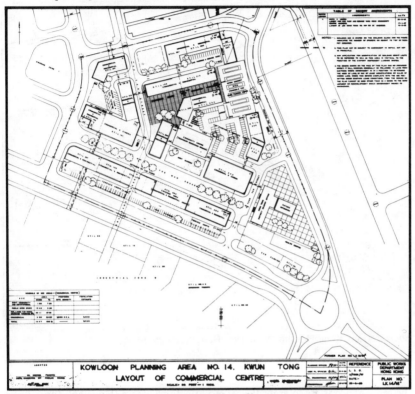

Source: Territorial Development Department, Hong Kong government.

of all, however, with the rapid expansion of the town's population targets
these facilities soon became grossly inadequate.

Factory workers want the same sort of recreational facilities as commercial workers.
Statue Square in Central and Yue Man Square in Kwun Tong are good examples
of the type of thing that is required ... Readers will probably be more familiar
with the greenery, trees and fountains of Statue Square than the dust, tree stumps
and dried up ponds of Yue Man Square.[74]

In 1967, it was noted that the area of the Kwun Tong commercial centre
had been kept deliberately small with the intention of establishing a compact and lively centre for the town.

This object has now been largely achieved and the time is opportune to consider
how best commercial floor space can be expanded. I have come to the conclusion
that in view of the present population and early large increases expected it would

Fig. 2.5   Hong Kong Housing Authority Kwun Tong Estate, Phase 1, 1961 (Plan
              HA 7/13) — this estate was the first public housing to be built in a new
              town other than the Resettlement Estate 'H' Blocks, which can be seen
              to the west of this estate.

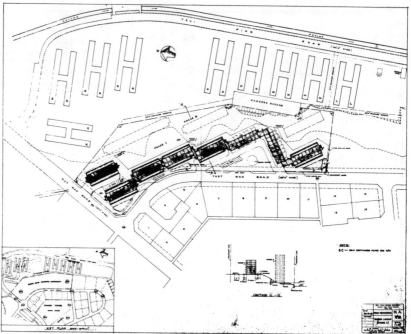

Source: Hong Kong Housing Authority, Hong Kong government.

be more appropriate to grant [lease] modifications within [Housing] Zones I and
II to allow certain commercial uses rather than to enforce present restrictions against
such uses.[75]

The old centre had clearly outgrown itself in less than a decade, and the
original zoning concept of the new town had become obsolete. From the
mid-1960s onward the planners were faced with orchestrating a long and
painful adjustment to the realities of a much larger population than the
town had ever been designed for, and attempting to include the higher
planning standards that the planners and the community themselves were
then demanding.

   On the public housing side (see Fig. 2.5), Kwun Tong was seen as playing a pivotal role in the contemporary public housing programmes. As
early as 1955, it was recognized by the Commissioner for Resettlement
that a considerable number of sites for the new resettlement 'H' blocks
was going to be required, and Kwun Tong took its share — ultimately
six estates housing some 259,000 people. Providing public housing through
the new Housing Authority proved more problematical. A survey of potential tenants suggested that accommodation should be provided in five/six
person flats at an average monthly rent of between HK $55 and HK $65.

Given the two-and-a-half-hectare site allocated, and even developing a scheme of seven-storey walk-up flats where:

finishes are either eliminated altogether or cut down to a very low standard, the structure is designed to optimum limits, and no site amenities are provided other than paths to give access to the buildings,[76]

the initial cost-breakdown caused the Housing Authority to attempt to negotiate for a specially low land price, unsuccessfully as it turned out. Nevertheless, the scheme was built and it contained 864 flats and 16 shops in the seven-storey blocks of Phase I, followed from 1963 by a further 1,070 units in the newly designed high-rise blocks of Phase II.

The Wo Lok Estate at Kwun Tong once again represented a first; both in design terms — for the block designs incorporated local standardized layouts as far as possible (rather than the specialized design of the Authority's first estate at North Point on Hong Kong Island); and secondly, because it illustrated an organizational principle for public housing in new towns that has remained to this day, namely that estate design for public housing estates has always been the prerogative of the Housing Authority itself within site boundaries laid down by the planners of each town. It is a division of responsibility that has had some important implications for the subsequent history of new-town design in Hong Kong (see Chapter 7).

It is therefore difficult to escape from the already expressed conclusion that Kwun Tong was indeed the place where the initial mistakes, and hopefully the first learning processes to do with new-town planning in Hong Kong were made. Later, the mistakes had to be rectified:

It no longer matters how and why this situation in Kwun Tong has arisen, but what can we do to retrieve it.[77]

Furthermore, the high degree of overcrowding, lack of environmental beauty, recreation and entertainment facilities, the problem of traffic congestion, shortage of spaces for commercial/business undertakings, all these problems reflect that an urban district is neither sufficiently nor well planned.[78]

This is clearly a verdict with which few in 1973 would have disagreed. Yet, one must not deny the achievement either: in a decade, a new and vibrant manufacturing centre had been created where before only a municipal rubbish tip existed. Without the economic wealth created in its factories, the development possibilities and subsequent history of Hong Kong in the 1970s and beyond might well have been rather different. For that, at least, Hong Kong requires to be thankful.

The Search for a Development Strategy

We have already noted that as early as mid-1952 new-town development had been mentioned within government as a possible development option for Hong Kong. Kwun Tong, though the first manifestation of such a policy, really came about as a specific solution to a specific problem, rather than as a response to these wider questions about an overall development strategy for the long-term development of the Territory as a whole.

Such concerns, however, resurfaced in some correspondence at the end of 1955 between the Commissioner for Resettlement and the Director of Public Works, in which the latter noted that as a response to space demands for the natural increase in population, for immigrants and refugees, and for people then in sub-standard housing, three planning solutions suggested themselves — increasing the density of existing areas; placing housing developments in underdeveloped areas of the existing urban area; and new-town development in the New Territories.

Where the problem is so big as it is in Hong Kong it is impossible to rely on any one solution and therefore [I would] recommend a combination of all reasonable solutions i.e. new suburbs, under-populated suburbs and new towns. Proposed action [would be to] secure funds for development of both suburbs and new towns to provide for site formation, reclamation, public services and public buildings. A programme of successive developments to be drawn up; boundaries of suburbs due for development to be decided; likewise for new towns in the New Territories (Tsun Wan, Castle Peak Area, Shatin, Tai Po Area, Sai Kung, Lantao, Lamma). Planning [would] need to be stepped up: First a regional plan, then town plans, while a decision is also required on the future role of the Housing Authority and on housing policy generally.[79]

Clearly, pressure was again mounting within government for some longer term strategic planning decisions. But there were also jurisdiction arguments. In early discussions during 1954 on the possibility of developing Sha Tin, one of the Assistant Colonial Secretaries commented:

it is not, I think, the function of the Housing Authority to develop 'satellite towns', an idea which is or was fashionable with town planners in England and which seems to have a fascination for some members of the Housing Authority. The question whether satellite towns should or should not be developed and where they should be sited is surely a matter of town planning, a function of the Public Works Department, which should be not be usurped by the Housing Authority.[80]

The debate was carried forward by a report from the Commissioner for Resettlement in November 1955 setting out a survey of the situation some eighteen months after the resettlement effort had begun in the aftermath of the Shek Kip Mei fire.

Our housing problem is completely and demonstrably insoluble by present methods ... the situation still amounts to a grave emergency, and one of its worst features is of course the shortage of land capable of immediate development.[81]

It was this warning that triggered the setting up of a special committee, following a Governor's conference in December 1955, to:

investigate and report on the Colony's housing situation, including resettlement of squatters, in relation both to the needs of the population, now and in the foreseeable future, and to the resources likely to be available for the purpose.[82]

The new committee got down to work rapidly, and in three months (by May 1956) was ready with its first interim report.[83] Besides a recommendation to continue and expand the existing resettlement programme, it also asked for a major change in the policy of government towards the development of land.

The Committee considers that the land shortage must be relieved and that it can be relieved only by the adoption of a new and positive policy towards land development...It is clearly impossible for new accommodation to be produced by any means on this scale [for 80,000 people per annum additional to the resettlement programme] and at this pace in the present urban areas or at the taxpayer's expense. What appears to be required is the equivalent of one new town ... each year. What then is practical? The Committee considers that the fundamental requirement is for a really adequate technical staff to plan and carry out the basic engineering works necessary to make new land capable of development on a very substantial scale. At this stage this is chiefly an engineering matter ... although of course town planning must proceed in step with engineering investigations ... The proposal is then, that the engineering problems associated with this type of possible new development should be investigated by the Government, with a view to the Government planning and carrying out the engineering works precedent to the creation of new towns or suburbs, complete with everything but the buildings. The land thus made available for urban or suburban development would then all be used in a combination of the following forms of development: a) sale for housing; b) sale for industry: c) construction of government-aided housing; and d) construction of parks, public buildings including schools, clinics, markets, etc. It is not contended that these operations would be necessarily profit making.[84]

Clearly, the Committee was influenced by the Kwun Tong model, then just getting under way, and it was of course too early to learn any of the planning lessons that were to become apparent there. So, with the approval of the main recommendations by the Executive Council and the Finance Committee of the Legislative Council in June and July 1956, a new-town programme for Hong Kong additional to development at Kwun Tong had become a firm commitment of government. The questions were now how, where, and when, rather than the if of previous years.

In fact the Committee had been strongly influenced in its deliberations and conclusions by a review produced by the planning staff within the Public Works Department entitled *Proposed Measures for the Accommodation of Surplus Population.*[85] It was effectively a worked-up version of the Director's note of 1955 referred to earlier, and it repeated the same three directions for future development. The redevelopment of existing areas at increased densities had now been catered for by the 1955 revision of the Buildings Ordinance, but the emphasis on urban infilling or new towns remained as possible choices. The review suggested that about

650,000 might be accommodated on maximum densities within Hong Kong Island and Kowloon, with a further 1.5 million on various new-town sites in the New Territories. The Committee, in endorsing the recommendations in its final report of 1958, was not, however, quite so enthusiastic as the planners.

The Committee considers, however, that the proposal for the creation of new towns in the areas suggested in Planning Memorandum No.1, although highly desirable from the point of view of the reduction of the high densities of population existing in the urban area, needs to be approached with considerable caution and is unlikely by itself to provide a solution to the housing problems of the urban area ... The strong possibility is that there is little scope for dormitory towns and that new towns can only be located around new centres of employment [the origin of the self-containment argument in Hong Kong]. But in Hong Kong the main sources of employment are commerce and light industry; it is not possible to calculate with any certainty their future development, and in the case of commerce the centre of employment is bound to remain in the city and around the harbour shores. New towns may follow industrial expansion into new areas; industrial expansion may be facilitated, but it cannot be created, nor can new towns be created without it or without the prior establishment of other sources of employment. The Committee considers that, whilst all possible steps should be taken to encourage the creation of new towns outside the urban area... it is likely that for some time to come the major proportion of domestic accommodation for the increasing population must be found in the urban area and close to the city.[86]

A conclusion reinforced by the Committee's belief that some 68 sites capable of accommodating another 3 million people existed in the main urban area (see Fig. 2.6).

Government's implementation of the Committee's *Second Interim Report* in March 1957 by appointing a new Commissioner for Housing as government's professional housing adviser, also proved significant for the development of Hong Kong's new towns, for it brought to Hong Kong (in December 1958) J.M. Fraser, a former Chairman of the Singapore Improvement Trust, who was soon to prove a fervent supporter of both new towns and comprehensive town planning — a policy position which did not always go down well with his new colleagues. 'I do not share his respect for Master Plans in a territory such as ours',[87] was a typical comment of the time, particularly in response to Fraser's thorough review of the Committee's three reports. Fraser also argued that the new Public Works Department Development Division:

will not meet the situation and that something like a Development Department [to come eventually perhaps in the formation of the New Territories Development Department in 1973/4] is needed to conceive, investigate and oversee development schemes ... The aim should be to build houses in planned communities which are as far as possible self-contained with shops, markets, schools, clinics and workplaces in close proximity. The idea of building housing schemes anywhere a site becomes available is fundamentally bad ... Land should be regarded as a permanent Government asset and not a commodity for sale. Land policy requires careful considera-

Fig. 2.6 Hong Kong's Urban Expansion Proposals of 1960 — drawn up by the Town Planning Office as *Planning Memorandum No.4*, it was the Territory's second attempt at a comprehensive development strategy, following Abercrombie's 1949 proposals.

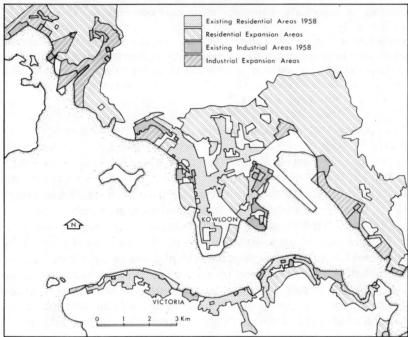

Existing Residential Areas 1958
Residential Expansion Areas
Existing Industrial Areas 1958
Industrial Expansion Areas

KOWLOON

VICTORIA

0   1   2   3 Km

Source: Based on Plan III, *Urban Area — Possible Expansion*, at 9/1 in BL 2/5282/61, Building and Lands Registry, Hong Kong.

tion, directed towards its most beneficial use. Town planning should be given a more prominent place in the Government organisation.[88]

The impact of the Special Committee's deliberations can also be judged by examining subsequent work from the Town Planning Office. December 1958 saw the production of Planning Memorandum No.4 (see Fig. 2.6) for discussion within government, which attempted to set out the development trends for the coming ten years 'to give a lead to the policy to be adopted particularly in relation to the question of satellite towns'.[89] After reviewing current population trends, a number of planning assumptions were set out as a basis for formulating future development policy. The average housing density per net hectare over all residential zones was set at 1,000 persons per acre, (2,471 persons per hectare) with uses divided up at 40 per cent housing, 12 per cent community buildings, 8 per cent open space, and 40 per cent for roads and services. The proportions for industrial zones were similarly set at 200 employees to the net acre (495 per net hectare), with 60 per cent industrial, 6 per cent community facilities, 4 per cent open space and 30 per cent roads and services respectively.

Examination of potential land resources led the planners to suggest that:

although on theoretical planning grounds the establishment of new towns is highly to be desired on economic and political grounds, the trend will be towards further expansion of existing urban centres ... Assuming that Government policy will continue to be to facilitate private enterprise rather than to control and direct it, development policy should be in the short term to expand the existing urban districts and develop Tsuen Wan/Kwai Chung ... and in the long term to revive one or more of the New Town projects.'[90]

In summary, the suggestion was that immediate attention should focus on the harbour frontages between Tsuen Wan and Lei Yue Mun, with later expansion westwards in the direction of Lantau and Castle Peak. It is interesting also to note that at this time Tsuen Wan was already thought of as an extension of the existing urban area, like Kwun Tong, rather than as the separate new town then being promoted.

Despite such initial caution, the examination of new reclamations (see p. 70), and the decision to go ahead with major expansion of Tsuen Wan and Kwai Chung, by 1960 prompted the planners to put forward a further submission to government on the whole future of town planning in Hong Kong.[91] In part, the review stemmed from a perceived need to expand the existing planning staff in order to deal with the anticipated expansion of the urban areas and the development of the New Territories; but it was also a response to a:

need for more comprehensive planning and more detailed control of development expressed by many individuals and authorities ... during the last few years.[92]

In particular, R.C. Clarke, the Assistant Superintendent of Crown Lands (Planning), argued that the preparation of a guideline regional plan for the whole Territory had now become necessary, together with a major data collection exercise to back up the planning work required.

With more comprehensive data available and with a generally approved Regional Plan the preparation of planning and development schemes for township areas would proceed with greater confidence,[93]

even though the paper came down firmly against the master plan concept then being advocated by the Commissioner for Housing based on his Singapore experience. In forwarding the paper to the Secretariat for comment the then Acting Director of Public Works supported the idea fully:

there is an urgent need for a Regional Plan for the Colony within the framework of which individual town plans can be prepared and related.[94]

Initial response to this pressure in the Secretariat was that even this idea was too ambitious, and it was suggested that regional planning was probably only needed in limited areas[95] — a fundamental misunderstanding of the concept. Nevertheless, the Secretariat response did eventually prove favourable, even though the result was a direct bid to take over the task itself.

What we need is an Economic Planning (or Development) Committee ... This committee would consider *ab initio* but in broad outline all major planning developments and ideas not only in the town planning sense but also major projects such as the Ocean Ship Terminal, Harbour Bridge, land development schemes, etc.[96]

This new suggestion was strongly supported by the Financial Secretary, and at a Secretariat meeting on 10 November 1960,

it was agreed that the fundamental problem at present lies in lack of coordination of planning policy and proposals in relation to the financial and economic resources of the Colony. Much time can be spent on grandiose schemes for which the funds cannot be provided ... It was decided that close liaison is necessary between the Public Works Department and the Secretariat and that this could be achieved by setting up a Committee, to be known as the Land Development Planning Committee.[97]

Thus, planning policy-making at the strategic level effectively began, perhaps not surprisingly for Hong Kong, out of financial necessities. The new committee met for the first time early in 1961.

Establishment of the new committee delayed consideration of the regional planning idea, and it was not until February 1962 that the Chairman of the new committee reported that:

the Committee, after considerably more discussion than is apparent from its minutes, has reached the conclusion that the preparation of a regional land use plan for the Colony is necessary.[98]

As a result of this decision a new section within the Town Planning Office was created to prepare a Colony Outline Plan on the basis that:

overall planning must be flexible and able to be frequently revised; it must be the guide, not the master. The plan should be used as a guide for the Town Planning Board when formulating district town plans, but should not be published and should not have statutory force.[99]

Nevertheless, when it eventually appeared in 1970, it did represent the government's agreed strategic thinking for the future development of the Territory, against which new-town planning, first considered in the 1950s, and partially implemented in the 1960s, had to be set. But by then, the plan had itself become a prisoner of past decisions:

Whilst there are a number of possible alternative development strategies [see Fig. 3.2] that could be adopted for long-term planning purposes, it is considered that government's basic policy should be decentralisation to new towns and improvement of the environment in the existing urban areas ... This gives positive expression to the strategy which in recent years has been followed but not stated in explicit terms by Government.[100]

It is now necessary to explain why such an outcome arose in the decade within which the plan was being formulated.

The Beginnings of the New-town Programme

In establishing the origins of Hong Kong's new towns it is apparent that a number of policy streams within government were developed in parallel. Thus, while the 1960s were a decade in which there was a gradual yet determined progression to an overall strategy for the development of Hong Kong, that process was rapidly overtaken by *ad hoc* responses to more immediately pressing demands for the production of more development land, particularly to meet housing requirements. It is therefore appropriate to return once again to the work of the 1956 Special Committee on Housing which we have considered earlier in this chapter.

While government was willing to accept the Committee's recommendation of 1956 that there should be a new Development Division set up within the Public Works Department to produce serviced sites, it became apparent that it could not be set up rapidly, not least because of problems with staff recruitment. The urgency of the problem (both to produce new land quickly, and to plan for a new town) therefore led in 1957 to the Public Works Department seeking approval to employ consultants to undertake the preliminary engineering and planning assessments of major possible projects.

After considerable discussion within government as to the priorities to be attached to the many schemes put forward as possibilities,[101] a final list of six was eventually put before the Executive Council in October 1957 for approval; following which Scott Wilson Kirkpatrick & Partners were engaged to proceed with preliminary engineering studies. The six were reclamation and town development schemes at Tai Po, Gin Drinker's Bay (Kwai Chung), Junk Bay, Sha Tin, and Castle Peak (Tuen Mun), together with a proposed road across the Lead Mine Pass from Tai Po to Shing Mun, with the possibility of then proceeding immediately to an implementation study for the Tai Po scheme. An additional scheme was later added and given to University of Hong Kong consultants for the expansion of Tsuen Wan. Of the reclamation schemes selected, there was general support within government for those proposed at Tai Po, Sha Tin, and Kwai Chung, while Junk Bay was included since it did not involve transport demands on already crowded roads into Kowloon; but Castle Peak only got its place because of its priority in the demands of the then District Commissioner, New Territories.

The consultant's reports were submitted to government over the period December 1958 to October 1959, and went before Executive Council at the end of the latter year. Some of the proposals will be considered in some detail later (as part of our study of some of the first-generation new towns); for purposes here, it is sufficient to note that on financial grounds it was argued strongly within government that only one scheme could proceed immediately, and that that scheme should be the one for Kwai Chung and Tsuen Wan. This was agreed to by the Executive Council, with an addendum that consideration of beginning the Sha Tin scheme could be reconsidered in three year's time should circumstances then appear to justify it. New-town development was thus firmly committed in Hong Kong, even before strategic planning for the Territory had properly begun. Yet another case of immediate priorities pre-empting reasoned strategic thinking.

Conclusions

The decade and a half following the reincorporation of the Territory in 1945 demonstrates a fragmented and sometimes tortuous search for an appropriate and implementable development strategy. This can usefully be broken down into a number of sometimes disparate elements representing particular, and often immediate, policy requirements of the Hong Kong administration.

The first of these was a requirement to develop an appropriate planning machinery which eventually was required to determine and control the unforeseen urban expansion that by the end of the 1950s was universally recognized within government as being a somewhat unwelcome necessity. Yet such requirements had been foreseen and advocated by Abercrombie after the war, had suffered a severe relapse at the hands of the highest levels of government in the early 1950s, and were still unresolved in the early 1960s as new-town building in Hong Kong began in earnest.

The second element was the gradual evolution, sometimes forced along by the pressures of external events, of a coherent housing policy, particularly for the nascent public sector. This was set to drive forward all subsequent new-town development programmes. At first, this was inexorably linked to attempts to deal with the squatter problem. While it was realized early on that government would have to involve itself, financial constraints and policies gave rise to a clear impression that the government's hand was being forced by outside pressures and circumstances, rather than that its involvement came from a determination or even a voluntary willingness to intervene. Yet having begun, effectively from 1953, it was an involvement that progressively deepened, and became all pervasive; so by the 1980s almost half of Hong Kong's population, and much of it in new towns, was housed in publicly subsidized accommodation.

The third area was the government's needs to respond to the fundamental change that took place in this period to the Territory's economic structure. By moving from one based primarily upon trading, to one dominated by manufacturing, this change created a demand for land and provided a market for the incoming labour supply. These factors led directly, as we have seen, to the first major attempt at urban expansion and new-town building. In fact, excluding the later public housing programmes, more land was sold to the private sector in the decade after the war for industrial purposes than it took for housing. Land production for industry continued to remain a major policy issue in all subsequent decades up until the present.

A final conclusion would be to note that the fact that the search for a strategy seemed so tortuous is symptomatic perhaps of a more general problem that the Hong Kong government has seemingly always had, perhaps of its own making: that of relating financial resources to aspirations. Even when overwhelming support for a policy initiative could be found, money was not always made available or willed to be given, and worthy initiatives had to wait. Many have blamed this on a stringent and conservative public finance policy.[102]

Nevertheless, by the end of the 1950s, new-town building in Hong Kong had become an accepted and major part of the government's public works programme, and it is to an examination of that process that the remainder of our discussion must turn.

Notes

1. 'Report of the Housing Commission 1935', *Hong Kong Sessional Papers*, No. 12/38 (Hong Kong, Local Printing Press, 1938), para. 95, pp. 282–3.
2. Sir David Owen, *Future Control and Development of the Port of Hong Kong: Report by Sir David J. Owen* (Hong Kong, Government Printer, 1941).
3. Letter of 11 October 1946 to the Colonial Secretary in GEN 2/25/58/46, Public Records Office, Hong Kong.
4. Quoted in *Colonial Development and Welfare Advisory Committee Notes*, No. 953, August 1947. A copy can be found in CO 129/614/2, Public Record Office, London.
5. As part of Abercrombie's *County of London Plan 1944* (London, His Majesty's Stationery Office, 1945), he suggested ten sites for new-town development around London, each of about 60,000 population, of which eight were to be developed at a distance of around twelve and a half to fifty kilometres from the central city. The towns were envisaged as self-contained, independent communities, and were planned to relieve the perceived overcrowded and congested conditions in London.
6. As suggested by K.S. Pun, 'New Towns and Urban Renewal in Hong Kong', in D.R. Phillips and A.G.O. Yeh (eds.), *New Towns in East and South-east Asia: Planning and Development* (Hong Kong, Oxford University Press, 1987), p. 45.
7. Prof. Sir Patrick Abercrombie, *Hong Kong: Preliminary Planning Report* (Hong Kong, Government Printer, 1949), para. 6, p. 2.
8. Abercrombie (1949), see note 7 above, para. 102, p. 20.
9. Abercrombie (1949), see note 7 above, paras. 12, 14, and 15, pp. 3 and 4.
10. Abercrombie put forward the following targets for his suggested new development areas:

    A. Hill District, east of Ho Man Tin, 81 hectares; 57,000 pop.
    B. Kau Lung Tsai east, 132 hectares; 92,700 pop.
    C. Kowloon Tong west, 111 hectares; 78,500 pop.
    D. Castle Peak Road area, 51 hectares, 35,600 pop.
    E. Kwun Tong reclamation, 71 hectares; 50,000 pop.
    F. Hung Hom reclamation, 61 hectares; 75,000 pop.
    G. Gin Drinkers Bay, 81 hectares; 57,000 pop.
    H. Tsuen Wan, 78 hectares; 55,000 pop.
    I. Overspill north of Kai Tak, 142 hectares; 100,000 pop.

Of these schemes, Kwun Tong was to become the first official new town in the mid-1950s, to be followed by Tsuen Wan and Kwai Chung (Gin Drinkers Bay) in the early 1960s. Abercrombie (1949), see note 7 above, para. 18, p. 4.

11. Abercrombie (1949), see note 7 above, para. 4, p. 1.

12. Report of 18 September 1945 by A. Nicol, Port Engineer to Col. Rouse (Department of Public Works); para. XVI. Copy in GEN 2/25/58/46, Public Records Office, Hong Kong.

13. Referred to in BL 52/641/46, Public Records Office, Hong Kong.

14. Minutes of Executive Council (CO 131/125, Public Record Office, London), 5 December 1950, pp. 135–6.

15. Comment of 7 May 1946, in BL 1467/45, Public Records Office, Hong Kong.

16. Memorandum of 5 May 1946 from the Colonial Secretary to the Governor, in BL 1458/45, Public Records Office, Hong Kong.

17. Governor's Minute of 19 November 1946 in BL 6/4921/46, Public Records Office, Hong Kong.

18. Governor's Minute of 19 November 1946, see note 17 above.

19. See for example the letter of 29 March 1950 in BL 1/5281/50, setting out the views of a special committee of the Kowloon Residents' Association on Abercrombie's proposals (Hong Kong, Public Records Office).

20. Memorandum of 25 August 1950 from the Financial Secretary to the Deputy Colonial Secretary, in BL 1/5281/50, Public Records Office, Hong Kong.

21. Memorandum of 24 December 1951 from the Acting Financial Secretary, in BL 3/5282/51, Public Records Office, Hong Kong.

22. Reported in BL 3/5282/51, see note 21 above, Public Records Office, Hong Kong.

23. Governor's Memorandum of 8 November 1950, in BL 3/5282/51, Public Records Office, Hong Kong.

24. Colonial Secretariat, *Memorandum for Executive Council: Town Planning*, No. 23, 5 January 1952, in BL 3/5282/51, Public Records Office, Hong Kong. A full account of the vicissitudes of town planning during this period can be found in Roger Bristow, *Land-use Planning in Hong Kong: History, Policies and Procedures* (Hong Kong, Oxford University Press, 1984), pp. 69–72.

25. Governor's letter to the Rt. Hon. Oliver Lyttelton, Secretary of State for the Colonies, 19 February 1953. Copy at 30 in BL 3/5282/51, Public Records Office, Hong Kong.

26. Minute at 18/1 in BL 3/5282/51, Public Records Office, Hong Kong.

27. Correspondence on this issue can be found in items 15 to 30, BL 3/5282/51, Public Records Office, Hong Kong.

28. Memorandum 22/1 in BL 3/5282/51, Public Records Office, Hong Kong.

29. Memorandum of 25 November 1954, in BL 1/5281/47, Public Records Office, Hong Kong.

30. Paragraph 6 of a note prepared by the District Commissioner, New Territories on 13 February 1950 (7 in BL 7/3801/48, Public Records Office, Hong Kong).

31. Memorandum from the District Commissioner, New Territories to the Colonial Secretary in January 1950 (BL 7/3801/48, Public Records Office, Hong Kong).

32. Minute 3 of 21 January 1946 in BL 4/4921/46, Public Records Office, Hong Kong.

33. Memorandum at 4 in BL4/4921/46, Public Records Office, Hong Kong.

34. As reported in a speech by the Colonial Secretary when introducing the 1954 Housing Bill in the Legislative Council; *Hong Kong Hansard* (Hong Kong Government Printer, 7 April 1954), p. 150.

35. Colonial Secretary (1954), see note 34 above, p. 150.

36. General information about this scheme can be found in CO 129/626/5, Public Record Office, London.

37. *Housing Committee Report: Singapore* (Singapore, Government Printer, 1947).

38. *Housing Committee Report* (1947), see note 37 above, paras. 44–54, pp. 11–12.

39. The full debate can be found in BL 110/3091/47, Public Records Office, Hong Kong.

40. Memorandum of 14 February 1949 by the Assistant Colonial Secretary, in BL 3/5282/48, Public Records Office, Hong Kong, p. 9.

41. Assistant Colonial Secretary (1949), see note 40 above, p. 9.

42. The plans can be found at 8/2 in BL 21/736/49, Public Records Office, Hong Kong.

43. J.T. Wakefield, *An Outline of the Activities of the Singapore Improvement Trust and Recommendations for the Constitution of an Improvement Trust (to be called a Housing Council) in Hong Kong* (Hong Kong, Hong Kong Government, 1952). Copy to be found at 34 in BL 18/736/50II, Public Records Office, Hong Kong.

44. Wakefield (1952), see note 43 above, para. 41, p. 13.

45. Wakefield (1952), see note 43 above, para. 42, p. 13.

46. Letter from the Chairman of the Urban Council, at 37 in BL 18/736/50II, Public Records Office, Hong Kong.

47. Memorandum of March 1953 from the Financial Secretary, at 49 in BL 18/736/50II, Public Records Office, Hong Kong.

48. Paragraph 16 of a memorandum from the Chief Building Surveyor to the Director of Public Works, at 50 in BL 18/736/50II, Public Records Office, Hong Kong.

49. Fuller discussions on squatter settlement in Hong Kong can be found in the general references on housing in Hong Kong, such as L.S.K. Wong, 'The Squatter Problem', in L.S.K. Wong (ed.), *Housing in Hong Kong: A Multidisciplinary Study* (Hong Kong, Heinemann Asia, 1978), pp. 204–32; while more recent and specific research has been published in: A. Smart, 'The Development of Diamond Hill from Village to Squatter Area: A Perspective on Public Housing', *Asian Journal of Public Administration*, Vol. 8, No. 1, June 1986, pp. 43–63; and E.G. Pryor, 'Squatting, Land Clearance and Urban Development in Hong Kong', *Land Use Policy*, Vol. 1, No. 1, July 1984, pp. 225–42.

50. Interdepartmental Committee on the Squatter Problem, 'Report of Interdepartmental Committee on the Squatter Problem' *Hong Kong Sessional Papers*, No. 4/48 (Hong Kong, Government Secretariat, 1948). Copy at 5/1 in BL 6/3091/48, Public Records Office, Hong Kong.

51. Interdepartmental Committee on the Squatter Problem (1948), see note 50 above, para. 8, p.4.

52. Report by the Senior Health Officer, December 1949, at 51/1 in BL 6/3091/48, Public Records Office, Hong Kong.

53. Letter of 19 July 1950, at 66 in BL 6/3091/48, Public Records Office, Hong Kong.

54. J.T. Wakefield, *Report on Squatters, Simple-Type Housing for Squatters and Permanent Housing for Employees of Government and Utility Companies* (Hong Kong, Social Welfare Office, 1951). Copy in CR 13/4802/51, Public Records Office, Hong Kong.

55. Emergency Regulations Ordinance Chapter 241 — originally passed in 1922 and the Emergency (Resettlement Areas) Regulations (three sets) 1952, followed later also by the Emergency (Squatter Clearance) Regulations 1953.

56. Speech by the Colonial Secretary, *Hong Kong Hansard* (Hong Kong Government Printer), 14 April 1954, p. 178.

57. Memorandum from the Social Welfare Officer to the Chairman of the Urban Council, 10 December 1952, at 3/1 in BL 11/3181/52, Public Records Office, Hong Kong.

58. Minute M2 of 28 July 1953 to the Deputy Colonial Secretary in BL 11/3181/52, Public Records Office, Hong Kong.

59. *Report of Interdepartmental Committee, 14 May 1954: New Industrial Areas*, at 24/1 in BL 2/5282/53I, Public Records Office, Hong Kong.

60. As on the public plan produced in November 1956, and upon which Fig. 2.3 is based. Crown Lands and Survey Office, *Kwun Tong New Town Plan* (Hong Kong, Government Printer, 1956).

61. Memorandum for the Executive Council at 24 in BL 2/5282/53I, Public Records Office, Hong Kong.

62. Memorandum for Executive Council, 19 May 1955, at 75 in BL 2/5282/53I, Public Records Office, Hong Kong.

63. *Report of the Working Committee on the New Industrial Area at Kun Tong*, April 1956; at 40/1 in BL 2/5282/53II, Public Records Office, Hong Kong.

64. Full details of the scheme are given in Annex IV to the *Report of the Working Committee on the New Industrial Area at Kun Tong*, see note 63 above.

65. Memorandum from the Commissioner of Labour to the Colonial Secretary, at 184 in BL 2/5282/53III, Public Records Office, Hong Kong.

66. Covering letter for general circulation from the Secretary for Chinese Affairs, 17 May 1958, accompanying the report *Development in the Ngau Tau Kok, Kun Tong Area*; at 9 and 9/1 in BL 3/5282/58, Public Records Office, Hong Kong.

67. Letter from the Colonial Secretary to the Chinese Manufacturers' Association, 19 January 1960, at 72 in BL 3/5282/58, Public Records Office, Hong Kong.

68. City District Officer, Kwun Tong, *Report on the Provision of Community Requirements in Kowloon Planning Area 14* (Hong Kong, Kwun Tong District Office, 1970), at Float in BL 3/5282/58, Public Records Office, Hong Kong.

69. Memorandum from the Secretary for Home Affairs to the Colonial Secretary, 25 August 1970, at Float in BL 3/5282/58, Public Records Office, Hong Kong.

70. City District Officer, Kwun Tong (1970), see note 68 above, para. B2, p. 1.

71. Memorandum from the Director of Urban Services to the Colonial Secretary, 16 October 1970, at 113 in BL 3/5282/58, Public Records Office, Hong Kong.

72. Secretariat for Home Affairs, *Planning and Development of the Kwun Tong Industrial Area*, September 1969; at 1/1 in BL 9/5282/69, Public Records Office, Hong Kong.

73. While there is no evidence of direct British influence, the Public Works Department was aware of contemporary British new-town practice. In particular, in 1953, a member of its staff had visited Stevenage, Harlow, and Crawley, and examples of layouts were included in his report. See, File BL 4/5282/53, Public Records Office, Hong Kong, *Visit of A.R. Giles (Crown Lands Surveyor, PWD) to Crawley, Stevenage and Harlow, August 1953; to study compulsory purchase and betterment.*

74. City District Officer, Kwun Tong, *Planning and Development of the Kwun Tong Industrial Area*, October 1969, para. 17, p. 6. Copy at 4/1 in BL 9/5282/69, Public Records Office, Hong Kong.

75. Memorandum from the Superintendent of Crown Lands and Surveys to the Colonial Secretary, 11 March 1967, at 47 in BL 5/736/56, Public Records Office, Hong Kong.

76. Memorandum from the Acting Commissioner for Housing to the Superintendent of Crown Lands and Surveys, 5 September 1960, at 2 in BL 7/2/18/736/50, Public Records Office, Hong Kong.

77. Memorandum from the Director of Urban Services to the Colonial Secretary, 16 October 1970, at 113 in BL 3/5282/58, Public Records Office, Hong Kong.

78. Y.K. Chan, *The Rise and Growth of Kwun Tong: A Study of Planned Urban Development* (Hong Kong, Chinese University of Hong Kong, Social Research Centre, 1973), p. 63.

79. Notes prepared by the Director of Public Works, dated 31 December 1955; at 8/2 in BL 3/5282/55, Public Records Office, Hong Kong.

80. Minute of the Assistant Colonial Secretary, 24 July 1954, at M16 in SEC 8/5282/54, Public Records Office, Hong Kong.

81. Commissioner for Resettlement, *Report on Squatters and Resettlement*, November 1955, p. 3. Copy at 1/1 in CR 16/4802/55I, Public Records Office, Hong Kong.

82. Set out in 3 in CR 16/4802/55I, Public Records Office, Hong Kong.

83. Special Committee on Housing, *Special Committee on Housing: First Interim Report* (Hong Kong, Government Printer, 1956). Original copy at 30/1 in CR 16/4802/55I, Public Records Office, Hong Kong.

84. Special Committee on Housing (1956), see note 83 above, paras. 5–7.

85. Town Planning Office, *Planning Memorandum No. 1: Proposed Measures for the Accommodation of Surplus Population*, February 1956. A copy was published as Appendix E to the *Final Report of the Special Committee on Housing 1956–58* (Hong Kong, Government Printer, 1958). The memorandum was one of a series prepared by the Town Planning Office as preparatory work for regional planning in the Territory.

86. *Final Report of the Special Committee on Housing* (1958), see note 85 above, para. 42, pp. 20–1.

87. Remark by the Assistant Superintendent (Crown Lands and Survey) — the chief government planner of the time, at 125/1 in CR 16/4802/55I, Public Records Office, Hong Kong.

88. Extracts from a memorandum prepared by the Commissioner for Housing, at 126 and 126/1 in CR 16/4802/55I, Public Records Office, Hong Kong.

89. Town Planning Office, *Planning Memorandum No. 4: Ten Year Development Programme*, January 1960, para. 1. Copy at 7/1 in BL 2/5282/61, Buildings and Lands Registry, Hong Kong.

90. Town Planning Office (1960), see note 89 above, para. 15, p. 8.

91. R.C. Clarke, *Town Planning — Future Policy*, 13 August 1960. Copy at 4/1 in BL 2/1/5281/47, Buildings and Lands Registry, Hong Kong.

92. R.C. Clarke (1960), see note 91 above, opening paragraph.

93. R.C. Clarke (1960), see note 91 above, para. 16, p. 3.

94. Memorandum from the Acting Director of Public Works to the Deputy Colonial Secretary, 15 August 1960, at 4 in BL 2/1/5281/47, Buildings and Lands Registry, Hong Kong.

95. See minutes at M1 and M2, in BL 2/1/5281/47, Buildings and Lands Registry, Hong Kong.

96. Minute by the Deputy Financial Secretary, 5 September 1960, at M4 in BL 2/1/5281/47, Buildings and Lands Registry, Hong Kong.

97. Stated in Minute M13A of 10 November 1960, in BL 2/1/5281/47, Buildings and Lands Registry, Hong Kong.

98. Minute of 12 February 1962 from the Deputy Economic Secretary to the Colonial

and Financial Secretaries, at M18 in BL 2/1/5281/47, Buildings and Lands Registry, Hong Kong.

99. Memorandum at 42/1 in BL 2/1/5281/47, Buildings and Lands Registry, Hong Kong.

100. Colony Outline Planning Division, *The Colony Outline Plan: Book 3, Vol. I — Concepts and Outline Proposals* (Hong Kong, Crown Lands and Survey Office, 1969), paras. 3.1–2, p. 2.

101. The various new-town sites put forward for consideration are shown on the maps included as endpapers in this book. Taken from *Plan of 1 October 1957*, at 32/2 in BL 1/5282/56I, Public Records Office, Hong Kong.

102. For example see N.C. Owen, 'Economic Policy' in K. Hopkins (ed.), *Hong Kong: The Industrial Colony — A Political, Social and Economic Survey* (Hong Kong, Oxford University Press, 1971), pp. 141–206.

3. Strategic Planning and the New Towns

NEW-TOWN planning in Hong Kong effectively began with the Scott Wilson Kirkpatrick & Partners reclamation proposals of 1959, but it was not until the Executive Council's decision in November of that year to proceed with land formation in Gin Drinkers Bay (Kwai Chung) that comprehensive urban planning procedures for the new towns became a vital necessity. This process began with the planning for the new town of Tsuen Wan.

Tsuen Wan New Town — The Early Years of New-town Planning

Tsuen Wan really began as an urbanized settlement in 1935, when over fifty two-storey houses were built by developers to form Chung On Street and Market Street. The decade before the Pacific War also saw the first factories set up in the area, and demand had progressed sufficiently by 1937 for the first layout plan to be required from government in order to guide the development of the growing settlement. Yet, even after the major up-date of 1954, some twenty years later, which allowed for the first time for possible extensions on to reclamations in Tsuen Wan Bay, development still largely proceeded haphazardly by individual permissions, with the required public infrastructure following on behind as necessities demanded.

Even so, by 1958, the area had already grown to a population of:

over 80,000, the majority of whom were recent immigrants from central China, and Tsuen Wan had become one of the greatest industrial centres in Hong Kong. It contained 20% of the Hong Kong labour force and produced more than half its textiles, enamelware and beer. Much of the industrial population is shifting — men who worked in Tsuen Wan factories and lived in squatter shacks or bed spaces, but belonged to larger family units back in Kowloon... Of the families in Tsuen Wan, many are unhoused and live in squatter accommodation on hillsides, or in bed spaces rented on a shift system.[1]

Thus, there already existed a major squatter settlement, 13 original villages, and additional resettlement from elsewhere (principally resulting from the Tai Lam water scheme) — all contributing to a complex, incipient, urban landscape upon which it was now proposed to impose a new town (see Plate 4a). While planning up until then could be described as achievable, transforming it into a viable and comprehensive form for a major city proved to be something else. It was this new planning that began at the end of the 1950s in two phases, concerning itself with the new reclamation in Gin Drinkers Bay and the development of Tsuen Wan itself.

Unlike some of the other reclamation studies completed by Scott Wilson Kirkpatrick & Partners, the study for Gin Drinkers Bay completed in January 1959[2] was almost entirely concerned with the engineering requirement of providing sufficient fill from the terracing of the nearby hillsides to allow the infilling of the bay to some 14 feet (4.27 metres) above sea level (some quarter of a million cubic metres of material). Although the consultants did show a simple grid-iron road layout on their plan, with contour roads on the terraces, no suggestions were made for the allocation of the new land uses that might form the basis of a major new-town development.

For the separate consultants from the University investigating Tsuen Wan proper, the situation was much more complex. Reclamation in Tsuen Wan Bay (Plate 4a) had already begun in accordance with the Public Works Department's 1954 plan, although by 1959, despite the construction of over a hundred Chinese tenement houses, progress by the private sector had proved to be slow. This had resulted in 1957 in a decision to complete the initial 49 hectares of reclamation by public dumping of fill material resulting from the building of the Tai Wo resettlement estate — Tsuen Wan's first. This estate, replacing an earlier cottage estate, was also envisaged as accommodation for squatters and others displaced by early local new-town development.

However, it was the general pressures for formed sites in Tsuen Wan in 1958 that were cited by government as the prime reason for briefing consultants for new-town development in Tsuen Wan.

The task of the consultants is to produce a staged programme for completion of the portions of Tsuen Wan reclamation known as Housing Zone IV and Industrial Zones I, II, III, and V. Filling material is to be obtained from sites in and around Tsuen Wan which will thereby be formed into suitable areas for housing, industrial and civic development. The formation of areas for agricultural areas may also be included if convenient. The Consultants are to provide outline layouts for such areas.[3]

While it is proper to suggest that the Hong Kong government at this time really saw their new proposals as an ongoing extension of existing policies to meet demands for new development sites, particularly for industry and public housing, the consultants (an architectural team from the staff of the University of Hong Kong) interpreted their brief widely, and produced a design for comprehensive urban development, including both engineering aspects of the land production as well as proposals for the development and management of what to them was a complete new-town proposal. It represented for Hong Kong the first attempt to design a new town from first principles.

The initial constraints laid down were that the town should be planned within a designated area of just over 405 hectares, and that it should be industrial on a self-contained and balanced basis. In the absence of Territory-wide planning standards at that time, net residential density was set at 2,470 persons to the hectare, with 0.002 hectares per worker gross for the new industrial areas. The total design population of the scheme was to be 216,000 (43,000 were allowed for on the already designated 87 hectares of the Public Works Department's plan). For the new reclamation 4.35 million cubic metres of fill material was to be taken from two areas to the north-west and south-east of the town, which would create 72 hectares of developable land, sufficient to house about half of the designed population of the new town.

In general, the zoning proposed by the consultants followed the earlier government requirements (Plan LTW 17C), but with the major exception that a complete new town centre was designated, based on the existing shopping area in Tung On Street.

This area should be planned in detail as a unit to create an environment which would foster civic pride and interest and to become the focal point around which the town is balanced.[4]

It was also asserted elsewhere that:

the principle of establishing self-contained easily identifiable communities in the true sense of 'neighbourhood units' cannot easily be applied.[5]

Nevertheless, the principle was used as far as possible with three in the north-west, but avoided on the terraced areas of the Texaco Peninsula to the south-east. There, the high density public housing areas were set out as units of some 12 to 15,000 people, interspersed with 'residential centres' in which it was proposed to centralize the shopping, local markets, service industry, and local administration — effectively a series of district centre functions. Associated with these were the proposed primary schools. Open space, apart from the recommended use of the urban fringe areas, was confined to a sea-front promenade and a major new stadium and sports ground. Roads were seen essentially as distributors within the town, and were not to penetrate the proposed housing areas. Finally, a new bypass road from Lai Chi Kok to the western side of the new town was proposed, to replace Castle Peak Road (a proposal which was finally to reach fruition in the 1980s).

The proposals were also innovative in another way.

The success of any New Town project depends very much on developing and maintaining a sense of civic pride and responsibility among the population. This can only be achieved if the town is first of all designed as an entity and then administered as such...It is realised that this would be a new departure from established practice in the Colony, but 'Town Development' is something new...It would seem also, initially, that development on the scale and at the speed contemplated will require an organisation to be set up; similar in many respects to the Development Corporations of the New Towns in the United Kingdom.[6]

Correct though these proposals may now seem, with hindsight, these ideas proved totally unacceptable to the government: it was not yet prepared to revise its traditional ways of tackling urban development. Thus, in May 1960, it was agreed within the Secretariat that the Kwai Chung (Gin Drinkers Bay) development would be handled under the usual Town Planning Ordinance procedures, and in July it was agreed that the new-town plan would cover the whole watershed area — that is both Tsuen Wan, Kwai Chung, and the adjacent island of Tsing Yi. It was also confirmed that the plan would 'show only the main road framework and broad zoning, leaving details to be filled in departmentally',[7] thus reaffirming a principle that was and is basic to land-use planning in Hong Kong. This agreement, to utilize statutory planning procedures, even though only in outline, did however have to overcome opposition from the District Commissioner New Territories, who up until then had had the responsibility of controlling the development of the area. But the move to statutory control was justified on grounds of necessary consultation, public information, and the authority that statutory power would give to the new plan, and it was pushed through. It was to be the first involvement of the formal town-planning processes of Hong Kong in new-town planning in the Territory.

The opposite point of view was expressed in a contemporary report by the Commissioner.

For the Tsuen Wan town area covered by the University Consultants' report it would be necessary to spend $40 million on engineering works, and this makes no allowance for resettlement measures. The political opposition would in my view . . . be great enough to pose a real threat to the security of the Colony. It would come not only from the few thousand descendents of the original villagers but from everyone whose livelihood would be affected and from investors in existing land who saw their investments in a sense appropriated. The most practical approach will be a somewhat untidy and piecemeal one whereby we develop the areas where there are no major administrative difficulties and for the time being leave the others in the hope that private owners will follow suite of their own accord . . . Piecemeal development implies a continuous process of digging and dumping, lots being auctioned as they come into existence, and roads and services being developed as there is land to put them on. . . From the engineering point of view the sort of programme of works which is likely to emerge may well seem scrappy and in some ways unsatisfactory. But to develop a new town on an area containing 6,000 indigenous villagers and inumerable squatters is necessarily a more costly process than to do so in an area containing no human problems.[8]

Despite the imposition of the statutory control, the New Territories administration's arguments were those that were heeded. Indeed, it can be said that the Commissioner's comments proved perceptive, for the development of Tsuen Wan in the early 1960s threw up major periods of conflict with local interest groups in the subsequent period of implementation.[9]

When the government's own proposals finally saw the light of day as a statutory plan in October 1963 (Outline Development Plan LTW 75 [see Fig. 3.1]), the proposed structure for the new town was changed dramatically.[10] The three areas of Tsuen Wan, Kwai Chung, and Tsing Yi were now to become a major city of some 1.2 million people.

The basic concept of the plan may be summarized as follows: (i) To provide additional land for industrial development within the framework of a balanced land use pattern designed to allow people to live within a reasonable distance of their

Fig. 3.1 Tsuen Wan Outline Development Plan, 1963 (Plan LTW/75, now termed an Outline Zoning Plan) — the first plan drawn up in Hong Kong for a complete new town, it was based on earlier consultants' reports prepared in 1958–9 (see also Plates 4a and 4b).

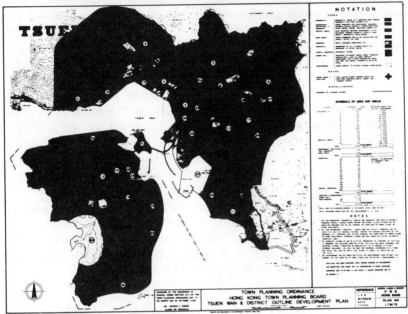

Source: Town Planning Office, Buildings and Lands Department, Hong Kong government.

place of work; (ii) To estimate the population and intensities of land use so as to enable adequate public services to be provided in the most economical manner; (iii) To make provision for satisfactory lines of communication; and (iv) To provide reasonable community facilities for the welfare and well-being of an estimated population of 1.2 million.[11]

Utilizing a survey of existing conditions elsewhere in Hong Kong, the planning standards applied to the zoning within the plan were now 865 workers to the gross hectare for industrial land, with a ratio of 1 to 5 industrial workers to the total population; while three gross residential densities of 405, 120–405, and below 120 per hectare were used for the various residential areas. The highest gross densities thus worked out at around twice those suggested by the earlier University planning team, and the new plan therefore equated roughly with the earlier estimate of a final developed population target of 600,000 for the whole city area (including Kwai Chung) suggested by the consultants, that is, a doubling of population was now proposed for approximately the same area. The attempt of the Town Planning Board to fix population maxima in the plan did, however, generate lively debate within government about the density standards and open-space provision that were implied; a debate that led eventually to the general introduction of density standards throughout Hong Kong from 1965.[12]

The 1963 proposals that finally emerged hid, however, the loss of a battle by the planners within government, for the final plan differed significantly from the planners' first proposals which followed the ideas of the consultants much more closely.[13] Those had set a new target population at only 640,000, with 15 residential zones on 688 hectares, and 258 hectares of industrial land. The industrial worker density was also lower (at 494 per hectare instead of 865), while the residential gross densities were 988–1,977, 494–746 and below 247 respectively. The initial open-space standard applied had also been more generous at 0.3 hectares per thousand population, giving a total of 194 hectares for the whole town. What were perceived then as over-generous standards came under attack within the government, and were rejected at the discussions within the Town Planning Board.

Perhaps more interesting to us now are the discussions which were influenced by the views of a visiting mission from the World Bank, who were then being approached as a possible benefactor for the financing of the Kwai Chung reclamation. They criticized the economic returns expected from the industrial part of the scheme. Thus, overall:

in the course of its deliberations the Board considered that the comparatively low population densities shown on the draft plan, as well as the scale of provision of active recreation space and space for community projects, were neither economic nor realistic when considered in relation to the growing need for housing sites.[14]

Other factors forcing government's hand were the increasing need to accommodate large quantities of government housing at densities similar to those used elsewhere, and the impracticality of attempting to enforce lower densities over private development in the new town as opposed to those available to developers elsewhere. Yet, it was not to be the last time that the professional planners in Hong Kong were to be accused and defeated on the grounds of unrealistic idealism. Now, however, financial returns and the pressures of public housing requirements were already dictating planning policies for the Hong Kong new towns.

The planners had also incorporated another change, this time from the experiences learned from the Kwun Tong development. It was firmly resolved that adequate housing land must be provided to enable workers to live within walking distance of their work, and thereby removing the need to commute. This led to the use of reclaimed land for housing, and also, later, areas in north-east Tsing Yi were provided with sufficient residential sites to balance the employment potential of the planned industrial areas. It also introduced the concept of balance between industrial land/worker requirements and the population targets for the whole town and its constituent parts. The planners now envisaged that their more detailed area plans for the residential areas:

will result in a breakdown of these areas into neighbourhood units of varying population size with provision for local shops, schools, open spaces, institutions and other community requirements associated with a predominant residential use;[15]

a straight copy of contemporary British new-town planning conventions.

Another major change concerned the town-centre uses. The area of the consultants' proposed town centre in Tsuen Wan itself was much reduced, though:

the Tsuen Wan central zone is likely to become the predominant focal point owing to its earlier development from an existing nucleus of older villages and shops.[16]

Instead, attention was now focused on a new three-centre pattern, with separate developments for Tsuen Wan, Kwai Chung, and Tsing Yi, where:

it is proposed that comprehensive schemes including three-dimensional control, car parking segregation of vehicular and pedestrian traffic, etc. will be prepared[17] (see pp. 234–7 and Fig. 7.4).

Finally, throughout the town, an open-space standard of 0.04 hectares to each hectare of developed land was now to be applied, reducing the total to only 121 hectares for the now doubled population of the new town.

Yet, in spite of these revisions, and perhaps even in spite of the planners, development of the first major new town in Hong Kong failed to materialize as an effective comprehensive scheme. It was not until the establishment of the New Territories Development Department in the next decade (pp. 121–3), and incorporation of Tsuen Wan within the Territory-wide new-town programme of the mid-1970s, that true comprehensive control of the development of Tsuen Wan proved possible. By settling for existing procedures and the adaption of planning machinery and development capabilities on a piecemeal and *ad hoc* basis, the Hong Kong government not only missed an opportunity, but also set in train the development of a physical environment that resulted in major problems in the 1970s and 1980s.

Development in the 1960s was mainly concentrated on the building of public housing and the formation of land for industrial development with the very minimum of community facilities being provided.[18]

This situation was only slowly put right from 1972 onwards.

Unlike the other New Towns there has never been any formal staging of development in Tsuen Wan and for the purposes of this programme it has been necessary to divide the town into various areas which can be treated to a large extent as self-contained development. The works within these have then been programmed to be completed or 'balanced' so that all essential services, community facilities and communications in the area are provided in accordance with the approved or draft Outline Zoning Plans and at a rate to match the population build-up.

However housing and industrial development are in different areas and the balancing of employment opportunities against population build-up can only be attained by ensuring that both types of area develop concurrently.[19]

But, that plan was for the 1970s, and was introduced and developed with the benefit of hind-sight; by then, there were 400,000 people living in the town, three-quarters of them in varied forms of public housing, itself an indictment of earlier planning policies and outcomes.

The Development of Strategic Planning Policies

The initial planning for Tsuen Wan took place against a background of more general questioning at all levels within the Hong Kong government about the development and planning future of Hong Kong.

You said that World Bank finance for either a water scheme or reclamation might make it possible to consider other desirable schemes involving capital expenditure which either had a return or which at least did not involve heavy recurrent expenditure. The obvious direction to turn to in such circumstances is to development schemes. . . There is an increasing coordination on technical and procedural matters on land sales but there was, in my time at any rate, little attempt to rationalise policy or assessment of demand on a Colony basis. No one did, and possibly no one does now, know how much land is required for development. . .So far as I know there has only been one attempt to calculate the amount of land we need. This was the very rough and incomplete paper Planning Memorandum No. 4 [see Fig. 2.6]. . .Nevertheless, I think this is the most important paper yet produced on development and believe that until we can produce a realistic and fully considered version of it, all expenditure on development works must be based on tuition, blind faith or just good guess work. . .To sum up if we get an unexpected supply of cheap capital it should be spent on development and urban expansion. We cannot tell how, or where, or at what rate it should be spent until we know how much land is needed. This we do not know. We should find out.[20]

To answer such questions proved to be the major planning task of the 1960s, though, as we have seen, there were in fact earlier attempts to set the strategic growth pattern for the development of Hong Kong.

Further initial views were also put forward at this time by the New Territories Administration in a paper prepared in 1959 and entitled, *Urban Expansion into the New Territories*.[21] The paper laid down some important general principles. It pointed out that:

development will be piecemeal unless there exists a reserve of Crown land which can be carved up and offered in a methodical way in exchange for agricultural land surrendered at random over an area when urban development is taking place. . .In practice this means that to speed up the development of a valley adjoining the sea it is necessary to undertake a reclamation so that part of the reclamation can be used to exchange for the surrender of agricultural land.[22]

The report went on to suggest that for new towns proximity to Kowloon would be a factor, to allow for interdependence, and that expansion of an existing centre would be preferable with adjoining flat land or shallow sea. Of the potential sites, Tsuen Wan/Kwai Chung was placed first, with Sha Tin as a possibility. Elsewhere, in the suggested inner ring, Ho Chung and Junk Bay were rejected; while in an outer ring of later possibilities Tuen Mun (Castle Peak), Tai Po, and Sai Kung were thought to be feasible. At the time, the inclusion of Sha Tin gave rise to a major difference of opinion within government — the District Commissioner argued strongly for immediate implementation of the consultants' 1959 scheme, there having already been a six-year moratorium on development in the valley imposed because of the lack of an overall scheme and suspected flooding dangers; while the Director of Public Works remained much more cautious. Overall, however, the fears were summarized as follows:

But all development depends on communications and planning. Unless at the very least the Government is prepared to improve communications and keep development planning well ahead of demand a 'land shortage' will be created. It will not be a shortage of land as such but a shortage of land ready for development. This is the present position.[23]

Comment of a different kind also came at the time from the Director of Commerce and Industry.

The fundamental lesson to be learnt from the reclamation at Kwun Tong is that facilities for adequate road communication, drainage and road access should be made available *pari passu* with the provision of factory sites. Similarly, housing development for workers should be concomitant with the development of factory sites. I am convinced that this cannot be achieved if left solely to private enterprise.[24]

But more imperative and specific requirements even than these were to push the Hong Kong government finally in 1962 into major new planning initiatives and a formal new-town programme.

One of these triggers has already been mentioned — the move formally to prepare a Colony Outline Plan for the Territory;[25] suggested by the Colonial Secretary following the 'Regional Plan' proposals of the land-use planners in the Public Works Department. But, the next steps towards the new-town programme were precipitated by other factors. The new Land Development Planning Committee had already noted that:

some kind of outline plan for the Colony is necessary if only in connection with the land required for industrial development and the continuation of the Resettlement Programme after the next four/five years,[26]

and the theme was taken up in LDPC Paper No. 14 put before the Committee in September 1962.

To keep the Resettlement Programme going at the average rate of 100,000 persons resettled per year it is necessary to find the land and start planning the layouts,

particularly roads and services, some four or five years before the sites are required to be formed ready for the letting of building contracts. It is the Public
Works Department view that Shatin, if developed in accordance with the approved Town Plan [as a dormitory satellite town, first envisaged in 1954] is unlikely
to make any great impact on the general housing or industrial situation. They are
of the opinion that the demand for housing sites (including Resettlement) and the
parallel need for industrial sites may force Government into another large scale
development scheme comparable with Kwun Tong or Kwai Chung. Experience
at Kwai Chung has shown that it takes a long time to set a major development
scheme in motion. Though there is still a lot to be done at Kwai Chung it is not
too early to consider the question of its successor.[27]

In fact, commitments already under way were beginning to force government's hand. Public works already agreed to and commenced included
initial reclamation works and water supply at Castle Peak (committed
to meet land exchange requirements resulting from drainage works
being undertaken in Yuen Long in the north-west New Territories), while
the Castle Peak Road was already being improved. At Sha Tin the works
associated with new water supply schemes for the urban area, and the land
requirements of the new Chinese University, had also encouraged limited
land exchanges and given rise to road improvements and drainage works
in the valley, which served to increase existing private development
pressures. These were further exacerbated by knowledge of the new Lion
Rock road tunnel to the south that was being proposed as part of the water
supply arrangements for the main urban area. Thus localized decisions
were already beginning to modify the Executive Council's policy of 1959
that development resources should be concentrated at Tsuen Wan/Kwai
Chung. They also caused some to doubt the efficacy of the newly introduced strategic planning mechanisms:

The Sha Tin Town Plan envisages an area of fairly low density residential development. The maximum densities shown on the approved Town Plan are in Areas
7 and 8 with 250 people to the acre [618 to the hectare]. Such development is unlikely
to make great impact on the general housing or industrial situation during the
next ten years at least. The impending development of Kwai Chung is a different
matter. Within a short time its population is likely to exceed the ultimate population envisaged at Sha Tin. The centre of gravity of industrial development is likely to move from Kwun Tong to West Kowloon, first to Kwai Chung/Tsuen Wan
and then, following on the completion of the dual carriageway road, on to Castle
Peak. The Colony Outline Plan is intended to provide the answer to the question
of where to go after Kwai Chung/Tsuen Wan. But it will be a long time before
we get the Colony Outline Plan and I do not not think we can afford to wait for it.[28]

To summarize therefore, public housing requirements, *ad hoc* infrastructure provisions made to meet individual programme requirements, and
private development pressures, all conspired to force government's hand,
and to break down the general order of priorities that they were attempting to establish. Thus, it was not before time, that the Land Development
Planning Committee came to reconsider the possible development of Sha
Tin in 1961/2, in line with the 1959 Executive Council decision.[29] Discus-

sion centred around the comparative costs involved over land production at Sha Tin or Tuen Mun (Castle Peak), particularly as those for Sha Tin seemed so high (HK $372 million as against HK $144 million). One result of this was a general agreement that the proposed population densities and target for residential development at Sha Tin[30] would have to be increased, and accordingly the Public Works Department was asked to revise the whole scheme. Even so, further examination in September 1963, and in particular in response to a paper on the development of Sha Tin and Tuen Mun (Castle Peak) prepared by the New Territories Administration,[31] led the Committee to prepare a report, which was submitted to the Secretariat early in 1964, on the urgent need for the development of both Sha Tin and Tuen Mun (Castle Peak). In parallel to these discussions, the Public Works Department was preparing schemes for both Sha Tin and Tuen Mun (Castle Peak), and these, prepared by the Department's Development Office, duly appeared in 1965.[32]

To a degree the plans had already been pre-empted by events, for by March 1964 it had already been agreed that Tuen Mun (Castle Peak) Stage 1 should go ahead, with a target population of 100,000 by 1968, 'because the development of at least one of the areas was vital to the future of the Colony in view of the 1970 resettlement requirements'.[33] This had come about because of the deliberations of the government's Working Party on Squatters, Resettlement, and Government Low-cost Housing which had been meeting from June 1963, and whose recommendations had been largely endorsed in a major government policy statement in 1964.[34]

This committed government to provide 900,000 resettlement units over the six-year period to March 1970, with a further possible one million units to April 1974, with an additional 170,000 and 120,000 low-cost public housing units over the same two periods. As we shall see later in Chapter 7, much of the immediate impact of this series of decisions was felt in the design of Tsuen Wan/Kwai Chung,[35] but for the long-term strategic impact the decisions acted as a major spur to the discussions about new-town development, for it was thought that it was likely that at least two further new towns would now become necessary to meet the proposed housing targets. Hence there was now an immediate need to see whether or not Sha Tin and Tuen Mun (Castle Peak) were to be the required two sites.

There was also an immediate impact upon the Public Works Department's plans of 1965. In accommodating sites at Tuen Mun (Castle Peak) for about 500,000 people as a part of the government's new housing requirements, it immediately became apparent that the overall target population for the town as a whole was likely to approach over one million (similar to that of the earlier Tsuen Wan scheme). Similarly, at Sha Tin, the pressures to improve the economic viability of the scheme, and applying residential densities similar to those of Tsuen Wan and Tuen Mun (Castle Peak) both resulted in a similar prospect of a one-million population city for the valley site. Thus, in both cases these new concepts were incorporated into new statutory plans for the proposed towns, which were finally put before the Hong Kong public during 1966 (see Figs. 5.1c and 5.4b).[36]

The Public Works Department's initial plans had come before the Land Development Planning Committee in April 1965.[37] Discussions were lengthy,[38] but despite misgivings about the tying of development to rigid commitments, set by the ten-year programme of engineering works required to produce the land (doubts were expressed about the possible social and property market aspects of such a programme), it was nevertheless recommended that rather than proceeding sequentially,

the Committee now considered that it was not appropriate to envisage that the two areas should be developed consecutively and felt that a broader base for development was required which would be more flexible and permit a wider deployment of resources. In view of this it was agreed that both schemes should be accepted in principle at the outset, in the realization that development in each area would proceed at different rates and with differently phased works programmes; and that once the first phase of development had begun for both schemes, progress thereafter should be subject to periodical review.[39]

Following approval in the Executive Council, 1966 saw the commencement of work on Tuen Mun (Castle Peak) Stage 1A as a first step, following the decision in the Public Works Sub-committee of the Legislative Council that Stage 1 of the Tuen Mun (Castle Peak) scheme should be subdivided into two, a decision reflecting the general downturn in the Hong Kong property market of that time.

The subsequent history of the development of the two towns is dealt with in Chapter 5; here, we must turn again to the ongoing evolution of strategic planning that continued to interact with the detailed planning of the first three new towns as they developed, and which was to lead to further major expansions of the new-town programme in the 1970s and early 1980s. Associated with this strategic policy development was the recognition of a requirement to impose general standards over development in the Territory, and it is to these specifically that we must now turn first, as the next part of the Hong Kong new-town story.

The Imposition of Planning Standards

We have already noted that matters of planning densities and open-space standards to be applied in the new towns had been raised at various times during the early planning of Tsuen Wan/Kwai Chung. This was, in fact, merely one part of a wider debate over the extent and method of controlling the intensity of building development in Hong Kong as a whole, and as to what might be regarded as acceptable development maxima in urban areas.

Density zoning in Hong Kong originated as a policy from a suggestion within the Secretariat in 1950,[40] and it was first endorsed by the Executive Council in 1955 for use in mutual covenants incorporated within Crown land leases issued for properties in the Kowloon Tong garden suburb in Kowloon. The idea was then extended generally in the *Density Zoning*

— *Residential Properties: Urban, Suburban and Rural Coverage Scales* of May 1958, which gave maximum plot coverages for buildings of various heights, and which formed the basis for the lease controls and discretionary powers available to the Building Ordinance Office under Clause 9B(1) of the 1955 Buildings Ordinance. As we have seen, the whole matter then came under further review in 1962,[41] with a proposal from the Planning Office to impose standardized plot ratio controls throughout the urban area, following internal investigations by a Public Works Department working party on height and density controls that had been sitting since 1961.

By February 1963, the Land Development Planning Committee had agreed that three density zones should be suggested — a general control over the whole Territory of a maximum plot ratio of three, while a few areas were to be allowed to go to five, while the Zone 1 controls set out in the proposed amendments to the planning regulations[42] were to be confined to the main urban areas. The New Territories Administration however resisted the extension of formal controls to the New Territories, except for in the major towns. The final proposals were placed before the Executive Council in October 1963, and formed the basis of the density zoning controls published by the Crown Lands and Survey Office at the end of the year,[43] thus setting out for the first time a set of development control parameters to which urban development in Hong Kong was expected to conform, and to which the new towns were also now to be designed.

These density controls proved important for the new towns, not so much because they could be used to control the intensity of private or public development (indeed the public housing always remained formally excluded from the coverage of these controls), but because the use of the control standards when preparing plans and approving developments formed the basic framework for forward land-use planning throughout the Territory from the early 1960s, and imposed a standardized urban form whether under statutory or departmental frameworks. Thus for the new towns, the early density formulations that were introduced in Tsuen Wan, based on comparisons with existing known density patterns elsewhere in Hong Kong, were now replaced by formalized and standardized density calculations applied on a general basis, and which came to be periodically reviewed professionally as social demands and aspirations changed.

This concept of designing to set standards was very much extended and formalized in the ongoing work for the new Colony Outline Plan which began in earnest from late 1964, when the idea of standards was applied to many other planning requirements than simple zoning densities. In the preamble to the final document it was stated:

the standards and locational factors specified in this section should be used as a guide in the assessment of land requirements for various uses and their disposition in the preparation of outline zoning plans, outline development plans and layout plans. The standards for urban areas apply particularly to the planning of new town areas and the main rural service centres...As new information becomes available, the standards and other information contained herein will be reviewed.[44]

The standards finally summarized in each of the nine parts of the volume had been determined by each of the Colony Plan Working Committees and presented standards of provision, mainly on population bases, for the multitude of infrastructure and community services that government was now expected to provide. The principle followed subsequently has always been that while service departments in making comments on draft plans have tended to use the standards quite rigidly in checking their requirements against proposed provisions in the plans, the standards themselves have remained under almost constant revision as both experience of their use and the availability of higher levels of funding have allowed more generous levels of provision. Some idea of the general improvement can be seen from the representative figures in Table 3.1, and some aspects of the impact of the changes are discussed further in the design comments set out later in Chapter 7.

Initially, specific standards were set down in the plans for the new towns. For Sha Tin and Tuen Mun (Castle Peak) it was agreed that the vast majority of the residential population would live in residential areas developed at Zone 1 standards, three-quarters of which would be for public housing of various kinds. Using the planning standards set out in the plan, and with eight hectares of open space per 100,000 population, this gave an overall gross density of about 2,076 persons to the hectare for the two towns. This compared with an actual figure of 1,542 persons to the hectare in the main urban area (average), and 2,916 to the hectare in the newest public housing estates of the time. In the case of Tsuen Wan rather different conditions applied. Because of the substantial amount of high density low-cost government housing concentrated in the town, and the low open-space provision of only five hectares per 100,000 population, the overall gross densities worked out at some 2,718 persons to the hectare, about the same as New Kowloon east, and an urban environment was being created that was, like Kwun Tong before it, to create planning problems for the future.

The pressures on land resources in the 1970s, which led to a whole variety of government policy changes to do with land use in Hong Kong, also had their impact on planning standards and their application in the new towns. A forecast shortage of housing sites for the later 1980s in particular encouraged the government in 1980-1 for example to look at ways of improving the utilization of its land bank, which in turn led to a tightening of standards. Hence the general density standard for public housing that had applied through most of the 1970s of 2,500 persons to the hectare was then increased to 3,000; a change made possible in part by improvements in design to the individual housing blocks. In general, this meant a reconsideration of planned densities on a site-by-site basis in the older new towns where planning was further advanced and existing facilities were already committed, while full implementation was reserved for the newer developments then commencing in Junk Bay and Tin Shui Wai. A similar change was also made for the private sector, where the domestic plot ratios allowed in new-town private estates were increased in September 1981, following a review by consultants who had reported the previous June.

For the purpose, the study prepared and evaluated a number of alternative layouts in terms of compliance with all current building, fire, and planning standards, the resultant level of environmental amenity, the implications arising in connection with transport services and the provision of roads and services, sociological and economic considerations and land utilisation.[45]

Put briefly, the result was an increase in the permissable plot ratio maxima from five to eight in Zone 1 areas, 3.3 to five in Zone 2, and 2.1 to three in Zone 3. For the Zone 1 areas it was thought that the new standards could save up to seven hectares of land for each 20,000 people housed.

The objectives of the 1980s exercise were well summarized in the 1982 Report of the Special Committee on Land Supply.

The increased domestic plot ratios in the new town areas may be applied either to achieve greater population capacity or to use less land. In the main opportunities for achieving greater population capacity for a given area of land will arise in 'second generation' new towns where there will be more scope for providing the necessary infrastructure...As with higher density standards for public housing estates, the application of higher domestic plot ratios in new town areas should help to achieve greater cost-effectiveness of land use and provide opportunities for making additional land available for other uses.[46]

In the event, while building densities increased in terms of units of accommodation per units of land occupied, falling household size meant that population densities, particularly in the new public housing estates, rose only marginally, or even in some cases fell, thus reinforcing another lesson already learned, that the Hong Kong planners could not easily control population levels through direct building controls.

There were also two other areas of more recent change that deserve a mention while we are discussing the implementation of planning standards in the Hong Kong new towns. Custom and practice have come to mean that the standards and guidelines are utilized primarily in planning land reservations to satisfy government's overall policy objectives. Clearly, as these policy objectives have become more sophisticated, particularly with regard to the delivery of community services, so the standards have had to adjust accordingly. In some cases this has actually led to the abandonment of population-based standards altogether, to be replaced by others based on performance or some other operational criteria, or to replacement by new standards of increased levels of sophistication or flexibility.

To illustrate this, two specific examples of revisions affecting the new towns, also from the 1980s, can be usefully cited. In 1982, the Special Committee on Land Supply noted that:

hitherto there has been no overall strategy for rationalising the distribution of commercial uses in new towns apart from the designation of town centres and the

Table 3.1 Selected Comparative Planning Standards Applied in Planning the Hong Kong New Towns

Facility	Standards Applied				
	First Proposal	Initial Standard	Colony Outline Plan Standards 1970	Hong Kong Outline Plan Standards 1979	Hong Kong Planning Standards & Guidelines 1987
Public housing	1,850 ppgh	6,095 ppgh	2,916 ppgh	2,500–3,000 ppgh	2,700–3,000 ppgh
Private housing	810 ppgh	2,560 ppgh	2,560 ppgh	1,300 ppgh (2,500 in special schemes)	1,740 ppgh
Manufacturing industry	494 wpgh	865 wpgh	740 wpgh	800 wpgh	25 sq.m. per worker
Service industry	—	—	0.4 ha per 100,000 p	0.08 sq.m. per person	0.08 sq.m./person
Shops	—	—	0.46 sq.m. per person	0.6 sq.m. per person	hierarchy/expenditure model
Market stalls	—	—	75 per 10,000 p	140 per 10,000 p	1 per 70 households (public housing)
Schools	—	—	1 bisessional classroom per 450 p	1 bisessional classroom per 450 p (primary) 500 p (secondary)	1 bisessional place per 75 primary 56 secondary age persons
Hospitals	—	—	4.25 beds per 1,000 p	5.5 beds per 1,000 p	5.5 beds per 1,000 p
Clinics	—	—	1 per 100,000 p	1 per 100,000 p (located on as needed basis)	1 per 100,000 p

Table 3.1 (*cont.*)

Facility	Standards Applied				
	First Proposal	Initial Standard	Colony Outline Plan Standards 1970	Hong Kong Outline Plan Standards 1979	Hong Kong Planning Standards & Guidelines 1987
Libraries	—	—	—	—	1 per 200,000 p
Cinemas	—	—	38 seats per 1,000 p	—	—
Community centres	—	—	—	—	6 per 120,000 p
Car parking (Public housing)			1 space per 10 flats	1 space per 10 flats	1 space per 10 flats
(Private housing)			1 space per 250 p	1 space per 250 p	1 space per 5 flats
(Industrial)			1 space per 930 sq.m.	1 space per 930 sq.m.	1 space per 930 sq.m.
Open space	30 ha per 100,000 p	1.9 ha per 100,000 p (District space)	12 ha per 100,000 p	20 ha per 100,000 p	15–20 ha per 100,000 p (10 ha District)

Notes: ppgh — persons per gross hectare
wpgh — workers per gross hectare
ha — hectares
p — persons
sq.m. — square metres
Where a range of standards exists only maxima are shown in this table.

Sources: Various official publications of the Town Planning Office, Buildings and Lands Department, Hong Kong government.

general requirement that each residential area should have its own provision of such uses. It has been the practice to apply territory-wide standards set out in the Hong Kong Outline Plan [the 1980s up-date of the earlier Colony Outline Plan]. Such standards have been criticised as being too insensitive to local conditions. However, steps are now being taken to develop an approach to the planning of shopping centres taking into account such factors as catchment areas, nodal points, household incomes and expenditure patterns, captive levels, etc.[47]

The other example concerns industry. In the early 1980s a potential over-supply of industrial land was identified on a Territory-wide basis. Partly to encourage industrialists to take up sites when full development to per-mitted plot ratios was not envisaged, an attempt was made to improve the take-up rates by modifying the density controls. Not only did the 1983 change reduce the maximum industrial plot ratios expected in Sha Tin and Tuen Mun (Castle Peak) in Industrial Zone 1A areas from 9.5 to an average of five, but each average concealed an expected variety of individually negotiated plot ratios ranging from 3.5 to nine within each zone.

A general conclusion, therefore, is that with regard to the use of stand-ards within new-town planning in Hong Kong there is now rather less standardization on a Territory-wide basis than before, and rather more consideration of the precise requirements and opportunities of individual sites. As it is put officially:

it is important to note that the planning standards and guidelines formulated for Hong Kong are generally applied with a degree of flexibility, having regard to such factors as local requirements, topography, the density and socio-economic structure of the population, and resource availability.[48]

They have become increasingly complex, especially with the general in-troduction of the additional ten volumes of the *Transport Planning and Design Manual*, prepared by the Transport Department from 1985, but they remain one of the cornerstones of urban planning method and prac-tice in Hong Kong. As such, they are a prime determinant of the detailed design of the new towns — a subject to which we return in Chapter 7.

Strategic Planning Changes

The later 1960s were the first real period of strategic thinking over future development prospects for the whole of Hong Kong, and within which new-town development was now expected to take a role — certainly since Abercrombie's report. The Colony Outline Plan of 1970[49] was based on a medium population forecast of 5.76 million over the twenty years to 1986 (from a 1966 baseline of 3.73 million), out of which 2.42 million were estimated to require new housing accommodation (1.74 million within the subsidized public sector). The Plan also assumed that the estimated workforce increase of between 1.43 and 2.47 million would continue to need traditional industrial manufacturing and commercial employment

Fig. 3.2 Alternative strategies for the development of Hong Kong, as suggested
in the Colony Outline Plan of 1969.

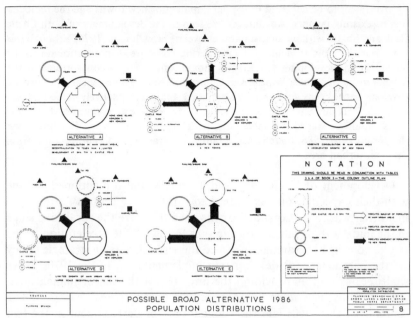

Source: Colony Outline Planning Division, *Colony Outline Plan, Book 3, Vol. I — Concepts and Outline Proposals* (Hong Kong, Crown Lands and Survey Office, 1969),
Plate 8, following p. 25.

with a high semi-skilled content, to which the new towns would have to
make a major contribution. In recommending an agreed strategy to be
followed, five possible alternatives were considered (see Fig. 3.2),

ranging from large-scale decentralisation from the main areas of Hong Kong Island,
Kowloon and New Kowloon to maximum consolidation within these same
areas. . . Ideally, the choice of one of these alternatives should be guided by a detailed assessment of the relative economics of each. Whilst it is possible that this could
be done after a prolonged study, it is considered that a decision has to be made
on the best information now available as large-scale investment of public funds
is inevitable and it is desirable for this investment to be distributed according to
an agreed population distribution. . . It is therefore considered that Government's
basic policy should be decentralisation to new towns and improvement of the environment in the existing urban areas.[50]

It was argued that full decentralization (see Strategies D and E in
Fig. 3.2) would constitute a radical departure from established trends and
policies, while concentration (Strategy A) would result in an unacceptable
level of congestion in the main urban areas.

A strategy which aims at a distribution between Alternatives B and C [see Fig.
3.2] would result in a more gradual evolution of urban functions, take account

of accepted development projects, allow a greater degree of flexibility in the planning and development of the existing urban areas and enable an appropriate balance of investment to be achieved in the development of new towns and the remodelling of existing layouts. Advantages are seen in the development of both Castle Peak and Shatin with an almost parallel level of growth from 1976, although this may be impossible to achieve if engineering costs are disproportionate to the advantages of development. . .Efforts should continue to be concentrated on the development of Tsuen Wan/Kwai Chung to which Government and private developers are already substantially committed. Initially, a relatively modest growth of Castle Peak and Shatin is recommended. . .Development works in both of these areas should be staged to enable large-scale expansion of urban functions over the period 1976–1986, thereby accelerating the strategy of decentralisation from the main urban area.[51]

Development of Yuen Long and Tai Po was also mentioned, in line with their expected roles as 'enhanced rural service centres', a development that was to be expanded by the need to utilize the rural townships in the mid-1970s as public housing sites following the acceleration of the public housing programme. In effect, these statements on strategic policy set the parameters for development implementation in the 1970s as we shall see, as well as providing the impetus for the major management changes in the new-town programme that were to come in 1973–4. The thinking of the 1960s laid the foundations for development in the two following decades.

The more detailed assessments of the Plan's Population and Housing Working Group also shed further light on government's new-town thinking of the late 1960s.

It is also apparent, however, that in the light of recent trends, there is a strong preference amongst households for accommodation in the main urban areas and conversely a reluctance to move to new towns. The reasons for this are many but a lack of community facilities in the new towns at the time when the population moves in and also a lack of appropriate transportation connections with the main urban areas appear to be fundamental problems. Furthermore, the heavy emphasis on industry in the new towns tends to narrow the scope for local employment to 'blue collar' positions whereas there is a heavy demand for office jobs amongst school leavers. The movement to the new towns of middle-income groups who cannot afford private accommodation and who are excluded from Resettlement and Government Low-Cost housing is also deterred by the lack of accommodation in Housing Authority and Housing Society estates.[52]

Measures suggested to improve this situation were to provide a wider choice of accommodation and employment, and to attempt to develop complete communities at each stage of growth of the towns.

In conclusion, the population distribution assumed as the basis for the Colony Outline Plan will not materialise of its own accord but will evolve only as a result of the application of policy decisions concerning the various means by which a strategy of decentralisation and new town growth can be achieved. In this latter respect, it is the practice in the United Kingdom for new towns to be built and managed by a development corporation so as to ensure the growth of a balanced and well-equipped community. Whilst it is not suggested that such an organisation be set up in Hong Kong, it is emphasised that the fulfilment of the new towns as self-contained entities at each stage of development will require the careful integration of effort by Government and private enterprise.[53]

Such integration proved very hard to achieve, especially in the early days.

As we have said, the commitment set out in the Plan, and endorsed by the government in its acceptance of the Plan's principles in 1971, determined policies towards new-town development in Hong Kong for the 1970s. But more immediately, two other events had important consequences upon the way that the programme was initially implemented. The first was the result of the 1971 population census, which showed a significant down-turn in the likely population growth-rates upon which the Colony Outline Plan's strategy had been based. This, together with the lower population targets that the Plan had itself postulated for Sha Tin and Tuen Mun (Castle Peak), meant that the one million target populations for those two towns had been rendered obsolete. Secondly, the government's commitment in the early 1970s, under the new Governor, Sir Murray MacLehose, to an ambitious expanded ten-year public housing programme from October 1972 resulted in both a reassessment of the public housing sites required from the new-town programme, and more particularly a revision of the potential population targets of individual estates, given an intention to improve the standards of community facilities to be provided.

All of these together resulted in a major replanning exercise and planning standards revision in all the new towns, which produced a substantial drop in each of the overall population targets for completion. Nevertheless, despite the disruption, the new-town programme for Hong Kong was firmly committed, and government's commitment found expression in major administrative reforms in 1973, when a new and specific development department (the New Territories Development Department) was set up within the Public Works Department to take overall responsibility for the expanding new-town requirements.

However, while implementation of the new-town programme showed a marked acceleration in the 1970s, monitoring of the Colony Outline Plan's forecasts rapidly revealed, as expected, scope for important revisions as the programme got under way. These eventually came for approval before the Land Development Policy Committee (as the Planning Committee had been renamed) in August 1979, as a new and revised plan.[54] By then, higher population projections, in part due to higher than expected immigration levels, and increasing rates of household formation and smaller households were all putting increasing pressure on the existing housing production targets, and hence the availability of developable land and the growth targets of the new towns. The land production question in particular had risen to prominence once again as it had in the early

1960s, and this had now given rise to the formation of a new high-level government committee to consider the specific problem — the Special Committee on Land Production (later Supply) which was to sit from 1977 to 1985.[55] Even so, the design populations for the new-town programme produced in 1977[56] remained little changed from those set at the beginning of the decade (Tsuen Wan at 870,000; Sha Tin at 550,000; and Tuen Mun [Castle Peak] at 530,000). Only the additional 440,000 now programmed for the three expanded rural towns of Yuen Long, Sheung Shui/Fanling, and Tai Po were essentially new; a fact to be recognized by their official designation as further Hong Kong new towns in 1979.

The initial objectives of the ten-year public housing programme were set out in 1972 as:

(i) To eliminate all squatter and licensed areas; (ii) To allow for the redevelopment of cottage areas; (iii) To provide self-contained dwellings for all those households at present sharing accommodation in private tenements; (iv) To relieve overcrowding in existing Government housing, including redevelopment and renovation of the estates where some such form of renewal is essential; and (v) To provide housing to those people who have to be rehoused in consequence of other Government schemes and policies.[57]

These were further amplified in papers prepared by the Secretary of Housing as part of the 1975 Housing Programme. They noted that the government's long-term aim was to provide a permanent self-contained dwelling for each household on an unshared basis, without overcrowding and at an affordable rent. Yet, by 1978, it was estimated that the shortfall still remained at about 206,000 units, excluding any possible demands from the one- and two-person households then excluded from the programme on eligibility grounds.

The outcome of this later reassessment was the realization that there would be a continued public housing need, and demand therefore for new building sites well into the 1990s.[58] It was estimated that the potential land demand outside of earmarked sites up until 1987 would amount to between 78 and 342 hectares, with a requirement that the first of the new sites would have to become available early in the 1980s. The potential source of such new sites seemed most likely to be, as before, from further expansion of the new-town programme. Thus, in addition to the already agreed extensions of Sha Tin (Area B — Ma On Shan [see Fig. 5.3], and Tuen Mun East [see Fig. 5.5]), which were already being examined, the Hong Kong Outline Plan revision of 1979 recommended as a first priority that North-east Lantau and Junk Bay should be protected as potential long-term development sites, even though the Plan can be criticized for failing to take any effective long-term overall strategic look at the Territory as a whole. This last requirement awaited a further round of strategic thinking that was to culminate in the Territorial Development Strategy of 1983, the refinement of which formed the basis of current strategic development planning in Hong Kong, within which ongoing new-town development forms a part.

Strategies for the 1980s

The most recent strategic review of development opportunities in Hong Kong began following the report of the Special Committee on Land Production in July 1977,[59] which noted that potential extension areas for the two new towns of Tuen Mun and Sha Tin had already been identified and were to be investigated by consultants in 1977 and 1978.[60] The report also suggested new areas for investigation as potential development sites, of which the major locations were near Tin Shui Wai in the north-west New Territories and Three Fathoms Cove to the north-east of Sha Tin.[61]

However, the possible sites:

were scattered and bore no relation to the pattern of existing development. Moreover, on the basis of past performance they might be expected to have high unit production costs. For this reason, it was considered that a comprehensive investigation of North Lantau should proceed as soon as possible and that, subject to the findings of that investigation and the identification of a deficit between the overall demand for and the production of land, it should be considered whether it might be preferable to proceed with its development in advance of some or all of the other areas identified by the Committee.[62]

This new, in-house investigation initiated the first of what was to become a series of five sub-regional studies of development potential, mainly done by consultants, which together over the period 1978 to 1982 provided background material for the development of the government's own new Territorial Development Strategy. The second area for investigation, both in-house and later with consultants, was the north-west of the New Territories, where a concentration of the smaller designated development sites of the Committee suggested the need for early, more detailed investigations.

It needs to be noted however that the formation of the Special Committee itself was but one outcome of a major review within government at the end of the 1970s, especially regarding land matters, but also relating by extension to the planning of future strategic land use in the Territory.[63] Part of this upheaval resulted in the formation of a new Strategic Planning Unit within the Environment Branch of the Secretariat to oversee the evolving programme that was then moving rapidly towards the formulation of a new development strategy for Hong Kong. Indeed, one of its specific terms of reference was to develop:

a territorial development strategy to provide guidance to the government for the long-term provision of land and infrastructure to meet needs arising from continued population growth. This work will require, in the first instance, the commissioning of various sub-regional development studies and the reassessment — from a transportation point of view — of assumed alternative population distributions.[64]

These twin objectives arose from two assessments within government, which were publicly expressed through the various annual reports of the

Special Committee on Land Supply — that there was likely to be a shortfall of sites for the public housing programme in the late 1980s and 1990s;
and that the self-contained, balanced planning objectives for the new towns
were not being attained, and hence yet more new policies towards their
development would have to be established. These assessments deserve some
closer consideration.

The Executive Council's housing objectives of October 1980, which were
the basis of the first of these reassessments, were in turn founded upon
demand forecasts done in 1979 taking into account affordability, demand
from clearances, overcrowding relief, redevelopment of old estates, and
the 1977–80 influx of illegal immigrants from China. These considerations suggested that an ongoing programme of 30,000 new units per year,
plus 5,000 each from the new home-ownership and private sector partnership schemes would be required in order to meet the original housing
objectives set out by the government in 1972. This annual target was
expected to last well into the 1990s. To meet these targets and if possible
exceed them was now seen as a political imperative, and the initial realization of a possible shortfall in the mid-1980s resulted in an immediate
decision to go ahead with site formation works at both Ma On Shan (the
north-eastern extension of Sha Tin [see Fig. 5.3]), and Junk Bay (see Fig.
6.3), in order to provide sites on stream in 1982–3 and 1984–5 respectively. Thus, short-term commitments forced by immediate housing
pressures pushed government into new strategic developments even before
any new strategic investigations were properly under way.

The same immediate housing pressures were also behind the decisions
to revise and increase the density standards applied in the new towns that
were mentioned previously (pp. 90–1), as well as more specific investigations to look at the possibilities of increasing the design capacities of particular proposed development areas such as So Kwun Wat (Tuen Mun
Eastern Extension). In 1981, such pressures were further increased by the
decisions taken to restrict the development of both Ma On Shan and Junk
Bay to population ceilings set by the need to avoid expensive rail links
within the developments, which were required if maximum population
growth was to be allowed. These pressures led in turn to a search for yet
further supplementary housing sites within the new towns and elsewhere,
of which about half was to come from rezoning what was held to be surplus
industrial land.

However, this was essentially a short-term measure, and by 1984 a clear
impasse had been reached:

we are concerned that for housing production after 1990/91, the estimated land
requirements will no longer be met by the continued selection of supplementary
sites without sacrificing environmental quality. We therefore recommend that
Government should now make planning decisions based on the results so far
available from various major strategic studies of future land use options to assure
a steady supply of land for public housing in the long term.[65]

Short-term demands were threatening longer-term strategies once again.

The whole question of balance in the planning of the new towns also came to the fore in the early 1980s, and was the background to the specific requirement that the Strategic Planning Unit should include transportation objectives in its new strategic planning exercises.

It is evident that in some areas the rapid build-up of development, particularly in the field of housing, has placed heavy strains on the capacity of arterial transportation systems. We are aware of the increased priority now being given to the upgrading of such systems and would not propose that current major development projects, particularly in the new towns, be held back until the additional transportation capacity has been provided. However, with the benefit of hindsight we would express a degree of concern over the need to keep land development programmes and the provision of major infrastructure in a reasonable state of balance, particularly in such new development areas as Junk Bay and Ma On Shan where provision of arterial transportation links and services should be the forerunner of urban growth.[66]

This had been expressed as a warning as early as 1977, and one of its effects was the conscious decision to restrict the growth of both Junk Bay and Ma On Shan to 120,000 each, the knock-on effects of which elsewhere within the new-town programme we have just described.

However, the most obvious problem concerning transport investment, particularly in the New Territories, was the growing realization that the functioning of the new towns as they grew in the 1970s was not quite as assumed and planned for. Balance, at least as far as the provision of facilities was concerned was reckoned to have improved:

we are satisfied that the administrative mechanisms in new town areas provide an adequate means to achieve 'balanced' development in respect to ancillary community facilities.[67]

But doubts were beginning to appear in other areas.

For housing, the public/private split came under review.

The forecast surplus of land supply in both the Urban Areas and in the New Territories [for the *private* sector it should be noted] could lead developers to concentrate on private sector housing in the Urban areas leading to an imbalance in the new towns. In this connection we consider that a detailed study of the socio-economic background of private and public sector housing as well as the pattern of private sector housing investment would be useful in determining the most appropriate housing mix to meet the needs of people in various income brackets and the ways in which this could be achieved.[68]

We consider that advantage should be taken of the present supply situation to review existing planning standards. For example, the opportunity should be taken to reconsider what is an appropriate housing mix in the New Towns and how this can best be achieved. In recommending this approach, we are not necessarily suggesting less intensive use of individual sites but an approach which would improve the cost-effectiveness of land use, having regard to the need for balance in development in new and redeveloped areas.[69]

Thus by the mid-1980s, the whole future of housing policy in Hong Kong had come under review, particularly in the public sector, where, by the middle of the decade, long-term reviews were beginning to detect a discernable shift from renting to home-ownership for the 1990s. The outcome of this was the beginnings of a design shift in the final round of the 1980s new towns.

Of more concern though to the strategic planning considerations being considered here, at least as far as 'balance' in the new towns was concerned, was the looming problem of employment and the operation of the labour markets being formed by the various new towns.

The concept of 'balanced development' has been a fundamental principle for the planning and development of new towns. This concept proposes that in each new town the number of local employment opportunities, particularly in respect of service trade and manufacturing industries, should generally equate with the number of resident workers. Such an objective is seen to have considerable socio-economic value, particularly in helping to minimize interzonal travel demands. However, it is seen that whilst the concept of balanced development should remain a long-term goal, past trends indicate that a high degree of worker mobility is likely to be the general pattern for some years to come suggesting that the distribution of jobs should be considered in a territorial context which would carry with it the implication of diverting more resources to improving transport systems.[70]

Reviews for the Special Committee on Land Supply reinforced this assessment in that they suggested that by 1991 over four times as many job opportunities were likely to be available in the main metropolitan area as in the employment centres outside. Such concerns were confirmed and reinforced by the findings of a 1983 survey by the Hong Kong Productivity Centre into industrial mobility in the Territory.

Whereas workers who live in the new towns have a strong wish to work near where they live, employers have shown a far greater reluctance to move beyond the metropolitan areas mainly because they see the New Towns as unable to provide labour of the right type and quality. While employment balance remains a desirable planning objective a high degree of job mobility is likely to exist in the New Towns for some years to come and the prospect of achieving balance will be subject to changes in the pattern of industrial development. While we feel that the concept of employment balance on a sub-regional level may be supported in principle, an in-depth examination in respect of the implications on the existing and planned transport infrastructure would be necessary.[71]

This last request was to materialize in the second Territory-wide Comprehensive Transport Study of 1986–8, the first having been completed a decade before in 1976.[72]

Bringing these varied strands of unease together suggests that by the mid-1980s, for a variety of reasons, the original concepts about strategic planning for Hong Kong had come to be questioned. While the population decentralization envisaged in the Colony Outline Plan had indeed occurred, the new towns were beginning to function in ways not quite intended. They were not yet balanced, in that they displayed marked biases towards public housing — in part due to their uncompleted states; and they were not self-contained, in that they were generating large commuting flows, particularly for work purposes. In fact, in labour market terms, the older established urban area labour market had now merely spread to embrace the larger labour pool represented by the nearby new-town populations. Hong Kong had come to operate as a single metropolitan labour market, within which various sub-markets were operating on either a sectoral or spatial basis. Recognition of this in planning terms meant that the Hong Kong new towns could no longer realistically be considered and planned for as separate entities, but were now in fact and operation merely parts of a wider single metropolitan city region that was requiring to be planned on an integrated and wholistic basis. The older concepts of central core and independent satellites that underpinned their origins had now become obsolete, and in fact were probably never ever particularly viable.

This recognition of the unity of metropolitan Hong Kong is likely to be further reinforced by 1980's strategic policies which suggest a return to concentration of development around the harbour, rather than further urban decentralization in the next century. This was in part realized by an *ad hoc* working group set up within government in 1984–5 to consider the whole question of balanced development in the new towns. They concluded that balances between public and private housing, and between population and community facilities were achievable in the new towns, but that balances between the local labour force and local job opportunities were much more difficult to achieve in a free market situation, as applies in Hong Kong. Short of withholding land where there is a demand or discouraging worker mobility, both of which would adversely affect the Hong Kong economy, it was recognized that it could be many years before employment balance could be achieved for all sub-regions in the Territory, if at all. Realistically, consideration of the Hong Kong new towns as independent labour markets had disappeared, and with it emerged the necessity for a fundamental reassessment of their roles within the Hong Kong urban system.

The New Towns and the Territorial Development Strategy

The current Territorial Development Strategy began formally in 1980 with the establishment of the Strategic Planning Unit within the government's Environment Secretariat. However, its origins can be traced directly to the work of the Special Committee on Land Supply. The new unit was set two basic objectives:

To reassess in broad terms future priorities for investment in land development and major infrastructure; [and] to produce a long term land use/transportation strategy for Hong Kong to cater for a derived target population and associated socio-economic activities in a manner which will produce the highest quality environment within constraints set by resource availability and the time frame within which the needs of the target population have been met.[73]

Lesser requirements were maximum benefits from public investment; forecasts of land production, including targeting; sub-regionally-based programming for land-use development proposals; and, providing a framework for safeguarding conservation principles and implementing the final agreed strategy.

The steps by which such objectives were to be met were formulated, as is often the way of planners, in a well-differentiated series of separate tasks. Having set goals and objectives and identified key issues which might affect future development, the major investigation, after completing estimates of housing and employment trends, was to make a major reappraisal of the regional development potential for each of the five sub-regions into which Hong Kong had been divided. With the exception of the North Lantau Island studies, which were intimately bound up with the investigation of Chek Lap Kok as a new site for Hong Kong's international airport, the remaining four studies for the north-west and north-east New Territories, Junk Bay/Sai Kung, and the Harbour Area were all put out to various consultancy teams, and were completed over the 1980–3 period.[74]

Essentially, they were land-use, sub-regional planning studies, which attempted to derive maximum feasible target populations for their areas, taking into account the specific problems of each area and selecting the best sites for further development. As might be expected, in the New Territories major extensions to the existing and planned new towns formed a major part of the potential that was investigated (see Fig. 8.3). This was particularly so since major determinants of potential were the availability of land fill (that is, potential borrow areas), and drainage, transportation, and servicing constraints.

The five studies between them suggested that potential development sites offered capacities capable of providing settlements for some ten and a half million people, some three and a half million more than the 7.1 million then forecast for the target year of 2001. Clearly the next stage of the investigation involved choices, even though committed land development already meant that the locations of the 1991 forecast population distribution were already largely determined (see Tables 3.2 and 3.3). After 1991, the effective choice of a strategy therefore concerned the placing of an incremental addition of:

about 900,000 people and an increase in jobs of about 200,000. These projections translate into requirements for about 1000 hectares of additional land and for corresponding expansion of the transport network after 1991.[75]

Within these forecasts it was estimated that additional public housing for about one and a half million people would be likely to be required over the 20-year period 1981–2001.

The remaining stages of the study,[76] involving the setting of investment

Table 3.2 Actual, Forecast, and Potential Population Distributions, 1971–2001 (population in hundred thousands)

| | Areas | | | | | | Sub-regions | | |
	1971	1976	1981	1986	1991	1991	2001	Ultimate Potential
Main urban area	3,181	3,394	3,736	3,660	3,534	4,240[1]	?	5,800
Rural New Territories	240	265	317	360	408	910[2]	?	1,900
New towns	436	685	1,019	1,594	2,226	70[3]	?	800
Marine population	80	59	53	47	42	790[4]	?	1,700
						160[5]	?	400
Total	3,937	4,403	5,125	5,661	6,210	6,170	7,089	10,600

Notes: The sub-regions are as follows: 1. Metropolitan Area; 2. North-east New Territories; 3. South-west New Territories; 4. North-west New Territories; 5. South-east New Territories.

Source: Strategic Planning Unit, *An Outline of Strategic Planning in Hong Kong: A Positional Statement* (Hong Kong, Strategic Planning Unit, 1982).

Table 3.3 Revised Regional Population Forecasts of 1985 — Strategic Options (population in hundred thousands)

Sub-region	Current Programmes	Future Opportunities	Potential by Area	Strategic Choices	
				New Territories Option	Harbour Option
Metropolitan area	4,056	1,342	5,398	4,425	4,928
NE New Territories	1,022	555	1,577	1,048	1,022
SW New Territories	57	700	757	57	57
NW New Territories	839	546	1,385	1,316	839
SE New Territories	206	142	348	206	206
Total	6,180	3,285	9,465	7,052	7,052

Source: Government Information Services, *Planning for Growth* (Hong Kong, Government Printer, 1985).

objectives, the generation and evaluation of the alternative strategies, and the selection and implementation of a first-stage development strategy for the 1990s, have now come to be seen as more controversial[77] — particularly in terms of the methodology used (see Chapter 8). These affected the possible outcomes and the policy constraints, which set further limits within which the potential strategies could be formulated and compared. In the planners' own words, the outcome was to focus the examination:

to produce some very broad evaluations for each strategic development option in terms of land development costs, territory-wide transportation costs and the economic consequences thereof ... The development costs assessments would need to be in terms of unit costs, cash flows, lead times for the production of land, and economic evaluations ... With regard to territory-wide transportation studies, assessments would seek to determine for an assumed population/employment distribution the likely person travel demands between major traffic zones,[78]

thus giving peak-hour traffic loadings and modal split forecasts which were then to be assigned to current and planned transport networks in the classic land-use transportation-model manner.

It has been reasonably argued that this methodology places too much emphasis on the economic considerations generally, and the public expenditure considerations for the government in particular. This is largely a direct outcome of the quantifiable data used for the analysis — public sector capital costs, net financial and resource costs to the community, net public sector costs, transport operating costs, and travel times. It was stated that:

each sub-regional study has defined areas for strategic urban growth taking into account a wide diversity of geographic, social, economic, transport and environmental considerations. The areas so defined may thus be regarded as the best local choice for major urban development when being evaluated at a strategic planning level.[79]

The fact that the statement specifies 'local' emphasizes the consequence that submergence of these more nebulous planning virtues, when subjected to the quantitative criteria of the Territory-wide analysis and evaluation, led to an outcome that tipped the balance, inevitably, in the government's specific favour as provider of the public capital, and took lesser account of wider strategic issues.[80]

The relevance of this whole argument to our story of new-town development in Hong Kong is that its outcome has largely determined the future of the Hong Kong new towns into the 1990s and the next century. The alternative strategy evaluations which the Strategic Planning Unit undertook concentrated on two broad strategy options — either to leave the existing international airport at Kai Tak or to relocate it at Chek Lap Kok, and within both to derive three alternative strategies which would either minimize public sector capital costs, minimize community costs, or minimize net public sector costs.

In general, the first series, which minimized land acquisition and major interzonal transport infrastructure costs, meant an outcome that produced a balance between limited new reclamations around the harbour and continued New Territories growth particularly in the north-west (including the major expansion of Tin Shui Wai as a new town). Minimizing community costs, on the other hand, favoured concentration of future growth in the main urban core around the harbour. The third set of evaluations, where potential urban population distributions were primarily influenced by the patterns of assumed transport costs, were eventually discarded as being too variable and impracticable in policy terms. They required active control of transport costs by government intervention through such mechanisms as road tolls and fare controls — political non-starters as far as Hong Kong is concerned.

In the event, the final outcome of the exercise in quantitative terms proved indecisive: cost-benefit differences, expressed as differences between public expenditures and expected revenues to government, proved to be marginal between the Territory-wide options.

That being the case, if it is considered desirable to make a choice between the options presented then it may be expected that subsequent evaluations would have to depend heavily on a high degree of intuitive judgement. However, before any action is taken in such a direction it is considered that attention should be focussed on the commonalities between Growth Patterns A and B [that is to concentrate on the harbour area, or to continue with urban expansion in the New Territories] with respect to both base growth [that is the already committed and expected growth] and strategic growth [future expansion] land use — transport components. Acceptance of commonalities would provide a firm basis for subsequent detailed planning and the programming of works which will be required regardless of long-term strategic development options.[81]

Thus, in the time-honoured way, the Hong Kong government took a cautious view of the future. Using the common elements of both strategic options, approximately 310,000 people were expected to be located in public sector housing schemes at Green Island (207,000) and Yau Ma Tei (87,000) on new reclamations, with a balance of 16,000 on a group of small schemes near Pokfulam. There are also likely to be some additional possibilities on other reclamations such as Hung Hom Bay (begun in 1986–7 primarily to provide expansion space for the Kowloon–Canton Railway terminals), and Wanchai, both likely to be for the private housing sector. These schemes (see Fig. 8.1) were designed to meet the land production requirements of the mid-1990s, thus deferring further incremental strategic decisions for a decade or more.

A general conclusion seems to be that there would be a case for a substantial commitment to strategic growth in the harbour area to keep development programmes going to at least the mid-1990s.[82]

It has therefore been decided that a flexible line should be adopted by planning initially to proceed with the implementation of components common to the two main growth patterns in the medium term and deciding on subsequent steps from time to time with the benefit of up-to-date information. This would be better than seeking to define a final plan up to the end of the 1990s, which would inevitably be affected by, and need modification in the light of changing circumstances in the meantime.[83]

Such pragmatism has, with hindsight seemed wise. Decisions, taken in 1988, to allow full expansion of Junk Bay in the 1990s and to develop fully the Tin Shui Wai reclamation, also in 1988, re-emphasize the importance of the new towns, while *Metroplan*[84] and the strategic review of harbour expansion and airport relocation begun in the late 1980s are fully in line with the Territorial Development Strategy's objectives. Apparently the eventual outcome of the balance between these competing strategies has not yet been decided.

Conclusions

Reading between the lines, one is tempted to wonder how far such pragmatism is influenced by the future 1997 handover to China, or uncertainties over possible levels of developer confidence from the private sector in the 1990s. Yet, whatever the cause, for the shorter term, the development focus in Hong Kong has now begun to return once more to the urban core, as it was in the 1950s and early 1960s. Perhaps decentralization and new towns will turn out to have been but a 20-year phase in the development history of the Territory. The nagging doubt however is that the basis on which such a major change has been founded is less than adequate, as we shall see in Chapter 8. The long-term future of the Hong Kong new-town programme, particularly of its fourth-generation phase, seems hardly yet to have been addressed, particularly as to how the Territory as a whole might be expected, or planned, to function as a complete metropolitan area. Already, exercises like the second Territory-wide transportation study, begun in 1986, and the keeping in place of the Strategic Planning Unit itself, suggest that we have not yet heard the last of discussion as to what the strategic development future of Hong Kong should be. It seems that we cannot yet consider the new-town story of Hong Kong as closed, whatever the premonitions of the Territorial Development Strategy might suggest, and whatever the outcome of *Metroplan* in the 1990s.

Perhaps the clearest point to come from any overall look at the place of new-town development within the wider policies of the Hong Kong government, is that its detailed evolution has always been subservient to, and an outcome of, other wider considerations of social and economic policy. This is, in fact, but a particular example of the more general role that land-use planning as a professional discipline has always had in Hong Kong — as a tool of the public works initiators, who in turn have been propelled by the social and economic imperatives of government. Thus new-town planning in Hong Kong has turned out to be not unlike new-town planning elsewhere, for example, the new-town planning in the United Kingdom, where so many of the detailed concepts originated.

The particularly unique contribution of the Hong Kong policy-making process lies in the overwhelming dominance throughout of the need for immediate response to the quest for public housing sites (land), which has been set at various stages by the vagaries of the public-housing programmes and the varied priorities put upon them by government, followed closely at various times by industrial land requirements. The variance in these demands over time clearly led to an incremental approach being taken to new-town development, which, associated with the Hong Kong government's well-known addiction to financial viability, in turn brought about the rather specific form of new-town organization that characterizes the way that new towns have been planned, built, and developed in the Territory, and which we shall look at in the next chapter. Associated with this administrative process is the very particular land acquisition, conversion, and preparation process that is also a unique aspect of Hong Kong's new-town development programmes.

The overwhelming impression therefore is a somewhat surprising one. At first the sheer scale and magnitude of the new-town programme in the 1970s and 1980s suggests common purpose and the great objective. Yet, detailed examination betrays the incremental approach and the pragmatism for which the public sector in Hong Kong is renowned. There is, in fact, a somewhat stumbling progression towards any integrated concept for the strategic development of Hong Kong, of which the new-town programme forms a major part. Moreover, despite appearances, that remains incomplete in the late 1980s, and as we have just argued, it remains hedged about with rather too many 'ifs and buts'. It seems clear that new-town development in Hong Kong is destined to remain within an overall policy of incremental shifts and balances, within a strategic development scenario that is itself to be determined by wider shifts in economic, social, and political fortune, to which Hong Kong will be subjected. This is perhaps not a surprising conclusion overall, given the origins and fortunes of new-town programmes elsewhere in the world: they, too, remain so often dependent on wider outcomes of varied national economic and social policy.

Notes

1. W.J. Smyly, 'Tsuen Wan Township', *Far Eastern Economic Review*, Vol. 33, No. 9, 31 August 1961, p. 397.

2. Scott Wilson Kirkpatrick & Partners, *Report on Reclamation at Gin Drinkers Bay* (Hong Kong, Government Printer, 1959).

3. W.G. Gregory, S. Mackey, J.R. Firth, C.H. Wong, K.W. Leung, *Tsuen Wan Development: A Feasibility Report* (Hong Kong, Cathay Press, 1959), p. 1.

4. Gregory, Mackey, Firth, Wong, and Leung (1959), see note 3 above, p. 8.

5. Gregory, Mackey, Firth, Wong, and Leung (1959), see note 3 above, p. 8.

6. Gregory, Mackey, Firth, Wong, and Leung (1959), see note 3 above, p. 11.

7. Memorandum from the Director of Public Works to the Colonial Secretary, 12 July 1960, at 2 in BL 4/5282/60I, Buildings and Lands Registry, Hong Kong.

8. Report on Tsuen Wan by the District Commissioner, New Territories, quoted in Smyly (1961), see note 1 above, pp. 404–5.

9. Some major examples were the disruption of early main drainage work due to clearance difficulties; the opposition of the Tsuen Wan Rural Committee to land exchange arrangements in the summer of 1963; more recently, the persistent village opposition to major redevelopment proposals for the Kau Wah Kam valley near to Lai Chi Kok (New Kowloon); and the so-called Four Villages dispute on the island of Tsing Yi near to the proposed town centre.

10. Plan LTW 75 was approved by the Governor-in-Council on 8 October 1963, after major revisions from the Town Planning Board.

11. Planning Division, *Tsuen Wan and District Outline Development Plan — Statement to accompany Plan No. LTW/75* (Hong Kong, Government Printer, 1963), pp. 1–2.

12. See memorandum of 8 February 1962 by the Deputy Economic Secretary, Chairman of the Land Development Planning Committee, at 15/1 in BL 2/1/5281/47, Buildings and Lands Registry, Hong Kong.

13. Prepared as Plan LTW 57, *Tsuen Wan District Outline Development Plan*, 15 August 1961.

14. Memorandum for Executive Council XCR (63)17 of 22 January 1963, at 47 in BL 4/5282/60I, Buildings and Lands Registry, Hong Kong.

15. Planning Division, *Tsuen Wan and District Outline Development Plan* (1963), see note 11 above, p. 2.

16. Planning Division, *Tsuen Wan and District Outline Development Plan* (1963), see note 11 above, p. 3.

17. Planning Division, *Tsuen Wan and District Outline Development Plan* (1963), see note 11 above, p. 3.

18. Tsuen Wan New Town Development Office, *Tsuen Wan New Town Development Programme: Forecast of Expenditure, Aug, 1974* (Hong Kong, New Territories Development Department, 1974), para. 1.3, p. 1.

19. Tsuen Wan New Town Development Office (1974), see note 18 above, para. 2.

20. Minute M123 by an Assistant Secretary, 23 June 1961, in BL 1/5282/56I Public Records Office, Hong Kong.

21. District Commissioner New Territories, *Urban Expansion into the New Territories: Note by the District Commissioner, New Territories* (Hong Kong, New Territories Administration, 1959). At 70/1 in BL 1/5282/56I, Public Records Office, Hong Kong.

22. District Commissioner New Territories (1959), see note 21 above, para. 4, p. 2.

23. District Commissioner New Territories (1959), see note 21 above, para. 4, p. 16.

24. Memorandum from the Director of Commerce and Industry to the Colonial Secretary, 6 October 1959, at 75 in BL 1/5282/56I, Public Records Office, Hong Kong.

25. See Colony Outline Planning Team, *Hong Kong: The Colony Outline Plan, Planning Report 1* (Hong Kong, Crown Lands and Survey Office, 1964), for a discussion of how to prepare such a regional plan. The proposals were prepared by the professional planners, but rejected firmly by government, who objected, especially to the proposed public involvement and participation suggested. A copy can be found at 34/1 in BL 2/1/5282/47, Buildings and Lands Registry, Hong Kong.
The title change from 'Regional Plan' to 'Colony Outline Plan' had been suggested two years before in a memorandum from the Colonial Secretary to the Director of Public Works on 24 February 1962; at 111 in BL 1/5282/56I, Public Records Office, Hong Kong.

26. Memorandum at 111 in BL 1/5282/56I, Public Records Office, Hong Kong.

27. Land Development Planning Committee Paper No. 14, *Large Scale Development in the New Territories*, Public Works Department, 14 September 1962. Copy at 114/1 in BL 1/5282/56I, Public Records Office, Hong Kong.

28. Memorandum from the Director of Public Works to the District Commissioner New Territories, 25 August 1962, at 114/1C in BL 1/5282/56I, Public Records Office, Hong Kong.

29. Land Development Planning Committee Paper No. 23A, *Sites for New Towns and Large Development Schemes*, Public Works Department, 19 April 1963.

30. Prepared by the Town Planning Board in 1961 as Outline Development Plan LST 19, for a residential town of 360,000.

31. Land Development Planning Committee Paper No. 36, *Urban Development in the New Territories*, New Territories Administration, 23 September 1963.

32. Development Division, *Report on Development at Sha Tin* and *Report on Development at Castle Peak* (Hong Kong, Public Works Department, 1965). Copies in LSO 123/HPG/63, Buildings and Lands Registry, Hong Kong. Further discussion of this debate is in Chapter 5, pp. 168–70.

33. Comment by the Director of Public Works at a meeting of the Public Works Department Policy Committee on 6 March 1964; at M1 in LSO 123/HPG/63, Buildings and Lands Registry, Hong Kong.

34. *Review of Policies for Squatter Control, Resettlement and Government Low-Cost Housing 1964*, White Paper (Hong Kong, Government Printer, 1964).

35. See Items 41, 42, and 45 in BL 4/5282/60V for a discussion of the impact of this programme on Tsuen Wan New Town. It involved a major reallocation of sites which increased the proportion of high-density housing, removed Kwai Chung town centre, and radically altered the planned form of the new town. The file is in the Buildings and Lands Registry, Hong Kong.

36. Published as Outline Zoning Plans LCP 32 (Castle Peak) and LST 47 (Sha Tin), Crown Lands and Survey Office, Hong Kong, 1966.

37. Land Development Planning Committee Paper No. 71, *Proposed New Towns at Castle Peak and Sha Tin*, Public Works Department, 9 April 1965.

38. Minute M21 in LSO 123/HPG/63, Buildings and Lands Registry, Hong Kong (Extract of the minutes of the fiftieth meeting of the Land Development Planning Committee, 9 April 1965).

39. Conclusions in Minute M21, LSO 123/HPG/63, Buildings and Lands Registry, Hong Kong.

40. Minute of 24 July 1950 in BL 21/3181/50, Public Records Office, Hong Kong.

41. Planning Division, *Planning Memorandum No. 5: The Application of Population Density Control to Outline Zoning and Outline Development Plans and Related to Building Heights and Coverage* (Hong Kong, Crown Lands and Survey Office, 1962). Copy at 24 in BL 2/1/5281/47, Public Records Office, Hong Kong.

42. Set out in the First Schedule of the *Building (Planning) (Amendment) (No. 2) Regulations 1962* (Hong Kong, Government Printer, 1962).

43. *Building (Planning) (Amendment) (No. 2) Regulations 1962* (1962), see note 42 above, and Density Zoning Plans for Hong Kong Island and Kowloon.

44. Colony Outline Planning Division, *The Colony Outline Plan: Book 3, Vol. II — Standards and Locational Factors* (Hong Kong, Crown Lands and Survey Office, 1970), p. 1.

45. Special Committee on Land Supply, *Special Committee on Land Supply: Report to His Excellency the Governor, March 1982* (Hong Kong, Government Printer, 1982), para.3.23, p. 22.

46. Special Committee on Land Supply (1982), see note 45 above, para.3.25, p. 24.

47. Special Committee on Land Supply (1982), see note 45 above, para.5.11, p. 37.

48. Town Planning Division, *Information Pamphlet: Hong Kong Planning Standards and Guidelines* (Hong Kong, Lands Department, 1985), p. 2. This document is always available and is updated from time to time.

49. The whole plan documentation was produced in three sets of documents. Book 1 consisted of the background working papers; Book 2 contained the reports of the six Working Committees which prepared the detailed studies, subject by subject; and Book 3 contained the final proposals in two volumes — on concepts and proposals, and planning standards respectively.

50. Colony Outline Planning Division, *The Colony Outline Plan: Book 3, Vol. I — Concepts and Outline Proposals* (Crown Lands and Survey Office, Hong Kong, 1969), pp. 23–4.

51. Colony Outline Planning Division (1969), see note 50 above, pp. 26–7.

52. Colony Outline Planning Division (1969), see note 50 above, p. 31.

53. Colony Outline Planning Division (1969), see note 50 above, p. 32.

54. Colony Planning Division, *Hong Kong Outline Plan* (Hong Kong, Town Planning Office, 1979).

55. The debate over land policy can be followed in Roger Bristow, *Land-use Planning in Hong Kong: History, Policies and Procedures* (Hong Kong, Oxford University Press, 1984), pp. 116–9.

56. Land Development Policy Committee Paper No. 19/77, *Main Urban Areas Design Population*, Town Planning Office, July 1977.

57. Quoted in Colony Planning Division (1979), see note 54 above, para.2.1, pp. 13.1–13.2.

58. The assessments were summarized in the following Land Development Policy Committee Papers: No. 23/78, *Broad Assessment of Future Demand for and Supply of Housing*; No. 24/78, *Demand for Public Housing*; and No. 32/78, *Long Term Land Requirements for Housing*. These were all prepared by the Town Planning Office during 1978.

59. Special Committee on Land Production, *Report of the Special Committee on Land Production* (Hong Kong, Government Printer, 1977).

60. The respective reports were: Maunsell Consultants Asia, *Sha Tin Stage II Engineering Feasibilty Study* (Hong Kong, New Territories Development Department, 1977); and Scott Wilson Kirkpatrick & Partners, *Tuen Mun Stage II Extension Study* (Hong Kong, New Territories Development Department, 1978).

61. Special Committee on Land Production (1977), see note 59 above, Appendix 9.

62. Special Committee on Land Production (1977), see note 59 above, para.30, p. 17.

63. A fuller account of these changes can be found in Bristow (1984), see note 55 above, pp. 112–8 and 133–4.

64. *Hong Kong Annual Report 1981* (Hong Kong, Government Printer, 1981), p. 107.

65. Special Committee on Land Supply, *Special Committee on Land Supply: Report to His Excellency the Governor, March 1984* (Hong Kong, Government Printer, 1984), para.3.8, p. 14.

66. Special Committee on Land Production, *Special Committee on Land Production: Report to His Excellency the Governor, March 1981* (Hong Kong, Government Printer, 1981), para.7.7, pp. 41–2.

67. Special Committee on Land Supply (1981), see note 66 above, para.2.20, p. 10.

68. Special Committee on Land Supply (1984), see note 65 above, para.3.33, p. 19.

69. Special Committee on Land Supply, *Special Commitee on Land Supply: Report to His Excellency the Governor, March 1985* (Hong Kong, Government Printer, 1985), para.9.4, p. 31.

70. Special Committee on Land Supply, *Special Committee on Land Supply: Report to His Excellency the Governor, March 1983* (Hong Kong, Government Printer, 1983), para.4.3, p. 17.

71. Special Committee on Land Supply (1984), see note 65 above, paras.4.19-4.20, p. 22.

72. Wilbur Smith and Associates, *Hong Kong Comprehensive Transport Study* (Hong Kong, Wilbur Smith and Associates, 1976), 3 vols.

73. Strategic Planning Unit, *An Outline of Strategic Planning in Hong Kong: A Positional Statement* (Hong Hong, Strategic Planning Unit, 1982), pp. 1–2. The quotations are taken from Land Development Policy Committee Paper No. 40/80 of 31 Oct. 1980.

74. The main reports of the various study teams can be found under: North Lantau Island — Town Planning Division, *North Lantau Study* (Hong Kong, Lands Department, 1981). North-west New Territories — New Territories Development Consultants, *Development Investigation of the North Western New Territories* (Hong Kong, New Territories Development Consultants, 1981), 4 vols. North-east New Territories — Freeman Fox & Partners (Far East), HFA Hong Kong, EBC Hong Kong, and Watson Hawksley Asia, *North Eastern New Territories Study: Final Report* (Hong Kong, New Territories Development Department, 1982). Junk Bay and Sai Kung — Maunsell Consultants Asia, Shankland Cox, and Brian Clouston and Partners, *Junk Bay Development Study* (Hong Kong, New Territories Development Department, 1982). Main Harbour Area — Scott Wilson Kirkpatrick & Partners, Robert Matthew, Johnson-Marshall and Partners (Hong Kong), Coopers and Lybrand Associates Limited, and Collier Petty Ltd., *Harbour Reclamations and Urban Growth Study — Final Report* (Lands Department, Hong Kong, 1983).

75. Government Information Services, *Planning for Growth* (Hong Kong, Government Printer, 1985), p. 9.

76. The structure of the studies was set out in — Strategic Planning Unit, *Hong Kong Territorial Development Strategy* (Hong Kong, Strategic Planning Unit, 1984), and was produced in 7 volumes, as follows: 1. *Introductory Statement* (1982); 2. *Broad Method and Policy Assumptions* (1982); 3. *Demographic Inputs* (1982); 4. *Review of Current Development Programmes* (1983), 5. *Alternative Strategies and Evaluation* (1983); 6. *Territorial Development Strategy — Initial Results* (1984); and 7. *Initial Development Strategy* (1984).

77. B. Taylor, *Rethinking the Territorial Development Strategy Planning Process* (Hong Kong, University of Hong Kong, Centre of Urban Studies and Urban Planning, Seminar Paper, 1986).

78. Strategic Planning Unit, *Territorial Development Strategy: Initial Results* (Hong Kong, Strategic Planning Unit, 1984), p. 12.

79. Strategic Planning Unit (1984), see note 78 above, p. 12.

80. M.R. Bristow, 'The Role and Place of Strategic Planning in Hong Kong', *Planning and Development: Journal of the Hong Kong Institute of Planners,* Vol. 4. No. 1, March 1988, pp. 14–20.

81. Strategic Planning Unit (1984), see note 78 above, p. 24.

82. Strategic Planning Unit (1984), see note 78 above, p. 41.
83. Strategic Planning Unit (1984), see note 78 above, p. 42.
84. Town Planning Office, *Metroplan* (Hong Kong, Government Printer, 1988).

4. New-town Development Procedures and Controls

Organization and Structures

As both Endacott and Miners have pointed out elsewhere,[1] a definitive and unique aspect of Hong Kong's government is the role and status of its committees.

One must conclude that the key to government in Hong Kong is the number and dominance of committees ... It is these that provide the key to land-use planning in Hong Kong, rather than the operational departments that implement their decisions.[2]

Thus, in considering the procedures and organizational methodologies that grew up and were concerned with new-town development in Hong Kong, it should come as no surprise to find that there has evolved a complex and specific committee structure which is uniquely concerned with all aspects of the development of major new communities in the Territory.

This specific structure fits within a government that remains a bureaucracy, which is still unhindered by a fully elected legislature. Since the McKinsey administrative reforms of 1973,[3] this has consisted of, in summary, a Colonial Secretariat in which major policy issues are debated and decided upon and made up at the highest levels of Secretaries responsible for major policy areas like housing, building, public works, or land policy, with administrative departmental groupings below them deployed to implement policy and deliver services and other public duties. The reason for the dominance of the committees is that they remain the principal method by which policy is discussed and determined. They also often act as co-ordinators between separate policy interests, as the means of reconciling conflict within government, and as the major means of generating the collective view of the executive branch of the government which is always required to advance new policy initiatives.

It should not be assumed, however, that committees only have a role as policy-makers. As important, though often at lower levels of the Hong Kong government, are those with implementing functions, especially within the line departments. In short, committees permeate all actions of government in Hong Kong, and therefore, given the magnitude and complexity of new towns, it is not surprising that, at all levels, we find a committee structure. In fact, as with land-use planning generally in Hong Kong, in seeking to understand how the planning and development of the new towns has been undertaken, we are faced with unravelling a fairly complex network of interconnecting parts — all concerned in various ways with policy, organization, and control. For this purpose we need, therefore, to take both a sequential and analytical look at the organization and procedures of government in Hong Kong that are concerned with new-town development in the Territory.

Town Planning in Hong Kong

It is not appropriate here either to attempt to give a detailed analysis of how the Hong Kong government as a whole operates, or to describe in detail the entire set of arrangements that have developed for determining and operating land-use policies in Hong Kong, even though both set a crucial context within which the new-town programme has to work. Fortunately, there are already two excellent texts elsewhere to which the interested reader is referred should he or she wish to explore further.[4]

An important criterion to remember, however, about town planning as a whole in Hong Kong, is that there are principally two separate planning systems in operation, although they are linked administratively and procedurally. These are the statutory planning system, which acts primarily through a zoning system of control and which is largely supervised through the Town Planning Board (a committee of both officials and Legislative Councillors), and a parallel system of departmental non-statutory planning which is formally under the control of the Land Development Policy Committee and its lesser committee structures. The most usual linkage operates sequentially, in that the statutory Outline Zoning Plan is based on the more detailed Outline Development Plan and most often follows it, but such a system also allows planning to proceed on a non-statutory basis alone.[5] This has led, and particularly in Hong Kong new-town planning, to an endless debate about which process is the most appropriate for areas of new and rapid urban change, with the result that statutory planning has not always been applied, particularly at early stages of development.

The relationship of new-town planning, therefore, to the formal statutory planning system that is meant to operate in all potential urban areas has at times been ambivalent. For example, even by 1988, not all the new towns were covered by publicly approved statutory plans (see Appendix 1). While from the beginning, Tsuen Wan and Sha Tin were covered by statutory frameworks which were regularly updated, the first town of Kwun Tong was specifically excluded from the Town Planning Board's normal procedures, and Tuen Mun (Castle Peak), while it began with a statutory plan in 1966, had to wait for 17 years before its initial plan was formally revised. Of the more recent new-town designations, five in all, by 1988, only Tai Po and Sheung Shui (Fanling) had been brought within the statutory net.

Such procedural variations stem from when the planning process was determined within an ever-shifting set of government perspectives on the suitability and purposes of statutory land-use planning in Hong Kong. We have already seen the initial debate on statutory planning for Tsuen Wan as an example. The reluctance to employ it was in part a result of an initial ambivalence to the public exposure of plans, and a fear that the rigidities of the system would slow down to an unacceptable degree the rapid pace of conception, development, adjustment, and change that characterized new-town development in Hong Kong. This need 'not to interfere' has been accentuated by the high-profile, politically endorsed nature of the new-town programme itself, and reinforced by its involvement as a major implementor of the Territory's mainstream social welfare policies, particularly in the public housing field. Thus, although there have been arguments for public accountability within the new-town programme, they have until comparatively recently tended to be drowned by the perceived requirement to get things done whatever the niceties of procedural systems.

Initial Committee Structures

Getting things done was initially quite simple. The Hong Kong government has long had a time-honoured way of dealing with large public works projects. As we have already seen with Kwun Tong, initial feasibility is studied by a special committee of government officials specially formed for the purpose — in more recent years often with the help of specialized consultants hired to undertake any necessary investigative work and sometimes to float unpalatable solutions which the government itself may not wish to be seen initiating or supporting. This is usually followed by the setting up of a further committee formed to review the recommendations, and perhaps to oversee the initial implementation of the project should the project be accepted. This simple structure still remains in principle, even though the complexities of major projects like the new towns have resulted in the breakdown of the task into component parts, with a resultant proliferation and specialization of the ensuing committee structures. The current structure is given in Fig. 4.2 and perhaps the best explanation is to see how this structure has evolved since its beginnings in the first new town of Kwun Tong in 1954.

At the time that investigations into the feasibility of developing Kwun Tong began, town planning in Hong Kong was still in its infancy. The reformed Town Planning Office had only been created for less than a year, and the Town Planning Board had only met twice (in 1951) and was not to meet again until 1955. It is therefore perhaps not surprising that the Board was not to be involved with the new town, and that the planners took a subsidiary role to the engineers in the planning for the reclamation. Even so, the chief planner at that time, Mr R.C. Clarke, was a member of both the investigatory and implementation committees,[6] the second of which remained in being for most of the early reclamation period. Towards the end of its life it also adjusted to another major change — with the setting up of the new Development Division of the Public Works Department in 1958. This resulted in direct representation from the new Division (for the Kwun Tong Stage III Reclamation became its first development task), and reforming of the committee as the Kwun Tong Advisory Committee in August 1958. Since in its final form this represented the government's first attempt at controlling new-town development by committee, it is perhaps worth quoting its terms of reference in full.

It was required:

(i)   To coordinate, where necessary, the activities of departments concerned with the development of the Kwun Tong reclamation and the neighbouring area.

(ii) To keep under review the practical implementation of the special arrangements agreed for disposal of industrial sites at Kwun Tong.

(iii) To advise Government on any major change in policy so far approved thought desirable in the light of experience.

(iv) To advise Government in accordance with the accepted principles of the report of the Working Committee on Kwun Tong, on any important adjustments in the allocation of sites for individual factories, factory boundaries, lanes and roads in Stages I, II and III of the reclamation.

(v)   To advise Government on the apportionment of sites for flatted factories in the Kwun Tong area.

(vi) To advise Government on the sale of land for workers' housing to suitable persons or organisations.[7]

In some ways, the situation at Kwun Tong was simple from an administrative point of view. While technically within the New Territories, it was from the beginning treated as an extension of the existing urban area, and was almost exclusively under the direct control of the Public Works Department and its sub-departments for both planning and development. Moreover, there was only a minimal amount of squatter relocation required and no permanent settlement to allow for or relocate, since the site consisted largely of barren hillside, the former municipal rubbish tip, and new reclamation and borrow sites.

The situation was not at all so simple when the decision was taken in 1959 to develop Gin Drinkers Bay and to extend Tsuen Wan. As noted previously, the development sites already contained a population of over 80,000, some of whom had already been relocated at least once. This complexity formed the real basis of the New Territories Administration's initial caution about initiating a full-scale development programme in the area. In fact, it was clear immediately that to initiate successful urban development on the scale contemplated, nothing less than a major reorganization of the government's methods was required, in particular in relation to the need for land assembly for the public development of the new town.

That necessity was met almost immediately in 1960 with the setting up of District Land Conferences (committees) in the New Territories, and the introduction of a new policy on land resumption and exchange (the so-called Letter 'B' system) whereby existing landowners were encouraged to surrender land within new-town areas to the government in exchange for an entitlement (conferred by the Letter 'B') to exchange sites made available in the town after site formation, or alternatively for future use elsewhere in the New Territories. Letter 'B' entitlements rapidly developed a market of their own and became a popular method for private sector developers to build up large land banks for future property development and speculation.

There is no immediate record that the government set up any special committee to oversee or evaluate the Scott Wilson reclamation studies, but once implementation of Gin Drinkers Bay had been agreed, from October 1960, a new working committee was once again put into place to control the implementation of the scheme. This was expanded in 1963 to form a Tsuen Wan/Kwai Chung Co-ordinating Committee within the Public Works Department, and this was charged with organizing the physical development of the engineering requirements up to site-provision stage for the whole of the new-town area except Tsing Yi. Tsing Yi was first investigated seriously in the mid-1960s and responsibility for the island, was given to a later separate Planning Co-ordination Committee (set up on the Sha Tin/Castle Peak model of that time — during 1965). This was later reconstituted in 1972–3 when a further investigation was undertaken which began the present Tsing Yi development as a part of Tsuen Wan new town.[8]

The Tsuen Wan/Kwai Chung Co-ordinating Committee was to remain in place as the co-ordinator of the physical development of the town until overtaken by the major procedural reforms of 1973–4, but difficulties in achieving planning objectives forced other changes by 1970. It was found that:

the development of a major new urban area presents problems in coordination and timing which require an exceptional degree of cooperation between the various departments concerned, and it is now [February 1970] considered that an inter-departmental management committee is necessary to ensure that the new town is developed as a balanced urban community.[9]

But talking of events of 1970 here is anticipating things a little; first, we need to return to the early 1960s.

The year 1960, as we have already learnt in Chapter 3, was an important year for the Hong Kong new-town story, in that it saw the first meeting of the new Land Development Planning Committee, later reformed in 1975 as the Land Development Policy Committee. While the Committee's origins lay in a debate within the government about the need for strategic development planning — indeed, at first, it was thought that it should be concerned with economic development matters, it very rapidly became the government's principal land-use planning adviser, and, as such, was the primary forum for discussion and decisions about the need for, size and scope of the rapidly expanding new-town programme. This dominant policy-making role remained and continues today.

But to return again to the specific, localized administrative machinery for the towns themselves: in one sense, the early planning mechanism set for Tsuen Wan represented a regressive step. While total planning of Kwun Tong, at least in the professional land-use planning sense, did not appear in the terms of reference, at least it had a full series of government committees to oversee its development, and they did at least attempt in their membership to provide an interdepartmental co-ordinated approach. The Public Works Department's Co-ordinating Committee for Tsuen Wan/

Kwai Chung did not operate in this way. It was basically concerned only with the production of formed and serviced sites. These could then be handed on to others, either public or private, for development within a general planning framework, which was provided by the departmental and statutory plans drawn up by the land-use planners (also within the Public Works Department).

The implementation problem, which had been identified by 1970, was that the site development, especially for public housing (though built by the Department) and industry, was in the hands of others, notably the Commissioners for Resettlement and Housing and the New Territories Administration respectively, with of course the private sector dictating the actual take-up of many of the newly formed sites. This private sector involvement proved particularly difficult when much of the development came on-stream in the later 1960s, for that was the time of a major property slump in Hong Kong with resultant private sector disinterest and the public sector had to take up the slack as best it could. Thus, effective development of Tsuen Wan new town on the truly 'balanced' basis that was in the minds of its original planners proved extremely hard to implement in practice, without the control and intervention of the strong implementing and managerial mechanism first suggested and advocated by the University consultants in 1959.

The steps to create the new towns of Sha Tin and Tuen Mun (Castle Peak) in the mid-1960s allowed a new experiment in control mechanisms to be tried. The initial step was to repeat the Kwun Tong model, rather than that of Tsuen Wan, but with a more specific recognition of the 'planning' responsibility. In April 1964, two Planning Co-ordination Committees were set up, one for each of the new towns, as part of the Public Works Department Development Division investigations into the possible development of the sites. Each Committee was chaired by the government's chief planner, again the Assistant Superintendent of Crown Lands (Planning), with two other permanent members (the Deputy District Commissioner New Territories, and the Chief Engineer of the Development Office of the Public Works Department), supplemented by representatives from other engineering and architectural sections, and the District Officers for each new-town area, as required. These two Committees determined the form and structure for the towns, and they were disbanded when their proposals (to be described in Chapter 5) were presented to the government in January 1965. Each Committee met on only five or six occasions.

The decision of 1965 to go ahead with these additional schemes led to a search within the government for appropriate mechanisms to control them. An initial Secretariat proposal in February 1966 suggested that a Progress Committee should be set up to discuss policy questions and other matters of major importance falling outside the competence of the Land Development Planning Committee.[10] The suggested members were to be the Principal Assistant Colonial Secretary (Lands), the Deputy Financial Secretary, the Director of Engineering Development and the Deputy District Commissioner New Territories. Further discussion within the government revolved around perceived problems of directing and co-ordinating works operations (seen as primarily a Public Works Department responsibility) and:

complex sociological and political problems inescapably bound up with the acquisition of land and the advancement of the two new towns projects. It was generally agreed that, unlike in Britain where absolute parliamentary authority could be vested in an overall controller, the situation locally was quite different. While the schemes were essentially Public Works Department projects, it none the less rested wholly with the District Commissioner New Territories to resolve problems associated with the acquisition of New Territories land and to assess and advise on political and social considerations affecting the advancement of the New Town Schemes.[11]

Such a solution was of course entirely political, indeed, for much the same reasons that previously had led the government to reject the University consultant's suggested development corporation mechanism for controlling the development of Tsuen Wan in 1959. It was related to the fact that land matters in the New Territories had always remained sensitive for the Hong Kong government ever since the signing of the original master lease at the end of the nineteenth century, and the New Territories Administration always saw itself within the internal politics of Hong Kong as the long-term guardian of the special interests of the area. Given the need both to co-ordinate the public works, and to safeguard the special interests and political sensitivities, the only feasible solution came to be seen as a dual committee structure for each town, with a central Progress Committee taking on the steering committee function to control the overall policy. Thus, in April 1966, final proposals for a committee framework headed by a central New Towns Works and Management Committee were forwarded to the Secretariat. This Committee was to be assisted by separate New Town Works Committees (responsible for engineering, planning, and land development matters) and New Town Management Committees (concerned with the provision of services, and co-ordinating development to achieve the planned aim of 'balance' within each town).[12] The new structure was introduced in both Sha Tin and Tuen Mun (Castle Peak) during 1967 as far as the central Secretariat Committee and the two Town Works Committees were concerned, but the parallel Management Committees under the New Territories Administration had to wait until 1968 and 1971 respectively before they were formally in place. In 1970 also, as we have seen, the new management committee principle was extended to the existing situation in Tsuen Wan.

This initial implementation structure remained in place within the government until the McKinsey reorganization of 1973–4, and as these caused a major review of the new-town planning mechanisms, it is to these that we must next turn our attention.

The New Territories Development Department

Pressure for reforming the machinery of government as a whole in Hong Kong had been building up throughout the late 1960s, and there were recurrent criticisms in the Legislative Council during the period.[13] The outcome of this debate was the appointment in 1972 of the American management consultants McKinsey and Company to review the whole system of administration and to make recommendations. This review was put before the Legislative Council in May 1973.

Apart from a radical reorganization of the central Secretariat on a policy programme (sectoral) basis, the central argument that rolling programmes of investment should be set up in major areas of social and economic policy to target government spending, and that decision-making should be delegated, put particular pressures on the existing management structures for the existing new towns, giving a major impetus to the need to expand the programme to meet part of the new social and economic targets then being formulated. The outcome was to initiate not only a review of the existing bureaucratic structures at the level of each new town, but also to create a completely new and major division within the Public Works Department as a successor to the old Development Division to take overall control of all aspects of the new-town programme. In a way, there had been a precedent: in 1967–8, within the Public Works Department, a special Castle Peak New Town Division had been set up briefly, but it had rapidly been re-absorbed within the main Development Division with the cut-back in new-town construction that occurred during the difficult economic conditions at the end of the 1960s.

The New Territories Development Department formally came into being when 61 new posts were created by the Finance Committee of the Legislative Council on 1 August 1973. With its formation, Hong Kong gave itself the nearest that it has had to the development corporation concept that has been so common for new-town development elsewhere. (As an aside, it can be mentioned that the development corporation idea was to surface again in 1981–2, when the Working Group on Private Sector Participation in Land Production suggested it as a possible mechanism for major private sector participation in the new-town development of the 1980s.[14]) The most important difference to note is that the Hong Kong model left the public developer as a planning and implementing agency, while financial controls and funding remained elsewhere within the government. Also control was centralized, rather than being devolved to separate bodies for each new town, even though detailed work was perforce done in each of the separate new-town development offices (see below). The basic functions of the new department were defined as follows:

(a) preparing overall balanced development programmes for the New Towns and the New Territories rural centres, and ensuring their implementation according to programme both effectively and economically;

(b) preparing development programmes for engineering works and buildings to be constructed by Consultants or by other Public Works Department Offices;

(c) preparing layout plans, outline development plans and land use planning relating to New Towns and rural development areas;

(d) carrying out development work associated with the 10-year housing target in the New Territories by providing formed land, roads, drainage and the full range of infrastructure required;

(e) liaising with the New Territories Administration and the Housing Department
in order that land acquisition and clearance programmes are implemented in
the sequence required for engineering and building programmes to proceed
on schedule;

(f) coordinating the work of utility undertakers and the activities of private
developers where these affect the overall programme of works; and

(g) overseeing major comprehensive private development schemes.[15]

It is clear however from the beginning that:

the raison d'être of the Department is to concentrate on development related to
the Public Housing Programme, which of course also includes a considerable element of the other forms of development necessary to support it.[16]

Some idea of how this complex reorganization looked in its initial form
can be seen in Fig. 4.1, which represents the development mechanism for
Sha Tin by 1976.

To meet its objectives the new department was initially organized into
five divisions — a Headquarters, three New Town Development Offices
(for each of the three new towns and located in each), and a general New
Territories Development Branch set up to oversee the committed expansion of the rural market towns for public housing purposes — then, principally Tai Po, and general development elsewhere in the New Territories.
The divisions were headed by the Director, three Project Managers (Principal Government Engineers), and a Government Engineer respectively
(it was not until much later that, in some cases, the new-town offices came
to be headed by planners!). The new concepts for control proved both
successful and resilient, with expansion of the original three new-town
offices during the 1970s, and an eventual extension of the pattern to the
whole of Hong Kong with the creation of the Territory Development
Department and its area offices in April 1986. The formation of the
Department also marked an important shift in town-planning responsibilities in Hong Kong, for, with the taking on of detailed new-town
planning from 1973, the reorganization marked the beginnings of the
splitting of detailed planning work from the Town Planning Office that
was also to be completed in the later changes of 1986.[17]

The three New Town Development Offices were the first examples in
Hong Kong of an integrated, devolved, multi-disciplinary form of
management, that was given responsibility for the detailed planning and
the implementation of the public works programme in each new town.
Under the Project Manager, each Office was required to prepare an overall
balanced development programme for its town. This required the Office
to prepare the necessary planning documents and infrastructure construction programmes. The Offices also took a leading role in arranging the
necessary land acquisition and clearance programmes with the New Territories Administration and the Housing Department. They were also
responsible for advising and servicing the local Works Progress and
Management Committees, and appointing and controlling the professional

Fig. 4.1 Division of responsibilities for new-town functions.[1]

Mapping	Outline Zoning Plan	Detailed planning	Feasibility study	Components	Schedule of accommodation	Preliminary or sketch plans	Legal formalities, G.Ns. etc. (other than land)	
Crown Lands & Survey Office	Town Planning Office (for Town Planning Board)	New Territories Development Department/Town Planning Office (using planning staff or consultants)	New Territories Development Department (using consultants)	Storm Drainage			New Territories Development Departm (using consulting en or P.W.D. branches agents)	Component Responsibilities
				Sewerage				
				Portworks				
				Roads[4]				
				Amenity treatment				
				Water supply			Waterworks Office	
				Sewage treatment			Civil Engineering Office	
				Public utilities			Public Utilities Compani	
				Public housing	Housing Dept./Architectural Offic P.W.D.			
				Public buildings and facilities, Recreation facilities	Departments concerned	New Territories Development Departm supported by A.O., P.W.D.[3]		
				Mass Transit	Mass Transit Studies			
				Private housing	Private developers			
				Industrial buildings	Private developers			
				Private community buildings	Private Developers			

Clear-ance	Site formation and recla-mation	Design, estimates, and construction	Main-tenance	Co-ordina-tion	Pro-gress con-trol	Control of funds	Acc-ounts	Obtaining approvals for P.W.S.C. items and funds	Endorse-ment of layout
New Territories Development Department (using consultants or P.W.D. branches)	New Territories Development Department	New Territories Development Department (using consultants or P.W.D. branches)	C.E.O. & H.O.	New Territories Development Department	New Territories Development Department			New Territories Develop-ment Depart-ment	New Territories Development Department
			C.E.O. & H.O.						
			C.E.O.						
			H.O.						
			U.S.D. & H.O.[5]						
		Waterworks Office				Waterworks Office			
		Civil Engineering Office				C.E.O.	P.W.D. H.Q.	C.E.O.	
		Public Utilities Cos.				Public Utility Cos.			
		Housing Dept./ A.O., P.W.D.	Housing Dept.			Housing Department and A.O., P.W.D.			
		New Territories Dev. Dept. supported by A.O., P.W.D.[3]	A.O., P.W.D.			A.O., P.W.D.	P.W.D. H.Q.	New Territories Dev. Dept.	
		Mass Transit Organization				Mass Transit Organization			
		Private developers				Private developers			
		Private developers							
		Private developers							

Housing Department

Notes: 1. The organizations shown are those primarily responsible for the functions; it has to be recognized that other organizations may have a secondary or minor responsibility, and many may have a close interest in the particular component, and require consultation.
2. C.L. & S.O. will provide the control points for the setting out, but thereafter the responsibility for setting out and the co-ordination of setting out will be the responsibility of N.T.D.D. (See D.T.I. No. 18/73.)
3. Design and construction of the bulk of public buildings will be undertaken by the P.W.D. Architectural Office or by the use of private architects. In either case the construction of buildings will be within the general programme of development controlled by the staff of the N.T. Development Department. When private architects are employed, technical and administrative services will be provided by the Architectural Office who will also approve designs and contract documents. The overseeing of the private architects and site liaison will, however, be undertaken by the staff of the New Territories Development Department. The Housing Department will deal with all public buildings which are integral with the housing estates it is constructing.
4. Design data and advice on timing to be provided by Highways Office.
5. Highways Office responsible for roadside verges only.
6. Key to abbreviations:

AO	— Architectural Office;
CEO	— Civil Engineering Office;
CL & SO	— Crown Lands and Survey Office;
DTI	— Department Technical Instruction;
HO	— Highways Office;
NTDD	— New Territories Development Department;
PWD	— Public Works Department;
USD	— Urban Services Department.

Source: J.S. Don, 'Organisation for Development of the New Towns in Hong Kong', in *Symposium on Social Planning in a New Town: Case Study — Shatin New Town* (Hong Kong, Hong Kong Council of Social Service, 1976), Appendix A, pp. 97–8.

consultants that were brought in to provide much of the specialist expertise required for planning and constructing each town.

Each Office had an engineering and planning team from the beginning, each headed by an appropriate professional officer and from the late 1970s a small landscape design team was added. Architectural services for the public buildings were initially centralized in Headquarters under a Chief Architect (New Territories Development), and the engineering and planning functions were also represented by senior officers at Headquarters level. On the planning side a formal liaison with the Colony Outline Planning Team in the Town Planning Office was maintained by the Headquarters Senior Planning Officer, thus, at least in theory, linking the strategic planning thinking with the day-to-day detailed planning of the towns. However, the statutory planning for the towns remained with the reformed Town Planning Office, back at the Public Works Department, though within that Office there was again a new specific appointment made at a senior level to take responsibility for statutory planning in the New Territories, most of which was in fact centred on the new towns.

In 1976, the size of the Department was doubled, partly because experience showed that trying to use consultant planners in the new towns was not practicable. The period of financial stringency within the public sector during 1974–5 also induced a major change in the financial control and programming for the new towns. The enforced breakdown of the schemes into separate components on a 'package' basis (shown in

Fig. 4.3) while allowing separate consideration of smaller financial demands, greatly increased not only the amount of planning and preparation work required, but also the number of staff. A third element which increased the work-load was a major review of the public housing programme and the resultant agreement of the new New Territories Development Progress Committee that sites should be found within the New Territories for an additional 200,000 housing units. This expansion was endorsed in a special report of the New Territories Public Housing Subcommittee of the Public Works Priorities Committee in August 1976. Once again new-town development was being driven by the fortunes of the Territory's public housing programme.

A further expansion in manpower took place in 1977 with the formation of an additional Development Office for Tai Po and Fanling, consequent upon the decisions to accelerate the expansion of Tai Po (from 101,000 target to 220,000), and to expand Sheung Shui/Fanling from 81 to 170,000, both initiated to meet forecast shortfalls in the public housing programme. This growth was further supplemented from 1980 with the formation of a fifth Office to commence the planning work for Junk Bay new town, the first of the fourth-generation towns. This last Office also established a new managerial principle in that the area covered included a large part of the town's hinterland (in Sai Kung) as well as the town site proper. This was a specific reaction to a meeting in September 1978 between the Sai Kung District Advisory Board and the Governor concerning development generally in the area.[18] Not only did the Office in the short term become responsible for developing one of the new sub-regional studies (as part of the build-up to the Territorial Development Strategy), but it acted as the prototype for the extension of the older new-town offices into true sub-regional development organizations that was to come with the formation of the Territory Development Department in 1986. At the present time, therefore, the requirements of new-town development are now subsumed within wider sub-regional responsibilities associated with the towns and their surrounding hinterlands, and together five Offices now cover the whole of the New Territories.

New-town Committees from the Seventies

The setting up of the new organization to oversee new-town development from 1973 affected the local committee structure that had been put in place earlier to control the development of the original three new towns. Procedures were now standardized, with the setting up of reformed Work Progress Committees in each of the three existing new towns in September 1973.

With the setting up of the New Territories Development Department, detailed and day-to-day coordination and action will be the responsibility of the New Town Project Manager in direct consultation with other departments and bodies, and the Progress Committee will be concerned mainly with major problems which are likely to affect the progress and planning of development in the New Towns ... The membership is limited to those directly involved in the preparation and implementation of the programme for the development of the new towns. The consultants responsible for the major development work will attend meetings by invitation ... Progress reports will have to be submitted to the Progress Committee so that they can (a) compare progress with approved programmes; (b) identify problems and agree remedial action; (c) identify the effect of each department's activity on other departments' activities; (d) update programmes in the light of progress and other factors.[19]

Regular reports were suggested to be prepared for planning matters, land acquisition and clearance, land formation and servicing, public housing, land availability and disposal, and the provision of community facilities. The membership requirements were set out as: the Director of New Territories Development (Chairman), the Project Manager (Vice-Chairman), the District Officer(s), Chief Engineer, Chief Architect, Chief Planning Officer, District Estate Surveyor, the Housing Department representative, and a secretary. It is interesting to note the requirement for the Director of the Department to be involved with each Committee, no doubt both to co-ordinate and to transmit policy decisions from the centre.

The formal terms of reference for each of these new Progress Committees are also worth noting in full:

1. To review and coordinate progress on planning layouts and development plans and programmes.
2. To recommend acceptance of necessary revision of draft and approved planning layouts, and feasibility studies.
3. To review and coordinate progress on the preparation of sites for public and private development through the various stages, i.e. land acquisition and clearances; land sale programmes; site formation; infrastructure with the aim of balanced development; public and private building.
4. For the purpose of 3, to prepare and review programmes of these activities.
5. To keep approved plans and programmes under review in the light of actual progress on private development, comments of Heads of Departments and the New Town Management Committee, so as to ensure balanced development.
6. To consider, as necessary, any means of expediting progress on land acquisition, clearance, site formation and infrastructure, and eventual land disposal.[20]

The earlier role of control of physical implementation was now therefore absorbed within a broader multi-disciplinary structure even wider than the professional multi-disciplinary team manning each Development Office. This control role for local senior professionals and officials remains in place today for current new-town development in Hong Kong.

In a rather similar way, the Management Committees which had also been formed by the beginning of the 1970s also proved to be durable features of new-town development management in Hong Kong. The first step in their transformation to the realities of the new decade was the modification of their memberships to reflect the new structures of the government brought in in 1973. Thus, the committees were now chaired by the Deputy Secretary for the New Territories (New Towns) — a new post heading a new New Towns Division within the New Territories Administration. It also had the appropriate District Officers and Project Manager as principle members. The committees' general roles were still to advise the administration on the provision and running of community facilities in the towns and to assist with the promotion of recreational and cultural activities, but the co-ordination to achieve the 'balanced' development objective had by now largely been taken over by the activities of the new Progress Committees. While further Management Committees were set up in 1979–80 to deal with the expansions of Tai Po and Sheung Shui/Fanling, their roles came rapidly to be overshadowed by the wider development of district administration in the New Territories which was to come in the 1980s, and which also concerned development in the new towns and brought the beginnings of real community involvement for their rapidly increasing populations.

Public Participation

So far, in discussing the committee structures set up to determine the development of the Hong Kong new towns, we have not considered what in Western planning terminology would be called 'public participation' within the development process. Until the 1980s, most of that opportunity in Hong Kong rested within the statutory planning system, and the use of that system within the new-town planning process. It is not appropriate here to open up a debate about the openness to the public of the whole Hong Kong planning system — that is available elsewhere[21] — but it is appropriate to assess what public reaction there was to the new-town proposals as they appeared, and to try to evaluate what influence it had as the planning of the towns progressed.

We have already pointed out that there is ample evidence of a fairly ambivalent attitude to the place of the statutory planning system within new-town planning in Hong Kong. One clear result of this is that the formal exhibiting of proposals and the formal opportunity for appeals from those directly affected has not always been possible for those already living within the new-town boundaries. From the beginning, rather, the more traditional routes of representation were followed; that is, through the use of local spokesmen provided through local community élites such as the Rural Committees in the new-town areas. The main sources of friction, as one would expect, proved to be the related questions of land acquisition, clearances, and the possible relocations and other effects upon the life of the villagers in the new-town areas. This, of course, has always been one of the main reasons for the active involvement of the New Territories Administration and its successors in the new-town administrative structures and why, here, it is necessary to consider the evolution of that Administration's consultative machinery, since it was through that that the local inhabitants had a voice.

While the use of these two mechanisms has meant that both local people directly affected by the proposals and developers and land owners have always had some interaction with the new-town development processes, at least in the beginning, there was also some evidence of a wider interest. Thus, when the draft statutory plans for both Sha Tin and Tuen Mun (Castle Peak) were put on exhibition in 1966, both the three main industrialists' associations and the professional groups of the Hong Kong Society of Architects and the Hong Kong Branch of the Town Planning Institute submitted lengthy and critical memoranda on the proposals. This was despite the fact that formally, under the requirements of the Town Planning Ordinance, their comments could not be considered by the Town Planning Board, since none of the organizations were directly affected by the proposals.[22]

By far the most important influence upon the development processes came from either the local Rural Committees, made up of local notables, and the traditional medium of contact between the government and the New Territories inhabitants, or, in some major instances, from the Heung Yee Kuk, which looked after the special interests of the New Territories as a whole. For both Tuen Mun (Castle Peak) and Sha Tin, initial reactions to the proposed developments were favourable. Subject to satisfactory detailed negotiations on the possible effects on the local villages and on land compensation matters, both Rural Committees tended to regard the proposals as bringing wealth to their communities and allowing development that, in the case of Sha Tin in particular, had long been campaigned for.

In Tsuen Wan, however, the position was rather different. The site was more highly developed. It had a large *in situ* squatter population, and the site enveloped some of the largest traditional villages in Hong Kong, which had powerful and vociferous supporters. When one notes that the Tsuen Wan Rural Committee was also highly politicized, it is not perhaps surprising to discover that at times it proved to be something of a thorn in the side of the town planners, especially in the early days of the new town — sufficiently so, that the Heung Yee Kuk got drawn directly into the fray on squatters, resettlement, and compensation matters in the early 1960s.[23]

In the 1970s, as the new-town programme rapidly expanded, and the adjacent rural areas became engulfed in an incipient suburbanization that was spreading out from the main urban area, the New Territories Administration realized that its long-established consultative machinery based on the local District Officers and the Rural Committees was no longer adequate. This recognition brought about the setting up in 1977 of new District Advisory Boards on an appointed basis, to cover the whole of the New Territories, and perforce the new towns, in seven areas. With their formation came an extension to the necessary consultative roles of the professionals in the new-town development offices.

These requirements were further magnified with the implementation of the District administrative reforms instituted following the Green and White Papers of 1980–1.[24] Not only did this bring about the adaptation of the former Management Committees to a new District administration structure (there are now 18 throughout Hong Kong), but by introducing directly elected members into local administration, the changes resulted for the first time in a direct channel of communication between the planners and those planned for in the various new towns. As the 1980s have progressed that channel has become more widely used, and demands have grown for more power to be given to the District Boards now responsible for each new-town area.

The current District Management Committees have now assumed the role of providing the local administrative response to the new District Boards.

The Chairman stressed that if district administration was to succeed, the suggestions made by the District Board had to be taken seriously by the District Management Committee. The District Management Committee would discuss the suggestions to arrive at a joint decision to see whether they should be implemented, partially implemented, delayed, modified, or even turned down.[25]

Clearly, agreement was not always expected from the beginning. The terms of reference were now concentrated on the identification of District needs, and setting priorities to ensure that government programmes provided adequate District services and facilities. To ensure this the revised committees were expected to have both co-ordinating and consultative roles in the new towns so as to 'advance the interests of residents and improve conditions in the district'.[26]

Using Sha Tin as an example, the new core membership of the committee now consisted of the District Officer in the Chair, the Project Manager, the Assistant Director (South) of the New Territories Services Department, the Assistant Director (East) of the Housing Department, the Chief Transport Director from Traffic Management (Transport Department), the Regional Recreation and Sports Officer (New Territories East) of the Recreation and Sports Service, and the Sha Tin Divisional Superintendent from the Police. To these were added other representatives as required to make up a total membership for each committee of some twelve to thirteen representatives.

The new-town management structures were further elaborated from 1981 with the formation of series of sub-committees charged with overseeing particular specialized areas of policy and implementation in the towns. Again utilizing Sha Tin by way of example, here eight sub-committees were eventually formed, in four groupings — community building (culture, recreation, and general), development (district services, traffic and transport, and planning), living environment, and internal administration.

In general, despite the complexity, the new structures represented a genuine attempt at devolving service delivery and local policy to the local level in Hong Kong, and setting up a reactive administration that could respond to local demands coming up through the District Boards. The new sub-committees also came to reflect comparable specialized groupings within the elected Boards, some of which like the Tuen Mun Commerce and Industry Committee were to become influential in the development of their towns. While the new structures applied throughout Hong Kong, they proved particularly important for the new towns, in that they were

Fig. 4.2 Organizational structure for the development of the new towns in Hong Kong (as of May 1987) — at that time, there were five development offices in Hong Kong with new-town development responsibilities: (a) Tsuen Wan (Tsuen Wan/Kwai Chung and Tsing Yi new town); (b) Sha Tin (Sha Tin and Ma On Shan new town); (c) New Territories Northeast (Sheung Shui/Fanling and Tai Po new towns); (d) New Territories North-west (Tuen Mun, Tin Shui Wai, and Yuen Long new towns); (e) New Territories South (Junk Bay new town).

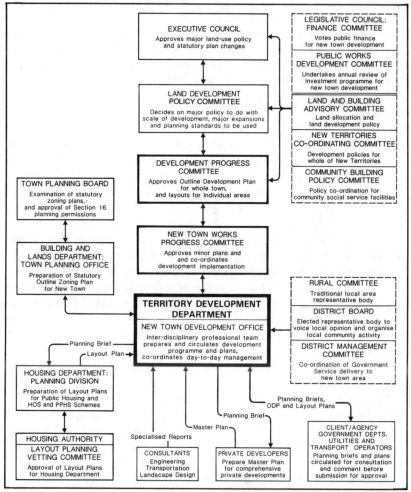

the first real attempt to meet adequately the deficiencies in the building up of the social and community life of the towns that had been identified so clearly in the early histories of Kwun Tong and Tsuen Wan.

To sum up (see Fig. 4.2), the current situation in the new towns of the 1980s is that each town is currently being developed under the control of a local Works Progress Committee, under the direct control of the Territory Development Department, which has the direct responsibility for approving and guiding the physical development programme for the town. This in turn, is formulated, controlled, and implemented through its operational arm, the area Development Office under the Project Manager. This Office is required to co-ordinate the physical and service inputs to the new-town programme. These are provided by the varied public sector agencies and the private developers and contractors. Alongside this works-orientated structure is a parallel interdepartmental management structure under the leadership of the City and New Territories Administration, which is designed to interact with the demands, requirements, and aspirations of the local communities, as interpreted through the new directly elected local administrations of the District Boards. Only one exception has ever been made to this generalized structure. Briefly, in 1976–7, in the case of Tsuen Wan, a specialized New Town Recreation and Amenities Advisory Committee was formed to meet the particularly acute community problems of that new town; but that solution, while perhaps a prototype of what was to come later, was absorbed within the introduction of the District Advisory Boards of 1977.[27]

Other Committees Affecting New-town Development

So far, apart from mentioning the background to the setting up of the Land Development Planning (Policy) Committee and later the New Territories Development Department in 1973, we have been concentrating on the administration of the new towns at the local level. If we return for a moment to the structure set out in Fig. 4.2, it becomes obvious that major decisions affecting the day-to-day planning of Hong Kong's new towns are made elsewhere. It is to those structures that we must now turn. As with land-use planning matters generally, a hierarchical committee structure exists in Hong Kong within which new-town policy and planning procedures take place.[28]

At the lowest level, planning of the Hong Kong new towns comes before both of the new-town committees that we have just described, though it is the Works Progress Committee that is concerned with the approval process for planning documents. In the main the work is consultative, in the sense that planning proposals in draft form are discussed by the Committee as they are prepared and amended by the professional planning staff. All major plans require formal approval at higher levels in the hierarchy (see Fig. 4.2). The principal approving agency for new-town planning work is the Development Progress Committee, which was first set up in its present form following the splitting up of the old Public Works Department in May 1982. The Committee acts as the approval agency for most of the planning work of the Territory Development Department, and for the new towns, as elsewhere, it approves all planning briefs and layout plans. In earlier periods its role was taken by the New Territories Development Progress Committee (from 1974 to 1982), and before that, the New Towns Works and Management Committee mentioned previously. In the early period of major new-town development, between 1974 and 1982, the Committee also had a specific responsibility to:

be concerned with the general progress and to look after the practical problems of development in the New Territories [and] to be responsible for the implementation and coordination of policies in respect of physical development.[29]

The major planning proposals and plans for the new towns as a whole proceed even higher up the government's committee hierarchy. The most important remains the Outline Development Plan for each town, which is the basic detailed planning document that exists for the whole of the designated new-town area (see Figs. 5.2, 5.3, 5.5, 6.6, and 6.8 as examples). Approval of this, and subsequent revisions, is the outcome of sometimes prolonged examination and discussion within the Land Development Policy Committee, whose members are some of the highest officials within the government. The Committee of course has wider responsibilities than for the planning of the new towns alone, but as its views have proved crucial to how the new towns have been developed, again it is worth looking in detail at its terms of reference:

In the light of the social, economic and financial needs of Hong Kong and resource constraints, to advise the Chief Secretary on:
(a) the formulation, monitoring and adjustment of development strategy, including the identification and assessment of options;
(b) the initiation, evaluation and coordination of sub-regional, and sectoral planning studies of strategic significance;
(c) the adequacy of development plans and programmes in the medium and longer term context;
(d) major proposals for land development in both the public and private sectors before they pass beyond outline planning;
(e) policies for the production, acquisition, use and disposal of land;
(f) land use planning standards of major significance; and
(g) the need for the preparation or replacement of statutory plans.[30]

Only a moment's consideration leads to the immediate conclusion that almost all these tasks affect the vital futures of all the new towns, and thus point to the dominating role of this Committee in our new-town story. The Committee also has special sub-committees, some of which have remained permanent, to look in detail at specific topics such as population change and distribution, industry, and planning standards; and it works closely with the new Land and Building Advisory Committee, which from 1985 replaced the earlier Special Committee on Land Production/Supply (itself formed in 1977).

The statutory plans for the new towns, Outline Zoning Plans, have always had to pass through a more complex approval process. These are prepared by the Statutory Planning Section of the Town Planning Office. Preparation is therefore a liaison exercise between the headquarters' planners and those in the appropriate sub-regional Development Office responsible for the new town for which the plan is being prepared. The latter Office will also have previously prepared the latest Outline Development Plan upon which the statutory plan is based. Pressure for revisions usually comes from the new-town planners, as planning for the town evolves;

but formal control of the process, once approval to start has been agreed by the Land Development Policy Committee, is in the hands of the Town Planning Board, and final approval is by the Executive Council — the highest organ of government of all in Hong Kong. Thus, where the statutory planning route is used to determine the structure of the town, as it was in the early days of Tsuen Wan, Sha Tin, and Tuen Mun (Castle Peak), then approval for the form and structure of the town has rested with the highest levels of Hong Kong's decision-makers.

Consideration of the committee hierarchy which is directly involved with the land-use planning of the new towns almost completes our consideration of the complex web of committees whose responsibilities impinge upon the new-town development process. Apart from those, like the Public Works Priority Committee, which are primarily concerned with financial and investment controls and priorities and will be discussed in the following section of this chapter, the remaining group that are of some importance are those associated with the City and New Territories Administration. We have already commented at some length about the individual District Management Committees that function for each of the eight new towns. Above these, in hierarchical terms, are two further committees that deserve some mention.

In 1982 a New Territories Co-ordination Committee was formed, made up of, at Secretary and Director level, those major departments of government involved in New Territories affairs. Its general field of responsibility is set as within 'the overall coordination of social and physical development'[31] and it is concerned with the effect of planned developments on people and the environment. It remains, however, primarily consultative — a 'talking-shop' — and it has no executive functions or power over the planning processes, for example.

Alongside this committee — which might be seen perhaps as an headquarters' equivalent of the management committees at the new-town level, from 1986 onwards a new Regional Council has been elected;[32] that is, a New Territories' equivalent of the much older Urban Council which has existed for the main urban area since the 1930s. While its functions are limited largely to service delivery, it provides a public and elected forum for New Territories matters as a whole, many of which emanate from the more specialized requirements of the eight new towns. Once again, it is an elected body that requires to be kept informed and consulted, where before the mid-1980s no such body existed other than the Heung Yee Kuk. At the least, it represents a further extension of accountability for policies towards the new towns.

The final committee that requires a mention, is the relatively newly formed Community Building Policy Committee. Set up in 1983, this Committee has as its central concern the co-ordination of government's efforts at developing community awareness and cohesion — not least in the new communities of the new towns. Besides the apparent social engineering ramifications of the task, the Committee also oversees the provision of the physical assets that are required for such a strategy, whether from public or voluntary sector sources. As an aside, this is a function of government common in other East and South-east Asian countries, but quite recently to be formally organized at the highest levels in Hong Kong.

Summary

The above has been an attempt to set out a reasonable guide as to how new-town policy is currently determined in Hong Kong, and how the day-to-day planning is affected. While the committee structure depicted in Fig. 4.2 appears complex, it represents a hierarchical division of responsibilities that has evolved sequentially from the earliest town-planning exercise at Kwun Tong in the 1950s. Major steps can be identified with the splitting between Public Works and New Territories Administration responsibilities in the 1960s, and the formation of the New Territories Development Department and its successor Territory Development Department in 1973 and 1986 respectively. But throughout, in its time-honoured way, the Hong Kong government has adjusted its new-town policy structures as demands have occurred, its internal perceptions become modified, and as external requirements have dictated. Whatever the complications of *ad hoc* changes, the result has been an administrative structure that has planned the development of eight major new settlements that ultimately will house some three and a half million people, over a space of twenty-six years in all, since the main programme began in 1973 — some achievement!

Financial Control Mechanisms

Pryor has pointed out elsewhere the uniqueness and importance of the system of financial management controlling the implementation of public works in Hong Kong, and how that relates to the building of the new towns in particular.[33] In assessing the effectiveness of the new-town development programme, some understanding of the workings of this system is necessary in order to understand the how and why of the progression of each town's programme, and in particular, to assess the reasons why certain planning goals have not always been met.

As with the financial control of public investment programmes elsewhere, Hong Kong development needs to be constrained within wider budgetary requirements set each year by the Territory's Financial Secretary. Again, as elsewhere, this essentially involves a 'bid' procedure, whereby funds required for future capital and recurrent expenditure are bargained for against competing requirements for the revenue resources available to the Finance Branch of the government each year. As one might expect, for Hong Kong, this involves the workings of yet another set of committees, with a formal set of procedures which are followed each year. New-town development has always been considered within the financing processes for public works as a whole, and as such, forms an integral part of each year's Public Works Programme. The current procedures effectively date from the McKinsey reforms of 1973, although they echo earlier practices.

The start of the annual cycle commences usually in the February of the year previous to that of the anticipated expenditure.

A key point in the review process is the setting of an overall expenditure guideline for all new towns with respect to new commitments to be entered into the following year.[34]

This is set by the Secretary (until recently — for Lands and Works) following negotiations with Finance Branch (who are, of course, constrained by their forecasts of the expected overall financial situation and changes in the government's budgetary policies). The implications of these expenditure limits are then discussed by the New Towns and Public Housing Sub-committee in April each year, in order to set the parameters within which each of the Development Offices at the new-town level is required to update its own 10-year development programme (the first of each series was produced for each town in 1974, and they have subsequently been revised annually).

These draft revisions are then prepared by each Office for submission to and agreement by the Sub-committee by the following September; from where they are sent to the Public Works Priorities Committee (chaired by the Chief Secretary), which is required to assess priorities for the whole of each year's proposed public works programme during October and November. The final stage is for the Committee to make recommendations to the Public Works Sub-committee of the Legislative Council as to which projects should go forward for inclusion in the spending programme of the coming year, and which eventually will appear in the annual budget documents the following February. The fortunes of the new towns are therefore very much affected by the annual budgetary cycle, especially since loan and deficit financing has rarely been used in Hong Kong to finance public capital expenditures.

So far, financial constraints and deficit budgeting have seriously affected the progress of the Hong Kong new towns on only three occasions. The first was during 1966–7, when, following the collapse of the building boom associated with the revision of the Building (Planning) Regulations, the first stage of development at Castle Peak had to be severely cut back and the commencement of Sha Tin was both delayed and also revised. The second involved budgetary cut-backs in both 1975–6 and 1979–80 which, while not so serious as before, nevertheless caused some rescheduling and deferment of projects within the planned programmes. The third involved the deficit budgets of the early 1980s, following another cyclical collapse in the Hong Kong property market, and lasted to 1985–6. During this most recent period, constraint again had to operate within the government's capital expenditure programmes, and the pace of new-town development was once again cut back for a while. A major effect of this curtailment was the restriction on the maximum possible growth allowed at both Ma On Shan and in Junk Bay to population thresholds which would not require expensive public investment in fixed rail links as envisaged in their early plans. As mentioned later, this resulted in a major search for alternative public housing sites, which is turn affected the whole new-town and public housing programming.

Individual projects within each new-town programme are processed through planning, preparation, approval, and implementation stages, just the same as all other public works projects in Hong Kong, via a system of priority assessment. Currently, all major projects are categorized into four priority levels. The lowest is approval in principle, where a project enters the Public Works Programme following assessment by the Public Works Vetting Committee, but with no work commitment for the sponsoring department. This confers a Category 'C' label. The next step to Category 'B' is undertaken by the Public Works Priorities Committee (and necessarily involves the ranking of projects in priority order) and occurs twice a year. This stage allows sponsoring departments to proceed with project planning up to the stage of preparing sketch plans or working drawings. It is designed to allow the government to assess the scope of a proposal in some detail before being required to give final approval. Projects at the next priority order above (Category 'AB') are allowed full site investigations, detailed design work and the preparation of tender documentation, and result from decisions of the Public Works Sub-committee of the Legislative Council's Finance Committee made during the annual financial appraisal procedures outlined above. The highest category of all (Category 'A' projects) are those that are currently under way in any year, or which, in the context of each year's review, are ready in all respects to proceed to tender and construction and which are given permission to proceed during the forthcoming financial year. Once again, assessment of Category 'A' projects, and any questions of downgrading or modification of projects are all considered together in the annual financial appraisal process. The Public Works Sub-committee is in any case duty-bound to review the progress of all projects and report its conclusions to its parent Finance Committee of the Legislative Council.

In general principles the above approval mechanism has always been in place throughout the whole of the new-town programme described in this book, but the current methods of organizing each new-town programme into discrete packages capable of independent implementation, and assessed through an annual assessment and prioritization procedure dates from the 1973 reforms. Those reforms introduced two new elements fundamental to all subsequent new-town development in Hong Kong. The first major change, the ten-year development programme outlined in the document produced each year by each of the development offices, centres around an assessment of forward capital expenditure requirements for each town, and a programming chart giving the expected timetable for the implementation of the planned programme. The timing is regarded as definitive for the first five years, and indicative thereafter, with a special emphasis on providing detailed assessments for projects timed to begin within the first two years of the finalized programme. The whole series of assessments are, of course, rolled forward for each year's new programme document.

The packaging innovation (see Fig. 4.3), introduced to meet the re-

Fig. 4.3   Development packages for the Hong Kong new towns — employed initially in 1973 by the New Territories Development Department as a means of programming the towns for financial budgeting purposes.

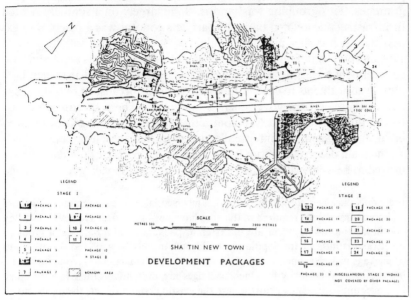

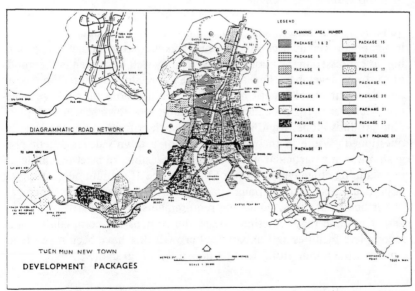

Sources: New Territories Development Department, *Hong Kong's New Towns: Sha Tin* (Hong Kong, Public Works Department, 1978), Map 8.
New Territories Development Department, *Tuen Mun New Town Development Programme, 1981 Edition* (Hong Kong, New Territories Development Department, 1981), Key Plan.

quirements of the new New Towns and Public Housing Sub-committee, was a method of grouping proposed development into separately implementable physical groupings, which could be financed as separate programmes. This grouping was, and is, done largely on a spatially related or infrastructure-related basis. In part, the concept was a reaction to experience with earlier public-expenditure control mechanisms in the late 1960s where, as in Stage I of both Tuen Mun (Castle Peak) and Sha Tin, commitment to large unified projects caused severe problems when last-minute adjustments to expenditure were required because of outside financial pressures on the government's budgeting. These specific problems forced the Public Works Sub-committee at the time to look for ways to break down the projects into smaller and more manageable pieces. Generally, the main determining criteria for drawing up 'package boundaries' have proved to be technical ones relating to drainage and servicing requirements.

Individual packages are 'balanced' in that all essential services, community facilities and communications required in the area have been provided. However, housing and industrial development are in different packages and a balance of employment opportunities with population build-up can only be achieved if both types of package proceed concurrently. This factor has been taken into account in assessing the order or priority in which packages are presented. Other factors taken into account in assessing priorities are the existing commitment, the public housing programme, land acquisition, comparative costs, land revenue and the possibility of private sector development.[35]

What is interesting about these decision criteria is the relatively low status of the planning requirements.

Determining packages by engineering criteria alone or financial requirements has meant that giving approval by individual package has inevitably broken up necessary planning linkages, even though later grouping, as expressed in the quotation above, may well have been in the minds of the town developers. One also gets the impression that sometimes costs and direct financial benefit have influenced decisions on package selection whatever may be the merit of particular new-town schemes on planning grounds alone. Rigid adherence to such criteria can at the least be questioned. While in theory restriction of a town's development programme at any particular package stage is feasible, to meet overall land-use planning objectives in terms of balance or self-containment, stopping at particular sets of development packages is often clearly more beneficial. Nevertheless, at times, budgeting requirements have dictated otherwise, and it is these that sometimes lie at the root of the complaints about incomplete facilities and unbalanced growth that have been made from time to time about Hong Kong's new-town programme.

Land-use Planning

We have already noted elsewhere in this chapter that the formulation of the planned form for each of the Hong Kong new towns has followed different routes. To recapitulate, Kwun Tong was entirely a departmental consideration and plan in its early days; Tsuen Wan was first considered by consultants, upon whose ideas an initial statutory plan was prepared, to be subsequently overturned by the demand to house much greater population densities; while Tuen Mun (Castle Peak) and Sha Tin both commenced with statutory plans based upon Public Works Department feasibility studies formulated in the early 1960s.[36] More recently, the expansion of the market towns of the New Territories to form the third wave of new-town building has largely remained a departmental exercise, as have also, so far, the latest proposals for Junk Bay and Tin Shui Wai; although as we shall see in Chapter 6, the last two have also once again been derived from major consultancy studies.

Such differences, however, mask a most important planning principle for Hong Kong. Whatever the mechanism, the new towns have come out of essentially a departmentally determined planning process. Whether in terms of influence over consultants' proposals, or determining statutory plans, the formulations of departmental planners, whether in headquarters or latterly the new-town development offices, have influenced the form of the towns as we now see them. In particular, it needs to be emphasized again that statutory planning, and hence the public influence over new-town design, has always followed departmental requirements, rather than the alternative of formally setting a framework within which departmental planning might subsequently take place.

It should, therefore, be no surprise to realize that in understanding the form of the new town and its underlying planning concepts, one need almost go no further than to study the appropriate Outline Development Plan. As with all such documents in Hong Kong, the plan, usually at a scale of 1.10,000 and containing zoning details, planning areas, communications, and site locations for government services, also consists of a detailed Planning Report which includes an Explanatory Statement setting out a reasoned justification of the various plan proposals, and various statistical and other appendices. The Explanatory Statement also sets out information on the planning history of the town, particularly regarding past cycles of plan preparation, current planning objectives for the town as a whole, and staging and implementation requirements. The planning objectives themselves are sub-divided into detailed proposals on population targets, overall structure, major land-use elements such as the town centre, retailing, housing, industrial, community, and open space uses, transportation and utilities. Overall, the plan forms the basic design from which all other planning documents required for the town are derived, and it forms the primary input into the drawing up of each town's annual ten-year development programme.

The plan formulation process for the new towns has followed in essence the same procedures as elsewhere in Hong Kong. Initial plans were formulated largely to accommodate forecast population targets. Subsequent revisions have come as those targets themselves have shifted, or as a result of the impact of changes in standards. Some of these standards have been in things like community service provision while others have resulted from the incorporation of new planning requirements, such as improved communication systems or landscape design principles. Development of each town itself, especially in the early days, also proved to be a significant cause of modifications, for implementation often proved to be a learning process too. One particular problem, as an example, was the recognition and overcoming of geotechnical site difficulties, now formally incorporated in the work of the Territory Geotechnical Control Office set up in 1977 as a response to the problem.

In essence the plan-making procedure is simple. The New Town Development Office prepares a new plan in draft form at the time it judges the previous plan to be sufficiently outdated. This assessment largely relates to the plan's normal use as a vehicle for informing other departments of government as a guide to their own policies and plans for the town. After initial completion, the plan in draft form is then circulated for comment to a wide variety of departments, as well as consultants and public utilities involved in the town; for example, for a recent Sha Tin plan this amounted to some thirty-two different consultees, plus another seven who received copies for information purposes. Often more than one circulation takes place as comments and suggested amendments are received by the Development Office and incorporated in the plan, or rejected with reasons, before the final draft is presented to the Works Progress Committee for initial approval. This takes place before final submission to the Development Progress Committee and if necessary the Land Development Policy Committee for final and formal adoption.

More detailed planning at the site level, which generally means for each of the individual planning areas shown on the Outline Development Plan, a number of which may be contained within a development package, is dealt with in one of three main ways. The predominant method, where the government is primarily preparing sites for normal onward development by the private sector or for general localized planning in the new towns, is the preparation of the individual layout plan. Prepared by the appropriate Development Office, the document consists of a large-scale plan of the proposed layout, together with an Explanatory Statement setting out the authority of the plan, land-use proposals, communications, and landscaping proposals. Again, as with the smaller scale plans, circulations of successive drafts provide the necessary legitimation of the plan before it is formally adopted by the Development Progress Committee. In some instances sketch plans have been circulated before the formal plan-making process has been begun, and in a few instances, in the early days of Sha Tin for example, some layout plans were actually prepared by consultants,[37] or three-dimensional sketches were prepared.

There are, however, two major exceptions to the standard procedures for detailed new-town planning work. These concern the planning of public housing estates, and areas of recent major private sector development. In both of these cases, because detailed control over the development lies outside of the hands of the appropriate Development Office, the planners set planning parameters by preparing as the first stage a planning brief for the site, for either the Planning and Research Division of the

Hong Kong Housing Department or the private sector developer, as appropriate. This sets out in some detail a set of development goals which the Office's planners would like to see achieved on the site, and additionally, usually includes target population figures, design parameters on services, densities, communications, and other planning requirements which are needed to link the site with its planned neighbours. A layout plan in outline form (that is largely the road and services layout) may also be provided in order to show to the potential developer how his scheme is required to be integrated into the larger requirements of the town. As with plans, planning briefs are circulated in draft form to other departments and consultees before approval by the appropriate committees, and onward transmission to the client.

The actual plan preparation process following the presentation of the planners' ideas in their brief varies slightly according to whether public or private sector development is involved. For public housing schemes, the Housing Department's planners prepare draft schemes for their public housing estates (see Fig. 7.8a–c) within the planning brief's requirements, and their proposals are circulated and amended through the same consultation mechanism as normal layout plans. Final approval, however, lies with the Housing Department's own Building Committee, following agreement from the new-town planners, rather than through the usual Development Progress Committee route. For major private sector schemes on large sites, successful tenderers are required to prepare their own master plan proposals (see Fig. 7.9) within the parameters set by the planners' brief. The possibilities here though are complicated further by the specific planning constraints that may be set by inclusion as restrictions in the developer's master Crown lease for the site, which act rather like the set of development control conditions that often exists in other planning systems.[38] These may well be imposed following negotiation between the new-town planners and the Buildings and Lands Department. Even more complication can be introduced if a planning permission from the Town Planning Board under Section 16 of the Town Planning Ordinance is involved,[39] where zoning restrictions require to be amended. Private master plans are again subject to the usual internal consultation and approval procedure within government.

All of the procedures so far mentioned are non-statutory, and yet determine the form and structure of all the Hong Kong new towns. Except in Tsuen Wan, development control, as thought of in many Western planning systems, is, as yet, hardly necessary — redevelopment of existing sites is rare in most of the Hong Kong new towns. Nevertheless, the need for eventual control of such a process is one reason for ensuring ultimate statutory control of all the new-town areas. It will be required to ensure that the detailed design of the town is maintained as an ongoing process. It has also on occasion already been required to prevent unwanted fringe development around the towns, and any absence, as around Tin Shui Wai, has demonstrated its value.

As noted previously, the statutory plan-making procedure is divorced from that for the general new-town planning that we have just described.

Essentially, it is a matter of liaison between the appropriate Development Office and the Statutory Planning Section of the Town Planning Office. As elsewhere, draft plans for the towns are publicly exhibited, and appeals considered, before final approval is given by the Governor-in-Council. Revision, of course, becomes necessary as the underlying departmental planning changes, since otherwise technical illegalities can occur.

Before closing this brief resumé on the land-use planning procedures, a further major input that requires a comment is the role of the consultants. From the earliest days, where expertise has been lacking, or personnel have simply not existed within the government, consultants have been used within the new-town development programme. Pryor has noted that:

wider use is made of consultancy services, particularly with regard to landscape projects and major engineering works for which a common arrangement is to enter into investigation, design and construction agreements.[40]

We can also note that with the major exception of Kwun Tong, all subsequent large new towns have commenced from an initial consultancy investigation. Engineering rather than planning interests have predominated, which has meant that there is to a degree justification for the jibe that the Hong Kong new towns have been 'engineering-led'. Nevertheless, consultant opinion about staging, land formation, servicing, and transportation design has provided much of the input to the basic town design process in Hong Kong, and the towns would not have come to fruition without them.

It is only from the late 1970s that further consultancy interests have added new dimensions to the development process. After some initial reservations, the pragmatic need to restore large areas of barren reclamation or devastated borrow slopes brought landscape design consultancy to the fore. From these more immediate requirements, with the encouragement of the Development Offices, their inputs have spread to subsequent projects like town parks and the landscaping of whole towns (Tai Po is widely regarded as the most successful example so far[41]). In this area in particular, the spread of new and innovative practice, often imported from outside, is beginning to have a major impact on new-town design in Hong Kong. This is likely to be most obvious in the towns of the 1980s (see Fig. 7.2) to which we refer in Chapter 6.

Some Conclusions

The important thing to note from this description of the organizational structure and the control procedures that guide the development progress of the new towns in Hong Kong is that it is no more than a special adaptation of more general procedural methods applied throughout government in Hong Kong. Thus, unlike new-town programmes in other countries, a policy for Hong Kong was initially tried of containing its development effort within the normal processes and procedures of the government. It was not until 1973, when the programme was well into its stride, that the varied pragmatic management structures introduced were judged to be less than effective, and under the impact of external consultants a new and specific machinery was put into place to control the development programme.

Yet even then, the new-town administrative and planning machinery represented merely a further pragmatic development of well-worn and well-tried bureaucratic principles. In earlier years, there seemed something of a glorification of the amateurism,

where, except in Hong Kong, would one see a government embark on the planning and construction of two new towns [Tuen Mun and Sha Tin], each to be capable of housing a million people by the 1980s, without setting up a vast and complex new department?[42]

The ultimate success of the programme, and the creation of eight new towns for some three and one half million people do, however, attest to the successes rather than any failures of the new machinery that had been brought into being.

Much of this chapter has been about the plethora of committees that are so much part of the planning and administration of the new towns, as well as a discussion of the procedures behind the planning and development processes. While it can be said that for the latter, the new towns have merely followed procedures and practices already in existence elsewhere, apart from the early innovations associated with the land acquisition requirements, their role in the administrative evolution of Hong Kong has proved pivotal.

In both the case of Tsuen Wan,[43] and later Kwun Tong, the planning and community welfare problems generated by the errors in their early planning caused them to require management innovations on the part of the government, and they later became prototypes for the local-level administration of the whole Territory. Thus, the evolution from the District Advisory Board in Tsuen Wan to the elected District Boards of the 1980s in Hong Kong, or the development of the corporate management structures of Kwun Tong into firstly the Urban Area Development Organization and then the Territory Development Department of 1986 is immediately apparent. In each case, the new-town environment provided the prototype and the testing ground whose successes led to emulation elsewhere. The new towns of Hong Kong have been as much laboratories for institution-building, as places for the building-up and growth of new social communities and physical development forms.

Notes

1. C.B. Endacott, *Government and People in Hong Kong 1841–1962: A Constitutional History* (Hong Kong, Hong Kong University Press, 1964), p. 239; and N.J. Miners, *The Government and Politics of Hong Kong* (Hong Kong, Oxford University Press, 1986), pp. 110–5.

2. Roger Bristow, *Land-use Planning in Hong Kong: History, Policies and Procedures* (Hong Kong, Oxford University Press, 1984), p. 173.

3. McKinsey and Co. Inc., *The Machinery of Government: A New Framework for Expanding Services* (Hong Kong, Government Printer, 1973).

4. Miners (1986), see note 1 above, and Bristow (1984), see note 2 above, are the relevant texts.

5. For a more detailed description of the Hong Kong system as a whole, see Bristow (1984), note 2 above, pp. 174–97.

6. The committee structures, and the report of 14 May 1954, are available at 24 and 24/1 in BL 2/5282/53I, Public Records Office, Hong Kong.

7. Copied from BL 2/5282/53III, Public Records Office, Hong Kong.

8. Development and Airport Division, *Further Report on Development at Tsing Yi* (Hong Kong, Public Works Department, 1973).

9. Colonial Secretary General Circular No. 4/70, *Appendix IV, Tsuen Wan/Kwai Chung Management Committee* (Hong Kong, Hong Kong Government, 1970), para.2, p. i.

10. See Minute M24 in LSO 123/HPG/63 of 1966, Buildings and Lands Registry, Hong Kong.

11. Minute M24 in LSO 123/HPG/63 (1966), see note 10 above, para.2.

12. Memorandum from the Planning Division, Public Works Department, April 1966, at 93 in LSO 123/HPG/63, Buildings and Lands Registry, Hong Kong.

13. Speeches worth examining can be found in the following pages of *Hong Kong Hansard* (Hong Kong, Government Printer, 1965–72): 11 March 1965, pp. 100–1; 25 March 1965, pp. 232–5; 13 March 1968, p. 85; and 15 November 1972, p. 164.

14. 'Report of the Working Group on Private Sector Participation in Land Production', in Special Committee on Land Supply, *Special Committee on Land Supply: Report to His Excellency the Governor, March 1982* (Hong Kong, Government Printer, 1982), Appendix II, para.5.1, p. 11.

15. Memorandum at 6/1 in ENV 35/05/07I, 25 August 1976, Buildings and Lands Registry, Hong Kong, para.1.21, p. (c).

16. Memorandum from the Secretary for the Environment to the Director of Public Works, at 13 in ENV 35/05/07I, Buildings and Lands Registry, Hong Kong.

17. Preparation of layout plans and other local planning work first passed out of the hands of the Town Planning Office generally in 1982, when it was given to the new Urban Area Development Organization following the earlier removal of New Territories planning work to the New Territories Development Department at the end of 1973. These two organizations were amalgamated into the Territory Development Department from April 1986, when all local planning work was centralized in that newly formed department and its area Development Offices.

18. Noted at 31 in ENV 35/05/07I, Buildings and Lands Registry, Hong Kong, para.2.3.7, p. 5.

19. Extracts from *Appendix* at 1/1 in ENV 25/46/03I, August 1973, Buildings and Lands Registry, Hong Kong.

20. Extract from 1/1 in ENV 25/46/03I (1973), see note 19 above.

21. See Bristow (1984), see note 2 above, pp. 273–6.

22. See 5 in PWD/G/TPB 11 — Town Planning Board Paper No. 108, 15 July 1966, Town Planning Registry, Hong Kong.

23. For example, see the dispute over resumptions for land for Industrial Area 24 from 1961 to 1964, reported at 5/1c in BL 7/5281/49, Public Records Office, Hong Kong.

24. Issued as *A Pattern of District Administration in Hong Kong: Green Paper* (Hong Kong, Government Printer, 1980) and *White Paper: District Administration in Hong Kong* (Hong Kong, Government Printer, 1981).

25. Note from the *Minutes of the First Meeting of the Sha Tin District Management Committee on the 22 April 1981*, at 9 in BW(T) 29/10/01I, Buildings and Lands Registry, Hong Kong.

26. *Civil and Miscellaneous Lists: Hong Kong Government — 1 July 1986* (Hong Kong,

Government Printer, 1986), Part C, District Management Committee Terms of Reference, p. 126.

27. *Civil and Miscellaneous Lists: Hong Kong Government — 1 July 1977* (Hong Kong, Government Printer, 1977), (47), p. 68.

28. A full description of recent administrative structures for town planning generally in Hong Kong is given in Bristow (1984), see note 2 above, pp. 166–74, and the most recent Annual Report volumes of the Hong Kong government for the period since 1984.

29. *Civil and Miscellaneous Lists: Hong Kong Government — 1 January 1975* (Hong Kong, Government Printer, 1975), p. 65.

30. *Civil and Miscellaneous Lists: Hong Kong Government — 1 July 1985* (Hong Kong, Government Printer, 1985), p. 101.

31. *Civil and Miscellaneous Lists* (1985), see note 30 above, p. 125.

32. Set up under the Regional Council Ordinance (No. 39 of 1985). It is also a partially directly elected body.

33. E.G. Pryor, 'Supplementary Notes', in J. Wong, *The Cities of Asia: A Study of Urban Solutions and Urban Finance* (Singapore, Singapore University Economic Society of Singapore, 1976), pp. 308–13, and E.G. Pryor, 'Project Management for Hong Kong's New Towns', *Asian Architect and Contractor*, Vol. 16, No. 1, January 1986, pp. 48–53.

34. Pryor (1986), see note 33 above, p. 50.

35. Sha Tin New Town Development Office, *Sha Tin New Town Development Programme: Forecast of Expenditure — August 1974* (Hong Kong, New Territories Development Department, 1974), p. ST/1/2.

36. Development Division, *Report on Development at Castle Peak* (Hong Kong, Public Works Department, 1965); and Development Division, *Report on Development at Sha Tin* (Hong Kong, Public Works Department, 1965).

37. For example, see Maunsell Consultants Asia, *Planning Report — Sha Tin Areas 7 and 2O; Layout Plan No. PST/2* (Hong Kong, Maunsell Consultants Asia, 1975), and plans, at 63/1 and 63/2 in BL 8/5282/61III, Buildings and Lands Registry, Hong Kong.

38. As an example, see *Sha Tin Town Centre Lease Conditions*, published as an appendix 'Example of Lease' in Yuncken Freeman Hong Kong, Scott Wilson Kirkpatrick & Partners, Jones Lang Wootton, and Levett & Bailey, *Tuen Mun Town Centre Study — Volume 2: Design Guidelines* (Hong Kong, New Territories Development Department, 1979), Appendix A.

39. Where proposed uses on a site subject to zoning controls imposed by a statutory Outline Zoning Plan do not conform with those listed in the plan's Schedule of Permitted Uses as permitted at all times, they may still be allowable if approved by the Town Planning Board under the planning permission system introduced in the 1974 amendments to the Town Planning Ordinance (now Section 16 of the Town Planning Ordinance (No. 20 of 1939).

40. Pryor (1986), see note 33 above, p. 52.

41. The proposals for Tai Po were first put forward in Urbis Planning Design Group and Brian Clouston and Partners Hong Kong Limited, *Tai Po Landscape and Recreation Study — Final Report* (Hong Kong, New Territories Development Department, 1979).

42. Speech by the Director of Public Works, *Hong Kong Hansard* (Hong Kong, Government Printer), 24 March 1966, p. 193.

43. J. Hayes, 'Building a Community in a New Town: A Management Relationship with the New Population' in C.K. Leung, J.W. Cushman, and G.W. Wang (eds.), *Hong Kong: Dilemmas of Growth* (Hong Kong, University of Hong Kong, Centre of Asian Studies, 1980), pp. 308–40.

5. The First-generation New Towns: Sha Tin and Tuen Mun (Castle Peak)

ALTHOUGH Tsuen Wan was the first real attempt in Hong Kong to plan a new town as a complete community, and is normally considered as a first-generation new town, only Sha Tin and Tuen Mun (Castle Peak) fully fall within our stricter definition, in that they were developed on mostly virgin sites as theoretically independent, self-contained, balanced settlements. There are also editorial reasons why we should concentrate our attentions on these two, for space itself precludes comparable treatment of many of the other Hong Kong towns, which in any case have grown under similar procedural systems, and have much the same development histories. Only during the 1980s has new-town methodology changed more radically in Hong Kong, and that is to be considered later. Here, the growth and management of Sha Tin and Tuen Mun represent the most advanced and successful fulfilment of Hong Kong's initial attempts at major new-town development in the Territory.

The Planning of Sha Tin

Initial Moves

Interest in developing Sha Tin first surfaced as a major consideration of the Hong Kong government in the 1950s, although it is recorded that possible reclamations were investigated there as early as 1923, and again in 1939.[1] Interest arose in the 1950s following the building of the three streets of Sha Tin Market adjacent to the railway station. This was followed by investigations to extend the railway reclamation, and proposals by Kwan, Chu, and Yang and the South China Textile Company to develop a new garden suburb to the north-east of the station.[2]

The idea of reclamation at Sha Tin is not a new one. There seems every reason to agree that in due course this valley, so close to the city, will become a satellite town, or at least a 'dormitory' for the city. It is already on the way to becoming the latter, and is a popular week-end and holiday excursion resort. Demand for land is vigorous, but at present, in the absence of any development plan, very few building sales or conversions are being permitted [in fact a moratorium lasted from 1953 to 1961]. What is needed is an overall development plan prepared by the Public Works Department.[3]

The response of that department was, however, predictable:

Sha Tin and district has always been regarded by the Public Works Department as a future dormitory and recreational area, but not as a satellite town since it is considered undesirable that any industrial development should take place there ... I am of the opinion that unless and until Government is prepared to make funds available for improving transport facilities (this means major road improvements in addition to providing a double track rail) and to provide mains water, there is little possibility of Sha Tin developing as a major residential area. Pending such time, development as a week-end recreational centre should continue.[4]

Nevertheless, the pressures did cause a plan to be produced to control development in the area (Outline Development Plan LST 2 of July 1954 — see Fig. 5.1a), together with a more detailed layout plan for the area adjacent to the railway station (Plan LST 3).

The new plans set out a simple main-road framework, and suggested areas for the development of traditional Chinese tenement housing, private villa residences, and dispersed low-density housing on an adjacent hillside. But implementation rested upon the requirement of major reclamation, and that was likely to be a government responsibility, and in the 1950s the government's priorities were, as we have seen, elsewhere. This wish not to get involved gave rise to ideas of throwing the area open to private enterprise, even though there was opposition to the Kwan, Chu, and Yang scheme:

I do not think the idea of a garden city as seems to be contemplated by the cotton people is at all desirable. The demand for industrial land is far too keen to allow one of the valuable flat areas like this to be wasted on villas.[5]

By 1955, it was noted that:

a draft outline plan of Shatin district has been prepared in the Crown Lands and Survey Office...but has so far received only preliminary engineering consideration. The working up of this preliminary draft into a full scale comprehensive plan is not proceeding at the moment because available staff is engaged on more urgent work.[6]

In fact, it had already been agreed that no private development should go ahead until land matters in the valley were transferred from the New Territories Administration to the Public Works Department, and that the required staff were not yet available. The plan, therefore, remained unimplemented, and the Sha Tin Rural Committee was not informed of its existence.

The private development idea is interesting, since it was an early precursor of proposals subsequently developed in greater depth in the early 1980s, and which then were to lead to the setting-up of the Land Development Corporation in 1986 for urban redevelopment purposes. The original suggestion was:

Rather than shelving all development for the time being one or other of the following proposals should be adopted ... A private development corporation or corporations should be formed to submit and carry out proposals for the reclamation and development of large areas of the Shatin district: this would reduce the function of this Department to one of merely approving schemes.[7]

Fig. 5.1 Sha Tin new town — development schemes, 1954–1986.

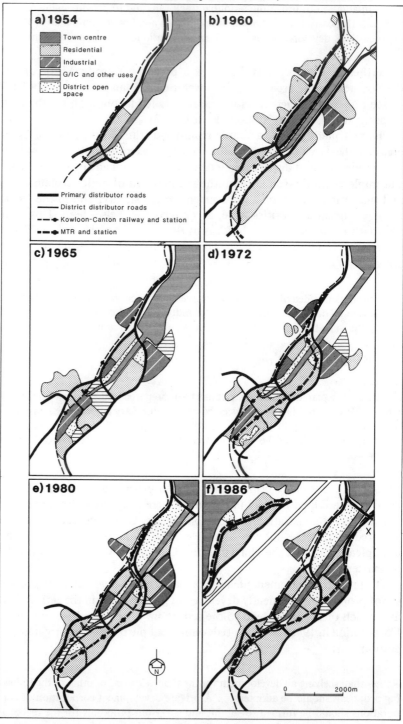

Source: Based on Outline Zoning Plans and Outline Development Plans, Town Planning Office, Buildings and Lands Department, Hong Kong government.

The idea was, however, dropped in favour of the alternative of giving the Public Works Department more staff to set up and extend the capabilities of its new Development Division which was becoming involved with the reclamation works at Kai Tak and Kwun Tong. Staff recruitment proved difficult though, and, it was this shortage that was one of the main reasons why consultants were eventually employed in Sha Tin in 1957 to study the reclamation possibilities in depth. These studies were a part of the Scott and Wilson series of studies first mentioned in Chapter 3.

The consultant's proposals formed the next major step towards the development of Sha Tin as a new town. Principally, their recommended scheme suggested artificially channelling the existing Shing Mun river down the south-eastern side of the valley, with a two-stage reclamation of approximately 239 hectares — the first stage providing land for a town of some 275,000 people. The whole of the new area was to be protected by a raised embankment to protect the site from flooding by predicted typhoon surges in Tolo Harbour. It was also agreed that the potential population target for the dormitory town was dependent on the capacity of the upgraded communication links with Kowloon. The expected commuting element was thought to be as high as 75,000; while some industry was to be provided to employ the balance.

The new housing areas were calculated on an average density of some 1,853 persons to the hectare.

Although we anticipate that the bulk of new industry would be sited on the reclamation, much of its area might be used for residential and other purposes. [The terraces of the three borrow areas were also suggested for residential use, as with the other Scott and Wilson schemes — following the Kwun Tong model.] The area in the vicinity of Sha Tin Station could, as at present, form a natural town centre and be developed as the main shopping district, surrounded by a high density residential belt. Industry could be sited further out on the reclamation, together with residential areas and public open spaces.[8]

While an immediate go-ahead for the proposals was refused in the comparative assessments of the government in 1959–60, preliminary planning work was begun, given that the Executive Council wished to review the scheme again three years later. At the time, it was argued that other public works in the valley (principally connecting works of the Plover Cove water project and the new Lion Rock Tunnel which was required to carry the water to the urban area, and, coincidentally, had been bored to include a roadway), would tend to increase development pressures, which would require a formal planning framework in place in order for them to be properly controlled. Accordingly, a formal request was made of the Town Planning Board on 29 March 1960 to begin a statutory planning process for the valley area.

On investigation, it was soon apparent that the consultant's recommendation to construct an embankment against flood dangers was not suitable, and the basic decision was taken to raise the reclamation level to remove the flood risk. This required the use of more borrow areas, and these were included in the new plan (LST 17, see Fig. 5.1b),[9] which was formally exhibited in 1961 and finally approved as Plan LST 19 at the end of that year. The main dispositions of the reclamation areas in fact reverted to those first put forward tentatively in the earlier 1954 proposals, with a new centrally trained river channel.

An important principle of the new plan was:

while allowing for a considerable increase in population and a modicum of industrial development ... in preparing the plan every effort has been made to maintain large areas of open green belt, space for recreation and picnicing and, as far as possible, to preserve the land and seascape down the centre of the valley.[10]

The suggested land-use controls in the green wedges between the residential and other neighbourhoods were that:

these reserves have been provided to separate physically the development zones and due account has been taken of the general topographical features and landscape possibilities. In general existing uses would be permitted to remain in this part of the green belt; applications for new development should not be considered unless they were for schools, Temples and other institutions, very low density residential development, village expansion or for forestry, agricultural or open space purposes. As detail planning proceeds specific areas for park development and tree planting should be scheduled.[11]

Although the green wedge idea was to disappear rapidly in the face of a soon-to-materialize onslaught for ever higher densities, these initial ideas represent an interesting forerunner to the landscaping ideas applied from the mid-1970s.

The 1961 plan provided a broad zonal classification of 11 residential zones of 118 hectares with two more zones, at Fo Tan and Tai Wai, becoming the basis of Sha Tin's present industrial areas, and a large 61-hectare central area. The new design population of the town had increased to 360,400. Major road proposals were also suggested, with the main Kowloon to Tai Po road transferred across the river to the south-east side, while at the draft plan stage the railway was also proposed for realignment alongside the new river channel. It is clear that the new residential zones were conceived of as neighbourhoods, in the new-town tradition, with local open space, schools, markets, and community facilities. Each was separated from its neighbours by the green wedges (not unlike Abercrombie's original model of the 1940s — as in Plate 2a). The industrial zones were planned at a plot ratio of 1 to 5, and 'are to provide for service industry and a small degree of manufacturing of a specialist nature suited to the surroundings e.g. suitable light industries'.[12] It was envisaged that half of the working population would be employed locally, and half would commute to the main urban area to the south.

Yet, the plan was in a very real sense still only tentative. Not only had there not yet been a proper investigation of its engineering implications, for of course the consultant's earlier study was now no longer entirely relevant, but the planners themselves stated that:

an ultimate population of 360,000 persons is proposed. Clearly this will not be approached, let alone reached, within this decade since there is no present intention for large reclamation or other works. The plan is intended only to indicate the basis on which private enterprise may proceed and the tempo of development rests largely with individual landowners ... The plan indicates only broad principles and ... detailed layouts will have to be prepared for each of the various use zones. It is understood that this will be put in hand for two of the zones as soon as approval is given, but it must be emphasised that the plan is a long term one.[13]

New-town development in Sha Tin as a public enterprise was clearly not yet envisaged; nevertheless, a number of key design parameters were now in place which ultimately were to affect the form of the present town. The positioning of the town centre and two of the principal industrial areas was now decided, as well as some of the borrow platforms, and the general line of the principal arterial road which passed the town. Active public sector involvement however had to await the Executive Council's next review, then expected in 1962.[14]

It is interesting to note that two organizations sent in general comments about this first public plan when it appeared in mid-1961. These were the Hong Kong Society of Architects (through their Planning Committee), and the Tsim Sha Tsui District Kaifong Welfare Advancement Association.[15] The latter put forward some comments on some of the zoning, but the architects were more fundamental in their criticisms. They suggested that, to maintain the regional importance of the valley as a recreational resource, the central valley should be developed with lagoons and landscaped open space, while the lower slopes of the surrounding hills should be the location for the main building development: 'the concept of preserving the valley and seascape as it is, is not practical with such a large amount of development'[16] was their main criticism of the government's plan.

The professionals also wanted to see tight design controls imposed by three-dimensional urban design regulations (rather on the model then being proposed for central Victoria on Hong Kong Island), as well as some 'traditional' new-town features such as an orbital road, separate road and footpath networks, and a phased development operation run by a new-town corporation on the British model. They did, however, welcome the introduction of this new type of generalized statutory plan well in advance of physical development on the site, which they agreed ought to be able to control the overall layout of the new town. But their comments were neither viewed favourably within the government, nor were they considered formally by the Town Planning Board, since the architects' status was not that of a formal objector under the terms of the Town Planning Ordinance.

In July 1963, active consideration was finally being given by government as to how the plan might be implemented. It was noted at the time, that the current discussions on housing policy[17] and the siting of the new

Chinese University of Hong Kong were likely to affect development, and, that the new road link with Kowloon was now to be complete by the late 1960s. It was accordingly agreed that 'on the grounds of cost, development should be concentrated on one area at a time starting at the head of the valley and moving downwards.'[18]

It was accepted at the time that the development would start in Area 1, the speed depending largely on private enterprise initiative, and, that consideration should be given to revising the statutory plan so as to exclude Areas 7, 8, 13 (part), 16, and 18 in order to reduce the immediate scope of the scheme. The Development Office of the Public Works Department was asked to prepare a feasibility study for the first stage, which:

should be based on the smaller scheme . . . thus considerably reducing the extent of the work involved; the levels should, however, be such as to enable the full scheme to go ahead in the very long term should this ever become necessary.[19]

The 1965 Scheme

The long term in fact came very quickly, as we have seen previously in Chapter 3. The Development Office's investigations into the Sha Tin scheme were undertaken during most of 1964 and it was accepted 'that the preliminary engineering investigations . . . should be completed before the Outline Development Plan is sent for revision'.[20] By June,

it had been established that adequate filling was available in the area to complete the reclamation more or less as shown on the statutory plan. If this were done and densities similar to those for Tsuen Wan and Castle Peak [Tuen Mun] adopted then the population of the new town at Sha Tin may well exceed one million people.[21]

Two important changes about the town had now been decided: the concentration on the reclamation, partially for land acquisition reasons, meant that the original idea of starting at the head of the valley and working down seawards was now discarded, while the target population and the resultant densities for the town were drastically altered. The second change had in fact been foreshadowed by a decision of the Land Development Planning Committee in October 1963 which set the policies to meet increasing needs for high-density housing sites, and which were made public in the 1964 White Paper. This strategic imperative had itself initiated the engineering investigation begun in March 1964, and led to the formation of a Planning Co-ordination Committee in April to determine the detailed plan for the town. The formal step of referring back the existing statutory plan for revision was also taken the following August.

By November 1964, draft copies of the new development plan (LST 41B) (see Fig. 5.1c) were being circulated for comment within the government. The suggestion at the time was for a 15-year, four-stage programme to produce a city of some 1,007,300 people on a 500 hectares site,[22] which was finally increased to 1,090,400 on 864 hectares in all (excluding green belt land within the plan area) in the final feasibility report of January 1965.[23] An important new element for the town was the inclusion of major areas of resettlement and low-cost public housing at gross average densities of 5,560 persons to the hectare, and estimated to provide some 540,000 units of accommodation on 94 hectares. The central area for the town also changed, in that it was much reduced to only 41 hectares.

The planning of the town itself is based upon the development of the residential and industrial areas located on the lower levels and reclamations to a high degree of intensity (zone 1 density) and the residential areas on the higher levels in a somewhat less intense manner (zone 2 and 3 densities). An area for the 'town centre' has been selected adjoining the present town and adjacent to the railway station as a natural extension [yet it was only in Stage II of the proposed staging of the project put forward by the engineers at this time] ... Industry has been distributed into three main zones around the town, again to give easy access from all parts of the town and conform with the anticipated stages of development.[24]

The industrial land was determined on the basis one hectare per 865 workers (one in five of the total population being estimated as requiring local work).

As with the earlier plan, the trunk road to the north-east New Territories from Kowloon was kept to the south-east side of the town, though its alignment was shifted again to skirt the main urban area. It was also designed to full motorway standards, with grade-separated junctions to a hierarchical road system of primary, secondary, and distributor routes within the town. Other changes were the general introduction of retailing uses on the ground floors of the high-density residential areas, and the provision of village resite areas to cater for anticipated village clearances within the new-town area.

In contrast to the earlier plan, the more intensive general development meant that only 10 per cent of the developed area was left as usable open space, principally in the form of a riverside park and the *fung shui* hill of Yuen Chau Kok. Staging of the development, put forward on engineering grounds (chiefly reclamation and sewerage requirements), was suggested in the following sequence; the south-eastern reclamation, the north-western, the Sha Tin valley, and finally Pak Tin. This staging also avoided large amounts of private land resumption in the early years. The first stage of 243 hectares was expected to support 395,000 people, of whom 350,000 were to be in resettlement estates.

It has been mentioned earlier that overall planning of the town was in the hands of the special Planning Co-ordination Committee. At its first meeting on 23 April 1964,[25] it set itself six principal tasks: to agree the main framework for the new outline zoning plan; to agree main drainage and levels; to set the limits for reclamation; to agree on water supply; to determine the phasing of works; and to assess the costs and timing of development, together with any development returns. At this stage, planning was still being done on the basis of a probable 500,000 population target for the town. It is also of interest to note that, at the time, road links with both Kwai Chung and Kowloon via Tate's Cairn came under discussion (both were finally to come to fruition at the end of the 1980s).

The second meeting, in June, proved critical to the final town design. Because of the engineers' findings that full-site development seemed feasible, the town's population target was increased to a million, and it was agreed that all future planning would proceed on this basis, developing the land at full urban area densities. This was accepted, even though increasing the population to this level meant that the prime function of the town as a commuting centre for the main urban area would now have to be changed to a more self-supporting one with its own industry, even though this would contradict the existing strategic policy of restricting new industrial development to the coastal strip between Junk Bay and Castle Peak. Later meetings were concerned with more detailed matters — sewage treatment and the staging of the project, and possible open-space standards (those mentioned were Abercrombie's half acre per 1,000 population [one hectare per 4,942], and the current practice at that time of 1 hectare per 10 hectares of formed land). The Committee finally met in December 1964 to adopt its draft Feasibility Report.

Meanwhile, alongside this departmental planning process, the formal revision of the statutory plan, through the Town Planning Board mechanism, was also progressing. The draft plan (Plan LST 46) was finally put before the Board early in 1966. With some minor zone boundary amendments and the addition of a new primary road loop at the head of the valley, the plan was published as a draft for public exhibition (Plan LST 47) on 15 April 1966. As with the earlier plan of 1961, there were two groups of objectors; those intimately concerned with particular sites, and those concerned professionally with the generalities of the proposals. Apart from a very few specific site issues, the main local concern turned out to be the revised routing of the trunk road around the town, which was argued by the villagers now affected to have adverse effects on their local hillslope — this was of *fung shui*[26] significance. Not for the first time in Hong Kong new-town planning, delicate and expensive negotiations between government and villagers were required.

More generally, both the Hong Kong Society of Architects and the Hong Kong Branch of the Town Planning Institute sent in comments. Together they objected strongly to the high densities proposed (as also did separate representations from Hong Kong industrialists), and the planners in particular argued that strategically there ought to be more concentration of development around the harbour area (shades of the Territory Development Strategy of the 1980s!) as an alternative to the expansion of the new town to the suggested levels. However, in their internal response, the government planners suggested that densities could not be reduced, given the pressing need to meet the public housing targets just set in the 1964 White Paper; and accordingly the Town Planning Board endorsed their view and passed the plan as proposed for final adoption.

Initial Implementation

Formal approval of the new statutory plan as late as 13 July 1967 did not of course affect further departmental work on the scheme. The Land Development Planning Committee recommended on 9 April 1965 that Stage I of the scheme on the south-eastern side of the valley should go ahead,[27] and at the third review of the 1965–6 public works programme it was included as a Category A item.

However, since that time, the problems of land availability, rate of development, population densities, rate of population growth [the 1966 sample census had just been published when these remarks were being made], etc. have been under review.[28]

All of these, and general budgetary constraints, caused a further change before actual implementation finally got under way, such that in September 1966 it was agreed that the lower expected demands of the 1970s warranted a revised and smaller first stage scheme, on the lines of Tuen Mun (Castle Peak) Stage 1A which was also agreed about this time, that is, on the basis of only 71 hectares for 100,000 people. Sewerage treatment requirements meant that 1976 was the earliest that any scheme was estimated to be ready for occupation, and since the population forecasts were now thought to be uncertain it was thought prudent to plan on the basis of an initial target of 145,000 in Sha Tin. The revised targets also allowed some reductions in the planned public housing densities. Finally, another new factor had entered the calculations of the new-town planners, for it was 1966 that saw the first firm moves to provide a new racecourse for Hong Kong in the Sha Tin valley, and a site was reserved on the north shore of the inlet adjacent to Fo Tan.

Two alternatives were put forward for consideration as locations for the suggested first-stage development. Scheme A was for some 158 hectares on the south-east side of the valley, adjacent to the new trunk road (a scaled down version of the 1965 proposals); with a target population of 120,000 to be accommodated on 25 hectares, and with 63 hectares of industrial land. Scheme B was smaller, and consisted of only 83 hectares for a population of 87,750 (on 18 hectares), of which 80 per cent was to be in public housing. The reclamation for the latter scheme was to be between the existing town centre and the new racecourse site to the northwest of the river, and included the development of the first stage of the Fo Tan industrial area (20 hectares). The population target and hence the size of the scheme was limited by the employment potential estimated for the planned industrial estate.

Initially, despite near unanimous preference by other government departments for Scheme B, the engineers recommended that Scheme A should go ahead on the grounds that it was more compact, had greater potential for expansion, could be developed independently, and had lower unit costs. Nevertheless, despite the theoretical advantages, the preference to develop on the opposite side of the valley adjacent to the existing development proved overwhelming, and Scheme B at Wo Che commenced on a phased basis (Phase 1 was for 30,000 people on 37 hectares, as the first part of the Lok Yuen Public Housing Estate),[29] following agreement by the Land Development Planning Committee in August 1967.

The next significant move in the development of the town took place in 1969. As a political move, to meet demands from local landowners to participate in the prosperity the new-town growth was bringing to the area (an approach had been made to the government by the Sha Tin Rural Committee), an investigation was carried out into the effects of allowing private development in Areas 3 and 4, and the adjacent industrial area (Area 17). Experience in Tai Wai village, where a layout plan had been in existence since 1959, suggested that only very slow progress was likely where private amalgamation of existing lots was required to develop sites in accordance with any new plan. Accordingly, for the new area, a new method was proposed, building on a Tsuen Wan precedent where land had been resumed in advance of public purpose requirements:

It is considered that a more comprehensive method should be used as follows: (a) a layout is prepared, circulated and adopted; (b) resumption proceedings are instituted to implement the layout. As an alternative to cash compensation an exchange entitlement on the 5:2 ratio would be issued if landowners surrender their land prior to the resumption date; (c) the land is formed to levels and serviced; (d) the formed and serviced sites are made available for development by way of exchange.[30]

A first phase of 13 hectares in Areas 3 and 17 was suggested to try out the new procedure, but it had to be postponed due to planning delays, for the detailed plan for Area 3 did not become available until late 1972.

Yet, already in 1969, detailed layout planning was underway for Areas 3 and 4, 7 (the central area), and 16 (the Fo Tan Industrial Zone), and those for the reclamation area were approved in principle in May. Detailed planning of the new town could now be said to have begun in earnest.

Subsequent Developments

It is not appropriate within the scope of this book to try to give a 'blow-by-blow' account of the development of every area in Sha Tin, even though we do need to try to pick out the more significant changes that affected the overall growth and conceptualization of the town. However, some additional detail is discussed in Chapter 7, when we will be looking at specific design aspects of items like town centres, public housing, and other elements of the Hong Kong new towns.

In the public sector, while the first stages of reclamation were under way, there was little incentive to complete new layout plan work. The next major impetus was yet another change in the town's planning targets as a result of Territory-wide revisions to the population forecasts following the 1971 census. 1985 forecasts had now fallen from 7.2 million (the 1968 estimate) to only 5.8 million, and this induced a major revision of the plan for the town as a whole (see Fig. 5.1d) and the initiation of a whole new cycle of Outline Development Plans, beginning with Plan LST 59A.

Additionally, improved standards of provision for various community uses such as open spaces, secondary schools, and off-street parking, together with greater space allocations in both public and private housing have had the effect of reducing considerably the overall population densities assumed in the design of new residential neighbourhoods. The corollary of this is that urban land requirements per head of population have increased. In view of these trends and also changes of major road alignments it became evident that it would be necessary to review the planning proposals for the new town of Shatin.[31]

The standards revision came from the work on the Colony Outline Plan that we have examined in the previous chapter, while issues more specific to Sha Tin included such questions as the racecourse provision, an alignment for the proposed mass-transit line, and a possible new permanent exhibition site for the Chinese Manufacturers Association.

In the resultant reformulation of the development plan (see Fig. 5.1d), a revised set of planning objectives was set down which were said to have guided the planning process.

It is considered that the basic concept should be the creation of a number of residential neighbourhoods for various types of housing with easy access by means of a high-capacity transportation system to three principal areas of industrial employment. A system of open spaces should be provided to give identity to and link the main concentrations of urban development.[32]

To facilitate the subsequent detailed planning work required, the town was now divided for the first time into 50 planning areas, each of which was likely to require a separate layout plan in the future. For the town as a whole the target population was now set at only 475,000, with 68 per cent in public housing at a new gross average density of 2,471 to the hectare. The town centre was again reduced in scope, now to only 16 hectares, but additional neighbourhood centres were to be planned for each of the housing areas. New density rules and plot ratios were adopted in the town,[33] and on the industrial side a new industrial land target was set of 136 hectares at a new worker density of 741 to the hectare. The plan also required that these industrial sites should be separated from adjacent areas by principal roads or open space 'buffer' areas. For the first time too, mention was made of the allocation of sites for a major cultural centre in the town centre, and for three tertiary education institutions. Clearly, as the planners' ideas were developing, so their concepts of what the town might be like were becoming much more sophisticated.

Open-space allocations were now divided into a new country park extension, 'active' and 'passive' open space areas, and local open spaces at 9 hectares and 8 hectares per 100,000 population for the district and local space respectively. On the transportation side there were yet more changes. A major new trunk road (Route 5) was included to connect Sha Tin through the mountains with Tsuen Wan, while an extension of the mass transit East Kowloon Line was envisaged to run along the south-eastern side of the valley, crossing to a new terminus alongside the racecourse. Trams were also mentioned as a possible internal public transport system, and it was laid down that at the detailed planning stage a fully segregated separate pedestrian network would be provided for the town.

Finally, to ensure fully integrated and balanced community development, it was argued that a properly staged programme of land formation and subsequent development was essential. It was thought that subsequent revisions to the plan 'that can be expected are likely to involve the detailed layout of individual planning areas rather than the overall structure of the new town';[34] a rash prediction, given the past history at the time, and one not to be borne out in practice. Nevertheless, the 1971–2 revision did set out the basic form of the town to which most subsequent development has conformed. Its ideas finally became public knowledge in August 1978, when its associated Outline Zoning Plan eventually reached public exhibition as Plan LST 69, though not without some further more minor revision.

Before the onset of the Ten Year Public Housing Programme and the administrative reforms of 1973–4, progress in Sha Tin was slow. Only Phase 1 of the First Stage was as yet under way. 1973, however, did see the first major step towards more rapid completion of the town with the appointment of Maunsell Consultants Asia to investigate how Stage I of the town should proceed to completion. For them it was the beginning of a long association with the planning of the town through their role as principal engineering and transportation consultants.

In 1974, they recommended the further development of 337 hectares gross, to cater for a population of 245,000 in the town by 1979; approximately 68 per cent of whom would be in public housing estates as before. Using these recommendations, the year also saw the production by the new New Town Development Office of its first ten-year development programme for the town. It divided Stage I into 11 development 'packages', of which the first two were already under way, with Package 3 for the associated sewerage works (see Fig. 4.3a). Substantial areas on the southeast side of the valley were suggested for development by the private sector. In Areas 5 and 48,

Mei Foo Investment are considering asking to take over part of the areas reserved for public and private housing. If this possibility eventuates there will be a considerable reduction in the expenditure forecast for this package ... Package 7 — Tender documents are being prepared for private developers to reclaim some 48 hectares of seabed which are zoned for residential and industrial use in Area 14. The private developer would retain about 15 hectares for his own Zone 2 [density] residential building and the remaining land would be handed over to Government.[35]

In the event, Mei Foo Investments withdrew, to be replaced by Chinachem, who successfully tendered for a smaller scheme of some 8 hectares for 9,000 people in Area 48, which finally got under way in 1977; but the public finance constraints of 1975–6 encouraged the government to press ahead more urgently with the other proposal for Area 14. The outcome here was to provide eventually a site of some 56 hectares which was put out to public tender in October 1975. The successful tenderer put forward their required Master Plan (see Fig. 7.9) for a major residential scheme, now known as City One, which was finally approved in July 1978. The scheme, as built, provides homes in 52 residential towers for 41,000, on a site area of 16 hectares, together with two major commercial complexes and other community facilities. It was the first major private venture for the new town.

As construction work on the separate packages within Stage I came on stream, and accelerated during the 1970s, so the required advanced planning work increased proportionately. Not only was the Development Office increasingly involved in the necessary layout planning work in advance of the actual reclamation and land conversion programme through to the provision of formed and serviced sites, but throughout the period, continuous adjustments were being made to the overall Development Plan as detailed examination of each area of development became necessary.

Additionally, as early as 1976, two more major planning inputs were under way.

It is proposed that consulting engineers [Maunsell's again] be authorized to proceed with the engineering feasibility study on stage II, so that land can be provided when required in due course for the later Sha Tin estates in the Public Housing Programme and other development to provide a balanced township [the original ten-year programme required Sha Tin to provide for nine new estates, to which others were added later]. It is also proposed that the study should include the preparation by the consulting engineers of an overall landscaping master plan for the new town. This plan would form the brief for the many agencies who will be responsible for the detailed landscape design of the various elements of the new town.[36]

In fact the job was split, with Maunsell taking on the Stage II investigation, and Yuncken Freeman Hong Kong the landscape study.[37]

The engineering study brief noted that:

at the present time land use proposals ... plan for a population of about 520,000 and a land area of some 350 hectares. However, having regard to likely land acquisition and clearance problems in the Stage II planning areas [they included much less reclamation, for example] and the need to achieve greater programming flexibility to meet Government's housing target it is now intended to establish the ultimate economic extent and best order of balanced development for Sha Tin Stage II taking into account all known constraints ... The study should consider further development on the eastern side of Sha Tin Hoi [Area B, now Ma On Shan, as well as an area in the bay to the north-west of the Chinese University, then termed Area 'A'].[38]

On the landscape side the consultants were required to produce a Master Landscape Plan stating 'appropriate main landscape objectives and policies to be followed in the future planning, development and management of Sha Tin'[39] together with detailed requirements, criteria, and techniques, using case-study examples taken from the area, to enable full incorporation of new landscape principles in the planning procedures throughout the town.

In effect, full incorporation of these two bodies of work represented yet another major upheaval in how the whole town was being conceived. The evaluation of Stage II now had to provide for a further major expansion of the built-up area towards the north-east, and possibly the north-west also; whilst the attempt to introduce full landscaping into the planning work involved, at least theoretically, a complete reworking of past detailed layout planning for the older areas as well as the new.

Both studies were completed early in 1977, and two major decisions resulted from their recommendations — the acceptance that Sha Tin should be extended into Area 'B', Ma On Shan, following completion of developments at the head of the Sha Tin valley; and agreement that the new town should get a professional landscape team within the Development Office to implement the landscaping proposals, and to provide a continuing professional input into the ongoing planning of the town. Two other decisions, on the transportation side, also had a major impact on the town form at this time.

With the government's earlier decision only to proceed with the development of the Mass Transit Initial System in the main urban area, the former mass transit railway alignment in eastern Sha Tin had earlier been replaced by a new branch from the main line of the Kowloon — Canton Railway. This solution was now also discarded, and a complete reassessment of the town's transportation needs was undertaken in a consultancy transport study begun in 1974. This study also led to a decision to go for a segregated pedestrian and cycleway system in Sha Tin, following principles first applied in the British prototype town of Stevenage some thirty years before.

It was 1977, therefore, that saw the final departmental planning stages that led to the form of the town as it now is (see Fig. 5.1e). That year brought the completion of a new Outline Development Plan (STP 76/2022), the first sketch plan for Ma On Shan (STP 77/502A) — for a target population of 80,000, and the incorporation for the first time in a ten-year development programme of the full 14 additional packages for the development of Stage II of the town.

Once again, general objectives for the development were set out, and these had become somewhat more sophisticated than those of five years before:

(i)   to create a balanced and vigorous self-contained community to meet the basic needs of all the residents;

(ii)   to provide new opportunities and freedom of choice for residents in location, type, standard of housing, education, employment;

(iii)   to create a meaningful community to which people can relate healthily with a strong sense of place and where people can develop socially;

(iv)   to provide ease, safety and convenience of movement for residents to and from their places of work, learning, shopping and recreation;

(v)   to use the available resources efficiently, wisely and imaginatively;

(vi)   to create an attractive and convenient city appropriate to the district.[40]

The plan now envisaged a final population target of 550,300, of which 56 per cent were to be in public housing.

The valley site of the new town and its division by major transportation corridors and the Shing Mun River realignment has dictated a linear framework for Sha Tin New Town. Within this linear framework, the basic concept has been the creation of residential districts for various types of housing, with easy access by means of a high capacity transportation system to three principal areas of industrial employment ... Recreational facilities [are linked] by developing a system of pedestrian and cycle pathways linking living and working areas to recreation areas, and providing strong pedestrian links to peripheral green belt and passive areas.[41]

To achieve this, the plan boundary now contained 65 separate planning areas, including a town-centre precinct of some 34 hectares containing 316,000 square metres of shop and office space, a cultural and administrative centre, new railway station, and a town park (see Figs. 7.3, 7.5, and 7.6, and Plate 7b). The latest planning standard density figures were applied for the housing and industrial land allocations, while the three tertiary education sites of previous schemes were now reduced to two, one having been replaced by the new Prince of Wales Teaching Hospital which was to be associated with the Chinese University. On the transport side, major infrastructure proposals were not altered (for example, a tracked transit alignment remained in eastern Sha Tin), though the plan's explanatory statement noted that since 1974 consultants had been developing a bus-based internal transportation network utilizing bus lanes, bus roads, and traffic priority measures at junctions. The new plan also gave details for the first time of the new grade-separated pedestrian and cycleway system envisaged for the town.

Development in the Eighties

The final, and most recent, stages of planning for Sha Tin fall into three distinct phases — the detailed refinement of the 1977 design in a series of departmental circulations of minor amendments, and interaction of these with necessary zonal and other changes introduced with the new statutory Outline Zoning Plan (LST 69) of 1978, and culminating in the revisions of 1986 and 1988 (Plans S/ST/3 and S/ST/4). A major Outline Development Plan revision in 1986 (Plan D/ST 1/1) (see Fig. 5.2 and 5.1f) took account of rezoning and density changes induced by the need to meet increased public housing targets and raised 'the population development in Sha Tin proper so as to fully utilise the infrastructure which has already been provided'.[42] The extension of planning and subsequent implementation to Ma On Shan achieved a total population target of some 800,000 for the whole urban complex by the early 1990s. Further rounds of fine tuning have taken place since, as the present town proceeds to final completion (Plan D/ST/3/1 was being prepared during 1988), while yet further expansion into Area A or north-eastwards into Three Fathoms Cove still remain as future possibilities.

A comment on Ma On Shan is an appropriate place to conclude our

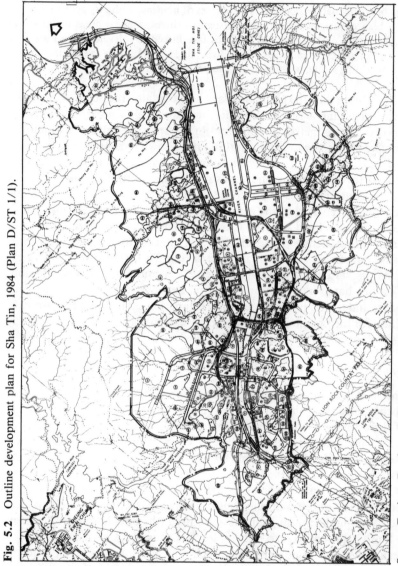

Fig. 5.2 Outline development plan for Sha Tin, 1984 (Plan D/ST 1/1).

Source: Territory Development Department, Hong Kong government.

Table 5.1   Land-use Distributions in Sha Tin and Ma On Shan

	Sha Tin		Ma On Shan	
	Hectares	Per Cent	Hectares	Per Cent
Special residential	135.6	8.6	64.5	13.5
Residential 1	62.8	4.0	40.5	8.5
Residential 2	34.0	2.0	51.5	10.8
Residential 3	106.7	6.8	15.3	3.2
Residential 4	114.9	7.3	—	—
Town centre	14.5	1.0	4.5	0.9
Village	132.7	8.4	21.4	4.5
Total residential and commercial	601.2	38.1	197.7	41.4
Government and community	213.4	13.6	50.2	10.5
Industry	121.3	7.7	18.2	3.8
District open space	76.3	4.8	34.9	7.3
Non-intensive open space	271.4	17.3	58.0	12.1
Roads	159.4	10.1	103.6	21.7
Other	133.7	8.4	15.2	3.2
Total	1576.7	100	477.8	100

Note: Residential 1–4 are densities, high to low.

Sources: Sha Tin Outline Development Plan D/ST 1/1 (1986), and Ma On Shan Outline Development Plan STP/OD/1 (1983); Sha Tin Development Office, Territory Development Department, Hong Kong.

brief look at the development history of Sha Tin, for it represents for that town the first real opportunity for the planners to incorporate the lessons learnt in the first round of new-town planning. As such, it presents an interesting contrast to the planning of the later independent new towns of Junk Bay and Tin Shui Wai with which it is contemporaneous.

The initial proposals (Plan STP 77/502A) envisaged 21 hectares of housing in two zones, 43 hectares of private residential development, and 22 hectares of industrial land on four sites, for a total population of some 81,600. The imposition of the new housing targets of the early 1980s produced a major expansion of these proposals, and the current scheme was first made public as Outline Development Plan STP/OD/1 in 1983 (later renumbered as D/ST 2/1B) (see Fig. 5.3). The area has now been planned virtually as a new town in itself (almost equal to Junk Bay Stages I and II, for example) since its target population has been increased to 315,500, and provides an interesting contrast (see Table 5.1) with Sha Tin itself in terms of its land-use make-up.

The town has its own town and district centres around which a public transport spine connects all areas with the main core of Sha Tin to the south-west. Although by 1988 only Stages I and II of Ma On Shan were formally authorized, in order to avoid the need to commence investment

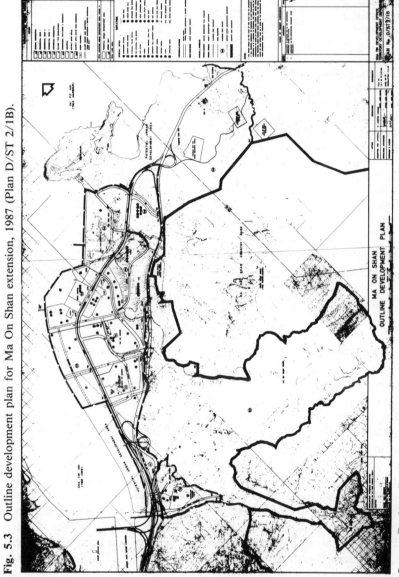

Fig. 5.3 Outline development plan for Ma On Shan extension, 1987 (Plan D/ST 2/1B).

Source: Territory Development Department, Hong Kong government.

in the fixed rail link to Sha Tin proper, the momentum of the development on the site is likely, as elsewhere in Hong Kong, to lead to full
development of the site's potential in the 1990s. Ultimately, the 68 new
planning areas of the town will provide a major extension to the linear
city of Sha Tin.[43]

On completion, a major urban ribbon, some 12 kilometres long by one
kilometre wide, stretching from the Beacon Hill Tunnel to beyond Lok
Wo Sha and housing approaching a million people, will have replaced a
rural valley containing only a railway and a few traditional Chinese villages
in the short space of some three decades (see Plates 5a and 5b). Yet, the
Ma On Shan of the 1980s is not quite the Sha Tin of earlier decades. As
Table 5.1 shows, the distribution of land uses and hence the function of
the town, albeit as a constituent part of greater Sha Tin, had changed.
Clearly, new-town planning had moved on by the 1980s, and it is a subject to which we shall return later in this book. For now, it remains for
us to examine further the first major round of new-town building, through
the development story of Sha Tin's twin city, Tuen Mun.

The Planning of Tuen Mun (Castle Peak)

Initial Moves

The planning history of Tuen Mun[44] in many ways mirrors that of Sha
Tin, at least procedurally. Indeed, at the beginning there was a long debate
within government as to which should proceed, and direct comparisons
were made between the two schemes (see Tables 5.2 and 5.3),[45] in order
to decide whether they should be proceeded with sequentially, simultaneously, or not at all. Yet there were important differences. In the early
days, Castle Peak, as it was first known, almost began by stealth, and
was commonly thought of within the government as the New Territories
Administration's brainchild.[46] Also, it has always been seen as, and promoted as, a factory town, a direct successor to Kwun Tong and Tsuen
Wan, and hence has grown up with a very different social and community
mix to its urbane rival across the New Territories' hills.

While Scott and Wilson had produced a report for a reclamation scheme
in Castle Peak Bay in May 1959, which estimated a possible design population of 285,000 for the proposed development, the recommendation was
put on one side by the Executive Council's initial decision in 1959 to proceed only with Kwai Chung. However, it was stated that:

there is no objection to the District Commissioner New Territories disposing of
land (or converting land) at Sha Tin, Castle Peak or Tai Po provided it is clearly
understood by developers that Government will not provide services requiring heavy
expenditure of public funds.[47]

As we have seen, for a variety of reasons, private development in the Sha
Tin valley was not able to proceed, but around the Castle Peak area the

Table 5.2 Comparison of the Proposed New Towns at Tuen Mun (Castle Peak) and Sha Tin

	Tuen Mun		Sha Tin	
Design characteristics: population				
Resettlement	438,500		442,500	
Other public housing	130,500		96,800	
Private housing	466,500		539,600	
Total	1,035,500		1,078,900	
Initial planned population build-up				
1968	5,000		—	
1970	51,000		5,000	
1972	216,150		189,400	
1974	521,000		545,100	
Land-use in hectares/per cent				
Settlement	72/17		72/13	
Other public housing	23/6		17/3	
Private housing	150/35		153/28	
Residential total	245/58		242/44	
Industrial	153/37		191/35	
Community	13/3		32/6	
District open space	10/2		82/15	
Total	421/100		547/100	
Costs of scheme HK$m./HK$ per square metre				
Village relocation	—	—	25	0.03
Clearance	10	0.02	73	0.04
Land formation	61	0.13	90	0.11
Roads	43	0.09	130	0.16
Water supply	109	0.22	81	0.10
Sewerage	114	0.23	352	0.44
Typhoon shelter	23	0.05	—	—
Total gross costs	432	0.88	878	1.07
Revenues in HK$m.				
Residential land (at $1.1/$7.5 per sq. m.)	135.7		418.0	
Industrial land (at $1.4/$3.7 per sq. m.)	333.3		254.0	
Totals	469		672	

story was rather different; indeed, development pressures were increased by a government decision of June 1960 to restrict major industrial development to the coastal strip between Junk Bay and Castle Peak.[48]

Thus, by June 1962, it was being reported that:

as you are aware, the Public Works Programme now includes items for development works at Castle Peak (Category Aii), a water supply (Category C), and extensions of the dual carriageway from Tsuen Wan (Category C) and from Yuen Long to Ping Shan (Category Aii) thence to Hung Shui Kiu (Category C). In other

Table 5.3 Advantages and Disadvantages of the Proposed New Towns at Tuen Mun (Castle Peak) and Sha Tin

Castle Peak	Sha Tin
Advantages	
Can become reasonably self-contained.	Good current transport links with urban area, easily improved.
Sewage into tidal stream.	
Direct sea access to harbour.	Employment and facilities can be provided in urban area.
Limited private resumption required.	
Disadvantages	
Trunk road to Tsuen Wan required.	No direct sea access to port.
Reluctance to move to town (remoteness).	Expensive road links to Kowloon and Kwai Chung if full development is required.
Inducements may be needed for industrial and community facilities.	
	Considerable private resumptions required.
	Full treatment of sewage.
	Loss of agricultural land.

Note: From Table 5.2 it can also be seen that Castle Peak was expected to be profitable, and Sha Tin was not.

Sources: Tables adapted from Land Development Planning Committee Paper No. 71, 9 April 1965; and assessment from Population and Housing Working Committee, *Colony Outline Plan, Book 2, Chapter 11 — Report on Population and Housing* (Hong Kong, Crown Lands and Survey Office, 1969), Appendices D and E, pp. 170–1.

words, a modest start is now being made with the first stage of the draft Castle Peak Outline Development Plan [LCP 8] and the associated communications, partly in order to facilitate the acquisition of land for public purposes at Yuen Long [the new area was being developed for anticipated use as a land exchange site].[49]

As happened elsewhere in Hong Kong, incremental decision-making on a project-by-project basis was already building up a momentum that was to push the government into a comprehensive and large-scale commitment.

By 1962, the general development pressures in the area caused the Land Development Planning Committee to review the whole position at its meeting on 28 September of that year. It was agreed at the time that Castle Peak was probably the most suitable site for government's next large-scale development scheme after Kwai Chung, since it provided an excellent site with a potential of over 283 hectares of new land. Not only was there a suitable nucleus of existing population for a new settlement, but also there was a showing of interest from industrial developers. In addition, the site enjoyed good sea communication with the harbour. The matter was clinched by the fact that government was already committed to public works in the area which formed a large part of the planned Stage I of any new-town scheme. The outcome of the September meeting was a checking position — the Public Works Department was asked to prepare a paper setting out the justification for proceeding with development of Castle Peak in preference to Sha Tin.[50]

By March 1964, the preliminary works for Stage I (the causeway and bridge across Castle Peak Bay) were already under way, and additional to the other items from 1962, the government had also agreed to provide a further new road for the new sawmill sites which were to be sold on the western side of the Bay to operators displaced from the main urban area (Kowloon). Additionally, investigation had already begun regarding expanding San Hui village in Area 10, in order to meet further Yuen Long land-exchange requirements, as well as additional reclamation work to the west and north of the new causeway.

Note was taken of the fact that if the Government Aided Housing Programme, particularly resettlement, was to be satisfied in the late 1960s and early 1970s, it would be necessary to build a number of estates in the Castle Peak District. In order to prepare the way for these, the steps referred to above [as previously mentioned here] were essential. It was generally agreed that Castle Peak represented a much better proposition than Sha Tin, the only difficult factor being that of water supply [which was required to come from Fanling and Tai Lam Chung by pipeline].[51]

The 1965 Scheme

The actual outcome of the 1962 request from the Land Development Planning Committee was the preparation of a development feasibility study for Castle Peak, prepared during 1964 in parallel to that for Sha Tin.[52] As in Sha Tin, a special Planning Co-ordination Committee was formed in April 1964 to prepare an outline plan of the proposed new town (Plan LCP 11B — see Fig. 5.4a). The basic requirement affecting the design of the town was the agreed commitment to find sites for 438,500 persons in resettlement estates (73 hectares at the standard average gross density of 7,413 to the hectare) and an additional 130,500 in low-cost housing 23 hectares.

Thus, in order to attempt to provide a 'balanced' population, it was argued that an additional 326,500 people should be catered for at two levels of high density (3,064 and 1,977 to the gross hectare respectively), which in turn resulted in the other design figures of 150 hectares of industrial land, a 13-hectare town centre, 12.5 hectares of community uses and 10 hectares of formed (district) open space. To these design populations were added the 17,500 existing inhabitants on site and a further float of 90,000, to give the overall target design figure for the new plan of 1,035,250.[53] This was a substantial increase on the planners' initial proposals of March 1964, which had proposed a figure of only 869,600; and, as in Sha Tin, the expansion was a direct response to the demands of the Territory's new housing targets set that year. Other more detailed planning constraints

Fig. 5.4 Tuen Mun new town — development schemes, 1964–1980 (see also Plates 6a and 6b).

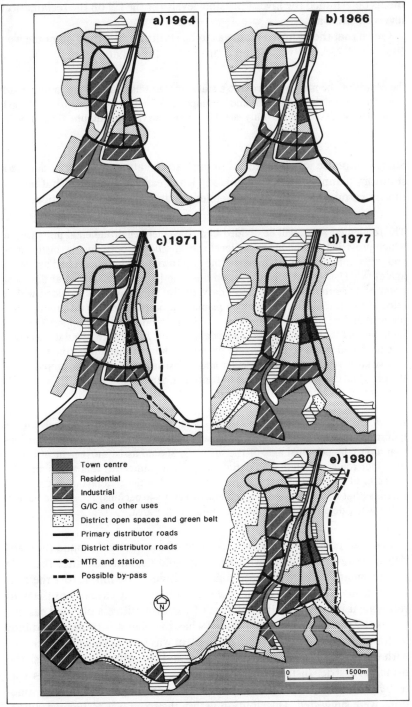

Source: Based on Outline Zoning Plans and Outline Development Plans, Town Planning Office, Buildings and Lands Department, Hong Kong government.

were set by engineering requirements. For example, water supply limitations kept development to below 15 metres OD, while the sewerage gra-
dients determined the lowest possible levels for the fill on the reclamation
levels in the Bay.

Given that the required plan was to be statutory (the final outcome was
Plan LCP 28A), it was pointed out at the time that:

the object of the plan is to provide a statutory land use pattern and major road
framework within which the use and development of land may be controlled. Broad
principles of development only are laid down leaving maximum flexibility in
details.[54]

Such a response was a reaction, in part, to the attempt to apply detailed
statutory planning elsewhere in Hong Kong early in the 1960s, but nevertheless certain basic design principles for the town were specified.

The residential zones will be divided into convenient environmental units within
which provision will be made for local shops, schools, open spaces, institutions
and other community requirements [the new town neighbourhood had appeared
again] ... The central zone shown on this plan [Area 11] is located at the focal
point of the proposed town. Secondary central zones may be provided within
selected residential zones as detailed planning proceeds [a rather different principle to that first applied in Sha Tin] ... It is intended that the upper floors of
buildings in the central area should be designed and used for residential purposes.
It is proposed that a comprehensive scheme including three-dimensional control,
car parking, segregation of vehicular and pedestrian traffic, etc. be prepared for
the principal central area [to come to fruition in the 1980s (see Figs. 7.6b and 7.7)
— twenty years later]. Smaller schemes may be prepared for the secondary central areas ... The industrial zones form two major groups, supported by a subsidiary group for specialized industries ... It is intended that ultimately all the
industrial areas will be developed for general light industries. Their general distribution along the principal axis of the town ... should assist movement of traffic
on minor roads within the industrial areas ... It is intended that a minimum of
0.1 acres of formed [open space] per acre of land in the area layout or per 2,000
persons [that is, 0.1 hectares per hectare, or per 4,940 persons] ... should be provided when detailed layouts are prepared for the area.[55]

The road pattern was designed as a limited-access radial around the high-
density core of the town, with ancillary land-uses outside after the style
of Buchanan.[56] There was also a central, high-grade link across the centre of the town adjacent to the town centre. The only casualty of the plan
refinement process was the deletion of the Committee's planned eastern
bypass by the Town Planning Board when the plan was transformed into
its statutory form in 1965. The road system was seen as being hierarchical,
with the ring as the primary distributor, and the central cross-link as the
principal district distributor. Direct access to these from frontages was
to be prohibited, and service roads for the frontages and limited junctions were suggested. Distribution within the town was to be by a subor-

dinate system of district and local distributor roads. There was no thought as yet of any segregated public transport system.

Unlike in Sha Tin, the initial plan (see Fig. 5.4a) set the basic form of a town that has remained to the present: that is the high-density core, including the industrial areas, set within a high capacity ring road, all on the floor of the valley, and principally on new reclamation. Outside of this core were developed the lower density areas and ancillary uses and major open spaces. Subsequent change has been either to change particular zonal uses; to accommodate changing standards; or, most recently, to look at the possibilities of major peripheral expansion to accommodate possible future housing pressures from elsewhere in Hong Kong. It is to all of these that we now turn.

Initial Implementation

The 1965 development report recommended an initial start on a revised Stage I scheme for a population of 135,000 on a limited reclamation to the north-west of the town centre, and it formed the basis of a decision to go ahead in principle by the Land Development Planning Committee in April 1965. Almost immediately afterwards, however, the decision was affected by a public expenditure cut-back, arising from which the Public Works Sub-committee decided in 1966 to divide the Stage into two parts. As at Sha Tin, the new sites to be begun were almost entirely to meet immediate public housing commitments.

Meanwhile, in April 1965, the draft statutory plan for the proposals was going through the internal consultation stages prior to publication. Particular attention was being paid to transportation matters. Firstly, it was confirmed that it was intended 'to provide grade separate vehicular and pedestrian intersections, thus segregating pedestrian from vehicular and local from through traffic'.[57] By February 1966, an important planning principle had also been determined for both Castle Peak and Sha Tin:

From such investigations as have been carried out by Government's consultants it appears probable that should the new towns develop to the population and at the intensity at present planned then some form of passenger mass transit within the town and between the towns and the existing urban area will become necessary. What form this will take cannot yet be stated nor can any provision be made in the Draft Plans.[58]

Yet, despite the initial pessimism, by draft publication stage the inter-town problem had already been tackled. Plan LCP 32, for the first time, included a main-line railway reserve on the eastern side of the town, part of a proposed line from Fanling to Yuen Long, Tuen Mun (Castle Peak), and Tsuen Wan. Another change was the deletion from the statutory plan of the proposed three-dimensional design controls — a move common to a more general Territory-wide retreat in this policy area.[59] In general terms, the plan stated:

the development of residential and industrial areas should be staged and coordinated to ensure that the increasing population has adequate employment opportunities in local industries. The provision of education, medical, community and public recreation facilities should be coincident with the increasing requirements of the population in order to create a homogeneous environment. A phased programme to serve an anticipated population of the order of 600,000 by 1976 has been prepared.[60]

The phasing requirement proved to be a hard objective to achieve, and in the event not always attainable, as we shall see.

The plan appeared almost simultaneously with the 1966 Sha Tin statutory plan mentioned earlier, and objections to both were considered by the Town Planning Board on 15 July 1966. The same general comments about the form of the town were made by the industrialists and professional groups as were made of Sha Tin (p. 156), but additionally the Tuen Mun Rural Committee expressed serious concern about the effects of the plan upon the existing villages, about which they had not been consulted; but, as no resite proposals were actually shown on the plan, and the complaint was received out of time, the Town Planning Board was able to avoid a formal response. The only important amendment made in fact was to delete the new railway reserve south of Area 37, the result of an objection from the military authorities at Gordon Camp and a realization that the line was now likely to be part of the Mass Transit System, which, its consultants agreed, was now most likely to arrive from the north.[61]

Following the endorsement for Stage IA in 1966, actual development on site began in 1968 with preparatory work for the San Fat public housing estate for 11,000 people in Area 10, using part of Area 4 to the northeast as a borrow area. However, advanced planning work for other areas was rapidly affected, as in Sha Tin, by the downturn in the population figures resulting from the 1971 census forecasts and the work on the Colony Outline Plan of 1969–70. In fact, Tuen Mun was used as a model for some detailed planning investigation work carried out for the Population and Housing Working Party of the Colony Outline Plan which affected all future new-town and other planning work in the Territory.[62] Not only did this lead to the strategic decisions about future development mentioned in Chapter 3, but more importantly, here it represented the first attempt to consider the detailed design of public housing areas in the new towns to a comprehensive set of planning standards.

The following procedure was used.[63] Using Plan LCP 33C and Area 2, the available area was assessed excluding major roads, the river, and other special uses. Theoretical standards of provision were then specified, separating out neighbourhood and town uses; and overall town densities were postulated to derive a total possible population. The town-centre requirements were then assessed, using specified, general space standards, which then left a residual total for dividing amongst the residential areas (such as Area 2, which was used as the test area). Although standards were of course very different, this procedure followed contemporary British practice as set out by the Ministry of Housing and Local Government. After determining the target populations between low, medium, and high density neighbourhoods, the land requirements for the low and medium density areas were then assessed and deducted from the residual first, thus leaving a remainder which was to be examined as to feasibility in accommodating the required high-density population target. Using an iterative revision procedure, the Working Group derived a layout which 'would result in the most appropriate form of development in terms of balancing the land requirements for public open space, GIC uses, service industry and commercial/residential development'.[64]

The test resulted in the derivation of the following density standards: Residential High-Density — 2,404 persons per hectare, Medium Density — 741 persons per hectare, and Low Density — 148 persons per hectare. With other population assessments at 99 to the hectare for GIC areas and 62 per hectare in the industrial zones, this produced the overall town density of about 1,235 to the hectare that was applied at the time to Tuen Mun (Castle Peak), Sha Tin, and Tsuen Wan, to give the new town targets of 685,000, 800,000, and 1,069,000 respectively.

Full implementation of these revised planning ideas came with the publication of the new 1971 Outline Development Plan (Plan LCP 43B, renumbered as TM/1C in 1974)[65] (see Fig. 5.4c). This reduced the Colony Outline Plan's target to only 476,000, of which 343,000 were to be in public housing. The plan also involved a major reclamation extension southwards into Castle Peak Bay to bring the plan area to a new total of some 809 hectares, of which only 101 were then under active development.

One of the most important new changes, and partially induced by the reclamation extension, was a complete revision of the town's highway network. The major alteration was the separation for functional reasons of the eastern side of the town's radial primary distributor from the north-south trunk road of the Castle Peak Road, while the Tuen Mun Eastern Bypass reappeared as a tentative alignment. The routing of the mass transit line through the town was also changed to a more central position, and once again extended towards Tsuen Wan. But the main effect of these transportation changes was to alter significantly the shape and size of the intervening spaces, in other words, the potential neighbourhoods and other areas, thus making major changes to the overall planning of the town.

Further changes came with the 1974 revision of the Plan, with further alterations to the southern reclamation limits following further engineering investigations. Another important change was the decision to extend the town centre across the Castle Peak Road into Area 37A, which introduced an interesting design problem for the future (see Chapter 7).

Perhaps the most far-reaching of the 1974 revisions, however, were the incorporation for the first time of an exclusive right-of-way public transport network (though the type of system was not yet specified), and a subsidiary pedestrian system throughout the town. Because the public transport network was a late addition, only in a few places were the alignments completely separate from the already determined road system; more usually the new routes were placed alongside the principal roads on widened rights-of-way. A final important alteration was an extension of the planning area to the far south-west at Tap Shek Kok to include sites for a projected power station and water desalter plant.

No sooner had the revised plan been formulated and circulated, however, than it was overtaken by further changes introduced to accommodate the public housing targets of the ten-year public housing programme of 1973. These called for four estates to be completed in Tuen Mun (officially renamed from 1973) by the late 1970s, over and above the already committed programme for 158,000 people.[66] These provided a major part of a revised public housing target of 344,000 out of an amended town target of 483,600. In fact, accurately forecasting the target was recognized at the time as being problematical. It was suggested in particular that 'the over-riding factor is that over the development period, there will be more secondary school children in the New Town than would be expected on the basis of the usual population projection'.[67] In the event, the initial problem of the 1980s turned out to be in the primary sector, which was to lead to an issue of territorial concern.

The next round of major revision in the development of Tuen Mun followed the completion of further consultancy studies in the mid-1970s. It followed on from the completion of the hydrological studies[68] into the alignment of the main nullah and the reclamation in the Bay, together with the Phase II engineering study by the main consultants (Scott Wilson Kirkpatrick & Partners) completed in 1975,[69] which recommended a three-stage programme to bring the town to completion. The major result was yet another change to the reclamation programme, and consequent road network and zoning changes (see Fig. 5.4d).

One of the dominant results of this was a decision to concentrate the light manufacturing zoning into just two areas, consisting of 100 hectares in a strip some 3.75 kilometres long along the western edge of the nullah, and another 40 hectares on the north side of the proposed new typhoon shelter to the east. While the planners decided once again to delete the line of the eastern bypass, the changes to the town's form accelerated the need to look again at the town's whole transportation needs, and they were put under scrutiny in a traffic and transport study that was put out to the consultants in 1976.[70] Nevertheless, Plan TM/1E, as it had by now become, formed the final basic design of the physical structure of the town upon which its present shape has depended. Subsequent change, as in Sha Tin, has been the result of internal pragmatic adjustment, or possible external expansion.

The Explanatory Statement for Plan TM/1E gives an interesting insight into the minds of the Tuen Mun planners of the time.

The planning of a new town presents a unique opportunity to design a total environment ... The structure of a new town is predetermined by general planning principles and land use allocation in accordance with the adopted planning standards. The form and character are then derived from the interpretation of this policy decision in building forms [the Colony Outline Plan Working Group approach lived on]. The physical elements which make up the environment, e.g. buildings, roads, the river channel, must be well related to provide a visual sense of coherence. Viewed from a distance, the new town should present the impression of a tapestry of urban forms amid green foliages. However, within this overall design there should be room for drama and contrast. The planning objectives must be to give visual pleasure, a sense of identity and the civic pride to the people of the town.[71]

It was ideals such as these, that led to the commissioning of the Tuen Mun landscape study.[72]

Consolidation and Expansion

In parallel with the departmental planning work that was determining the final form of the town during the early 1970s, there was also some consideration of updating the original statutory plan with which planning of the town had begun in 1967. Obsolescence had led to its formal withdrawal in 1971 and an instruction to prepare a revised statutory plan in 1973, yet it was not until TM/1E was in place that a final draft (Plan LCP 52) could be placed before the Town Planning Board in August 1977.

The planners' general objectives were reiterated:

The primary objective of the new town is to provide a balanced development of commercial, industrial and community services and an improved urban environment ... Consideration has been given to the need of a high quality townscape, a sense of identity and local civic pride. Great emphasis has also been placed on the provision of recreational and cultural facilities as the new town will be built as a self-supporting community. The major geographical features of the area have influenced the pattern of the town's zoning. The physical elements which make up the town's environment, such as the buildings, roads and waterways, have been carefully planned to provide residents with a sense of coherence in their community.[73]

While the Board wished to make the plan public,[74] it was in fact deferred, pending completion of the transportation and landscape studies that were then in hand. Perhaps even more than in Sha Tin, these studies were being utilized to make a thorough review of the principles upon which the town had been planned — a review that turned out to be quite protracted.

Irresolution remained when the matter came before the Town Planning Board again in February 1979. A number of reasons were advanced for the delay.[75] It was commented that the transport study, though completed, had not yet reached a conclusion. While the consultants had recommended a light rail tramway system for the public transport network (instead of buses),[76] and wanted major changes to the road network, the planners still thought that further consideration and investigation was necessary. Important revisions were also thought likely to arise from the work of the landscape consultants, since their Master Plan recommended:

a wide range of recreational opportunities of which the more significant in terms of the effect on land use zoning are a revision of the town boundary, the retention of Castle Peak Beach and the building of a lagoon in front of the beach, the extension of recreational uses including a larger town park, and a recreational 'spine' alongside the main nullah.[77]

In a completely different field, geotechnical problems on the western fringes of the town, on the slopes of Castle Peak itself, were now affecting both the routing of the new transmission line from the Castle Peak Power Station, as well as the designated public housing sites on the lower slopes. The resultant forced rezoning precipitated a study of zoning intensities elsewhere in the town to extract maximum density potentials, as well as adding additional urgency to the investigation of possible town expansion, which was introduced following the identification of potential land shortages for Hong Kong as a whole (identified by the Special Committee on Land Production at the end of the decade). The first of these extension studies, for a possible western extension in the vicinity of Lung Kwu Tan, was completed in 1979. Meanwhile, the most immediate effect of the zoning changes was a major rezoning exercise in Areas 3, 5, and 51, in the north-west of the town. This charge was circulated for approval in February 1979.

The net effect of all these changes was, of course, to force yet further alterations to the Outline Development Plan, and to defer still further the preparation and presentation of the derivative statutory plan. The first draft of the new round of development plan revision appeared as Plan TM 1/0/1 (see Fig. 5.4e and 5.5) in September 1980. In summary, the major revisions were a considerable expansion of the plan's boundaries to take in the possible new western and eastern expansion areas, a redesignation of the road hierarchy in accordance with the Transport Study's recommendation to abandon the role of the western side of the town's radial as a primary distributor, and the reinstatement of the draft alignment of the eastern bypass; while the railway reserves were deleted and all pretence was abandoned of including any comprehensive cycle-way network in the town.

In response to the Landscape Master Plan the town park in Area 16 was enlarged, while the detail of the typhoon shelter was modified to include the recommended lagoon scheme for the Castle Peak Beach. The plan also contained a considerable reshuffling of planned zoning uses, including the provision of sites for a polytechnic and district hospital, while the deletion of the housing sites on the western slopes meant adjustments and reallocations to make up the resulting deficits. All these changes meant further adjustments to the target population figure, now some 503,000, of which 315,000 were to be in public housing; while industrial land allocations were reduced to 115 hectares in total, consequent upon a realization that existing industrial developers were building at maximum plot ratios in the town. However, one bonus from the enforced zoning changes in the western fringes was a useful increase in the district open-space allocations, which now reached an average for the town of 20 hectares per 100,000 — twice the Hong Kong standard of that time.

Further planning boundary adjustments and zoning changes followed in 1981 (Plan LTM 1/0/1A) following consideration of suggested amendments after the internal circulation within government, and a further considerable number of detailed design amendments were processed through Plan LTM 1/0/1E in May 1982 as detailed planning of the various new-town areas progressed. In particular, the incorporation of further additions to the public housing targets raised the town's target population to 548,000 by that year, with 308,000 to be housed in the public sector, to which were added a further 63,000 in the new home-ownership estates which had been added to the government's housing targets for the area.

Plan LTM 1/0/1E contained a comment upon its role that is worth quoting, especially in explaining the long delay to the statutory plan for the town (which had formed a marked contrast to the procedures in Sha Tin).

New problems, opportunities and needs are regularly being identified in Tuen Mun and as a result, New Town planning proposals have had to be applied in a reasonably flexible manner ... The Outline Development Plan recognises the need to deal with, and make decisions regarding, a number of important planning matters on an incremental basis — as a result they are sufficiently flexible to adapt to any new or changing circumstance.[78]

Even so, despite the special pleading for flexibility, the plan did form the basis for the first new statutory plan for Tuen Mun to appear for 12 years — Plan LTM 2 of July 1983. While the new development in planning procedures represented the first opportunity for general public response on the features of the new town, only one objection required any formal amendment from the Town Planning Board, and the public participation opportunity in Tuen Mun planning generated relatively little response.

Of much more moment for the future of the town was the outcome of the moves for further expansion, also examined in the early 1980s. The already mentioned initial western extension study, which was concerned mostly with recreation possibilities and potential borrow sites, was subsumed within the wider investigations for the whole of the north western New Territories carried out at the beginning of the decade, as part of the lead up to the Territorial Development Strategy.[79] This was because of possible linkages with other suggested urban development sites further along the coast — particularly at Nim Wan, identified in the Special Committee for Land Production's 1977 report. Nevertheless, sufficient progress was made to enable the production and issuing of a planning guide for the area in October 1982, which was finally approved as Plan LTM 1/0/4I at the end of 1985. Apart from designating sites for limited recreational development on the coast north of the new power station, the main purpose of the plan was to select major new borrow sites adjacent to Deep Bay for future use in the reclamation of Castle Peak Bay as part of the future town.

Much more important, however, were the proposals developed for an eastern extension to the town, along the coastal strip towards Lok On Pai.

Fig. 5.5 Outline development plan for Tuen Mun, 1983 (Plan LTM 1/0/1G).

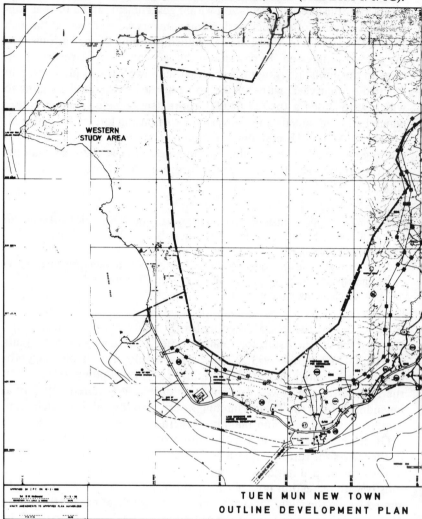

Source: Territory Development Department, Hong Kong government.

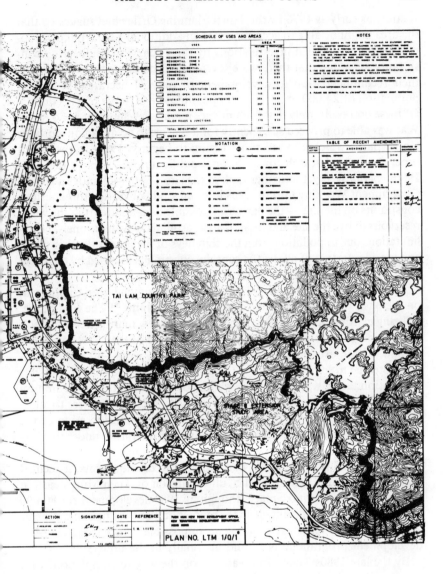

A study as early as 1976 by the Town Planning Office had suggested that the area might be able to accommodate an additional 130 to 180,000 people, but more detailed investigations by the Tuen Mun engineering consultants suggested that there were severe site constraints which restricted their recommendation to development of only 37 hectares for a total population of 24,000, out of a total possible site of some 680 hectares.[80] Of these proposals, only that for a private marina development at So Kwun Wat was able to proceed sufficiently for a scheme to go ahead on a private tender basis, which allowed construction to begin in 1986. In the meantime, the general search for additional public housing sites of the early 1980s encouraged yet a further look at the site's potential under a special Government Working Group. This internal study identified three serious constraints on the site — the danger of possible dam failure from the water reservoirs above the site and 'no-go' areas around the water tunnels, height limitations due to pollution from the chimneys of the nearby desalter plant, and most important of all, traffic capacity constraints imposed by the single road access possible to the main development site.

Yet, the final outcome in 1985 was still a recommendation to proceed, on the basis of a three-stage development programme.[81] The first phase, utilizing existing borrow areas, would, with the new marina development, allow for a population of some 24,000 by the end of the 1980s; while the second, within existing infrastructure provisions, would lift the population potential to some 87,000. The Group thought that the ultimate possible population target was likely to be about 130,000 after 1995. The interim outcome was a decision in the Development Progress Committee to allow detailed planning of the first phase to begin, while consideration of the remaining two phases was deferred pending consideration under the Territorial Development Strategy implementation arrangements. Given that strategy's initial propensity for harbour-related developments, it seemed unlikely in the late 1980s that the full expansion of Tuen Mun's eastern extension would ever take place, though by 1988 development for 80,000 was already committed. But given the momentum of existing commitment, such an outcome remains by no means impossible before the Tuen Mun development programme is wound up finally in the mid-1990s.

By the late 1980s Tuen Mun was well on the way to completion, with about half of the design population already in residence (see Table 8.2). A major event, too, was the inauguration of the first part of the new internal light rail system in 1988 — an innovation of major professional interest. Yet, some doubts remained about the viability of the town as a balanced, self-contained community as the planners had so often boasted initially. Of all the Hong Kong new towns it remained the one with the most problems, and those form the basis of some further comment in the final chapter. Nevertheless, in locational terms, Tuen Mun still remains the one new town in Hong Kong most capable of fulfilling in the long term the original new-town objectives of balance and self-containment.

Some Concluding Remarks

A full review of the overall new-town development process is provided in the final chapter. Here, it is appropriate to sum up the particular issues that Sha Tin and Tuen Mun demonstrate in particular.

As with so many new-town programmes, not least in Britain from whence the Hong Kong planners took much of their inspiration (Stevenage and Cumbernauld were specifically mentioned), incremental adaptation has been the dominant process that has affected the planning of the first major 'green-field' new towns in Hong Kong. This has not only been an understandable and necessary reaction to demands placed upon the planners' objectives from outside — most noticeably by continuous changes to the public housing targets and hence the target populations of the towns as a whole, but also adaptation to the planning process itself, both procedurally and theoretically.

In short, given the intense pressures to get on and produce results, new-town planning in Hong Kong has been very much an example of 'learning on the job' as planning methods and planning standards in particular have changed as the towns themselves evolved. In a very real sense, both Sha Tin and Tuen Mun acted as real-world prototypes for new-town planning in Hong Kong.

This learning process infected all aspects of the development process. In the professional planning field, from the beginnings of only two or three professionals grew and developed the multi-disciplinary teams of the present Development Offices, with landscape and transport specialists following the engineers of the early 1970s. The government's own machinery evolved too, until by the 1980s there existed embryonic, local government institutions in each new town; while the financial control and planning mechanisms themselves evolved in line with the magnitude of the public expenditure commitments required.

The lessons learnt in Sha Tin and Tuen Mun came to be applied retrospectively in the earlier scheme for Tsuen Wan, Kwai Chung, and Tsing Yi, and provided the base upon which the smaller expansion schemes of the 1970s for the three rural market towns got under way. Real opportunity for change and the effective implementation of lessons learned did not come, however, until the next phase of major 'green-field' opportunity in the mid-1980s, and it is to that that we turn in the next chapter of the Hong Kong new-town story — the new towns of the 1980s. For those, the planning and development of Ma On Shan had already provided some pointers.

Notes

1. Memorandum from the District Commissioner New Territories to the Colonial Secretariat, 17 September 1955, at 21 in SEC 8/5282/54, Public Records Office, Hong Kong.

2. A plan of the suggested scheme is at 5/1 in SEC 8/5282/54, Public Records Office, Hong Kong.

3. Minute by the District Commissioner New Territories, 16 June 1954, at M3 in SEC 8/5282/54, Public Records Office, Hong Kong. The first speculative development at Sha Tin, the three streets of Sha Tin Market, dated from 1950.

4. Minute by the Director of Public Works, 8 July 1954, at M9 in SEC 8/5282/54, Public Records Office, Hong Kong.

5. Minute by the Financial Secretary, 2 November 1954, at M24 in SEC 8/5282/54, Public Records Office, Hong Kong.

6. Extract from letter by the Colonial Secretary to the Hong Kong Civic Association, 22 September 1955, at 22 in SEC 8/5282/54, Public Records Office, Hong Kong.

7. Memorandum from the Director of Public Works to the Deputy Colonial Secretary, 14 October 1954, at 5 in SEC 8/5282/54, Public Records Office, Hong Kong.

8. Scott Wilson Kirkpatrick & Partners, *Report on Reclamation at Sha Tin* (Hong Kong, Public Works Department, 1959), p. 15.

9. An outline of the proposals in Plan LST 17 can be found in *The Hong Kong and Far East Builder*, Vol. 16, No. 1, 1961, pp. 50–1.

10. Planning Division, *Sha Tin and District Outline Development Plan: Explanatory Statement to accompany Plan No. LST 17* (Hong Kong, Crown Lands and Survey Office, 1961), paras.5–6, p. 1.

11. Planning Division (1961), see note 10 above, para.20, p. 3.

12. Planning Division (1961), see note 10 above, para.13, p. 2.

13. Planning Division (1961), see note 10 above, paras.10 and 26, pp. 2 and 4.

14. Executive Council decision of 17 November 1959, quoted at M107 in BL 1/5282/56I, Public Records Office, Hong Kong.

15. Copies of the correspondence, the Architects' Report and internal discussion on the matters raised can be found at 1–8 in LSO 4027/PD–TM 87/BMS/61, Town Planning Registry, Hong Kong.

16. Hong Kong Society of Architects Planning Committee, *Report to Government: Town Planning Ordinance, Hong Kong Planning Board — Sha Tin and District Outline Development Plan and Explanatory Statement* (Hong Kong, Hong Kong Society of Architects, 1961), para.B, p. 1.

17. Eventually to appear as *Review of Policies for Squatter Control, Resettlement and Government Low-Cost Housing*, White Paper (Hong Kong, Government Printer, 1964).

18. Minutes of a meeting, 5 July 1963, at 18 in BL 6/5282/56I, Public Records Office, Hong Kong, para.2(c) (i), p. 1.

19. Minutes of meeting (1963), see note 18 above, para.3(v), p. 2.

20. Minutes of 50th meeting of the Public Works Department Policy Committee, 6 March 1964, extract at M1 in LSO 123/HPG/63, Buildings and Lands Registry, Hong Kong.

21. Minutes of 53rd meeting of the Public Works Department Policy Committee, 5 June 1964, extract at M3 in LSO 123/HPG/63, Buildings and Lands Registry, Hong Kong.

22. Taken from the tables prepared by the Planning Division, September 1964, at 43B in LSO 123/HPG/63, Buildings and Lands Registry, Hong Kong.

23. Development Division, *Report on Development at Sha Tin* (Hong Kong, Public Works Department, 1965), Appendix B.

24. Town Planning Board Paper No. 70, 20 November 1964, *Sha Tin Outline Development Plan LST 42*, at 1 in PWD/G/TPB 11, Town Planning Registry, Hong Kong.

25. Full details of the discussion are in the Committee Minutes, in LSO 123/HPG/63B, Buildings and Lands Registry, Hong Kong.

26. The whole question of *fung shui*, the traditional locating of buildings and other features in the landscape, is a major issue for land-use planning in Hong Kong. It particularly affects major development proposals, and in the new towns has been important in influencing the detailed town designs in relation to already existing features, both natural and man-made. The general relationships of *fung shui* and planning are discussed in: P. Cookson Smith, 'Fung Shui and Architecture — Star-crossed Reality or Organised Superstition', *Building Journal Hong Kong*, February 1986, pp. 70–3; P. Cookson Smith, 'A Celestial Planning Guide' (Parts 1 and 2), *Building Journal Hong Kong*, February 1986, pp. 74–5, and March 1986, pp. 70–7; W.N. Chung, 'Fung Shui — A Structure does not improve on

Nature, it exists in harmony', *Building Journal Hong Kong*, February 1986, pp. 76–7; W.N. Chung, 'Fung Shui: contrast and neutral — the modern interpretation of Yin and Yang', *Building Journal Hong Kong*, March 1986, pp. 78–9; M. Chiang, 'Fung Shui in the Design of Regions and Cities' (Parts 1 and 2), *Asian Architect and Contractor*, September 1986, pp. 26–30; M. Chiang with M. Chiang, 'Fung Shui and its Application in City Planning', *Asian Architect and Contractor*, May 1986, pp. 19–20.

27. Minutes of the 50th meeting of the Land Development Planning Committee, extract at M21 in LSO 123/HPG/63, Buildings and Lands Registry, Hong Kong.

28. Development Division, *Report on the Development of Sha Tin New Town, Stage I (Revised)* (Hong Kong, Public Works Department, 1967), para.2, p. 1. Copy at 8/1 in BL 8/5282/61II, Buildings and Lands Registry, Hong Kong.

29. Land Development Planning Committee Paper No. 233, 31 January 1969, at 38 and 38/1–3 in BL 8/5282/61II, Buildings and Lands Registry, Hong Kong.

30. Land Development Planning Committee Paper No. 261, 26 September 1969, at 50 in BL 8/5282/61II, Buildings and Lands Registry, Hong Kong.

31. District Planning Division, Town Planning Office, *Shatin Outline Development Plan: Explanatory Statement — Plan LST 59A* (Hong Kong, Crown Lands and Survey Department, 1972), para.1.3, p. 1.

32. District Planning Division (1972), see note 31 above, para.2.1, p. 2.

33. District Planning Division (1972), see note 31 above, Schedules I–IV.

34. District Planning Division (1972), see note 31 above, para.14.1, p. 12.

35. Sha Tin New Town Development Office, *Sha Tin New Town Development Programme: Forecast of Expenditure, Aug. 1974* (Hong Kong, New Territories Development Department, 1974), Packages 5 and 7, p. ST/1/3.

36. *Public Works Sub-Committee — Second Review 1975/76: Sha Tin New Town, 2. Civil Engineering — Amendments and New Items, (ii) Development*, para.4, p. 99. At 2 in ENV 70/24/05I, Buildings and Lands Registry, Hong Kong.

37. Maunsell Consultants Asia, *Sha Tin New Town, Stage II Engineering Feasibility Study* (Hong Kong, New Territories Development Department, 1977): and Yuncken Freeman Hong Kong, *Sha Tin New Town Master Landscape Plan: Phase One Report* (Hong Kong, New Territories Development Department, 1977), 2 vols.

38. *Agreement No. CE 10/76: Sha Tin New Town Stage II — Engineering Feasibility Study: Brief* (Hong Kong, Public Works Department, 1976), at 2 in ENV 70/24/05I, Buildings and Lands Registry, Hong Kong.

39. Sha Tin New Town Development Office, *Draft Landscape Brief — Brief for a Study and Preparation of a Master Landscape Plan for Sha Tin New Town* (Hong Kong, New Territories Development Department, 1976), para.6.7, p. 6.

40. Sha Tin New Town Development Office, *Planning Report: Sha Tin New Town Outline Development Plan — Explanatory Statement to Outline Development Plan STP 77/2028A* (Hong Kong, New Territories Development Department, 1977), para.2.2, p. 2.

41. Sha Tin New Town Development Office (1977), see note 40 above, para.4, p. 4.

42. Memorandum of 14 November 1985, at 74 in TPD D/ST/200I, Town Planning Registry, Hong Kong.

43. There were also proposals during the round of sub-regional planning studies of the early 1980s to extend Ma On Shan even further north-westwards towards Three Fathoms Cove. The North Eastern Study of 1982 suggested a possible maximum target population of 197,500 for this further addition to the linear town. Some doubts were expressed at the time on the population forecasting done for the Study, and also the problems caused by the capacity constraints of possible transport links — particularly through Ma On Shan towards the main centre of Sha Tin. In the event, the proposals were omitted from the Territorial Development Strategy's recommendations, and now seem unlikely to proceed. Details of the proposed design can be found in Freeman Fox & Partners (Far East), Halcrow Fox and Associates Hong Kong, EBC Hong Kong, and Watson Hawksley Asia *North Eastern New Territories Study* (Hong Kong, Hong Kong government, 1982), pp. 39–50.

44. During its early life as a new town, Tuen Mun was always known officially as Castle Peak New Town, after the English name of the nearby mountain range. The reversion to the Chinese local name was officially gazetted in 1973.

45. Land Development Planning Committee Paper No. 71, 9 April 1965, *Proposed New Towns at Castle Peak and Sha Tin*, and supporting papers, at 78 and 78A–C in LSO 123/HPG/63, Buildings and Lands Registry, Hong Kong.

46. In the lead-up discussions for the Scott and Wilson reclamation investigations, the District Commissioner New Territories ranked the proposals in the order Tai Po, Junk Bay, Castle Peak, Gin Drinkers Bay, Sai Kung (not proceeded with), and Sha Tin. 'No-one ex-

cept the DCNT holds any particular brief for the Castle Peak scheme but it has been added in view of the priority he has given to it' (comment of Colonial Secretary in October 1957). See M58 and 32/1 in BL 1/5282/56I, Public Records Office, Hong Kong.

47. Confidential note on land development schemes from the Assistant Colonial Secretary (Lands), 23 November 1959, para.4, p. 1, at 80/1 in BL 1/5282/56, Public Records Office, Hong Kong.

48. The question was raised as an issue by the planners in April, and a final policy direct-ive issued by the Secretariat in June. See M117–8 and 92–8 (*Sites for Industry*) in BL 1/5282/56I, Public Records Office, Hong Kong.

49. Memorandum from the District Commissioner New Territories to the Director of Public Works, June 1962, at 114/1B in BL 1/5282/56I, Public Records Office, Hong Kong.

50. Minutes of the Land Development Planning Committee, 28 September 1962, Item 3, at 115 in BL 1/5282/56I, Public Records Office, Hong Kong.

51. Minutes of a Planning Meeting, 5 July 1963, para.9, p. 3, at 18 in BL 6/5282/56I, Buildings and Lands Registry, Hong Kong.

52. Development Division, *Report on Development at Castle Peak* (Hong Kong, Public Works Department, 1965). Copy at 11A in LSO 123/HPG/63A, Buildings and Lands Registry, Hong Kong.

53. *Castle Peak District — Outline Zoning Plan LCP 11A* of 20 March 1964 — this was the circulated version of Plan LCP 8.

54. Planning Division, *Proposed Castle Peak District Outline Development Plan: Ex-planatory Notes for Plan No. LCP 28A* (Hong Kong, Crown Lands and Survey Depart-ment, 1965), para.B2, p. 1.

55. Extracts from Planning Division (1965), see note 54 above.

56. This refers to C. Buchanan, *Traffic in Towns: A Study of the Long Term Problems of Traffic in Urban Areas* (London, Her Majesty's Stationery Office, 1963). The style is referred to by Wigglesworth, one of the Castle Peak planners, in J.M. Wigglesworth, 'The Development of New Towns', in D.J. Dwyer (ed.), *Asian Urbanisation: A Hong Kong Casebook* (Hong Kong, Hong Kong University Press, 1971), p. 60.

57. Minutes of a meeting on 5 April 1965, para.22, p. 3, at 36 in LSO 123/HPG/63B, Buildings and Lands Registry, Hong Kong.

58. Town Planning Board Paper No. 100, 18 February 1966, *Castle Peak and Shatin Outline Zoning Plans Nos. LCP/31A and LST/46A* (to be renumbered as LCP 32 and LST 47 respectively when published), para.8, p. 2, at 1/1 in TPB 10/11II, Town Planning Registry, Hong Kong. Proposals for a mass transit rail network in Hong Kong were under considera-tion at this time by consultants. The results were published as Freeman Fox, Wilbur Smith and Associates, *Hong Kong Mass Transport Study* (Hong Kong, Government Printer, 1967).

59. See Roger Bristow, *Land-use Planning in Hong Kong: History, Policies and Procedures* (Hong Kong, Oxford University Press, 1984), pp. 234–7.

60. Planning Division, *Castle Peak District Outline Zoning Plan No. LCP/32: Explanatory Statement* (Hong Kong, Crown Lands and Survey Department, 1967), para.12.2, p. 8.

61. Part of the consultant's investigations, published as Freeman Fox, Wilbur Smith and Associates (1967), see note 58 above.

62. Reported in Population and Housing Working Committee, *The Colony Outline Plan: Book 2, Chapter II — Report on Population and Housing* (Hong Kong, Crown Lands and Survey Office, 1969), pp. 111–27 and Appendix A, pp. 128–36.

63. Population and Housing Working Committee (1969), see note 62 above, pp. 111–2 with Plates 2.18–23.

64. Population and Housing Working Committee (1969), see note 62 above, pp. 124–5 with Plate 2.24.

65. Tuen Mun New Town Development Office, *Tuen Mun (Castle Peak) Outline Develop-ment Plan TM/1A–D* (Hong Kong, New Territories Development Department, 1974).

66. The four estates were Hip Wo (Area 37B) — 21,000; Sau Shing (Area 8) — 65,000; On Ting (Area 13B) — 23,000; and Leung Tin (Area 1) — 149,000. The full programme for new estates was given in Architectural Division, *10-Year Housing Programme — Part 1: New Estates, Housing Department* (Hong Kong, Housing Department, 1973).

67. Tuen Mun New Town Development Office, *Tuen Mun (Castle Peak) Outline Develop-ment Plan TM/1E: Explanatory Statement* (Hong Kong, New Territories Development Department, 1977), para.5.4, p. 5.

68. National Hydraulics Research Station, *Tuen Mun New Town: Physical Model Studies of Proposed Harbour Development* (Hong Kong, New Territories Development Department, 1978).

69. Scott Wilson Kirkpatrick & Partners, *Tuen Mun New Town Stage II Engineering*

Feasibility Study (Hong Kong, New Territories Development Department, 1976). This study was later extended in 1978 to include the three additional areas of Kwan Wat, Siu Lam, and Tai Lam Chung.

70. Scott Wilson Kirkpatrick & Partners, *Tuen Mun New Town Transport Study* (Hong Kong, New Territories Development Department, 1978).

71. Tuen Mun New Town Development Office (1977), see note 67 above, para.14.1, p. 19.

72. Yuncken Freeman Hong Kong, *Tuen Mun New Town Landscape Master Plan* (Hong Kong, New Territories Development Department, 1978).

73. Town Planning Board Paper No. 388, 17 June 1977 (Hong Kong, Town Planning Office, 1977), paras.3.1.1–3.2.1, p. 3.

74. See 15 to 30 in TPB 10/11II, Town Planning Registry, Hong Kong, for Town Planning Board discussions during this period.

75. Town Planning Board Paper No. 428, 2 February 1979 (Hong Kong, Town Planning Office, 1979).

76. The Tuen Mun Public Transport Strategy II was endorsed by the New Territories Development Progress Committee in October 1975. Following subsequent approval by the Transport Advisory Committee and the Executive Council, negotiations were under way by late 1979 with Hong Kong Tramways (the operator of the much older system on Hong Kong Island) as the potential operator of the new network. A special Transport Plan Implementation Group was also established to consider the implementation requirements of the new system.

77. Town Planning Board Paper No. 428 (1979), see note 75 above, para.2.3.2, p. 2.

78. Tuen Mun New Town Development Office, *Outline Development Plan: Explanatory Statement to ODP No. LTM 1/0/1E* (Hong Kong, New Territories Development Department, 1982), para.1.8, p. 2.

79. See New Territories Development Consultants, *Development Investigation of the North Western New Territories* (Hong Kong, New Territories Development Department, 1981), 4 vols.

80. Scott Wilson Kirkpatrick & Partners, *Tuen Mun New Town Stage II Extension Engineering Feasibility Study* (Hong Kong, New Territories Development Department, 1978).

81. Tuen Mun New Town Development Office, *Tuen Mun New Town: Eastern Extension Area Planning Statement* (Hong Kong, New Territories Development Department, 1985), para.1.4, pp. 1–2.

6. The New Towns of the Eighties: Junk Bay and Tin Shui Wai

JUNK BAY and Tin Shui Wai represent a foruth wave of new-town building in Hong Kong, if one allows for the inclusion of Kwun Tong as the first, and the expanded towns in the New Territories — finally designated as new towns in 1979 — as the third. The so-called 'market towns' (the third) are, in fact, something of a hybrid. Their initial expansion began purely as a series of suitable sites for individual public housing estates introduced as part of the new ten-year housing programme of 1973. It was not until the potential impact of these major units of new immigrant populations upon the existing small towns was realized, and further expansions were thought necessary as the public-housing targets were revised, that planning and designation as 'new' towns was deemed necessary. In design terms too, while some lessons were learnt from the development history of the earlier and much larger first-generation towns, so-called, the procedures used and the design principles followed very much replicated those being applied elsewhere. Only in one or two instances were there cases of real innovation, such as the landscape treatment of Tai Po; and for significant change, Hong Kong had to await the new virgin-site developments of the 1980s. The planning of the two towns of Junk Bay and Tin Shui Wai, therefore, represents most comprehensively the current state of the art of Hong Kong new-town planning.

There are a number of reasons for concentrating our attention on these two sites. It has already been mentioned that much of Hong Kong new-town planning has consisted of incremental learning by experience, but also over the twenty or so years of the programme there have been long and sustained periods of economic growth which have led to a rapid rise in people's living standards and expectations. It is only natural to expect, therefore, that later new-town developments should reflect both these influences by utilizing better methodologies and by implementing higher design standards.

Both these revisions are in evidence here, but for these two sites other important influences have also been at work. Tin Shui Wai began as a private enterprise initiative, and while its siting can be regarded as something of a planning problem, the design initially presented a refreshing reworking of Hong Kong government and private-sector requirements into a new urban form. Junk Bay also proved innovative in another way, partly because the same planning consultants were involved with it as with Tin Shui Wai. More particularly, for Hong Kong, it represents the first of the eight new towns where major and explicit planning choices were made and described as part of the strategic design of the town. Perhaps for the first time also, form, function, and detailed design can be said to have been fully integrated in the approach taken. However, it is a form of new-town planning that has not been without its problems, particularly in the incrementalist environment of new-town development in Hong Kong.

Junk Bay New Town

Initial Moves

While Junk Bay new town, as planned now, (see Fig. 6.6) is essentially a creation of the 1980s, it began life contemporaneously with the other early large new towns of Hong Kong as one of the possible reclamations of Scott and Wilson's 1950s studies.[1] Because of deep water in the main bay, their proposed scheme was confined to the larger of the two inlets, extending towards Tseung Kwan (as in Fig. 6.1). New access roads would have been provided to Ap Chai Wan from Clearwater Bay Road and from Kwun Tong, serving new terraces formed by the reclamation borrow areas on the hills to the west of the bay. The draft scheme put forward by the consultants was for 158 hectares, including 68 hectares of terracing to house an estimated population of about 150,000.

Certain problems were, however, recognized even at this initial stage. For example, 'quite apart from considerations of visibility on the airport, Junk Bay is largely enclosed and sheltered by hills, and in these circumstances pollution of the atmosphere should be avoided',[2] while on the western side the terraces for housing were all at altitudes over 76 metres above the industrial areas on the reclamation, which made for access problems. The reclamation itself was also viewed unfavourably.

A number of factors adversely affect the prospects of large-scale reclamation at Junk Bay. These are the depths of water in the bay, the unfavourable foundation conditions, the relative inaccessibility of the area by land and the difficulty of providing an adequate water supply [tunnelling was required].[3]

It is not surprising therefore, that Junk Bay appeared low on the list of government development priorities of the time.

Yet, as with Sha Tin, there was in fact a still earlier proposal for town development at Junk Bay, for in 1956 the planners had prepared a tentative sketch plan (Plan L/JB/1/1, see Fig. 6.1) setting out proposals upon which Scott and Wilson no doubt based their own design. The design concept utilized was very similar to that then under way contemporaneously in Kwun Tong, just across the dividing hills. Again the main reclamation was for industry, with a small area specified for workers' housing adjacent to the north end of the reclaimed main inlet. The borrow-area terraces, as in Kwun Tong, were set aside generally for housing purposes, while a new township centre was suggested for the Hang Hau area in the eastern inlet. No population or industrial target figures were supplied with the plan, so it is not possible to be clear what size exactly the new town was expected to be, though a figure not unlike that devised for the 1959 scheme would be about right.

Junk Bay did not figure seriously in government's 1959 review of where its second new town should be, though it was stated that 'the Consultant's proposals are still being considered in detail. When development proposals are settled the area should be town planned to let private developers build

Fig. 6.1   Junk Bay new town — development schemes, 1956–1987.

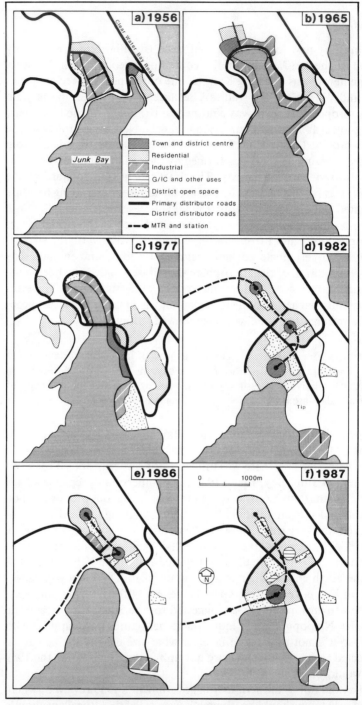

Sources: Based on consultants' reports, Outline Zoning Plans and Outline Development
Plans, Town Planning Office, Buildings and Lands Department, Hong Kong
government.

here'.[4] In the same paper it was also noted that a search for alternative sites for the shipbreaking industry and related steel rolling mills that were then about to be displaced from Gin Drinkers Bay and elsewhere had become urgent, and, in the event, the chosen site proved to be Junk Bay. Thus, the area became a repository for unwanted or obnoxious industries that could not be sited elsewhere in Hong Kong. By the following year, 1960, the District Commissioner New Territories was writing:

as regards Junk Bay, I doubt whether the proposed layout ... conforms closely to the Consultant's proposals and, as in the case of Sha Tin, I think that we should more properly regard the Consultant's report as having been scrapped.[5]

In fact, already in the previous December, the Public Works Sub-committee had agreed that Junk Bay should be left to the shipbreakers for the next five to ten years, and Junk Bay as a new-town site had effectively been shelved.

Nevertheless, the planners continued to refine their own long-term proposals, for when they produced a suggested layout for the new industrial area in October 1961 (Plan LJB/10A) it proved to be virtually an update of their 1956 ideas. The new industrial sites were now to be on reclamation platforms on each side of the bay's western inlet, while housing was once again proposed for the western hill terraces formed from the borrow sites, together with a smaller area of land at the head of the inlet. This latter area also contained a site for central services as well as similar suggestions for Hang Hau town. While the plan was formally endorsed in May 1962,[6] little happened on the ground other than reclamation for the industrial development, and it was not until the search for resettlement estate sites brought a proposal for such an estate in Junk Bay in 1965 that urban planning in Junk Bay really began in earnest.

In February 1965, a new draft outline zoning plan was presented to the Land Development Planning Committee with the aim of controlling development over the whole of the Junk Bay/Clearwater Bay Peninsula area.[7]

It is intended that the plan should introduce definite zoning proposals to coordinate and control future development. One of the main objects is to maintain the major part of this attractive peninsula in its natural state ... For this reason it is proposed to stop any further isolated ribbon development along the Clearwater Bay Road by providing low density residential areas grouped in appropriate places to meet the future demand.[8]

Given the sale of 32 hectares of new reclamation in the western arm of the bay for shipbreaking and allied industries, the planners again recommended utilizing the adjacent new borrow areas for high-density housing, including a new resettlement estate for 160,000 people, ostensibly to provide labour for the new industry. The design population for the whole town was envisaged at 279,000. It will be noted from Fig. 6.1b that sea access for the industrial sites was maintained, while new road links were now to connect the proposed settlement with Clearwater Bay Road, Kwun Tong, and Lei Yue Mun. It was stated that: 'it is anticipated that the plan will be implemented over a period of ten to fifteen years as a result of co-ordinated action by Government and private enterprise',[9] the by now classic Hong Kong new-town development model.

In practice, while it was agreed within government that the plan would be treated as an informal interdepartmental guideline, any further progression of the plan in its statutory or even departmental form was thought premature, particularly due to the lack of any essential public services, especially water supply, in Junk Bay itself. There was also no programmed road link to Kwun Tong either, and both were felt to make the new plan impossible to implement. The plan, therefore, got no further than a draft, and statutory planning for Junk Bay was deferred for more than twenty years.

The year 1965 also marked the end of the boom years for the new Junk Bay industry, for while 15 firms moved to Junk Bay between 1962 and 1965, none came thereafter, and a number of the reclaimed lots remained empty even though some were theoretically taken up. Industrial recession hit the Territory's local steel industry (for which the shipbreakers provided most of the raw material). The situation proved particularly difficult, not only because of problems in the local building industry, from the property cycle downturn, but also because of severe price competition from overseas competitors.

Despite pleas, the government refused to assist, believing in the long-term non-viability of the industry anyway, with the result that development in Junk Bay ground to a halt. Eventually, in June 1970, the Industrial Sites Co-ordination Committee (a sub-committee of the Land Development Planning Committee) finally agreed to a relaxation of user restrictions for the existing sites in the Bay in an attempt to revive the area's fortunes and to fully utilize the sites already provided. However, this attempt was hindered by a continuing lack of proper facilities, particularly the water supply, and this topic became a matter of intensive debate between the existing industrialists in the area and the government during the 1970–2 period.

The next major step towards a more integrated development approach to the problems of the area came in February 1974, when the renamed Land Development Policy Committee agreed that Junk Bay should be re-examined as the largest remaining reservoir of potential industrial land near to the main urban area.[10] It was argued at the time that the area had potential for capital-intensive, low-density industries, particularly based on engineering and chemical processing, which were not very suitable for urban locations but which were very much needed to provide raw materials for other Hong Kong industries.

Accordingly, Maunsell Consultants Asia were appointed in the first instance to determine, in broad terms, 'the area of land in Junk Bay which can be economically formed and serviced and whether the impact on the environment from industry which could be accommodated on that land

1a Construction under way at Kowloon Tong Garden Suburb, December 1926
Source: Public Records Office, Hong Kong, ref. 3/4/99

1b Kowloon Tong Garden Suburb in May 1983
Source: Survey and Mapping Office, Buildings and Lands Department, Hong Kong, ref. RC10.48713.16–5–83

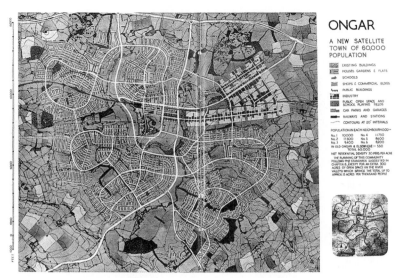

ONGAR

A NEW SATELLITE
TOWN OF 60,000
POPULATION

2a Sir Patrick Abercrombie's prototype British new-town design
Source: Abercrombie, *Greater London Plan 1944* (London, His Majesty's Stationery Office, 1945), drawing — detailed studies — Ongar, between pp. 170–1, Crown copyright reserved; reproduced with the permission of the Controller of Her Majesty's Stationery Office

2b Aerial view of Cumbernauld New Town central area, Scotland
Source: Cumbernauld New Town Development Corporation, United Kingdom, 1987, copyright reserved

3a Stage One of the Kwun Tong New Town reclamation in progress in December 1960
Source: Hong Kong Government Information Services, ref. 754/1

3b Kwun Tong New Town in May 1963
Source: Hong Kong Government Information Services, ref. 2164/1

4a Tsuen Wan in March 1960
Source: Hong Kong Government Information Services, ref. 592/6

4b Tsuen Wan New Town in June 1972
Source: Hong Kong Government Information Services, ref. 8216/58

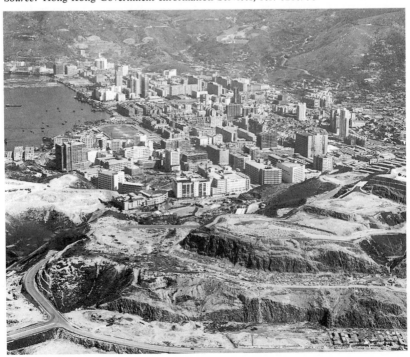

5a Sha Tin New Town in July 1978
Source: Hong Kong Government Information Services, ref. 18408/55

5b Aerial view of Sha Tin New Town in April 1986
Source: Survey and Mapping Office, Buildings and Lands Department, Hong Kong, ref. 1.04916.28–4–86

6a Early stages of the Tuen Mun (Castle Peak) reclamation, February 1971
Source: Hong Kong Government Information Services, ref. 7134/100

6b Tuen Mun New Town in April 1986
Source: Survey and Mapping Office, Buildings and Lands Department, Hong Kong, ref. 1.04805.28–4–86

7a Model of the initial 1976 design for Sha Tin Town Centre
Source: Hong Kong Government Information Services, ref. 13881/6

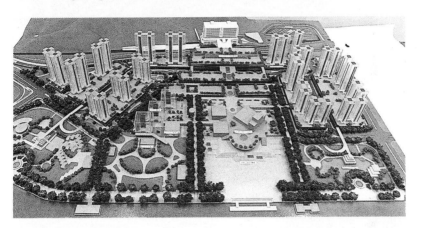

7b Sha Tin New Town Centre — the conceptual model of 1982 prepared by the consultants,
   Yuncken Freeman Hong Kong
Source: Hong Kong Government Information Services, ref. 26864/5

7c Model of the initial government design for Tuen Mun Town Centre, 1976
Source: Hong Kong Government Information Services, ref. 13878/11

8a Public housing design in the new towns — Sun Chui Estate Sha Tin
Source: Hong Kong Housing Authority, Hong Kong, 1987, copyright reserved

8b Fo Tan Industrial Estate, Area 16, Sha Tin in 1982
Source: Hong Kong Government Information Services, ref. 32572/15

was acceptable'.[11] The whole exercise was controlled by a special sub-committee of the reformed Industrial Land Sub-committee (of the Land Development Policy Committee). While it was mentioned at the time that the government planners had tentative proposals for residential develop-ments in the area for up to 58,000 people as a target, 'it was agreed that, as residential development was not the prime purpose of the study, the Stage I report should assume no plans for residential development other than that arising from the existing local residents'.[12]

The outcome of the consultant's initial studies was a clear warning that the physical features and topography of the area would lead to the con-centration of any pollutants that might be emitted in the valley. It was therefore argued that any industrial development allowed would have to be non-polluting — that is, to have no aerial or liquid emissions from the factories. It followed from this that any advantages from developing the site for industry were likely to be very limited, and accordingly the govern-ment's steering group advised the Industrial Land Sub-committee in October 1975 'that the ... Sub-Committee should view with serious doubt the advisability of marking a commitment to the industrial development of Junk Bay and proceeding with the [proposed] Stage II Study'.[13]

The recommendation was duly accepted, and the whole matter came before the Land Development Policy Committee the following August (1976). In a paper prepared by the New Territories Administration it was suggested that the whole future of Junk Bay should be reviewed once more.[14] It was noted that the Rennie's Mill cottage area in the south-west needed upgrading or redevelopment, that the shipbreaking sites had never been fully utilized, and that Hang Hau, though a long-established centre, badly needed improvement. It was also argued that 'as a composite unit they [the above problems] could provide the basis of a more extensive development scheme'[15] to put them right.

Additionally, the paper pointed out that:

a need has been recently identified for the provision of more sites for public hous-ing. It would seem that Junk Bay has something to offer in this respect: it cannot be used for the purpose originally projected, but much of the ground work con-nected with the original intention would be relevant, and would perhaps reduce the time necessary to put in hand other development of the area. Development of the area as a new town to provide public housing would require the provision of more employment opportunities, and the provision of light industry. In the three existing areas of Junk Bay there is a basis on which to build a new town, and at the same time the development proposed would deal with the problems of those existing areas which must, at some time, be faced.[16]

The outcome was, therefore, an agreement that Maunsell should con-tinue their stage two investigations, but on the basis that they were to ex-amine possible staged development as a seventh new town for Hong Kong. The development process for Junk Bay as a new town had now effect-ively begun, though not without some hiccups along the way.

The First Proposals

The consultants were required in their brief of 1976 to conform to the following guidelines.

Planning is to be in accordance with an outline planning strategy and design parameters to be agreed with the Town Planning Office [note *not* the New Territories Development Department that was then overseeing the other new towns in Hong Kong] ... A draft outline zoning plan will be produced by the Consultants ... which will provide for a balanced development, comprising public and private housing, supporting amenities and facilities, employment opportunities, and compatible industry, to approved standards.[17]

The consultants then formulated an investigative programme on the format set out in Fig. 6.2, which was an adaptation of the classic survey-analysis-plan scenario so familiar to planning students everywhere.

In the course of their analysis, a considerable amount of attention was paid to the new Junk Bay controlled tip to the south-east of the site, which formed an essential part of the ten-year Solid Waste Disposal Programme that had been agreed two years before in 1974 and which was to start in 1980. While the concentrated lorry traffic would create problems, the large borrow-area platforms created to provide the land-fill to cover the tip presented a much better proposition for high-density public-housing estates than the more confined areas previously considered on the western slopes of the Bay.

This affected the strategic analysis of the options undertaken by Yuncken Freeman Hong Kong as the planning consultant in October 1977 (see Fig. 6.3). They recognized five sub-areas around the bay as having rather different characteristics, and within each of which, they argued, were various planning options giving varying land-use mixes ranging from single-use zones to different combinations of housing and industry. The town-centre function was thought possible on one of two possible sites on the main reclamation. Nevertheless, development appeared likely to be extremely dispersed when compared with more traditional urban settlement patterns in Hong Kong, especially because of the major horizontal and vertical differences between the scattered developments. This was thought to be likely to favour a district-centre-based urban form.

The preferred strategy proposed that the platforms to the north-west and south-east should be largely public housing, each supporting their own district centres (see Fig. 6.1c and Fig. 6.3 top), while the area around the town centre was to concentrate on private housing provision. Rennie's Mill was left to be selectively developed with only a small additional population target. Industry was split into two, each side of the remaining water inlet. The strategy suggested an additional population in the Bay area of some 266,000, with 71 per cent in public and 21 per cent in private high-density housing. About 35,000 additional jobs were likely to be provided — slightly below the balanced target, while given the target population figure it was thought that a viable extension of the mass transit railway

Fig. 6.2   The consultant's planning task for the Junk Bay Development Study, 1977.

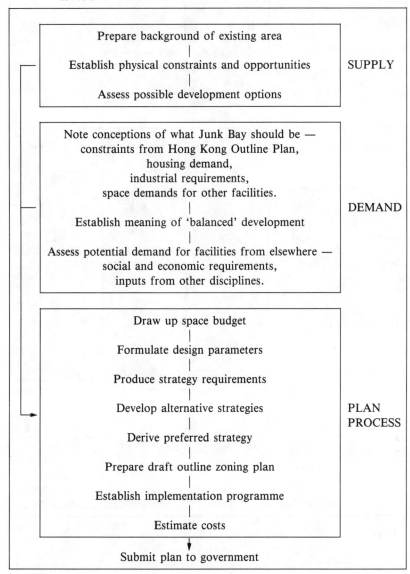

Prepare background of existing area Establish physical constraints and opportunities Assess possible development options	SUPPLY
Note conceptions of what Junk Bay should be — constraints from Hong Kong Outline Plan, housing demand, industrial requirements, space demands for other facilities. Establish meaning of 'balanced' development Assess potential demand for facilities from elsewhere — social and economic requirements, inputs from other disciplines.	DEMAND
Draw up space budget Formulate design parameters Produce strategy requirements Develop alternative strategies Derive preferred strategy Prepare draft outline zoning plan Establish implementation programme Estimate costs	PLAN PROCESS

Submit plan to government

Source: Adapted from Maunsell Consultants Asia, *Junk Bay Urban Development Study: Input from Town Planning Office* (Hong Kong, Maunsell Consultants Asia, 1977), at 17/A1 in BL 6/5282/56III, Public Records Office, Hong Kong, pp. 2–5.

from Kwun Tong was not likely, thus leaving access to the town to be by a new trunk road from the west including a short tunnel near Yau Tong.

In effect, these new proposals for a new town rested on three essential assumptions: an acceptance that the existing industries at the head of the

Fig. 6.3   Alternative design scenarios for Junk Bay new town.

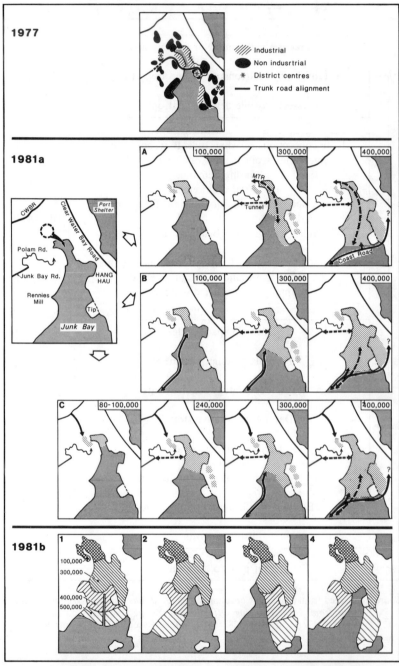

Sources: *Junk Bay Development Study Technical Note No.2 — Junk Bay Town: Alternative Development Concepts Initial Evaluation* at 40/3 in LW (SPU) 70/61/02 VI, Lands and Works Registry, Hong Kong.
Also shown as Diagram 10 in Junk Bay Development Office, *Junk Bay Development Study: Inception Report, February 1981* (Hong Kong, New Territories Development Department, 1981).

Bay should remain; an attempt to minimize the amount and cost of rock excavation required to form platforms; and a limit of reclamation works to areas of moderate water depth. The result was a pattern of dispersed areas of development at major differences of level; a concept that was neither economical of space nor transport. It is not surprising therefore that it failed to find favour with the government's planners.

In reviewing the proposed strategy in 1978, the steering group noted that only about one-third of the required reclamation fill was to come from the Junk Bay area itself (which made it an expensive proposal), and that the preferred strategy produced a very linear town strongly dependent on the efficiency of its internal road system. However these problems did not prove to be the main doubts expressed within the government about the scheme, even though a decision was taken within the Public Works Department in November 1978 to support the consultant's proposals.[18]

It is considered that the industrial land provision at Junk Day should be a Colony-wide target particularly in relation to Kwun Tong development and the Territory-wide demand. It should not be based on a balanced urban development for Junk Bay New Town as proposed since both design and projected population of Hong Kong in 1996 may not justify another New Town at Junk Bay, unless long term Government Policy would allow further migration from Mainland China ... All planning strategies suggested in the so-called Outline Zoning Plan are considered too subjective and rather premature at this stage. In fact a more detailed planning study is required before any such recommendations can be accepted and a proper Outline Zoning Plan can be prepared.[19]

Doubt was also expressed on just what exactly the 'clean-up' recommended for the existing industrial areas might actually involve; but perhaps the most damning comment came from elsewhere within government:

Even looking at the present figures, I cannot support the proposed strategy because of the (highly under-stated) *imbalance* between forecast cash outlay and forecast receipts. If we are to have public housing in this new town we should at least try to strike a balance in the equation, by having a significant proportion of the public housing under the Home Ownership Scheme. It is unreasonable to try to achieve balanced development, socially and environmentally, but not balanced finances.[20]

The normally unmentioned meaning of 'balanced development' in Hong Kong had now formally been brought into play — that the government expected its commitments in terms of costs and benefits ultimately to return the cost accountant's required profit margin upon completion, and Junk Bay, as proposed, did not comply. As a further delaying tactic, it was also suggested that the requirement for Junk Bay ought to be looked at within the wider questions of land availability in Hong Kong then being investigated as part of the initial studies for the proposed Territorial Development Strategy,[21] and this last question was to bedevil planning in Junk Bay for most of the early 1980s.

Yet, it was consideration within the government of the land question which provided the next impetus to implementing the new-town proposal.

In 1978, the Secretariat was under some pressure: 'it is highly desirable politically to be in a position to demonstrate a continuous plan for land production on a regular basis, and the Governor wishes to make some announcements in the October speech'.[22] Also:

the recent Report of the Working Group on New Territories Urban Land Acquisitions, which was approved by the Governor-in-Council, recommended that greater priority must be given to making available land for exchanges. This recommendation cannot be passed over, as a much improved Government performance in making land available for exchanges was recognised as being crucial to the continued acceptance by those affected of the Government's systems of acquisition.[23]

It was, in part, a recognition of these concerns that led to an immediate decision in Land Development Policy Committee in August 1978 to upgrade the Ma On Shan scheme (Sha Tin) to Category 'A' in the public works programme. But, although it was noted that Junk Bay was the largest potential area then available, and that the New Territories Administration was pressing for an early start, it was decided that full consideration of the consultant's 1978 report was required first.[24] Nevertheless, some preliminary steps were put in hand. Investigation work for a water supply, and the main access road from the west were upgraded to Category 'B' in the 1979 programme, with a view to commencing two areas in Junk Bay as a first stage. Once again, preliminaries born of necessity were beginning to pre-empt the long-term decision, as in Tuen Mun in the 1960s.

The immediate result of these moves was a requirement to deal with the already known and expected environmental problems in the new-town area, particularly from pollution. This especially meant the effects of the existing industry upon the now planned adjacent public housing estates. It was already thought that while the industry might be able to be brought up to an acceptable standard, though at a high cost, it would still remain noisy and visually intrusive. Removal would either mean allowing the resident industrialists to convert their sites to other uses at a suitable premium, or for the sites to be bought back by government. However, any resiting of the industries elsewhere in Hong Kong — most likely on Tsing Yi island, was also thought likely to pose further problems. It was, however, clear at the time that there was insufficient information on these issues, at least in terms of formulating a government policy, and so a further study was commissioned early in 1979 from the Hong Kong Productivity Centre,[25] in order to look at the viability of the Junk Bay industries long-term, and to assess potential policy options and costs for the government.

The conclusions, which were finally presented in May 1981, suggested that the shipbreaking industry was not likely to be viable as a long-term prospect, and was of little benefit to its 'downstream' industries. Steel rolling was seen to have some advantages in terms of being a local supplier for the Hong Kong construction industry, but was stated as being vulnerable to price competition from overseas. Others, such as the existing industrial gases plant were argued to be efficient and likely to remain.

The whole discussion was consolidated within an internal government report on the whole future of policy towards the Junk Bay industries that was prepared for consideration in June 1981.

In parallel with this set of investigations, the Land Development Policy Committee was still deliberating on how to proceed with the main proposal. At its meetings at the beginning of 1979 it decided to authorize the feasibility studies into water supply, environmental and geotechnical background, roads and potential fill; while a new steering group was formed to co-ordinate the studies and to safeguard the development potential of Junk Bay.[26] The terms of reference for the new group were:

to coordinate preparatory investigations of Junk Bay;
to identify and resolve problems encountered during the preliminary investigations;
to review the development proposals of the Consultants in the light of the preparatory investigations;
to recommend to the Land Development Policy Committee by the end of 1979 a development strategy for Junk Bay; and
to ensure that the development potential of Junk Bay is not prejudiced.[27]

General consideration of the Territory's land production problems were, however, still continuing and came to a head in August 1979. Consideration in the Land Development Policy Committee of a paper prepared jointly by the New Territories Administration, the Secretary for Housing, and the New Territories Development Department[28] resulted in a final decision to implement development at both Ma On Shan and Junk Bay, in order to forestall a projected shortfall in land for the public housing programme. It was this decision that led to the setting up of a new new-town development office for Junk Bay and Sai Kung in 1980 (to undertake work on the new town, and sub-regional planning work as part of the Territorial Development Strategy preliminaries), as well as reappointment of Maunsell's as main consultants for the proposed town (but now with an enhanced support team of professional planning, landscape, tunnelling, pollution, and property experts).

Another interesting innovation in 1980 was evidence of the direct interest of the new Strategic Planning Unit, set up in that year, in the planning parameters being discussed for the new town. It is clear that they wished to see the highest densities applied as reasonably possible to allow 'the full development potential' of the area to be exploited. It was argued that the town should be almost entirely high density: 'as far as high-class housing is concerned, in order to achieve a "balanced" town, it is felt there are ample opportunities for such development in other parts of the Sai Kung Peninsula'[29] (that is, of the low-density variety). Also 'the concept of "balanced" development should be given a broad interpretation in that I would wish to see that full account is taken of employment opportunities at San Po Kong, Kwun Tong, and even Chai Wan [on Hong Kong Island] assuming that it will be practical to provide satisfactory transportation connections'.[30] For the first time, integration of the town within its sub-regional context was being argued as crucial to the development of a strategy for the town itself. New-town planning in Hong Kong was maturing!

Planning the Town

The first meetings of the staff of the Junk Bay New Town Development Office set out some basic design problems associated with the town which would require investigation and resolution. The status of both Hang Hau Town and Rennie's Mill concerning the amount of possible redevelopment required, the need for a comprehensive public transport network both internally and externally, and what to do about the existing industry, were all specifically included.

The study is a comprehensive planning and engineering study ... to draw up firm proposals for the provision of serviced land and infrastructure for the development of Junk Bay New Town, and to carry out investigations and design work for the development of Junk Bay Phase 2 [denoted as Zones A and E — the main reclamation at the head of the bay, and the slope platforms to the west]. Because the implications of the development of a new town will stretch beyond the immediate area it will be necessary to carry out studies in the Sai Kung District hinterland ... To achieve these objectives, a multi-disciplinary approach is being adopted.[31]

One consequence of this attempt at the broader approach was a strong objection at the first meeting of the Consultant's Steering Group in November 1980 to a policy directive to the effect that initial housing development should take absolute priority and be commenced at the earliest opportunity — political requirements with a vengeance and a rerun of the requirements of the 1960s. Yet, it was accepted 'that development must be looked at across a wider assessment of priorities than may have been the case in the past, and that questions of accessibility and land use programming balance must explicitly be taken into account'.[32] To these ends the study was organized into three parallel investigatory streams — on the new town itself, the initial areas for development, and the hinterland, with various specialist sub-groups within the teams for such topics as transport matters, Rennie's Mill, and Hang Hau.

Planning for the new town (and Shankland Cox were the new planning consultants, fresh from their experience with Tin Shui Wai) began with a target base of 300,000 people, which, utilizing Strategic Planning Unit housing guidelines issued in November 1980, suggested a site area of between 370 and 390 hectares. It was also thought that another basic parameter was likely to be that up to 70 per cent of the total trips generated were likely to be external to the town's boundaries. This caused an immediate and urgent search for means of providing sufficient transportation access to the new town in time for the expected first public housing intake in 1986.

By January 1981, despite some criticism of the breadth of the strategic analysis, a preliminary look at broad-brush forms of development based on possible mass transit routes was in hand, based on the 'tight' urban

form that was now favoured in place of the more dispersed pattern of
the 1978 proposals (see Fig. 6.3, 1981a). It was also thought desirable that
the water areas at the head of the Bay should be completely reclaimed,
and that the idea of an open space/airway corridor along the valley in
some form should be encouraged as a planning concept. Finally, it was
agreed that higher densities should be linked with any possible reserved-
track public transport system.

The Junk Bay Development Office set out the following initial markers
for the planning study:

The draft 1978 Outline Zoning Plan [from Maunsell's earlier study] should be
regarded as a minimum growth option for planning purposes. A 'residential
only' scenario should be examined — the 'unbalanced' town with employment
demand largely met in urban Hong Kong and Kowloon. Also to be considered
should be a 'no-car/use public transport' option . . . A maximum growth option
should be postulated and examined based on the physical limits of forming land
for developments rather than other thresholds such as transport.[33]

It was also argued that access was likely to be the key factor in planning
development of the town, and that even taking a longer term view the
structure and nature of the town's internal transport system would be an
important determinant in the distribution of land uses and facilities within
the new town. As with much of British new-town planning of the 1970s
(see Chapter 1), the urban form was now about to be determined by the
internal movement requirements (see Fig. 6.5).

Government also had its own objectives for the town:

Cost Effectiveness: study recommendations must be cost effective in terms of
Government expenditure;
Population Growth: the plan must make provision for substantial population
growth in the study area;
Comprehensive Framework: the plan must provide a clear framework for the
development and control of land use throughout the study area;
Feasibility: the plan must be robust, and together with any legislative and administrative changes proposed, must be capable of implementation within a clearly
defined programme.[34]

From these varied requirements the Junk Bay planners set out a full set
of goals and objectives (see Fig. 6.4),[35] which were taken up by the consultants, together with some initial thoughts on a development strategy
for the town (see Fig. 6.3, 1981a).

Four major constraints were recognized in formulating the design for
the town — the need to locate initial areas on easily developed land outside existing village boundaries (this favoured the eastern flank of the bay);
the capacity of the interim water supply; the transport threshold of the
upgraded Po Lam Road extension which would have to provide the initial
access for the town; and the constraints set by the existing and proposed
landscaping. Other controls were set by the land formation requirements
and the constraints caused by existing urban development.

Fig. 6.4   Goals and objectives for the planning of Junk Bay.

(a) Initial Goals set by the Junk Bay Development Office

The Economy: to provide a framework for the self-sustained economic development of the study area

Employment: to make available an adequate range and number of employment opportunities to provide full employment for the working population of the study area

Housing: to house all residents of the study area in permanent dwellings constructed to standards commensurate with anticipated social values

Accessibility: to ensure convenient access to a full range of social and economic activities and facilities

Public Health: to provide comprehensive utilities and make available health facilities for all residents of the study area

Social Facilities: to make available a comprehensive range of retail, cultural, educational, and recreational facilities for the population in the study area

Environment: to improve the quality of the physical environment of the study area

---

(b) Plan Goals set by the Junk Bay Consultant Team

Implementation Goals

Cost Effectiveness: minimum capital cost per head, especially related to land formation, provision of utilities, and transport links; earliest possible return on public investment

Feasibility: ease of implementation within current legislation, government procedures, and socio-economic practices, taking account of any desirable and feasible changes

Flexibility: plan to function at different levels of population and local employment and to accept internal changes in socio-economic profile and types of activity

Programming: continuous smooth development through related but self-contained packages of public investments, and associated private investments; final goals to be achieved so far as possible at each stage of development

Final Goals

Balanced Development: appropriate degree of balance between population, local employment, and services, taking account of interactions between Junk Bay, metropolitan area, and hinterland

Environmental Quality: integration of town with natural environment and creation of high standard of urban environment

Cost and Convenience in Use: promotion of socio-economic interactions by convenient and economical distribution of land uses in relation to movement networks (urban function and economics)

External Links: transport links to metropolitan area and hinterland adequate for target populations and expected degrees of interaction

Interaction with Existing Uses: minimum physical and socio-economic disruption of existing settlements and activities, and promotion of their improvement and integration with the new town

---

Note: Goal set (a) had 33 sub-objectives, and goal set (b), initially 48.

(c) Evaluation Process for Checking Draft Alternate Strategies against Goals

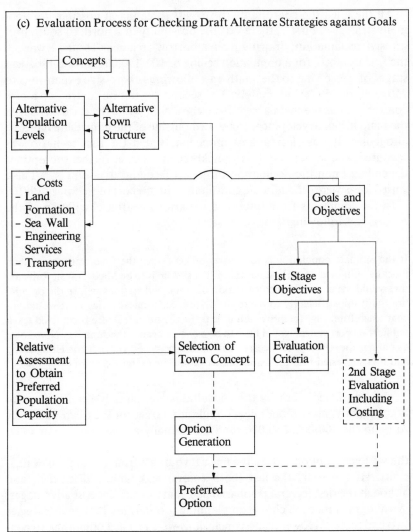

(d) Initial Evaluation of Strategic Development Concepts (See Fig. 6.3, 1981b)

| | Totals of | | | |
(Over 22 objectives)	1sts	2nds	3rds	4ths
Strategy A (1), centre of bay	7	3	8	4
Strategy B (3), east coast	5	5	8	4
Strategy C (2), west coast	7	10	2	3
Strategy D (4), both coasts	4	5	3	10

Sources: Junk Bay Development Office, *Situation Report*, November 1980, at 70/1 in ENV 70/61/02V, Buildings and Lands Registry, Hong Kong, p.21; Maunsell Consultants Asia, *Junk Bay Development Study, Junk Bay Town: Technical Note No.1 — Goals and Objectives, Initial Evaluation* (Hong Kong, Junk Bay Development Office, 1981), paras. 3.1–2, pp.2–3; and Maunsell Consultants Asia, *Junk Bay Development Study, Junk Bay Town: Technical Note No.2 — Alternative Development Concepts. Initial Evaluation* (Hong Kong, Junk Bay Development Office, 1981), p.8, fig.1, and p.22.

All these led the consultants to suggest three initial possible development strategies. Firstly, there was the possibility of a north to south progressive reclamation, drawing from a borrow area near Tseung Kwan, in the first instance, for a population ceiling of 100/150,000, with subsequent stages of borrowing to the south-east allowing progressive expansions to 250, 300, or 350,000 ultimately. The second suggestion centred on a new coastal road as the main access from the south; while the third envisaged the main urban development to be sited outside of the immediate bay area altogether. It was clear almost immediately that the first scenario was favoured, and within that, there quickly emerged three further sub-options depending upon the population target set (see Fig. 6.3, 1981a).[36] These varied ideas were set out in the consultant's first report of February 1981.[37]

In the comments from interested departments after circulation of the report, the following is of interest.

If the ultimate population is to be over 300,000 then the final transport system must be built in at an early stage and, if the system is to be Mass Transit Railway, this would mean the early construction of track and stations before the population built up sufficiently to make the system economically viable. It would appear, therefore, that the provision at least of the infrastructure for a fixed track public transport system would have to be a charge against the Junk Bay New Town as part of the development costs. This would be a new concept for Hong Kong and it is suggested that the implications should be examined at an early stage.[38]

Yet, continued work by the consultants was already leading them to argue that the most economical population target for the town was likely to be in the 300,000/350,000 range, eventually committed late in 1987, but with four possible location patterns (see Fig. 6.3, 1981b), of which the west coast option looked the most favourable from their initial evaluations. Of the four, the last (both coasts) was rapidly discarded, and although the first (central emphasis) had some significant cost advantages, it was agreed that the choice on planning grounds lay between strategies two and three.[39] However, no conclusions were reached other than to confirm the planning target as within the 300/350,000 population range.

By June 1981, some of the parameters affecting the detailed planning of the town had been resolved. The Housing Department had now decided that Rennie's Mill would be treated as a special improvement area, and it was agreed that the Junk Bay study should largely retain the existing 'village' and work around it as much as possible. It was also confirmed at the May steering group meeting that the planned housing mix should be set at 51 per cent public rented housing, 26 per cent public housing for sale, 22 per cent at private R1 and R2 high-density standards, and only one per cent low density private development (and that probably outside the new-town boundary). The major decisions now to be resolved concerned the industrial questions.

With regard to the existing industries, a special Working Group set up by the Junk Bay Development Office and the consultants produced a further report in June 1981.[40] They noted that at the head of the Bay less than half of the available land was, in fact, being used for industrial purposes, and that the shipbreaking and steel rolling industries in particular would be incompatible with urban development due to planning requirements and intolerable pollution levels. Accordingly, existing firms were placed into six categories[41] ranging from those which could be allowed to stay and would cause no problems to adjacent users, to those requiring various changes to their current processes, relocation within the Junk Bay area, or complete removal. The underdeveloped sites were recommended for immediate resumption.

For the future, a special paper was put before the Industrial Land Subcommittee in June 1981.[42] It was noted that while service employment related to the town itself might well be localized, other kinds of industrial employment were likely to be located nearby in the main urban core. This integration was particularly applicable to Junk Bay due to its proximity to the major industrial agglomerations at Kwun Tong and possibly Chai Wan. Later, Kowloon Bay, where there was a possible job surplus on the basis of current land zoning, was also thought likely to come into the picture.

In theory, this could allow Junk Bay to be planned purely as a residential commuter town, thus removing the pollution problems that industry would probably bring. On the other hand, the opportunity for waterfront industry on part of the reclamation represented the use of the last major opportunity of a location near to the main harbour, and hence it was argued that it ought to be encouraged in order to assist particularly with the then new policy initiative of diversifying the export industrial structure of Hong Kong. It was therefore argued that the concept of balanced development in Junk Bay should be maintained, particularly on grounds of avoiding sustained travel peaks on the town's transport links, with a concentration on high-rise, capital-intensive industry and some warehouse (godown) accommodation. This was agreed in committee subject to flexible application of the required planning standards and layouts.[43] Eventually this concept came to be reviewed again when Junk Bay was chosen as the site of Hong Kong's third industrial estate in 1988.

By August 1981, the consultants had agreed their first draft of a final design for the town (see Fig. 6.1d).[44] In addition to the 40 hectares of existing land, a new contiguous site was to be formed by 1996, from 283 hectares of reclamation and 95 hectares of borrow platforms, to house the 300,000 target population, with a first stage of 120,000 divided into five development packages. Development of the whole town would require improvements to Po Lam Road, followed by an extension of the Mass Transit Railway from Kwun Tong, and a major new road link by tunnel from the same area; while any further expansions would require yet more transport improvements in East Kowloon (investigated later, in 1986, as part of the Eastern Harbour Crossing studies). The land-use split for the town was set at 33 per cent residential, 17 per cent industrial, 11 per cent community uses, 13 per cent major open spaces, and 16 per cent for main communications. Two possible primary road networks were also considered — a box, or a single spine down the centre of the reclamation

Fig. 6.5 The consultants' district planning concept for Junk Bay new town.

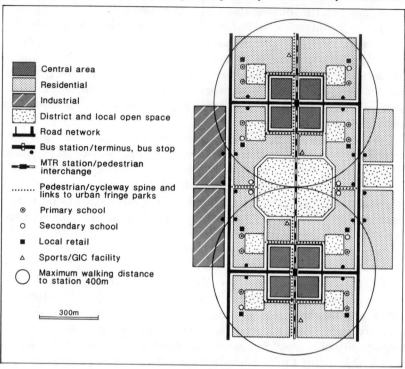

Source: Based on Figures 7.2 and 7.3 in Maunsell Consultants Asia, Shankland Cox, and Brian Clouston and Partners Hong Kong Limited, *Junk Bay Development Study: Interim Report, August 1981* (Hong Kong, New Territories Development Department, 1981), pp. 50 and 51.

— the latter being selected to allow for flexibility in the amount of material to be removed from Pak Shek Kok as the main borrow site to the south-east of the reclamation.

The key to the whole proposed urban form was the formation of three major districts of 80,000 each, concentrated in high-density developments centred on each district centre, which had a mass transit station as its focus (see Fig. 6.5) — the design allowed for 60,000 people to be within 400 metres of each station site. The town centre was placed on the waterfront at the southern end of the main reclamation, with a suggested floorspace of some 270,000 square metres, to which was added related office space. The largest industrial site, of 45 hectares, was placed south-east of the town beyond the existing controlled tip. As in Sha Tin, a separate network of pedestrian walks and cycleways was designed into the urban layout. The possibility of yet further expansion was suggested to be southwards along the western coast. However, it was apparent that crucial to the whole implementation of the scheme was a rapid government decision on both the removal of the existing non-compatible industries, and prompt commencement of the major new external transportation links, all of which were likely to expensive.

In coming to their conclusions the consultants emphasized that the population target was determined by the existence of major infrastructure thresholds, environmental constraints, and the costs of development for the different possible sizes of the town. Of the four urban options tested, those with the box-road network were rejected; while of those using the central spine, the western industrial area option had some cost and convenience advantages, but the eastern possibility was preferred on urban design and environmental grounds. This decision formed the basis of the final design (see Fig. 6.1d). Outside the town area itself, the preference was to concentrate low-density urban development in selected areas, and where urban and recreational uses clashed, to give preference to the latter, given the overall importance of the whole Sai Kung area to the recreational needs of Hong Kong as a whole.

The Steering Group, in commenting to the Land Development Policy Committee in September 1981 on the proposals,[45] endorsed the idea of a town of 300,000, provided that balanced development was followed as the design concept. They also noted that progress with the major transport infrastructure would determine the phasing of the town's development programme. Nevertheless, the proposals were accepted by the Committee, despite some doubts as to the costs and viability of the rail link that was the key to the town's design, and on the implications of the industrial policies suggested. Detailed planning for the town was now able to proceed.

The 1982 Plan

In early 1982, there was clear concern within government that having agreed to a planning concept for a 300,000-person town designed around a public transport rail link (on the classic Swedish new-town model), it had committed itself to long-term financial demands which it could now only modify with great difficulty: 'a town of 300,000 needs the MTR and the MTR needs 300,000 people in the town',[46] was a typical comment. It was a planning rigidity which some within the government heartily disliked. While the Housing Authority supported the proposals as they gave them a major public housing commitment, the strategic planners, then concerned with the Territorial Development Strategy, were much less convinced of the viability of a major ongoing commitment in Junk Bay, as against development possibilities elsewhere in Hong Kong.

Nevertheless, despite the doubts, detailed planning began with the circulation of the consultant's final proposals in March 1982.[47] The draft Outline Development Plan (see Fig. 6.1d) presented with the document envisaged a ten-year development programme for a final target population of 328,000, of which 300,000 would be in high-density towers. The expected work-force was estimated to be 159,000, of which 86,000 would be in industrial employment. The design followed the principles of the preferred strategy put forward by the consultants, and as in other Hong Kong new towns the proposed road network was hierarchical, based upon a tunnelled access road and central spine. Apart from 74,000 on two bor-row platform developments to the west, the remaining population was con-centrated around the mass transit stations, and the town-centre concept had now been enhanced by proposals for a multi-level development, major town park, and waterfront promenade. Also included in the main report were village concept plans for the existing small villages, and an overall urban fringe plan for the slope areas adjacent to the town itself. The whole scheme was now envisaged as a ten-package programme, associated with which were comprehensive transport and landscape planning proposals (see Fig. 7.2).

The comments from planners elsewhere in Hong Kong proved illuminating.

The statement that once commenced, the development momentum of Junk Bay cannot be curtailed below the point of maximum population potential (i.e. 300,000 persons) presumes that Junk Bay Outline Development Plan does not have the ability to respond to changing circumstances, be they economically, politically or physically orientated. If this is the case then Junk Bay is unique. The concept of adaptability is inherent in the structure of all other new towns, and is a basic premise of new town development planning, particularly so in the Hong Kong context.[48]

Other comments questioned the likelihood of sufficient industrial uptake to achieve the balance requirement, the non-likelihood of office develop-ment in the town, and the equity and wisdom of relying on a single high-quality public transport mode, especially as there was talk of giving the Mass Transit Railway Corporation a public transport monopoly in the town (as was to happen for the Kowloon–Canton Railway Corporation in Tuen Mun in 1986 as a part of the introduction of its Light Rail Transit system).

However, despite the reservations, papers were placed before the Land Development Policy Committee once again for decision in July 1982.[49] Already, the initial clearances for the first housing area of Package 1 had been completed, gazetting of the first new reclamation was ready to pro-ceed, and the first public housing intake of 49,000 was programmed for September 1986. Clearly, the public housing commitment was forcing the pace. It was argued that 'Junk Bay New Town can be viewed as a modest extension of the existing urban area meeting short term needs and this relationship tends to minimise the wider implications and impact of a com-mitment to development in this location'.[50]

However, it was noted that two problems still existed — the transport specialists were not in favour of a phased rail investment — it was argued to require 'all or nothing' from day one, while a recent request to extend the industrial land provision in the south-east needed further study.[51] The result was a decision that, while the consultant's proposals for the longer term were endorsed, only work on the first three packages should be com-mitted, both to meet immediate public housing needs and to allow some comparison within the Territorial Development Strategy investigations.

Nevertheless, it was agreed that there should be a further full review by mid-1983.

In the meantime, by August 1982, financial 'belt-tightening' within government had changed the situation such that it was felt that any approval of possible rail links should be deferred to the last possible moment, and that therefore Executive Council should be asked to give the go-ahead for the new town only in principle, with no population target specified and no commitment to a rail connection. The assent came in September, and from that date Junk Bay was officially and publicly born as Hong Kong's eighth new town, Tin Shui Wai having preceded it by only a few months.

Subsequent Developments

By December 1982, the strategic planners were arguing that:

it is now fairly clear that Junk Bay up to a population of about 175,000 persons will be required to maintain public rental housing targets and also to give us some flexibility to expand the scope of the Private Sector Participation Scheme/Home Ownership Scheme projects for which there is a substantial unfulfilled need.[52]

But actual implementation of the programme in terms of public works expenditures had now become enmeshed in wider financial debates brought on by the deficit budgets of the post-1982 economic downturn.

The government was faced with difficult choices between continuing the momentum of the existing new-town programme elsewhere, or committing itself to a major new programme at Junk Bay, as well as what to do about Tin Shui Wai. The choice was further complicated by another perceived option in that it was suggested that development of Area 14 in Junk Bay (which required major expenditure to remove the existing industry and a commitment to the new tunnelled access road) could be avoided or postponed by substituting public housing development on part of the under-utilized industrial estate at Yuen Long, for which the infrastructure was already in place. If it had been done, it would have been yet another case of *ad hoc* incremental utilization upsetting firm longer term planning commitments, rather on the lines of the Kwun Tong changes of 20 years before. Other possibilities were utilizing rezoned industrial land, as was in fact done; or hopefully deferring any long-term investment decisions on Junk Bay until 1984, when they could take advantage of the expected Territorial Development Strategy evaluations.

At this time, the Junk Bay planners were also expressing their own more immediate problems.

As the town is designed in an integral manner with the Mass Transit Railway it is increasingly difficult to keep options open. The linkage is very strong and the lack of positive decision on one element has an inexorable knock on effect on others. Can I hope that we shall not have to live with this new uncertainty for long and that a decision on the principle of MTR service can be taken soon rather than later?[53]

Yet, by December, the position was even gloomier, for then the Mass Transit Corporation announced that it had been unable to convince the government to support its plans for the extension with increased equity financing, and that accordingly, it felt that it could no longer commit itself to any further design work on the project.

Despite the setback, land-use planning work for the town continued unabated, and a new Junk Bay and Sai Kung Works Progress Committee met for the first time on 7 December 1982. More important, however, proved to be the ongoing strategic debate. While it was felt that curtailment of development at the 175,000 threshold (two districts) was possible (see Fig. 6.1e), it was pointed out that it would almost certainly require some remedial investment in higher order facilities such as a town park and swimming pool, for example, which originally would have come in later stages, even though the basic district pattern would not be compromised.

It was confirmed that at 175,000, access by the tunnel road only was possible, and that the rail link was unnecessary, though any subsequent growth and implementation of the rail link would bring about a much lower modal split in favour of the rail link because of already established road-based travel patterns. Some growth beyond 175,000 was also thought possible by increasing the public housing content of the town yet further. For the longer term, it was agreed that a rail decision could be deferred to 1987–8, while a likely relocation of the Shui Wing steelworks to the south of Rennie's Mill opened up the possibility of additional housing in that area and a new, fourth rail station there if the alignment into the town were from the south; with a resultant feasible population ceiling of 380,000 in all at full development.[54]

This latest review was put before the Land Development Policy Committee again for comment in August 1983.[55] The Committee agreed that Phase I development up to the 175,000 ceiling was appropriate, and that subsequent growth should be looked at in relation to the Territorial Development Strategy. In the meantime the suggestions on the rail link were endorsed, and it was agreed that it would be necessary to look at the complementary improvements in the East Kowloon road network. Nevertheless, the first Junk Bay Outline Development Plan (Plan JB/82/001B), based on the consultant's final report, was approved at this meeting as the basis for long-term development, with a subsidiary plan (JB/82/001A) for the now agreed Phase I scheme.

However, ongoing financial constraints during the economic depression of the early 1980s continued to affect the planning work. In particular, the wish to reduce costs led the Development Progress Committee in May 1984 to recommend that only the first tube of the new road tunnel need be completed by the first target date of 1988 — it was needed anyway to allow the new water supply to be provided — with a possible second tube deferred to 1990. This was even further restricted by a decision in

1985 to reduce the initial design to only one tube as part of a wider review of policy towards the Junk Bay development.[56]

This new review set new threshold ceilings by suggesting that 80,000 was the appropriate trigger requirement for the new tunnel, with 100,000 requiring it to be operational. The effect of this was to further lengthen the development period for the town, and thus spread the capital cost; yet, it remained agreed that Phase I remained necessary in total in order to meet the public housing commitments, and that if the project were halted at an earlier stage, particularly regarding the proposed expenditures on removing the existing industry, political pressures from the existing 80,000 people in the town would likely compel the government to complete the project in any case.

Yet, pressures for curtailment were clearly significant at this time. Not only had the Territorial Development Strategy come out in favour of developments elsewhere ahead of the Junk Bay proposals, but the government itself set up a special review working group to assess the viability of providing any continuing commitment to the town. In the words of the Secretariat, it was necessary:

to undertake a thorough review of the desirability or acceptability of such a pause [after completion of the committed works for the initial 80,000 public housing intake] and of how the housing programme might otherwise be sustained.[57]

Luckily for Junk Bay, immediate replacement of its projected housing programme elsewhere proved impossible.

Discussion of the review in the Development Progress Committee proved to be prolonged,[58] but by June 1985, it was agreed that the problem of the removal of incompatible industries would have to be reviewed again, that the effects on Phase II of the town of removing the rail access should be assessed, and that the development programme for Phase I should be revised and linked directly to the reduced scheme for the principal access road.

This led to a review of the Outline Development Plan (Plan JB/83/001C) which was circulated for the reduced scheme in October (see Fig. 6.1e). Reassessment of the transport capacities suggested a new maximum target of 220,000 for Phase I against a one-tube tunnel-constrained capacity of 200,000, with an additional 125,000 from the second tube if built. This, therefore, set an overall town limit of 325,000 now that the rail reserve was to be deleted. The major land-use change that resulted was the demotion of the northernmost district centre, which was now thought not to be viable without its nodal rail station, while the Hang Hau centre now took on the town-centre functions. It was this rezoning that allowed the increase in the Phase I population target.

These planned changes were put before the Development Progress Committee in January 1986 for approval,[59] where the proposed splitting of commercial and civic functions between the remaining two centres was queried. It was also noted, that although no rail access was shown, the disposition of the buildings and land uses still allowed future rail provision from the south (the original northern route was now rendered impossible by the proposed relocation of Lam Tin station in Kwun Tong on the new Eastern Harbour Crossing line). Nevertheless, despite the doubts, the new plan was approved as the basis of further planning work,[60] and published as Plan JB/83/001D.

Such changes were not, however, the end of the matter. Improvements in the Hong Kong economy in the mid-1980s allowed the Executive Council to request early in 1986 that the economic advantages of attempting simultaneous completion of both of the road-tunnel tubes should be looked at again, given the anticipated small additional cost involved. The result of this was a firm decision to go ahead with the full scheme, and construction of the twin tubes began later in that year. This, of course, reopened the whole question of viable target populations once again. Also, the criticisms of the planners' earlier revisions for Phase I caused yet further reassessments of the design, such that the whole form of the town came under review again in 1986–7.

Initial reconsideration of Phase I had suggested a reconcentration of service functions in one zone near to Hang Hau (Areas 37 and 38), and to rezone the areas as R1 residential and government/institutional/community uses so as to allow 'the level of commercial facilities allowed to respond to market forces'.[61] Limited commercial uses were now to remain in the former northern centre in Area 17, but most likely without a rail station. In fact, hope for an eventual rail link had by now increased again, such that a tentative alignment was reinserted on the revised plan, though in an arrangement that was an operator's nightmare — a short stub branchline within the town itself from a Kwun Tong branch terminus in the new town centre.

By October 1986 the Mass Transit Corporation was hinting that the extension to Junk Bay might be begun in 1992, following completion of their commitments on the Eastern Harbour Crossing extension. This, and the availability of the full-capacity road tunnel link from 1989, clearly reopened the whole question of how far Junk Bay development should proceed, since road constraints were now removed and the whole matter of viability for any rail link was effectively reopened. The result was that there was yet a further major planning review, resulting in the relocation of the new-town centre back to its original position on the southern waterfront, a reinstatement of the four district-centre concept, and a firm planning commitment to the idea of a rail link serving the town from the south. The new plan (see Fig. 6.1f and 6.6) — Plan D/JB/2, was in place by the end of 1987, and a firm commitment to the rail link was hoped for.

No sooner had the commitment to Junk Bay Phase II been made, however, that is to the population target of 320,000, than yet further review became a necessity during 1987–8. In April of 1987 yet another potential shortage of public housing sites was identified for the early 1990s in Hong Kong, primarily because the first sites on the new Territorial Development Strategy's harbour reclamations would not then be available. The result was that yet another search for potential sites was instituted, to which Junk Bay emerged as a major contributor.

Fig. 6.6 Outline development plan for Junk Bay, 1987 (Plan D/JB/2).

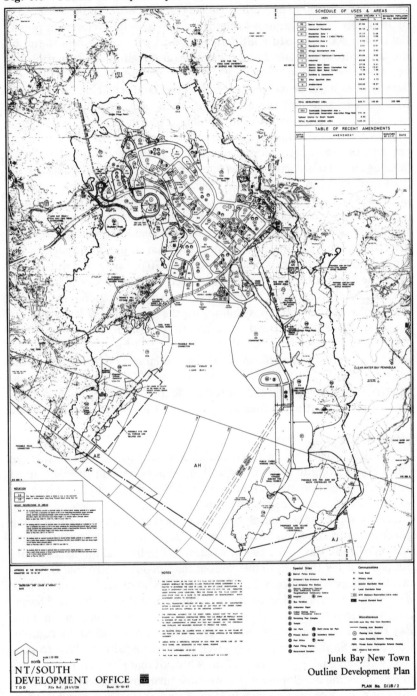

Source: Territory Development Department, Hong Kong government.

The outcome was a decision by the Land Development Policy Committee in April 1988 to authorize detailed planning work for the third phase of Junk Bay new town, thus bringing it up to its full development potential of 440,000 people (the ultimate limit set by the two access routes of the twin-bore road tunnel and the mass transit rail link). Primarily, the additional population (Plan ODP D/JB/3) will be housed in new high-density housing to be located on redeveloped land replacing the Rennie's Mill cottage area and the Shui Wing steelworks, together with some associated new reclamation. This enhanced fourth district, centred on a MTR station as elsewhere in Junk Bay, will provide for 110,000 of the required increase; with another two thousand in low density R3 and R4 housing to be constructed on the final borrow platforms of Pak Shek on the Clearwater Bay peninsular. Associated with this additional development, new industrial sites are expected to be developed to the south-west of the new town for port-related and hazardous industries, and to the far south-east (near Fat Tau Chau) for the third Hong Kong industrial estate. Nevertheless, despite these extensions, the final employment balance for the completed town is expected to reach only 70 per cent, and thus a considerable integration within the nearby metropolitan labour market is to be expected. This expected commuter flow, in both directions, should certainly enhance the traffic possibilities for the Mass Transit Railway Corporation. By 1988, it seemed not a question of when the railway would come to Junk Bay, tentatively thought to be 1993 for 1996 opening, but how. The negotiation within government was largely on how much of the rail reserve should be covered, and how far the MTR Corporation should be given land-development rights around the four stations in order to allow it to offset its construction costs against property development, rather along the lines of the development schemes associated with the Island Line, completed in the early 1980s.

The 1990s, therefore, will see Junk Bay taking its place alongside the other Hong Kong new towns as a planned development brought up to its full designed potential; perhaps a rather surprising outcome given the vicissitudes of its early beginnings. Such an outcome also raises interesting questions about the commitment of policy-makers within the Hong Kong government to any form of long-term strategy, for the incremental completion of Junk Bay in the 1990s, whatever its individual merits, can only put back further the shift to the harbour that the 1984 Territorial Development Strategy was supposed to implement. As so often in Hong Kong's new-town history, housing demands and incremental responses were beginning yet again to pre-empt strategic imperatives. The outcome in Junk Bay raises interesting questions for the 1990s with regard to the completion of Tin Shui Wai, especially given the decision also of 1988 to proceed with full land reclamation of the whole of that site. It is now to that most interesting development that we must turn, in order to complete the story of new-town development in Hong Kong, at least as far as it is determined for the handover to China in 1997.

Tin Shui Wai

The Private Sector Question

One of the many factors that gave rise to a growing interest in possible private sector involvement in new-town development in the 1980s was the attempt by the private sector to develop a new town of its own at Tin Shui Wai in the north-western New Territories. While the scheme in its original form did not materialize, it had important political and policy effects in Hong Kong, and is of interest to us in presenting alternative design ideas on how new-town development in Hong Kong might take place, less fettered by normal governmental constraints.

While the general area selected was related to some of the potential land production sites identified in the 1977 report of the Special Committee on Land Production,[62] it was not until early in 1980 that the private interest in the area became publicly known. The initial idea for the scheme had originated from an investment consortium which had bought speculatively a large parcel of 488 hectares of fish ponds to the west of Yuen Long. The original site assembly had been by local clan interests and Wimpey, the British housebuilding company who had also been involved shortly before with the Hong Lok Yuen residential estate near Tai Po. The early intention was again to develop low-density private housing, but the scheme was changed when the interests were bought out by a new consortium formed as Mightycity Limited — made up of 51 per cent China Resources, a People's Republic of China company operating in Hong Kong, Trafalgar Housing, Cheung Kong, and Wheelock Marden.

The new interests represented a major grouping of some of the largest of Hong Kong's Chinese property companies of the time, and with the high-profile mainland Chinese backing, they represented an important developer that the government in Hong Kong could hardly ignore. Moreover, the time seemed appropriate, given the government's expressed wish for greater private-sector involvement in major development projects and the state of the property market at the time. Business really began when the consortium appointed consultants to prepare planning proposals for the site in February 1980. As with all other major private development proposals in Hong Kong, the developers already knew that to obtain approval for their scheme they would need to submit a master plan for the site to the government for their approval, and the appointment of Shankland Cox, Binnie and Partners, and Peat Marwick Mitchell & Co. was for just that purpose.

In proposing an 846-hectare development scheme in November 1980, with a 15-year development period to a target population of 535,000, the private sector was making a proposition to the Hong Kong government equivalent to one of the government's own new-town commitments. While the scheme was conceived within the current Hong Kong planning standards, the detailed design was new, and the financing and development arrangements unique. Moreover, the dominant Chinese interest set the Hong Kong government a political dilemma that proved particularly sensitive, especially once the build-up to the 1984 Sino-British Agreement on the future of Hong Kong after 1997 had begun in the early 1980s.

In 1980, the developers had grounds for high hopes. Government had already made it clear that it wanted greater private-sector involvement in major development schemes, and already the Paramatta development in Sha Tin had shown the way for new-town schemes. Moreover, in 1975–6, 'the Government took this action to maintain land production for the housing programme at a time when public sector expenditure was under severe restraint',[63] and the developers for Tin Shui Wai advanced a similar argument for acceptance of their scheme.

It was suggested that the proposals provided for much needed public and private housing which would contribute towards the government's committed urban development programme. At full development the developers proposed 60,000 public housing units, 43,700 Home Ownership Scheme units and 43,000 private units. The total annual provision of public housing was suggested to represent between 15 and 20 per cent of the current Hong Kong annual public housing programme. The developers argued that their development offered a unique opportunity for the government to involve the private sector in making a significant contribution to resolving the housing problems caused by a rapidly increasing population. The use of private-sector finance and expertise to develop a new town would provide external support to government's own development programme, thus reducing demand on already overstretched resources.

To achieve these objectives the developer's consultants argued that four interests needed to be brought together, the developers themselves, government, funding agencies, and the local interests. It was accepted that the developer's interests made the project exceptional in new-town development terms. Apart from those related to all major planning projects, such as, for example, efficient and economical programming, three special objectives were argued as being necessary for effective private participation to materialize. These were to control the development so as to satisfy the shareholder's interests; to manage the project so as to gain and retain the confidence of the international financial sector; and to arrange the sale of the private-sector leaseholds on the site so as to earn an acceptable return on capital for the developers and maximize profits, whilst assuring sufficient cash flow to meet the development requirements of the enterprise.

To these ends, the development company was foreseen as being the overall controller of the scheme and its management — similar in role to that of the government's own new-town development offices, but with very important additional financial, marketing, and sales functions. These were stated to be both corporate and site management activities. Five major functional groupings were suggested for the organization of the proposed site development company: financial and administrative management; land clearance; plan implementation, project control, and professional servicing; operations and maintenance; and sales and marketing.

The anticipated role of government was also explicitly recognized. The ability of the government, once the decision had been made to develop the town, to complete the lease agreements, agree premium matters, and organize land resumption quickly and effectively was argued to be vital. Thus the developer saw the government as essentially 'enablers' to remove possible impediments and speed up the developer's own requirements; and it was a failure to recognize that the government might have other and wider requirements beyond this role that led to the effective breakdown of the initial negotiations on the scheme between the two parties. In particular, public-sector perceived costs, planning objectives, and differing financial requirements and expectations over the life of the scheme all pointed to possible formidable differences between the developers and the government.

Formal contact between the two potential partners was made during the preparation of the consultant's interim report between February and May 1980. The report set out the broad development objectives of the scheme and examined its potential for development. This initial information was put before the Territory's Executive Council in May 1980. On submission of the master plan the following October, the Land Development Policy Committee agreed that the proposals should be looked at within the government at three levels of analysis — territorial, sub-regional, and within the project itself.

In general terms, the resultant evaluation found that the urban design and detailed planning of the town was acceptable in terms of the criteria and constraints set by the government's own planning standards and guidelines — indeed it would have been a surprise to have found otherwise, given the consultant's original brief. At the sub-regional level, at that time, a similar response of broad acceptance was evident, even though detailed consideration of the new strategy for the area had only then just begun. Certainly the new sub-regional planning consultants were required to take the new scheme explicitly within their investigations. Much the most difficult question, however, proved to be the wider implications of the scheme within the government's policies for Hong Kong as a whole. In particular, the new strategic planners (the Strategic Planning Unit had been set up also in 1980) proved suspicious of this new-town upstart in a completely unforeseen location, and with a largely uncharted future.

There were a number of points of difficulty. While the proposals expressed a faith in designing a balanced concept for the town, experience elsewhere was already suggesting that this objective was likely to be unobtainable. In the New Territories, in particular, experience with the earlier and smaller private sector residential developments at Fairview Park and Hong Lok Yuen was suggesting that the government might well be faced with large infrastructure expenditures resulting from the new scheme, particularly if major commuting patterns were to develop. It was argued that such investment ought to compete in the normal way within the priority-setting of the annual public works programme rather than be determined by commitments from an independent private-sector scheme. Certainly government could already see major, and in its eyes more compelling, investment demands elsewhere for the early 1980s, and it had reservations about being tied to the programming of a private-sector scheme over which it thought it might have little or no direct control.

Most fundamental of all, however, was the uncertainty at the time over strategic development for the longer term. Just as the Territorial Development Strategy deliberations upset the Junk Bay development scheme, the same arguments were advanced against any definitive commitment towards Tin Shui Wai. It was argued conclusively by the strategic planners that any decision to go ahead would effectively pre-empt any worthwhile choices for Hong Kong as a whole as to future long-term development locations, since a new town of the size of the proposed new private-sector scheme at Tin Shui Wai represented an alternative rather than an addition to the existing major urban development suggestions then being examined. There was, therefore, every incentive to gain time to allow real strategic choices to remain open, and the more detailed problems of negotiation between the government and the developers proved something of a blessing in disguise in resolving this dilemma.

The core problem for government was made public by the Working Group on Private Sector Participation in Land Production in 1982.

Experience with large development proposals has demonstrated that very large scale land production and development by the private sector cannot be considered in isolation as the Government must be involved in producing major external infrastructure links and in the provision and running of community facilities. Private developments must be completed within a rigid timescale to ensure their profitability and we accept that it would be very difficult for the Government to assume the necessary long term commitment to meet its part of such a development, which would involve land acquisition, clearance and provision of Government facilities. Such a commitment would entail according an absolute priority to the development which the Government might later find it is able to meet only at the expense of other projects which at that time have a higher social or economic priority.[64]

There is little doubt of which project they were reminded at the time. Government, therefore, had a problem in 1980. On both planning and financial grounds there were excellent reasons for not proceeding, yet politically it felt unable to 'grasp the nettle' of immediate and outright rejection. The preferred solution was to try and wait.

The planners, in fact, offered four alternative policies to government. Because at the time possible relocation of Hong Kong's international airport to Chek Lap Kok, north of Lantau Island, was dominating strategic thinking, it was suggested that perhaps by means of a land exchange the potential developers might be linked into the north Lantau development as an alternative, with the Tin Shui Wai site being taken by the government as a longer-term development bank. Alternatively, should the airport go ahead, it was pointed out that the urban development of north Lantau might be deferred in order to allow Tin Shui Wai to proceed; or, that the airport site might be transferred to Deep Bay, adjacent to the proposed new-town site, even though it was agreed that this site caused operational problems due to its proximity to the international frontier with

Fig. 6.7   Tin Shui Wai new town — development schemes, 1983–1986.

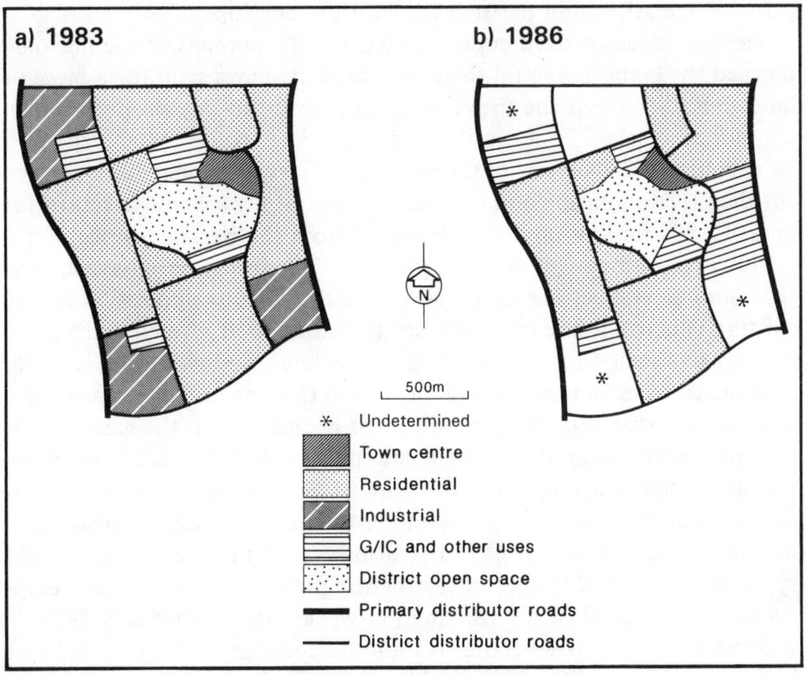

Sources: Based on initial ideas and later outline development plans, Territory Development
Department, Hong Kong government.

China. The last alternative was, of course, to turn down the scheme and,
because of its sensitivities, perhaps to buy out the developer. It was this
last option that the planners preferred.

The eventual outcome to the protracted negotiations is now well known.
The property market downturn of 1982–3 made the economics of the
original private scheme more difficult and the government was forced by
political considerations to intervene. The initial suggestion was a compromise — essentially one between the various factions within the government itself. It rejected the developer's full scheme for a target population
of 535,000, which it could do since about two-fifths of the proposal was
to be on newly reclaimed Crown foreshore, and instead suggested that
the consultant's first phase of 135,000 on 279 hectares in the south of the
area (see Fig. 6.7) would be more appropriate. However, the consortium
resisted this initial reaction, arguing that on viability grounds it required
all or nothing for the scheme. Negotiations therefore dragged on further
until July 1982, when external events precipitated a conclusion. The property slump of that year pressurized the developers to settle, and as the
government knew that serious negotiations with China on the future of
Hong Kong were about to get under way, they were already aware that
any collapse of the Tin Shui Wai scheme, given the Chinese involvement
in it, would be highly and seriously embarrassing. The result was a decision by the government to buy the developer's land-holding at a total price

of some HK\$ 2.26 billion, and eventually to utilize 170 hectares of it for a first-stage scheme in partnership with the developers.

The agreement proved controversial; for the purchase price not only marked the highest amount the government had ever paid for a piece of land; but also it was the first time it had agreed to buy property which was not earmarked for a specific and immediate project. Mightycity also gained, in that 39 hectares of the first-phase site was granted back to them for the private housing and commercial part of the scheme in return for an HK\$ 800 million premium deducted from the purchase price.

However, subsequent progress was slow. Following the agreement, the first land clearances began in 1984, despite vigorous opposition by the existing villagers to the terms offered (they had been offered much more initially by the developers), and these were completed at the end of 1986. Reclamation began that year with a view to the first public housing commencing construction during 1988–9 for occupation in the early 1990s, though this was delayed. The reclamation was unusual in that it was planned as a single-stage operation for the whole new-town site, using sea-dredged material from Deep Bay rather than nearby hillside terracing as normal in Hong Kong. It of course also created a partially unused land bank, which created further infrastructure pressures for the future, especially after Stage II of the reclamation works was approved in 1988. It was not until late in 1988 that full public endorsement for the scheme became apparent, with public backing from the Hong Kong government and a commitment from Cheung Kong to commence work on the first private-sector development on the site.

The experience of Tin Shui Wai led government to draw up for itself, in 1982, general criteria by which it should judge all future private-sector participation in major development schemes:

(a) The proposal should be compatible with Government's strategies and regional development planning and be sound commercially.

(b) There should be clear advantages in the private sector undertaking the work rather than the Government, and no over-riding disadvantages, particularly in terms of the use of resources.

(c) The area in question should be relatively self-contained, relatively free from land acquisition/clearance constraints and uncommitted in terms of the Public Works Programme.

(d) Private sector participation should not result in unacceptable loss of flexibility, programme constraints or financial commitments being placed on Government.[65]

Clearly, a major lesson had been learnt through the Tin Shui Wai negotiations. It was this lesson that also finally persuaded the government to conclude that the development corporation approach, involving private-sector participation, was not a suitable vehicle for new-town development in Hong Kong. The end result of investigation of that idea by both an internal working group in 1982[66] and consultants[67] was, however, the formation under an enabling ordinance of 1987, of a Land Development

Corporation in Hong Kong, which concerned itself solely with urban renewal projects. Only in Tsuen Wan was this likely to impinge upon new-town planning work in the Territory during the 1990s.

With regard to the new towns, the consultants' initial findings were that:

in respect of new town development there were possible disadvantages and no significant advantages in the use of a Land Development Corporation in the land formation and main infrastructure provision stages of a new town development mainly because of the rigid contractual conditions which would be required in order to ensure that private developers would proceed in a way and at a pace appropriate for the coordinated development of a new town. These conditions would inevitably reduce much of the flexibility required for the adaptation of new design to reflect changed circumstances. It was therefore felt that the use of a Land Development Corporation in a new town development situation was inappropriate.[68]

Private-sector new towns on the privatized American model were therefore rejected in Hong Kong.

Planning the Town

For the original private proposals, the principal features of their concept were the balanced provision of residential and employment areas at each stage of development, the ability for pedestrians and cyclists to move on traffic-free landscaped routes (termed boulevards) throughout the urban area and into the hinterland, and the provision of social, community, and recreational facilities close to residential areas. The town was planned on the basis of four districts, each with a population of between 100,000 and 150,000. Each district was to be made up of four residential neighbourhoods, which were designed to support a wide range of social, community, and commercial facilities. The central district was dominated by a major town centre which was to be the focal point for commercial and community activities.[69]

The basic urban form of the town as a whole was a derivative of Wilson's 'beads on a string/tartan grid' concepts linked to a one-kilometre directional grid similar to that employed at Milton Keynes in England (see Figs. 1.2 and 1.3). The result was a linear form, with an external primary road grid enclosing each of the four neighbourhood districts within a kilometre square. The dominant major routes were to form parallel north-south motorways routed along the western and eastern margins of the built-up area. Public transport was to be provided on an exclusive right-of-way running centrally through the neighbourhoods on the British Runcorn new-town model, while the pedestrian and cycleway networks and local open spaces were integrated with community uses and housing areas to minimize the walking distances to the appropriate local public transport stops. The concept was quite similar to that utilized later for Junk Bay (see Fig. 6.5).

In urban design terms it was suggested that the building masses should be so arranged such that the highest would form a central north-south spine for the town, with a concentration in the town centre. The estates on the fringes were planned at lower densities to allow the associated design scale to be reduced. This overall urban form was then linked into a three-tier open space system of town, district, and neighbourhood parks to form an integrated landscaped spatial system linking all parts of the town. Industry, in the classic new-town manner, was separated, and placed in two industrial estates to the south-west and north-east of the urban area, and outside the main primary road grid.

In summary, it was a design first for Hong Kong (since it preceded the same planner's work on Junk Bay), whereby the scheme proceeded from a setting out of first principles to an ever more complex integration at the detailed design stage of the many different facets that make up the functioning of a modern city. It was a major example of new-town design integration on the grand scale.

The events of 1982, of course, required a change in approach to the planning of Tin Shui Wai, and following discussions within the government, and the setting up of the Tin Shui Wai Consultant Management Group, Shankland Cox and Binnie and Partners were approached in December to undertake further work, now for the government, in order to bring their first-stage plan, originally prepared for Mightycity, into line with current government thinking.[70]

Since the new plan was concerned almost entirely with the first district, as a self-contained scheme on just part of the government's new land holding, significant changes to the original urban design concept had to be initiated (see Fig. 6.7). The population was now to be concentrated into five neighbourhoods rather than four, the fifth being focused around the town centre, which now enclosed the central district open space. Industry was also now to be included within the district boundary, and within the primary route network, to avoid resumption of additional land outside the government's initial land holding. Thus, four local employment areas were now designated for each of the four corners of the kilometre square of the enclosing primary road grid. The landscaped boulevard idea was retained, but the open-space network was now concentrated into green 'wedges' between the four periphery neighbourhoods which penetrated to the central-core district park.

In the consultant's revised Master Development Plan of October 1983,[71] the original developer's housing targets were amended to some 58,000 in public rented accommodation (43 per cent), and 10,000 in Home Ownership Scheme flats (7 per cent), thus leaving 67,500 (50 per cent) in private-sector housing. The overall target was increased on examination from 135,000 to 146,500, when higher-density planning standards were later applied, as elsewhere in the new-town programme of the early 1980s. The plan recognized that while it was set out on a balanced basis,

as this goal has not yet been achieved in other new towns in Hong Kong and there is no guarantee that employment opportunities will materialise as planned, the land use distribution has been formulated to allow flexibility for changes of use . . . As industrial land is already available in the sub-region, particularly at Yuen

Long Industrial Estate, it may prove difficult to attract industry to Tin Shui Wai in its early stages of development.[72]

This modification proved prophetic, for in the translation of the proposals into a departmental Outline Development Plan by the Development Office the following year (1984), the major change proved to be the deletion of the proposed industrial sites, and their addition to the designated land bank for possible future development (Plan MDP/TSW/1E — approved in November 1984). Subsequently, detailed design modifications, such as those for the town-centre scheme, proved necessary — up to Plan OD/TSW/3 (see Fig. 6.8) by 1986, and OD/TSW/3A in November 1987.

Another planning innovation included in the consultant's 1983 documentation was a planning scheme for the control and development of the fringe areas adjacent to the new-town boundary.[73] Unlike most of the earlier new towns, except Yuen Long and Sheung Shui/Fanling, the urban boundary for Tin Shui Wai could not be so clearly delineated in reality. It was suggested that to avoid unwanted and probably illegal building around the designated area, much tighter development control measures than currently available within the Hong Kong New Territories were going to be required. The scheme also took the opportunity to point out ways in which the initial scheme might be linked more effectively with its surrounding hinterland, particularly with regard to nearby existing settlement and possible major open space. This integrating documentation was formally entitled a 'structure plan' — the first formal use of that term in a Hong Kong context, though such a term was also under consideration by the government's planners at the time for use in rather different contexts.

Reaction to this last idea proved muted. While the late 1980s were witnessing a major effort to extend more comprehensive planning controls into the New Territories in Hong Kong, and a new sub-regional planning statement for the north-west New Territories was complete by 1987, neither solution seemed likely to be able to meet the planning objectives that the consultants had earlier argued for. Already there was, by 1987, good evidence of development pressures beginning to build again in the unplanned areas around both Tin Shui Wai and Yuen Long in the better property speculation conditions after the 1982–3 slump.

The result was that, once again, the planners at the sub-regional level were facing further incipient urbanization: a problem that had bedevilled planning work in the area over previous decades, and which the consultants for the north-west sub-regional study had specifically warned against in their earlier studies of 1980–1. One reaction to this, again arising out of the strategic review of planning policies for the north-west New Territories, was the active upgrading and improvement policies introduced late in the 1980s for the existing villages and industrial sites in the area.

While the programmes of resumption and land reclamation point to a firm commitment from government for the development of Tin Shui Wai, in the late 1980s uncertainty still surrounded the project in terms of its ultimate size and completion. In 1988, some preliminary work had

Fig. 6.8　Outline development plan for Tin Shui Wai Stage 1, 1986 (Plan OD/TSW/3).

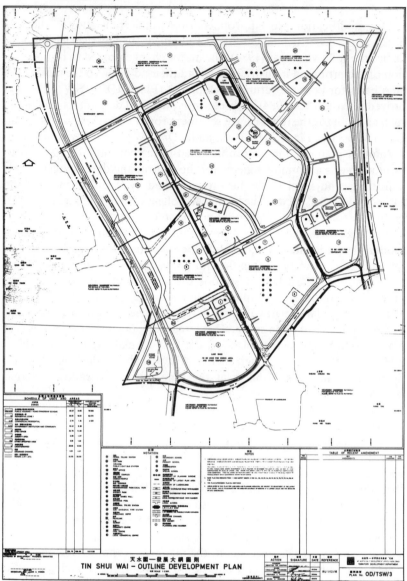

Source: Territory Development Department, Hong Kong government.

already begun on a tentative Stage II scheme for an additional 90,000 people, but any commitment to proceed further, even given the incentive that the Stage II reclamation agreed that year represents, seemed more likely to depend on major strategic options arising from the Comprehensive Transportation Study (CTS II) and further refinement of the Territorial Development Strategy. Certainly the locational advantages of Tin

Shui Wai looked set to change in the 1990s as the likely completion of
Route 'X' from Tsuen Wan to Yuen Long opens up a new western corridor to China, and as the completion of the Yuen Long Industrial Estate
further enhances the local sub-regional labour market to which the housing estates of Tin Shui Wai are planned to contribute. No one, it would
seem, would be greatly surprised were Tin Shui Wai eventually to proceed to full capacity in the 1990s, thus following the example of Junk Bay
and further delaying the strategic shift to the harbour first put forward
in the 1984 Territorial Development Strategy. Again, once committed,
government in Hong Kong seems somehow unlikely to say 'stop' before
full development and optimal financial returns have been achieved,
whatever any formal strategy might suggest.

Some Concluding Comments

The current development of both Junk Bay and Tin Shui Wai as new towns
of a more recent generation in Hong Kong raises some interesting planning policy issues for the Territory. On the one hand, they represent in
plan form the application of a fully integrated and relatively sophisticated
design process to both the concepts and the form of each town, comparable
in terms of advancement of the art of new-town planning and design to
the changes in Britain between the first and later generations of British
new towns. Yet, they also betray the hazards and difficulties of attempting the 'grand design' mode in the Hong Kong development context of
'ad hocery' and constant flux, where external circumstances and pressures
drastically alter the planning environment and policy constraints within
which the new-town planners and their town are expected to work. Junk
Bay, in particular, is an excellent example of this, in that the original public-
transport rail-oriented town design was 'tested' to virtual destruction by
1985, only to be resurrected again in the growing optimism of the late
1980s.

Tin Shui Wai is of course a very special case. Born of the 1980 speculative property bubble in Hong Kong, it might well have collapsed along
with the other victims when that bubble burst had it not been for the very
special circumstances surrounding the promoters and their timing. Whilst
the scheme was innovative, both in design and financing terms, it was that
very innovation that caused it to be viewed cautiously by both the planners and financial experts of the Hong Kong government. Certainly the
translation of the scheme by 1984 from a city into only another major
housing development, with resultant inevitable commuting flows, seemed
destined to bring about the very conditions of which government itself
had been so concerned in its initial evaluations of the full scheme in
1980–1.

Yet in some ways the consultant's design innovations continue to live
on. Certainly, the basic form of each town remains as originally conceived, even though so far the extent of final completion remains unclear,
at least for Tin Shui Wai. Doubts of course remain — just how much

of the original Tin Shui Wai will be developed, and should it remain at its present commitment? How far will government have left itself with a major sub-regional planning problem?

Only the 1990s will give the definitive answer to such speculation, but one would not be surprised if, in the time-honoured Hong Kong way, existing commitments in the form of the government's unused land bank or the momentum of existing development do cause further stages of growth to take place; even in spite of the suggestions in the Territorial Development Strategy to do otherwise, thus extending the Hong Kong new-town programme well into the twenty-first century. Certainly, for the 1990s, Tin Shui Wai, together with Ma On Shan and Tuen Mun East, will be the sites competing most strongly against the harbour reclamations for a major share of Hong Kong public investment. It is here that the strategic battle between metropolitan concentration or regional decentralization will be fought. The decisions of the late 1980s to expand Junk Bay to its full potential of 440,000 people perhaps give an indicator of which way that battle might go.

Notes

1. Scott Wilson Kirkpatrick & Partners, *Report on Reclamation at Junk Bay* (Hong Kong, Public Works Department, 1959). Copy at 7/1 in BL 6/5282/56I, Public Records Office, Hong Kong.

2. Scott Wilson Kirkpatrick & Partners (1959), see note 1 above, p. 12.

3. Scott Wilson Kirkpatrick & Partners (1959), see note 1 above, pp. 20–1.

4. Executive Council Paper No. 156, 17 November 1959, *Land Development Schemes*, at 79 in BL 6/5282/56I, Public Records Office, Hong Kong, para.6(c), p. 2.

5. Memorandum from District Commissioner New Territories to Colonial Secretary, 20 April 1960, at 92 in BL 6/5282/56I, Public Records Office, Hong Kong, para.2(a), p. 1.

6. Planning Division, *Junk Bay Outline Development Plan, Sheet One, Plan LJB 10J, May 1962* (Hong Kong, Crown Lands and Survey Office, 1962).

7. Planning Division, *Junk Bay and Clearwater Bay Peninsula Outline Zoning Plan LM/89A*, circulated 3 December 1964 and presented with Land Development Planning Committee Paper No. 68, 26 February 1965; at 20 in BL 6/5282/56I, Public Records Office, Hong Kong.

8. Land Development Planning Committee (1965), see note 7 above, para.6, p. 1.

9. Land Development Planning Committee (1965), see note 7 above, para.20, p. 3.

10. Land Development Policy Committee Paper No. 399, 22 February 1974, *The Potential Industrial Use of Junk Bay*, (Hong Kong, Town Planning Office, 1974).

11. Memorandum from the Secretary for the Environment, 26 March 1975, at 18 in BL 6/5282/56II, Public Records Office, Hong Kong.

12. Minutes of the Fourth Meeting of the Junk Bay Development Study Steering Group, 11 July 1975, at 48/1 in BL 6/5282/56II, Public Records Office, Hong Kong, para.4.2.4.5, p. 8.

13. Junk Bay Development Steering Group, *Recommendations on Junk Bay Development Stage 1 — Engineering and Environmental Study: for Industrial Land Sub-Committee of Land Development Policy Committee* (Hong Kong, Hong Kong government, 1975), Recommendation (a), p. 1. Copy at 76/2 in BL 6/5282/56II, Public Records Office, Hong Kong.

14. Land Development Policy Committee Paper No. 29/76, (27 August 1976), *Junk Bay*, at 90/1 in BL 6/5282/56II, Public Records Office, Hong Kong.

15. Land Development Policy Committee (1976), see note 14 above, para.2.5, p. 2.

16. Land Development Policy Committee (1976), see note 14 above, paras.5.1–2, p. 4.

17. Chief Engineer, Consultant's Management Division, Civil Engineering Office, *Agreement No. CE 1/75, Item NDE 18(1) — Junk Bay Development: Revised Brief and Schedule of Fees — November 1976, Draft I — 18/11/76* (Hong Kong, Public Works Department, 1976), para (C)(1), p. 5.

18. Maunsell Consultants Asia, *Junk Bay Urban Development — Feasibility Study* (Hong Kong, New Territories Development Department, 1978).

19. Memorandum of Senior Planning Officer, Outline Planning Division, Town Planning Office, *Draft Notes on General Comments for Junk Bay Urban Development Feasibility Study*, at 2 in TPD/924/COPI, Town Planning Registry, Hong Kong, pp. 2–3.

20. Minute M49 in ENV(SPU) 70/61/02IV, Buildings and Lands Registry, Hong Kong.

21. Memorandum of 18 May 1978, from Chief Town Planning Officer, Outline Planning, to Chief Engineer, Consultant's Management Division, at 5 in TPD/924/COPI, Town Planning Registry, Hong Kong, para.4, p. 1.

22. Land Development Policy Committee Paper No. 29/78, 18 August 1978, *Land Production*, at 63 in BL 6/5282/56IV, Public Records Office, Hong Kong, para.6(e), p. 4.

23. Land Development Policy Committee (1978), see note 22 above, para.5, p. 3.

24. Minutes of the Land Development Policy Committee Extraordinary Meeting of 18 August 1978, at 63A in BL 6/5282/56IV, Public Records Office. Hong Kong, para.6, p. 7.

25. Hong Kong Productivity Centre, *Junk Bay Survey* (Hong Kong, Hong Kong Productivity Centre, 1981).

26. Minutes of Land Development Policy Committee meeting of 23 February 1979, at 105 in BL 6/5282/56IV, Public Records Office, Hong Kong, Matters Arising, paras.3.18 and 3.32, pp. 9–10.

27. Appendix to Memorandum of the Secretary for the Environment, 1 March 1979, at 107/1 in BL 6/5282/56IV, Public Records Office, Hong Kong.

28. Land Development Policy Committee Paper No. 25/79, 31 August 1979, *New Development Areas for Public Housing — An Appraisal of Junk Bay, Sha Tin Area B, and Tuen Mun Eastern Extension*, at 19/1 in ENV(SPU) 70/61/02V, Buildings and Lands Registry, Hong Kong.

29. Environment Branch, *Junk Bay Development: Environment Branch Points of View* (Draft), at 66 in ENV(SPU) 70/61/02V, Buildings and Lands Registry, Hong Kong, para.3.3, p. 2.

30. Memorandum from the Strategic Planning Unit to the Project Manager Sha Tin, 5 November 1980, at 64 in ENV(SPU) 70/61/02V, Buildings and Lands Registry, Hong Kong, para.(d), p. 2.

31. Memorandum from Project Manager Junk Bay, 4 November 1980, at 67 in ENV(SPU) 70/61/02V, Buildings and Lands Registry, Hong Kong.

32. Minutes of Junk Bay New Town Consultants Steering Group, 17 November 1980, at 76/1 in ENV(SPU) 70/61/02V, Buildings and Lands Registry, Hong Kong, para.4.4 (xxxii), p. 8.

33. Junk Bay Development Office, *Situation Report*, November 1980, at 70/1 in ENV(SPU) 70/61/02V, Buildings and Lands Registry, Hong Kong, para.3, pp. 8–9.

34. Junk Bay Development Office (1980), see note 33 above, para.K1, p. 20. These objectives were first set for the north-west New Territories development investigation of 1978, completed in-house by the government.

35. These were further developed by the consultants and appeared in April 1981 as Technical Note No. 1, *Junk Bay Development Study — Junk Bay Town: Goals and Objectives — Initial Evaluation*, from which Fig. 6.4b is taken. A copy is at 40/2 in ENV(SPU) 70/61/02VI, Buildings and Lands Registry, Hong Kong.

36. Minutes of the Junk Bay New Town Consultants Steering Group, 2 February 1981, at 4/1 in ENV(SPU) 70/61/02VI, Buildings and Lands Registry, Hong Kong, paras.5.2–4, pp. 5–8.

37. Maunsell Consultants Asia, Shankland Cox, and Brian Clouston and Partners Hong Kong Limited, *Junk Bay Development Study: Inception Report* (Hong Kong, New Territories Development Department, 1981).

38. Memorandum from the Secretary for the Environment to the Project Manager Junk Bay, 17 March 1981, at 14 in ENV(SPU) 70/61/02VI, Buildings and Lands Registry, Hong Kong, para.2, p. 1.

39. This evaluation is contained in Technical Note No. 2, *Junk Bay Development Study — Junk Bay Town: Alternative Development Concepts — Initial Evaluation*, partially illustrated in Fig. 6.3, 1981a and b. A complete copy is at 40/3 in ENV(SPU) 70/61/02VI, Buildings and Lands Registry, Hong Kong.

40. Junk Bay Development Office and the Junk Bay Development Study Consultants, *Existing Industries in Junk Bay* (Hong Kong, New Territories Development Department, 1981).

41. Junk Bay Development Office and the Junk Bay Development Study Consultants (1981), see note 40 above, para.6.2.2, p. 32, and para.10.1, p. 53.

42. Industrial Land Sub-Committee Paper, 25 June 1981, *Junk Bay New Town: Provision of Industrial Land Therein and Relationship to other Industrial Areas* (Hong Kong, Strategic Planning Unit, 1981).

43. Minutes of the Industrial Land Sub-Committee, 25 June 1981, at 34 in ENV(SPU) 70/61/02VII, Buildings and Lands Registry, Hong Kong.

44. Maunsell Consultants Asia, Shankland Cox, and Brian Clouston and Partners Hong Kong Limited, *Junk Bay Development Study: Interim Report, August 1981* (Hong Kong, New Territories Development, 1981).

45. Land Development Policy Committee Paper No. 35/81, 25 September 1981, *Development of Junk Bay New Town: and Contingent Issues*, at 23/1 in ENV(SPU) 70/61/02VIII, Buildings and Lands Registry, Hong Kong.

46. Memorandum from the Project Manager Junk Bay to the Secretary for Transport, 14 January 1982, at 77 in ENV(SPU) 70/61/02VIII, Buildings and Lands Registry, Hong Kong, para.2, p. 2.

47. Maunsell Consultants Asia, Shankland Cox Partnership. Brian Clouston and Partners Hong Kong Limited, *Junk Bay New Town Study: Draft Final Report — March 1982* (Hong Kong, New Territories Development Department, 1982).

48. Memorandum from the Project Manager Tai Po/Fanling to the Project Manager Junk Bay, 26 May 1982, at 20 in LW(SPU) 70/61/02IX, Buildings and Lands Registry, Hong Kong, para.3, p. 1.

49. Land Development Policy Committee Paper No. 10/82, 9 July 1982, *Development of Junk Bay New Town and Contingent Issues*, at 36 in ENV(SPU) 70/61/02IX, Buildings and Lands Registry, Hong Kong.

50. Land Development Policy Committee (1982), see note 48 above, para.3.4, p. 7.

51. Commissioned and completed as Shankland Cox, Binnie and Partners Hong Kong, Maunsell Consultants Asia, *Junk Bay East Coast Study — Final Report* (Hong Kong, New Territories Development Department, 1983).

52. Minute by the Government Town Planner, Strategic Planning, at M29 in ENV(SPU) 70/61/02X, Buildings and Lands Registry, Hong Kong.

53. Memorandum from the Project Manager Junk Bay to the Director, New Terrtories Development Department, 8 November 1982, at 38/1 in ENV(SPU) 70/61/02X, Buildings and Lands Registry, Hong Kong.

54. Land Development Policy Committee Draft Paper, 29 April 1983, *Development of Junk Bay New Town — Outline Development Plan and Development Programme Review*, at 110/1 in ENV(SPU) 70/61/02X, Buildings and Lands Registry, Hong Kong, para.3.3.3, p. 14.

55. Land Development Policy Committee Paper No. 18/83, 26 August 1983, *Development of Junk Bay New Town: Outline Development Plan and Development Programme Review*, at 60A in TPO 924/COPII, Town Planning Registry, Hong Kong.

56. Development Progress Committee Paper No. 41/85, 11 April 1985, *1985 Junk Bay Development Review*, at 22 in TPD D/JB/300(SS)I, Town Planning Registry, Hong Kong.

57. *1985 Junk Bay Review: Background Report*, attached at 10 to Development Progress Committee (1985), see note 56 above, para.1.1, p. 1.

58. See Minutes M8, M10 and M11 in TPD D/JB/300(SS)I, Town Planning Registry, Hong Kong.

59. See Minute M14 in TPD D/JB/300(SS)I, Town Planning Registry, Hong Kong.

60. Land Development Progress Committee Paper No. 4/86, *Junk Bay New Town Phase I Outline Development Plan — Plan No. JB/83/001D*, at Minute M15 in TPD D/JB/300(SS)I, Town Planning Registry, Hong Kong.

61. Memorandum from the Project Manager Junk Bay, 8 March 1986, at 37 in TPD D/JB/300(SS)I, Town Planning Registry, Hong Kong.

62. Special Committee on Land Production, *Report of the Special Committee on Land Production* (Hong Kong, Government Printer, 1977), Appendix 10, Area 1, p. 3. This recommendation was carried forward in the government's own internal *Development Investigation of North Western New Territories — Phases I–III.*

63. Special Committee on Land Supply, *Special Committee on Land Supply: Report to His Excellency the Governor, March 1982* (Hong Kong, Government Printer, 1982), Appen-

dix II — *Report of the Working Group on Private Sector Participation in Land Production*, para.2.1, p. 4.

64. Special Committee on Land Supply (1982), see note 63 above, Appendix II, para.4.2, p. 9.

65. Special Committee on Land Supply (1982), see note 63 above, Appendix II, para.3.1, p. 6.

66. A Working Group on Urban Renewal was set up within the Special Committee on Land Supply in July 1982, and agreed that the Development Corporation idea should be investigated. See Special Committee on Land Supply, *Special Committee on Land Supply: Report to His Excellency the Governor, March 1983* (Hong Kong, Government Printer, 1983), Appendix II, p. 27.

67. Coopers and Lybrand Associates Limited, *Land Development Corporations Study: Executive Summary* (Hong Kong, Hong Kong Government, 1983).

68. Special Committee on Land Supply, *Special Committee on Land Supply: Report to His Excellency the Governor, March 1984* (Hong Kong, Government Printer, 1984), para.6.4, p. 25.

69. Shankland Cox, Binnie and Partners, and Peat Marwick Mitchell & Co., *Tin Shui Wai Urban Development Master Plan* (Hong Kong, Mightycity Co. Ltd., 1980).

70. Shankland Cox, Binnie and Partners (Hong Kong), *Tin Shui Wai Urban Development — Interim Report* (Hong Kong, New Territories Development Department, 1983).

71. Shankland Cox and Binnie and Partners (Hong Kong), *Tin Shui Wai Urban Development — Master Development Plan* (Hong Kong, New Territories Development Department, 1983) 2 vols.

72. Shankland Cox et al. (1983, Vol. 1), see note 71 above, para.2.3.1, p. 13.

73. Shankland Cox et al. (1983, Vol. 1), see note 71 above, Section 8.4, *Edge Area Structure Plan*, pp. 73–8.

7. Some Aspects of New-town Design

Design is a methodology that, when applied to policy, can help solve some of the problems of misallocated resources and misused land ... The process of designing a house allocates resources and resolves conflicts. You shouldn't need to go through the bedrooms to get from the dining room to the kitchen; the overall shape of the house should be economical; the structural and mechanical systems should make sense, but be subordinate to the rooms ... A city is far more complex than even the most complicated building, but there are ways of introducing into our cities some of the coherence and even beauty that are the products of design.[1]

New towns represent one of the greatest challenges and opportunities in this sense, and not only can they lead to great success, but also the comprehensiveness of failure can be all pervading. It is, therefore, appropriate here to utilize an evaluation of design as a first examination of the success or otherwise of the Hong Kong new towns, and to begin we need to look at the towns as a whole.

Urban Form in the New Towns

An examination of the procedures followed by town planners when designing new towns suggests that, as a generalization, we can discern four major steps between commencement and completion of the development programme. These might be labelled as site selection, land-use planning, infrastructure design and development staging, and final implementation and construction. In the context of our analysis so far, much the greatest attention has been paid to the site selection, particularly in so far as it has been a part of wider strategic policy issues in Hong Kong. Only briefly have there been comments on such site constraints as land assembly or engineering requirements. Consideration of land-use planning, too, has been confined mostly to the more macro-distributional issues. Finally, programming and implementation have remained as mainly administrative issues in our discussion.

Thus, relatively little has yet been said on the detail of the planning design work, without which the new towns would not have materialized. As elsewhere, that design has been conceptualized at two levels, that of the town and that of its component parts. It is useful, therefore, to begin with comment on that which concerns the town as a whole — the assembly of the parts which make it function effectively as an urban entity, complete and operational in its own right.

It is clear that for new towns, two basic considerations have a fundamental effect upon how the town operates. These concern movement (the disposition of the transport system in terms of layout and availability of modes) and the distribution of the land uses in terms of space and functional requirements. These come together conceptually in terms of activity patterns (the usage of the town's various facilities) that the prospective population of the town is expected to develop. The discussion at the beginning of the book, in addition to showing some of the design origins for the Hong Kong new towns, also shows us how new-town design evolved conceptually in Britain; with the result, given the origins of many of Hong Kong's professional planners, that its phases directly affected subsequent design principles followed in Hong Kong. Study of that process also shows us how various forms of layout, urban space distributions, and planned linkages to enable various activities to take place gradually evolved, were tested and implemented, and sometimes finally discarded, as experience of new-town design developed.

In Western new-town planning there is one major theme that can be picked out as dominating the form of modern cities. This can be summed up in a single word — 'separation'. The result is everywhere. To give just one or two examples: the whole idea of zoning, whether based on the American model of codified legal constraints on the types of development allowed within each spatial unit, or on the more generalized British system of discretionary permissions being granted within general concepts of separating incompatible land uses and removing those which do not conform, has produced an urban form based upon the policy of encouraging single-use spatial areas as the building blocks from which the modern, Western city is formed. Thus, despite occasional dissent from those who would argue for more integrated forms of development or who champion the causes of those who lack the required means to travel, which the design demands, Western planners have become wedded to an urban form that is a high consumer of space, and demands ever increasing levels of personal mobility in order to take advantage of the multiplying opportunities that the planned city offers. This has resulted in another modern characteristic of the Western city — the development of increasingly complex and sophisticated movement systems in order to allow the city's inhabitants to take full advantage of the social and economic advantages and facilities that are put on offer. A corollary also applies, of course, that if mobility is impaired, then that citizen's welfare is impaired proportionately.

This dominating concept for city development has not been without its critics. Perhaps the best known and most influential has been the American, Jane Jacobs, who as long ago as 1961[2] wrote of the vigour and vitality of the multi-purpose city street and campaigned for its retention in the face of the onslaught from single-use zoning legislation. Yet even single-use zoning is in fact a misnomer, for while there may well be a dominating use within each zone, invariably other servicing activities remain. Thus, the new-town neighbourhood, that has been paramount in various guises in new-town planning, remains in reality an area within which a variety of localized activities are placed, all basically associated with the home and the day-to-day requirements of family life. Only the workplace has usually remained separated from the living areas. More recently, as Chapter 1 describes, the conceptualization of the 'activity centre' and its linkages within and between neighbourhoods has come to dominate new-town form, and demonstrates a growing awareness of the increasing complexities of urban life as expectations grow. Thus, the balance between, rather than the exclusion of, these various uses is the real issue to be determined by the designers.

One of the more interesting aspects of both old and new development in Hong Kong has been the grafting of this Western-derived urban form upon the traditions of an almost totally Chinese culture. Direct planning control has been comparatively recent as a tradition; even for Kwun Tong, land-use planning initially remained little more than dividing up new land into convenient parcels to allow construction and activities to be introduced by the private sector. While at first there was an attempt to separate land uses on a bad-neighbour principle, lot boundaries and the resultant road network were determined by the requirements of adequate building lots, and little thought was given as to how the town might actually function. Hence, problems like the influx of hawkers to provide services that were not 'allowed', or the endemic parking, servicing, and other traffic problems of the area, both testify to inadequate and partial analysis and design at the conceptual stage of the town's development.

As with their British new-town models, the form of the Hong Kong new towns is dominated by the requirements of their movement systems, once the constraints set by land acquisition and reclamation are allowed for. As implemented, both Sha Tin and Tuen Mun are laid out according to the hierarchical principles of their road systems, while Junk Bay and Tin Shui Wai are the first to examine and adopt bi-modal approaches utilizing both road and public transport networks. The result, as in Britain, is to delineate a framework of spaces within which the neighbourhood, the industrial and commercial centres, and the open spaces and recreational sites have to be determined.

Yet for Hong Kong there has always been an uneasy marriage of Western concepts and local requirements and cultural acceptances. The prime example of this is in the intensity of use and activity that the urban form is expected to allow, support, and facilitate and which is quite exceptional by Western planning standards. This is not only a result of the problem of land shortage and resultant high land values, with which those who know Hong Kong are so familiar. More pervasive and dominating in terms of community expectations are cultural attitudes themselves. The Chinese acceptance of high-rise living or the existence of weekend 'rush-hours' for recreational purposes seem but two symptoms of just what cultural or life-style differences might allow. Thus, Hong Kong is widely recognized to be unique as a city, and it is a uniqueness that has spilled over to its new towns. No other new towns quite replicate the disposition, density, and form of the buildings and uses that make up the new towns of Hong Kong.

Perhaps the most controversial of all aspects is the whole question of acceptable densities. After all, in 1949, Abercrombie tried ineffectively to transfer British density notions to Hong Kong, and undoubtedly one of the later aims of the planners formulating the Colony Outline Plan at the end of the 1960s was the classic one of using new towns to 'decongest' the existing urban core. In part, the policy has proved successful — today almost half of the Territory's population lives in the New Territories, and average gross urban densities, which approached 2,000 per hectare in the urban area in 1961, had, by 1986, been reduced by one-third. Yet, in the most modern high-rise developments much higher densities remain (up to 6,000 per hectare).

The net building site densities are of course even more staggering. A densely developed project in Kowloon [Ba Man], for example, has a density of 16,000 persons per hectare. In the newer public rental housing estates, which are all comprehensively designed to provide a satisfactory environment with all the necessary local facilities, a gross population density of 3,000 persons per hectare is applied as a guide in the initial planning stage. This can result in a net residential building site density of about 16,000 to 18,000 persons per hectare ... There is so far no conclusive statistical or other evidence to show that urban problems are particularly serious in these areas.[3]

Given current disquiet in Western countries about high-rise living and high densities, such conclusions may seem unreal and a cause for concern. The lesson from Hong Kong would appear to be that environment itself is not a cause for social pathologies, but that when set against expectations, familiarity, and attitudes, only then may it become a recipe for social disorder. Experience so far in Hong Kong suggests that reasonable design, good management, and socially accepted levels of crowdedness provide better clues to the acceptability, or otherwise, of the high-rise living than density levels themselves. 'There is nothing intrinsically good or bad in high-rise housing. It all depends on the quality of design and on the state of social development within the community'.[4] There are, of course, some design alternatives to high-rise Hong Kong style, notably the low-rise high-density for medium housing densities practised currently in Britain, or for even higher densities, the perimeter housing concept first put forward in Cambridge by Leslie Martin, and suggested for use in Singapore by T.K. Soon.[5]

Yet, most now agree that culture is the key to Hong Kong's acceptance. 'Previous studies done in Hong Kong found that Chinese were successful in developing ways of managing space, time and people'.[6] It was noted, too, that in Chinese communities 'much of the crowding was voluntary. In traditional Chinese culture, there was little ideology of conspicuous consumption of space'.[7] Hong Kong can therefore be put forward as a particular example of the generalization that successful urban design must understand, make use of, and be formulated for the 'user culture' of its potential inhabitants. So far, the new towns of Hong Kong seem relatively successful at attaining that particular planning objective.

There are, however, other aspects of high-rise debate that deserve a mention in the Hong Kong context. More controversial perhaps, is the social planning argument that the success of high-rise living can be deduced from the fact that, 'planned social interventions aiming at improvement of neighbourliness are possible. Residents can be mobilized to form informal and semi-formal networks at the [block] estate or project level'.[8] Certainly these ideas have been prevalent in both Hong Kong and Singapore, and have been utilized in both territories as a means of both community development and nation-building programmes. Their relative success can again be linked back to another long-standing tradition — that of mutual assistance in rural Chinese society, a previous fact of life of the communities from which so many of Hong Kong's present new-town dwellers once came. It is interesting to speculate, therefore, if such traditions will outlast the current generation of new-town immigrants.

There are, of course, other aspects of high-density living, not least those concerning relative efficiency.

It maximises the utilization of valuable urban land. It also reduces internal travel demand ... and generates sufficient external travel demand to support public transport. It provides relatively larger open space areas for residents compared to low-rise development at the same density.[9]

This goes back to the 'towers-in-the-park' Western design concepts of the early post-war years. All can be demonstrated in Hong Kong, and, given the fact of land shortage, it is not at all surprising that these merits should be advanced as the positive trade-offs of an urban form which necessity has seemingly forced upon the Hong Kong planners.

But, if high density is perhaps the most obvious characteristic of the form of the Hong Kong new towns, there is another which is also all pervasive, and intrudes at even the most detailed level of urban design: and that is the multiple use of sites. The concept has a venerable history, since it clearly derives from the traditional Chinese shop-house found all over East Asia, and characteristic of earlier periods of Hong Kong development. While Hong Kong has attempted to introduce the American concept of zoning into the Territory, experience, and an unwillingness to face high costs, soon forced a realization that single-use zones were impractical, and that some form of looser multi-use zoning control would have to be employed to control the development of the city.[10]. Even if only on equity grounds, the same concept has since been carried over into new-town planning in Hong Kong.

Equally, the value of urban land has encouraged the integration of varied uses upon single sites, such that the multi-use building is synonymous with development in most of Hong Kong. It is, therefore, only a truism that the successful planners in Hong Kong, as well as in urban design, have to think and be accustomed to implement three-dimensionally. It is a fact first recognized formally in the Colony Outline Plan of 1969 (see Fig. 7.1).

Due to the high densities of development which have to be accepted in Hong Kong, an urban form is being created which, in effect, comprises cities within a city ... [This] may call for a new approach to land use planning and development so as to allow for a greater degree of vertical integration of urban functions which, it should be noted, already exists in a haphazard form in many districts. Among other things, this pattern of development helps to spread the traffic load, encourages the economic use of utility services, stimulates the growth of commercial and industrial enterprises, and enlivens the quality of urban living.[11]

Fig. 7.1   The new urban form concept introduced in the Colony Outline Plan, 1969.

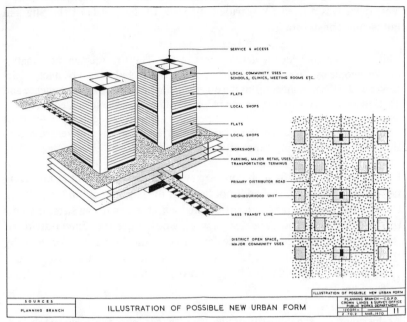

ILLUSTRATION OF POSSIBLE NEW URBAN FORM

Source: Planning Branch, Crown Lands and Survey Office, Hong Kong government, *Colony Outline Plan, Book 3* (Hong Kong, Crown Lands and Survey Office, 1969), Vol.1, Plate 11, following p. 37.

It is not surprising that both the public and private sectors in Hong Kong have perpetuated this urban style in their plans for new development, of which the new towns are an integral part.

   To sum up, the Hong Kong new towns in their present form present an interesting paradox. Their layout, disposition of land uses, planned linkages, and site designs all echo the fundamentals of contemporary British new-town design; yet, the inhabitants are almost entirely Chinese, and they are slowly beginning to impose their own ways and activities upon the alien form. The interesting question is whether the separation of uses and the careful management of functions within buildings in the new towns will gradually collapse under the pressures of small-scale individual en-trepreneurship as has happened elsewhere in Hong Kong, to bring about the bustling, uncontrolled, multivarious activity of the main urban area; thus replacing, in time, the current order and uniformity of the new-town neighbourhoods. The answer to that question may well be yes, and symp-toms of such a change are already beginning to appear.

The Landscape Design Input to the Hong Kong New Towns

A professional input to enhance the environmental design aspects of the Hong Kong new towns in landscape terms came relatively late in the design process. Indeed, it was, at first, largely remedial — what to do with the denuded borrow areas in the hills around the new-town sites, for instance. Yet, there was a need for a wider purpose. In the words of the Sha Tin landscape consultants:

> while the main goal for the development of Sha Tin is to accommodate half a million people by 1986, other important objectives include social balance, social choice and self containment. But the other standard objectives of convenience and attractiveness having to do with the physical, rather than the social, environment are noticed and felt by the majority of residents and non-residents alike — indeed their absence, particularly in the form of a 'soft' landscape, is now generally considered to be a mark of failure in a new town project.[12]

Up until the mid-1970s such concerns were indeed missing in Hong Kong new-town planning. Yet, had it not been for the requirement in Hong Kong to solve two specific problems associated with the new-town sites, it seems that professional landscape design work would have remained outside of the mainstream of new-town design work in the Territory, for even by the 1970s there was no tradition of professional landscape design work to be tapped locally. The problems, however, promoted a response, firstly for Sha Tin:

> At this point, . . . the similarity of Sha Tin with the typical new town largely ends . . . In this landscape brief there has been a special need to deal with the unusual problems of landscaping huge areas of filled land, and design for revegetation and development of the borrow areas from which the fill was derived.[13]

It was to deal with these issues specifically that the landscape design teams were introduced, but the result was a much wider, and all-pervasive influence upon Hong Kong new-town planning that appreciably altered the detail of the later new towns. That effect was noticeable first in Tai Po.[14]

The late incorporation of landscape design principles in the first-generation new towns, of course, made for problems. When the government's brief suggested that the consultant's master plan was 'intended to be an overall guide, but with specific examples of all the main or important features to enable the main landscaping elements of the new town to be appropriately planned and developed in later detailed planning',[15] it betrayed something of a misunderstanding of the role of landscape design work within that for the town as a whole. It is not, in fact, the 'prettyfying' role that seems implied. As the consultants politely commented:

> the timing of the Landscape Master Plan brief has required the study team to assess and recommend on a wide variety of degrees of commitment . . . The proposals developed for each level of land use commitment are progressively greater in scope as the degree of commitment reduces . . . As an example, in reviewing the possibility of development in Areas A and B [those to the north of the Chinese University of Hong Kong, and at Ma On Shan], it is appropriate to suggest, as a guide for planning, areas which have potential as open space or development land, the relationship of the massing or development to existing land forms, the recreation op-

portunities which should be preserved and incorporated in development, and guidelines for the townscape of key areas. In work on Stage I, however, where road alignments and development forms are more firmly fixed, attention was focussed more directly on the open spaces, and treatment of transportation networks, as a means of achieving a viable landscape system within the overall concept.[16]

For Tai Po, the master landscape plan became almost an alternative plan (to the outline development plan produced by the government's planners), but it was not until Tin Shui Wai and Junk Bay were begun in the 1980s that full integration of the landscape teams proved possible from the very beginning of design work on each new-town development (see Fig. 7.2).

Currently, the landscape elements of new-town planning are integrated at a variety of scales related to locations and functions. Thus, open space hierarchies, integration with fringe countryside, and recreational requirements — both active and passive — form important elements of the landscape professional's contributions.

These areas interlock with the intensively developed urban townscape, and assist with softening its character and form. They also provide opportunities for non-intensive recreation, and pedestrian [or cycle] movement through them to various parts of the town, and to upland recreation areas.[17]

They also act as a vegetated back-cloth, often seen as an appropriate foil, sometimes in the formal *fung shui* sense, to the mass of the town's built form, and thus integrating the urban form into its surrounding environment in design and activity terms (see Fig. 7.11).

There is little doubt that one of the principal innovations that the landscape designers brought to new-town planning in Hong Kong was a full exploitation of recreational opportunities and requirements. The first, the Sha Tin Landscape Master Plan, had to develop such provision standards from scratch, basing its ideas upon existing Hong Kong user patterns for the various recreation uses suggested. Such uses then had to be integrated into proposed district and neighbourhood open-space patterns (based on existing planned standards), which hopefully could be joined to form landscaped wedges and linkages containing the town's pedestrian, cycle, or other transport networks. In all the major Hong Kong new towns this network of open space has been designed to focus on a major town park as the key feature of each town's open space system (see Fig. 7.3), and where possible this has taken advantage of dominating natural features such as river or water frontages as major design features.

The treatment of the borrow areas has presented special problems. The traditional method of treating cut slopes in Hong Kong by surfacing them with concrete skim (*chunam*) leaves a permanent scar on the landscape, and was clearly inappropriate for large areas; especially as many of the sites were planned for high-class residential developments. Thus new land-restoration techniques had to be devised and implemented rapidly. One of the immediate recommendations of the various landscape consultants

Fig. 7.2   Junk Bay new town master landscape plan, 1982.

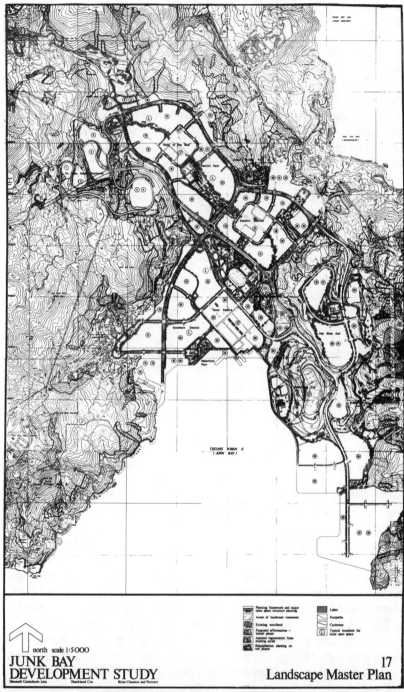

Source: Maunsell Consultants Asia, Shankland Cox, and Brian Clouston and Partners Hong Kong Limited, *Junk Bay New Town Study, Draft Final Report* (Hong Kong, New Territories Development Department, 1982), Plate 17.

Fig. 7.3   Schematic layout for Sha Tin new town park (Area 12).

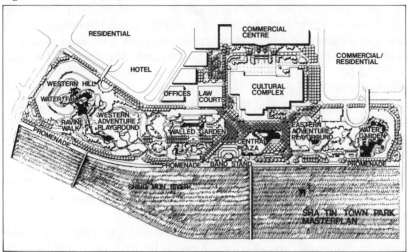

Source: Brian Clouston and Partners Hong Kong Limited, Hong Kong, 1986.

was that the borrow areas should not be selected and exploited purely on engineering grounds, but that they should be examined both for potential landscape impact at the macro-level as well as regarding potential reclaimability, particularly if they were to be returned to their natural state or to be used for recreational purposes. Together with their proper investigation on geotechnical grounds (since the formation of the Geotechnical Control Office within the old Public Works Department in 1977), the development of hydro-seeding techniques and the proper utilization of 'cut and fill' on reclaimed slopes has contributed to an immense improvement in the way that the Territory's land resources have been utilized in recent years as a contribution to the development of the new towns.

Today, while a few still regard landscape design as essentially a tree-planting exercise, and landscape management is likely to be the problem for the Hong Kong new towns in the 1990s, there is no doubt at all that landscape development as a part of urban design has come a long way in a decade, and that Hong Kong's new towns have proved to be a major catalyst in bringing landscape design to the fore amongst the design professions in Hong Kong.

Transport Networks and Strategies

Perhaps one of the more surprising things about new-town planning in Hong Kong until comparatively recently has been the ready acceptance of a transport philosophy based upon road hierarchies, and urban development laid out for easy communication by the private vehicle. Even allowing for the dominance of the bus, this seems odd when one learns that over 70 per cent of journeys in Hong Kong are currently made by public

transport,[18] and that car ownership is actively discouraged by high taxation policies. Given this encouragement of low car-ownership rates, and
the problems of car-parking provision in high-density environments, it
seems surprising that design of the public transport town came so late to
Hong Kong. The result is that with the possible exceptions of Tin Shui
Wai and Junk Bay (if, as now seems likely, the Mass Transit Railway is
eventually extended to that latter town), public transport fits ill with the
transport networks provided for most of the Hong Kong new towns. Traditional hierarchical road networks and neighbourhood environment areas
are very inefficient layouts from the point of view of the public transport
operator.[19] At best, public transport requires the most direct routes between high-density nodes, and performs even better if on reserved-track
unique routes. The relative experiences in the United Kingdom of Runcorn and Milton Keynes, pointed out in Chapter 1, are excellent demonstra-
tions of the issue.

Hence, in examining the transportation efficiencies of most of the Hong
Kong new towns it is arguable that all except the most recent are highway
towns upon which public transport networks are now being imposed. This
even applies in Tuen Mun, though there is now a dedicated-track transit
system there. This was an inevitable result of the way that the towns'
designs were produced.

Engineering development studies for each of the New Towns have included local
transport studies in the classical manner, using trip generation, distribution and
assignment models. These were initially used to estimate vehicular traffic for planning and detailed design of road networks. As development of the town progressed
the original transportation work has been extended to allow planning in detail
for public transport facilities.[20]

Sha Tin is a classic example of the problems that this approach generates.
Although a centralized bus network has been adopted as policy for Sha
Tin (that is, a radial route network focused upon the town centre to provide
maximum route interchange), the efficiency of the network is impaired
by the necessity to follow a road network designed on quite different principles, even though it includes special design features such as possible bus-
only lanes. An additional complication is the need to maximize route
interchange, and yet to allow separate networks to be developed focused
upon the railway stations within the town that provide for an important
part of the interurban public transport network to the main harbour area.
Such inconveniences are important in that they reduce the competitiveness
of public transport networks against the private car, or they increase the
costs of those for whom there is no alternative; both are important issues
in a town where its urban form assumes high mobility capabilities from
its inhabitants.

It might be suggested that the Tuen Mun light-rail system, first opened
in 1988, represents an important improvement over the Sha Tin model.
Yet close examination betrays a serious mistake. While separation of the
system from other road traffic is a definite advance on the Sha Tin model,

the system (except for a few minor exceptions) is tied to the layout of the road network along which it is mainly constructed. This perpetuates two disadvantages. The first is the simple one of access — wherever the tracks are placed, in the median strip or on one or other side of the road, pedestrians must cross roadways to board the tramway vehicles, and expensive and inconvenient footbridges or subways often have to be provided. The other issue is the same as for Sha Tin — the inappropriateness of road routings for optimally designed public transport route networks between traffic nodes.

Much the best solution would have been to design the light rapid transit network first, and then to place the urban forms around it, rather than the reverse, so that the system would have been at ground level and connecting the centres of the neighbourhoods (their traffic foci). For Tuen Mun, the savings in construction cost of locating the rail lines as a part of the road infrastructure have been judged to be more important than the longer term advantages of competitiveness and operating effeciency that independent location would have brought. Only in Tin Shui Wai (see Fig. 6.8) should the full advantages of integration be demonstrated, provided that the town eventually develops as currently planned.

Yet even optimally located systems have disadvantages. No fixed-track system can be as flexible as the motor bus in meeting fluctuations in demand location. So, it is apposite to note the justifications of those who recommended such fixed-track systems for the Hong Kong new towns.

The review of alternative public transport systems indicated that certain fixed track systems could offer lower operating costs and travel times than a bus service, with the most promising alternative being some form of tramway or light rail system using double-deck vehicles on surface track.[21]

Capital costs of installing a bus-only or rail-bus system for Tuen Mun were found to be almost identical. Although the concept of 'exclusive public transport right-of-way' was introduced at an early stage into the planning of Tuen Mun, and the first private sector interest in providing such a service arose in 1972,[22] the extremely long gestation period, and the fact that the eventual operator demanded and got a monopolistic public transport franchise for services in the town when the system was inaugurated in 1988[23] both indicate that even the operator wished to safeguard their investment in the system. The viability of such new public transport modes, even in Hong Kong, is not yet proven, at least not for the new towns.

Before leaving this rather cursory look at transport provision in the Hong Kong new towns, it is worth just a mention of the planning for the more personal modes, that is, for pedestrians and cycling. Attitudes to pedestrianization have become remarkably consistent. In all studies except the very earliest, the pedestrianization and later enclosure of shopping centres has been followed as a design principle; while at the town scale, the principle of segregated route networks independent of the road systems was introduced in both Sha Tin and Tuen Mun at an early stage, and has been continued subsequently.

The pedestrian system is an attempt to redress the balance between vehicles and pedestrians which has gradually been eroded over the years. It is recognised that the majority of all trips are made on foot and it is hoped that Shatin New Town will be a pleasant place not only to live but also to walk.[24]

Increasingly, these systems have come to be integrated with the proposed systems of open spaces and parks so as to provide a total environment at the human scale and an optimal one for human activities.

More controversial for Hong Kong has proved to be the provision for cyclists. In Sha Tin,

the footpath and cycle system has been designed to link the important areas of the Town, particular use being made of the designated areas of open space adjacent to the Shing Mun River. In addition to the recreational cycling which is so popular at present, it is anticipated that cycles will continue to be used extensively for the transporting and delivery of goods and journeys to and from work and school.[25]

For Sha Tin the planners clearly assumed that the traditional uses of the bicycle should continue and be encouraged. Yet, the transport consultants in Tuen Mun commented that:

it was possible to conclude that, despite the flat site of the new town, cycling will never cater for a significant amount of the total travel demand ... After considering a fully segregated network of cycle routes ... it was concluded that such elaborate provision would be difficult to attain at this late stage in the development programme and probably would never be fully justified.[26]

This sounds a little like special pleading to apologize for not thinking about the inclusion of such facilities within the town's overall design soon enough. Clearly cycling as a mode is continuing to remain of importance, since full segregated networks are already included in the town and site planning of later new towns in Hong Kong like Junk Bay. There,

the main cycleways are aligned primarily to provide direct routes between residential areas and industrial zones [the journey to work]. The total system, including secondary cycleways, would link to district and town centres, Mass Transit Railway stations, parks and recreation facilities.[27]

This faith seems justified by present usage rates in towns like Sha Tin that have already invested in such networks.

Once again, as with so much of new-town design in Hong Kong, there is a clear progression in sophistication and integration between transport modes and town design as the Hong Kong planners have become more experienced. However, if one asks which of the facets of past design make for the more obvious problems of the 1980s, then transport questions would be high on the agenda of complaints. That points to early errors, the lessons of which are only now being learned, digested, and sometimes acted upon.

Town Centres

One of the most impressive achievements of current new-town planning in Hong Kong is the quality of the town centres. But again, achieving that standard has been a long, and at times painful, process. It has already been commented that the first, at Kwun Tong (see Fig. 2.4), followed closely on British contemporary design principles. However, such a design was both land intensive and low rise; characteristics that were eminently unsuitable for Hong Kong conditions. It was not surprising, therefore, that at the next opportunity (in Tsuen Wan in the early 1960s) the opportunity was taken to design a centre more appropriate to Hong Kong's requirements.

Kwai Chung

The 1963 Outline Development Plan for Tsuen Wan (see Fig. 3.1) proposed that the new town should have three separate commercial centres, Tsuen Wan itself, Kwai Chung, and Tsing Yi. Kwai Chung provided the first opportunity for new thinking on design. In February 1964, a layout scheme (Plan LTW 79) for a large part of Kwai Chung, including Area 17 — the Central Area, went before the Land Development Planning Committee for approval,[28] following some preliminary planning begun the previous November. The new centre was envisaged as a subsidiary centre to that in Tsuen Wan, providing facilities for both commercial and administrative activities.

The principal focus is a two-storeyed commercial podium surmounted by residential point blocks [see Fig. 7.4], designed to incorporate a high level pedestrian circulation system segregated from vehicular traffic and providing the most direct and convenient lines of communication between the terraced residential area on the west through the commercial centre to the industrial area on the east ... The podium may be used either as private or public open space, or to provide a second level of shopping frontage when demands on the commercial centre so require ... Apart from the principle commercial and residential land uses, there are two cinema sites; a market and a terminal bus station each with provision for multi-storey car parks over; Government reserves to meet both specified and anticipated but as yet unspecified demands; and public open space.[29]

Despite some doubts over the level of investment required of any developer to implement the scheme, and over the three-dimentional planning control then proposed, the plan was endorsed and sent to the Secretariat for approval. The design controls suggested related to the heights of the podium structure, the layout of the pedestrian system, and the positioning of the residential towers. By December 1965, the Kwai

Fig. 7.4 Kwai Chung town centre scheme, 1965 (Plan LTW/36T) — this, and
a similar scheme for Tsuen Wan centre, though never built, are of great
interest as the first design in Hong Kong for a multi-purpose and multi-
level shopping complex. It was to be linked by pedestrian bridges with
the surrounding housing estates, and was to be built by private developers
according to detailed design controls: an early precursor for those to
be built later at Sha Tin and Tuen Mun.

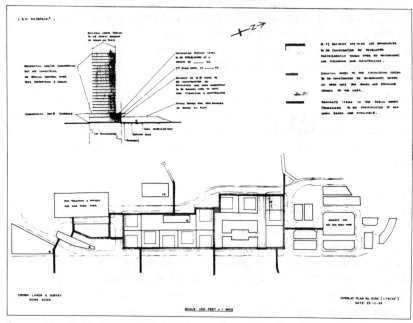

Source: 17/1 in BL 4/5282/60IV, Buildings and Lands Registry, Hong Kong.

Chung Co-ordinating Committee had agreed that the high-level pedestrian
walkways should be built by the developers where they abutted on to adjacent leased lots, while the other links and road footbridges would be
the responsibility of government.[30] Final approval, but not implementation, came in March 1966; just in time for the 1960s property slump.

The result was that take-up by potential developers for the scheme was
very slow. At the same time, the government's revision of its low-cost housing and resettlement programmes arising from the 1964 White Paper was
causing an urgent search for immediately available, additional sites. The
result was rezoning of available land in Tsuen Wan, and in October 1967
the District Commissioner New Territories suggested that premiums should
be reduced for the northern part of the Kwai Chung central area site and
that the remainder should be rezoned and used for government low-cost
housing[3] in order to expedite the take-up of reclaimed land in the area.
The result was the construction of the Kwai Hing housing estate, and the
loss of an effective town centre for Kwai Chung — not replaced even by
the late 1980s. There was, however, something of a postscript.

In 1981, it was pointed out that:

Kwai Chung has about half of Tsuen Wan New Town's area and ultimate population. It comprises twelve almost fully-developed Public Housing Estates, three major light industrial areas which will provide a substantial excess of factory jobs, Hong Kong's container port which still requires extensive back-up facilities, and ... very little else. Kwai Chung lacks private housing, non-factory jobs and leisure facilities. This socio-economic imbalance will be difficult to correct owing to the extent of committed development ... None of Kwai Chung's thirteen local commercial centres qualifies as a 'bright lights area'; that is a large, diverse, stimulating centre of community shopping, business and entertainment. It is too late to develop one town centre for the whole of Kwai Chung in the Kwai Hing area, but two town centres should be feasible via upgrading Kwai Fong and Shek Yam.[32]

Another case of *ad hoc* planning, missed opportunities, and sub-optimal solutions to attempt to solve resultant problems had become the planning outcome of the 1980s. The mistakes of two decades before had come home to roost.

Tsuen Wan Centre — A Special Case

Initial planning for a commercial centre in Tsuen Wan first followed very similar lines to that for Kwai Chung. In February 1965, a paper was produced outlining development proposals for that portion of the existing centre not developed on the north side of Castle Peak Road and west of Tai Ho Road in Area 18.

The intention is that the commercial/residential lots in question should each be sold restricted to a two-storey podium structure for commercial use only with a tower block above, which may be used for commercial/residential purposes. The levels of the three floors in the podium structure will have to be specified where necessary in order to relate them to adjoining building and provide for interconnecting high level pedestrian ways.[33]

Because the scheme was broken up by the existing road pattern, the planners recognized that a comprehensive single scheme on the Kwai Chung model was not practicable, but nevertheless, in their riew, the potential population served by the centre demanded a high-level circulation system to provide access to more shopping frontages on the restricted sites then available.

However, the proposals ran into opposition in the Land Development Planning Committee. Because the sites were split, it was argued that the level of detailed design control required to co-ordinate design amongst the various lot developers, and the constraints over tower development, would restrict and stifle possible private sector interest (no doubt recent experience on the Kwai Chung scheme was uppermost in their minds).

There was a very real danger of lack of sufficient coordination on the part of individual developers, thus isolated lots would be developed and have no architectural relationship to the rest of the development.[34]

Also, given the lack of upper-level shopping activity elsewhere in Tsuen Wan's existing commercial area, it was thought that the proposed two-level system would be unattractive. Hence it is not surprising that the scheme eventually approved in May 1965 incorporated conventional site development on larger lots, with ground-level circulation only, rather than the design principles of the original scheme.

The early outline zoning plans for the development of Tsuen Wan consistently proposed part of Area 6, as it had by then been designated, as the town centre, but immediate development became sterilized (by planning blight as it is usually termed) by the proposals for the new Mass Transit Railway being discussed and investigated at the end of the 1960s. Yet, as late as 1977, the hope still remained that it could be developed, even though detailed planning of the new rail link was already well under way.

According to the statutory draft Tsuen Wan Outline Zoning Plan No LTW/146, Area 6 is zoned for Town Centre for Tsuen Wan. This is the area in which cultural, administrative, commercial and social life of the town take place in their highest and most complicated form, and in which the most complicated central services supplied by the town are made available. The essential constituents of the town centre are: administrative buildings (e.g. town hall, town square, and other G/IC buildings), offices, banks, shops and important buildings for cultural and social purposes (e.g. library, museum, concert hall and theatre, etc.). These are services which are used by the population of the town as a whole and also by the inhabitants of its service area. The most important requirements for a town centre are geographical centrality and maximum accessibility for all modes of transport and pedestrians ... The role of this interchange [the MTR extension and bus terminus] should be designed, as in other city centres in other parts of the world, to incorporate all town centre facilities to serve the population of Tsuen Wan New Town and its neighbouring areas. It is considered that a great deal of rethinking is needed on the detailed design of Tsuen Wan Town Centre with a view to incorporating all town centre facilities, if possible, and terminal facilities with a high measure of compactness.[35]

Such a return to what would undoubtedly have been a high-rise multi-use centre was not to be however, for the decision to foreshorten the Tsuen Wan mass transit line and build the servicing depot in Area 6, in order to free land for the Kwai Chung container depot complex, removed the area from consideration as a town-centre site; the second major blow to the development of town-centre facilities in the town. Yet in 1976, the year before the above Report, events had taken an interesting turn. Following a visit by the Governor, Sir Murray MacLehose, when he had personally requested that a large meeting hall should be provided in the town, the Royal Hong Kong Jockey Club offered funds. By July, a site had been found by the New Town Progress Committee in Area 22, nearer to the waterfront, by adding to the government offices and magistracy that was already planned, with the result that the present Tsuen Wan Town Hall complex was born. Since this would affect the design concept of Area 6, by late in 1977 it was being suggested that community facilities should now be concentrated around the new town-hall site, while the old town centre in Area 6 should become, as an alternative, a self-contained residential/commercial complex centred on the new mass transit terminus.

These proposals were formalized in the plan revisions of 1977–8,[36] when the formal designation of 'town centre' was dropped, and the present civic centre was conceptualized. In the 1980s more improvements were gradually added — the redevelopment of the Yeung Uk stadium, a major open-space and transport interchange at the new ferry pier, and most recently a limited amount of redevelopment of the oldest commercial buildings in the area — such that, by the end of the decade, it looked possible that Tsuen Wan would at last have a town centre worthy of the name, and suitable for the then approaching one million population of Hong Kong's largest new town.

Sha Tin

As early as the Hong Kong Society of Architect's review of the Sha Tin plan (LST 17) in June 1961, suggestions were being made about the design of a new central area for the proposed town.

The railway line and one main through route could be left as mentioned and arranged so as to pass under the town centre, rather in the way it does in Vallingby New Town in Sweden [for in Cumbernauld in Britain (see Plate 2a)] ... and it is important to be able to move from the housing neighbourhoods to the town centre without crossing, at the same level, the main trunk roads.[37]

However, detailed planning work had to await the approval of Scheme IB by the Land Development Planning Committee in August 1967.[38] Stage IA as it came to be called, comprised Area 7 (zoned as 'central area'), 8, zoned as 'residential' — and to become Sha Tin's first public housing estate (Lok Yuen), and Area 16 (the Fo Tan industrial area, first stage). Thus, even though only part of Area 7 was to be reclaimed, planning of the whole zone was agreed as being necessary, and thus, town-centre requirements were being investigated at the earliest stages of new-town detailed planning work, unlike in Tsuen Wan. This work began in January 1969.

The first plan for the centre was put before the Land Development Planning Committee in May 1969.[39] Envisaged as serving an ultimate population of up to one million, the plan aimed to provide a full complement of administrative, cultural, educational, and commercial facilities. These were divided into three groups, of commercial in the north-east, educational in the centre, and the administrative and cultural to the south-west; each containing an associated open space of town square, active recreational area, and town park respectively; the whole being linked by a central pedestrian-spine routeway. Adjacent to the north-west was a major transport interchange alongside a much enlarged railway station. The whole scheme was to be surrounded by a ground-level ring road. The concept was, therefore, not unlike contemporary major schemes in British first-generation new towns or the prototypical city-centre scheme in Coventry.

While the plan was approved in principle, doubts were expressed by the Committee on the lavishness of the facilities provided, such as a museum and art gallery, and:

some members felt that pedestrian ways would be used for other purposes [no doubt hawking was being thought of] and that local considerations might affect the concept of providing pedestrian ways on this scale in Hong Kong. However idealistic this plan might be there was a feeling that the pedestrian ways might be overprovided and unrealistic. On the other hand if the pedestrian ways were replaced by roads the area of saleable land would be reduced, and the District Commissioner New Territories was concerned that the area of saleable land available would not meet the exchange commitments.[40]

It is clear that not all the constraints on the designers were planning ones.

It is interesting to note that the layout was prepared on the basis of providing sites of a variety of sizes to meet land exchange commitments expected under the New Territories Administration's Letter 'B' system. As it was expected that the sites would be allotted to a variety of owners, any kind of podium scheme was thought impossible to co-ordinate and implement — hence the ground-level solution, with pedestrian and vehicle separation by means of the pedestrian precinct, linked to surrounding areas by subways under the ring road.

Revision of the scheme, Plan LST 58 of September 1972,

was designed having regard to development within the framework of the Letter B exchange system with a view to comprehensive development by means of the aggregation of Letter B assignments if this was found to be desirable.[41]

It represented a first attempt to implement a scheme using larger sites, but it was again rejected by the Land Development Planning Committee.

Dissatisfaction with the proposals led to an attempt in 1973 to have the centre designed by outsiders. Maunsell Consultants Asia, the town's engineering consultants, brought in the British planners William Holford; and their proposals, presented in 1974[42] proved radical. Because of restricted space, limited access, vehicle and pedestrian servicing, and circulation requirements, it was argued that a continuous podium deck was required to provide vertical segregation.

The district commercial and community functions of Area 7 have been concentrated in a central, primarily commercial core. This area would be served by a raised pedestrian podium which would vertically separate the majority of pedestrian activities from vehicles. Surrounding this core, a primarily residential perimeter is envisaged, which would be linked to schools, public transport, commercial areas and district open space by pedestrian bridges at podium level.[43]

The central deck was to be dominated by three super-blocks rising above it, related to a town square, a market, and a cultural centre respectively.

Circulation of the consultant's scheme revealed sustained opposition to the podium scheme from within government,[44] particularly on grounds of the practicalities of implementing a comprehensive scheme amongst various developers. Doubtless, many were remembering the debacle of only a decade before with the Dockyard scheme on Hong Kong Island.[45] Many aspects of the detailed design were also criticized, sufficiently that the consultant's scheme was rejected and the government's own planners were instructed once again to have another try. This resulted in the issue of a revised planning brief by the Sha Tin New Town Development Office in October 1974, and release of a preliminary design as Sketch Plan C/SST/10A early in 1975.

The new scheme provided for a central commercial area with a podium, and high-rise office towers built over the railway station and bus terminus. The adjacent 'wings' were for normal commercial/residential development, linked to the commercial core by first-floor shopping podia. Between the commercial core and the adjacent major open space to the south-east in Area 12, two blocks were located to provide a major cultural complex and a government administrative centre. The disposition of the major land uses and the design blocks of the present day scheme (see Fig. 7.5) result from this exercise. The detailed planning work of the next ten years, in fact, was now only to fill in the detail and implement the scheme (Plates 7a and 7b).

It was envisaged that the new scheme could be developed in three major phases, proceeding from north-east to south-west, and Phase One (the residential northern wing) was the first to begin in 1977 as Sha Tin Town Centre Lots 15 and 16, for which the design control drawings were drawn up by the Public Works Department. It was noted that:

it is imperative that special controls be exercised with the letting of each phase of development particularly the commercial blocks which would be carried out by private developers. This is best done by letting off very large blocks of land to be comprehensively planned, designed and constructed within special parameters laid down under the terms of lease. Such parameters must include the construction and linking of shopping podia, predetermined levels and boundaries in accordance with plans and models. Such controls should also involve the integrating of acceptable standards of form, materials, texture and treatment of balconies, verandahs, advertising facilities and street furniture. These can be laid down with special conditions of lease similar to those used by development corporations for the private development of town centres overseas.[46]

This time the planners prepared their ground with care, and the result was an enthusiastic response from the Committee: 'We are very pleased in principle with the way the planning brief has been interpreted for the draft layout of the town centre'.[47] Following circulation, the formal plans for the site were finally approved in 1976.[48]

Fig. 7.5 Sha Tin new town town centre layout, 1983 (Area 7, Plan L/ST 7/1) (see also Fig. 7.6a and Plates 7a and 7b) — this was the third scheme for Sha Tin, and following a consultant's report formed the basis for the later development of the New Town Plaza scheme.

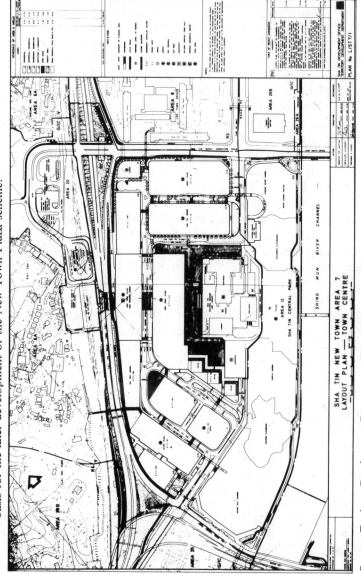

Source: Territory Development Department, Hong Kong government.

The last stage before final implementation of the town centre development at Sha Tin was the appointment of detailed design consultants in 1978 to draw up the detailed control requirements for the developers to implement the main scheme outlined by the government's planners. Yuncken Freeman Hong Kong were requested to provide a 'master architectural guide' for the scheme, setting out guidelines for later detailed design, development and maintenance of buildings, structures, and townscapes. They did introduce some design changes in their final report (Plate 7b): the office towers over the central shopping complex were removed, with the addition of a possible replacement site near the magistracy; while downgrading of the road network to district distributor status also allowed some savings in roadspace to be made; but the main features of the planners' layout remained.

Perhaps the most interesting aspect of the Report, which was accepted by government, was the final endorsement in Hong Kong of the principle of imposing detailed design requirements by lease conditions, as recommended by the planners in 1975. The consultants developed their recommendations from previous experience in Australia, especially Canberra (which also has a leasehold-based land development system).

The multi-level division of different land uses, the level 3 circulation systems and the functional connection between adjacent sites require comprehensive development control. This control will be exercised through lease conditions and administrative procedures within Sha Tin New Town Development Office. Controls on development are produced as a set of lease documents for each building site. These consist of written lease conditions to be read in conjunction with a set of drawings illustrating building envelope restrictions, design requirements and circulation connections for each development site. General information and concept material will accompany the legal documents to relate each development site to town centre design issues and indicate details of townscape elements required in both private and public spaces throughout the town.[49]

Control drawings were also provided by the consultants.

Thus, from a first attempt in the Dockyard proposals of 1961,[50] detailed site planning as a public/private partnership arrangement under overall public control came of age in Hong Kong in the New Town Plaza development of the early 1980s in Sha Tin (see Fig. 7.6a). No longer could Hong Kong's planners hide behind the statement that their control system lacks the means. The question about imposing good design had now become one of will. Subsequent progress in Sha Tin was rapid. Phase one was complete by 1980, while the central shopping plaza opened in 1985; this was followed by the cultural complex and the town park in 1987–8. The whole scheme was well on the way to final completion early in the 1990s, and already the centre has proved a major regional attraction, drawing customers from all over Hong Kong — testament, if any were needed, to the success of effective and attractive urban design.

Fig. 7.6 Cross-sectional diagrams for the multi-purpose town centres at Sha Tin and Tuen Mun (Castle Peak) (see also Plates 7b and 7c).

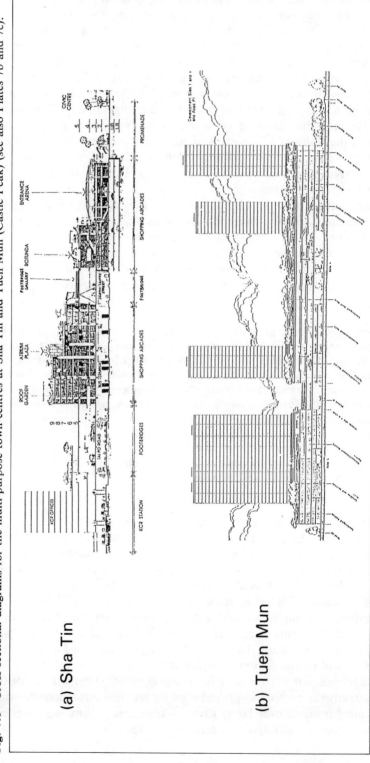

(a) Sha Tin

(b) Tuen Mun

Sources: Sun Hung Kai Properties Limited (New Town Plaza, Sha Tin); and Yuncken Freeman Hong Kong, Scott Wilson Kirkpatrick & Partners, Jones Lang Wootton, and Levett & Bailey, *Tuen Mun Centre Study: Vol.2 — Design Guidelines* (Hong Kong, New Territories Development Department, 1979), Section 3, p. 17.

Tuen Mun

As with Sha Tin, the location of a town-centre site for Tuen Mun new town was decided upon early, to be adjacent to the original population centre, near to the principal road through-route, and thus, off-set in relation to the urban area of the town as a whole. Initial thoughts of utilizing Area 11 alone were radically altered in 1973–4, when revision of the major road network led to the addition of the adjacent Area 37A to the site, which meant that Tuen Mun town centre now straddled the principal primary route through the town. This introduced major design problems in integrating the development of the whole site as one unit (see Figs. 7.7 and 7.6b). Despite the difficulties, the fact that planning proceeded more or less contemporaneously with that for Sha Tin, meant that many of the design solutions proved to be similar, as indeed has the final outcome (see Fig. 7.6).

Initial proposals were first circulated in January 1975 (Sketch Plan C/SCP/6), as a response to a planning brief issued by the Tuen Mun New Town Development Office late in 1974. They suggested a design concept based on a pedestrian precinct constructed above ground, and unlike the situation in Sha Tin the idea was not opposed, and it was able to be recirculated in October 1975 as a fully worked-up scheme. The two sites (Areas 11 and 37A) were considered separately, with connecting pedestrian bridges at podia level across the Castle Peak Road. The eastern Area 37A was to consist of a number of commercial and residential blocks linked by a first-floor pedestrian precinct structure over the service road network. To the west, a more complex arrangement of ground-floor structures and roads was again to be covered by a first-floor podium, above which commercial and residential towers were again proposed.

The land use pattern arrived ... at provides for a main north to south above the ground level internal service road and with residential buildings above the shops. The southern end of the pedestrian precinct joins up with the civic centre comprising a magistracy building, Government offices and a cultural complex grouped around a civic square.[51]

Unlike at Sha Tin, multi-storey car parks with direct access from the trunk road were proposed to be located adjacent to the centre. There was also an attempt to design in a variety of differently sized open spaces, vistas to the open area to the west (now the town park), and to provide design focal points both within the scheme and for the town as a whole. This was to be achieved by grouping the tall structures within Area 11 (see Plate 7c), Interestingly, while car and bus direct access to the scheme was possible, the exclusive public transport right-of-way was kept to the median strip of the adjacent district distributor roads, thus losing a possible opportunity for closer integration between public transport and land-use.

The result of the draft plan circulation was a comprehensive revision of the design in terms of both the blocking of the building masses and the distribution of the principal uses. An important change was the exten-

Fig. 7.7   Tuen Mun new town town centre layout, 1979 (Areas 11 and 37A, Plan LTM 2/11/4) (see also Fig. 7.6(b) and Plate 7c) — the scheme, while clearly related to its contemporary at Sha Tin, seems rather less successful, particularly in its integration with the road network. It suffered from the late inclusion of Area 37A and its resultant division by the main trunk road through the town.

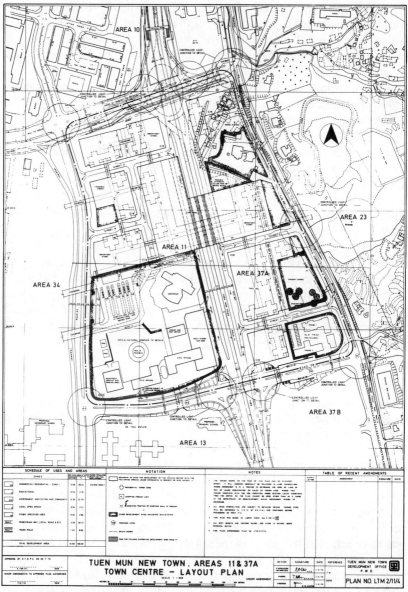

Source: Territory Development Department, Hong Kong government.

sion of the podium concept southwards into the civic area. However, in 1978, following the success of the final Sha Tin scheme, the whole design was given to the Sha Tin consultants, Yuncken Freeman, for further review and detailed design work. The outcome was yet another reworking of the original concept.[52]

While the original division of the site into a civic area to the south and a commercial core to the north was retained, the consultants completely revised and extended the design for the northern portion, utilizing a variant of their successful Sha Tin design. The main innovation was the introduction of an enclosed four-level retailing and parking complex bridging the Castle Peak Road, in order to provide a new and major focal point for the whole centre, and to integrate the east and west sites adjacent to the major bisecting highway. Linked to the central commercial complex by a system of overhead walkways were separate podia structures with residential towers above; the whole circulation system now being integral at third-floor level. The podia roofs were generally designed as landscaped recreational and open-space areas. There was also a separate ground-level pedestrian network to allow linkages to adjacent housing areas and to the town's public transport system (see Fig. 7.6b).

As with the Sha Tin scheme, the development was to be implemented in stages (seven), each of which would be subject to detailed design control through the site lease conditions and a general design manual.

The design and construction of the podium roof landscape areas, footbridges connecting the podium buildings, footpaths and landscaped areas between podium buildings and roads will be the responsibility of private developers. Accordingly a design brochure has been prepared to assist private developers in producing designs which will gain approval as will be required by lease conditions.[53]

The departmental layout plan incorporating the consultant's proposals (see Fig. 7.7) was approved finally by the New Territories Development Progress Committee at the end of July 1979. Full completion was almost accomplished a decade later.

Other Schemes

Since the late 1970s two other outline designs have appeared in Hong Kong for major town-centre developments, while two more, at an intermediate level, have been begun for both Ma On Shan and Tin Shui Wai. The major schemes were both designed by Shankland Cox for the first Tin Shui Wai master plan,[54] and shortly afterwards, for Junk Bay.[55] At present, both seem destined to remain as theoretical designs, for full implementation of Tin Shui Wai as a major new town still seems in doubt, and the planning of Junk Bay (see Fig. 6.6) has moved on somewhat from the consultant's original proposals. Nevertheless, the planning style brought to fruition in the twin centres of Sha Tin and Tuen Mun remains one of the most successful of the innovations that new-town planning has brought to Hong Kong, and points a useful way forward for the imposition of better town centre and retailing planning standards elsewhere in the Territory.

Housing Design

There is a considerable literature elsewhere on the development of housing in Hong Kong, particularly in the public sector,[56] and some of it specializing on design matters.[57] Nevertheless, it is appropriate in an analysis such as this to say something about the ways that housing has been dealt with within the overall planning of the Hong Kong new towns. This is especially apposite when practice in new towns elsewhere in the world is considered.

One of the first considerations is the place of the new towns in Hong Kong within the more general processes of the development of housing design, for it was notable in the examples from the West quoted in Chapter 1 that often new towns have been used as laboratories for the development of prototype and innovative designs. In Hong Kong, though one can point to examples of this kind, the fact that they occur in the new towns has been largely a matter of accident rather than intent. Innovative housing design, which in some twenty years has progressed through some seven 'marks' in public housing types for example, has been a requirement of public housing development as a whole rather than association with particular sites. Only with the disposition of the individual housing blocks on the site, and the surrounding landscaping and estate facilities, has local individuality come through as a major feature in the evolution of public housing estates. In other words, the programme has to be seen as a whole, rather than only that part associated directly with new-town development.

Housing in the Hong Kong new towns is, therefore, essentially derivative rather than innovative. Its delineation into neighbourhoods is but a local modification of almost universal practice elsewhere, while the public and private housing designs themselves derive from standardized models developed elsewhere in Hong Kong. In both sectors standardization is dominant over individualism at the estate level, while paradoxically perhaps, at the town scale the feeling is one of a discordant mosaic of independently conceived and unrelated three-dimentional modules scattered in a townscape in which they are only partially constrained by the special characteristics of their sites, and in which interrelationships between developments in terms of activities and design linkages are minimized. This impression is magnified for developments on the flat valley floors of reclaimed land, where topography is unable to relieve the blatant juxtaposition of completely unrelated designs.

The result is that meaningful comment on housing design remains at the estate or neighbourhood level; a reflection of the design 'packaging' that has come about in each planning unit, just like the engineering packaging that has so affected the basic planning of each town. In design terms the intrinsic failing is at the town scale rather than that of the individual scheme, and it is for this weakness that the planners can rightly be blamed.

However, the concentration on the neighbourhood was not always so. Examination of the earliest new-town housing layouts in both Kwun Tong and Tsuen Wan shows that they were direct derivatives of the general planning practice of the day, and could be traced back even as far as the principles utilized in the 1922 Town Planning Scheme. Basically, they were conceived as residential road layouts, adjacent to which were set out individual plots (lots) on which continuous frontages of conventional Chinese shop-houses or tenement buildings could be developed by private entrepreneurs. Yet, when a plan such as that produced in 1961 for Areas 12 and 13 in north Tsuen Wan is examined, if one was unaware of the location, the road layout could be argued to be absolutely identical to that of contemporary English suburbia, with its crescents, curving lines, and principal dual carriageways and roundabouts.[58] Only uncertainty on the availability of the site in the 1960s and changes in housing targets prevented its translation from British design manuals to Hong Kong reality.

The rejection of frontage development and the development of the estate model in the 1960s was largely a response to the necessity of accommodating the block designs for higher densities that the Public Works Department introduced into the public housing programme in that period. While for the resettlement housing 'H' blocks maximum concentration on site was demanded, and facilities other than the housing blocks themselves were virtually absent, even the earliest public housing estates (see Fig. 2.5) contained the rudiments of non-housing estate facilities within their designs. To take but one example, the Fuk Loi estate of 1963 in Tsuen Wan included both ground-floor shops, a kindergarten and open-play areas as an integral part of its initial design. Only for the cheapest levels of public housing (the low-cost estates) were such facilities excluded, where building costs were set to meet rental income targets, and unnecessary frills expenditure was frowned upon. The outcome of course was a typical Hong Kong solution: the provision of needed facilities by the private and informal sectors, and the proliferation of the hawker problems that haunted the planning and management of early housing estates all over Hong Kong in their early days.

It is, however, commonly recognized that public housing design came of age in Hong Kong when the first phase of the Wah Fu Estate near Aberdeen was opened on Hong Kong Island in 1968. The estate was truly innovative in that it introduced for the first time the concept of self-containment, with a full range of complementary services and facilities within the site, covered shopping, community facilities, education, local transport, and recreation. Only work activities were excluded from the estate design.[59] In fact, it set a design pattern that has remained ever since, subject only to design improvement and modification over the years. It also led the way for the private sector, who followed it up in the design for Mei Foo Sun Chuen, the first phase of which also opened in 1968, while Area 8, Stage IA of Sha Tin was the first new-town public estate to benefit from the lessons of Wah Fu.

Fig. 7.8   Public housing design in the new towns — successive plans for Sun Chui Estate, Sha Tin (Area 1B, Sha Tin): (a) Plan 78/P/1i of 15 September 1979 (*upper left*); (b) Plan 78/P/2i of January 1980 (*upper right*); (c) Plan 78/P/2x of January 1984 (*below*); (see also plate 8a).

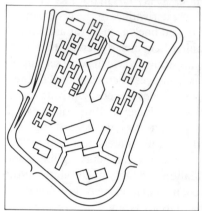
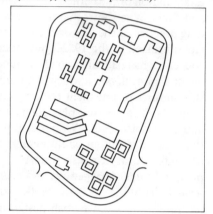
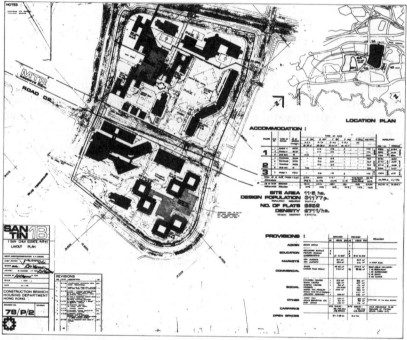

Source: Hong Kong Housing Authority, Hong Kong government.

The Lok Yuen Estate consisted of seven standardized multi-storey housing blocks set around a complex multi-level core containing two levels of shopping and market functions, a pedestrian deck, car parking, and a bus terminus. Also included within the scheme were public gardens, sports and recreation facilities, schools, clinic and welfare sites, and a cinema. The integrated housing estate thus came to Sha Tin from the beginning.

Even though Fig. 7.8 represents a design evolved nearly a decade later, the same basic design principles have remained. While the housing block designs have changed as resources have improved and demands have become more sophisticated, the same planning requirements have remained. These are essentially to accommodate population targets within the constraints of each individual neighbourhood site. Thus, as targets are reset or modified so the juggling of site designs progresses until a final scheme is accepted and agreed (see Figs. 7.8a, 7.8b, and 7.8c). Thus, the Housing Authority's site planners are basically solving a jigsaw puzzle of locating differing housing types and sizes within a fixed space, in order to meet target populations at site densities within current planning standards and guidelines set centrally. Only then is the complementary network of services and facilities designed in to meet the residents' requirements and to fill in the spaces between the housing blocks. The main advantage of recent design changes has been that as new building technologies have allowed higher and more sophisticated block designs, so increasing amounts of ground-level spaces have become available for more imaginative and innovative landscaping and servicing concepts to be designed and built in (see Plate 8a).

Before concluding, it must not be thought that the site planner in either the public or the private sector has anything of a free hand. In both, the demands of the market are paramount, in that accommodating the maximum in terms of target populations upon minimal sites is dominant as the constraining design parameter. This is particularly so for private developers (see Fig. 7.9). Even for them, not only does the site planner have to conform to the strait-jacket of planning standards and guidelines and the building regulations, but development of each area is now required to conform to the site-planning brief prepared by the relevant new-town development office planners. Such briefs not only provide the potential developer with information, especially about the planning context and site requirements set by the planners, together with relevant engineering, servicing, and infrastructure constraints, but they also often set quite precise planning requirements for the development of the site in terms of transport linkages, relationships with the road and other networks, housing mix to be accommodated, and any other special design criteria that the developer is required to incorporate. Lessons on integrated design are therefore slowly being learnt.

Yet, while the planning brief undoubtedly provides the vehicle by which overall design control at the urban scale might be imposed, the outcome to date clearly demonstrates that in the overall power balance the site developer is king, and the town designer remains weak. A prime example is the current paucity of design or transport linkages *between* schemes, rather than within. Until such relationships change, and the role of the urban planner is recognized in the negotiation that ought to take place at site level, the faults in urban design that currently afflict the Hong Kong new towns will remain. In short, current design failure represents a failure in procedure and responsibilities, rather than a failure in design itself at the urban scale in most of the contemporary towns.

Fig. 7.9 Private-sector high-density housing in the new towns — block plan for Sha Tin City One, Sha Tin New Town, 1986 (Area 14, Plan ML-ST-14A-5.2).

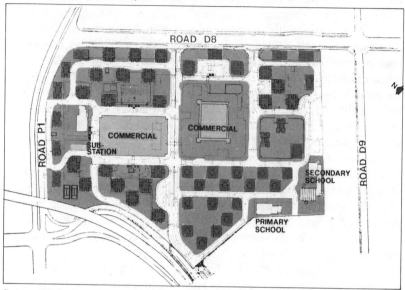

Source: Wong & Ouyang (HK) Ltd., Hong Kong, 1986. Copyright reserved.

Village Planning

There remains one further issue within Hong Kong new-town residential planning that deserves at least a passing mention. As with many new towns elsewhere, in Hong Kong, too, there has been an issue over the integration of existing settlement structures and communities. For most of the new towns considered here, it has been policy towards the traditional villages 'on site' that has been the main consideration; for Tai Po, Fanling, and Yuen Long the decision in the 1970s to locate major public housing developments alongside them created much more major design and social problems of integration. It is indeed for this very reason, that the latter remain much more akin to the theoretical concepts of expanded towns, rather than new towns, and hence were largely excluded from the discussion in these pages.

Village integration, where clearance has proved unnecessary within the wider considerations of urban design, is made more difficult in the Hong Kong case by the vast differences in scale between the high-density design of the new development itself and the traditional one and two-storey houses of the long-established villages that now have to live by its side. This relationship is further complicated by the long-standing building rights of indigenous villagers which require government to provide additional development sites adjacent to existing villages for further two- or three-storey village-house development in contemporary Hong Kong style.[60]

Fig. 7.10 Village resite layout for a new town — Leung Tin Tsuen in Tuen Mun (Castle Peak) new town, 1981 (Area 36B, Plan LTM 2/36/1).

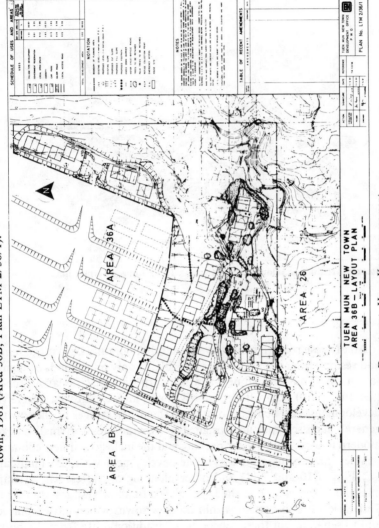

Source: Territory Development Department, Hong Kong government.

Fig. 7.11 Landscaping details for a village resite area in Tuen Mun (Castle Peak) new town, 1981 (Area 36B, Plan TM 6161 for LTM 2/36/1) (see also Fig. 7.10).

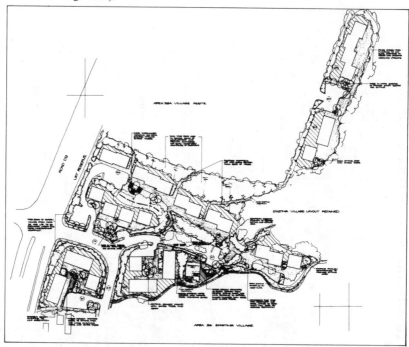

Source: Territory Development Department, Hong Kong government.

All of these requirements have meant that not only has village removal and resiting been avoided where possible, if only on grounds of compensation costs, but that all new towns incorporate specific layout schemes (see Fig. 7.10) for village improvement and expansion, where such developments can be incorporated on the urban fringes of the towns. In general, such schemes are designed to provide sites for small blocks of modern houses, to allow car parking and the inclusion of new community services, and to integrate the whole development with new landscaping (see Figs. 7.10 and 7.11) and other planning measures. The attempted integration represents, at the least, a wish to allow vestiges of older New Territories' life to remain within the new towns which have replaced it, and to separate out these 'cocoons' of traditional life from the bustling metropolises around them.

Industrial Areas

Planning for industry almost anywhere in Hong Kong, other than the two industrial estates at Tai Po and Yuen Long (soon to be joined by a third at Junk Bay), is entirely different to Western traditions (see Plate 8b and

Fig. 7.12). Only on those three estates does one find the low-rise, land-hungry industrial buildings so characteristic of modern industrial areas elsewhere, and utilized in the industrial planning of British and other new towns. As an aside, it is worth pointing out that at least as far as Tai Po and Yuen Long are concerned, the siting of the industrial estates is for-tuitous, rather than being an integral part of their new-town designs from the beginning. The alternative dominance in Hong Kong of the flatted factory block is well-known.[61] From its humble beginnings on the Kwun Tong reclamation in the 1950s (see Plate 3a), today's best factories have become very sophisticated buildings with lorry and container lifts, high-loading floors, and large support-free areas. In today's industrial areas, including the new towns, general plot ratios can be found of up to around 9.5, which allow up to 20 storeys of industrial production space on favourable sites, with generous roadways and areas for the development of necessary ancillary services.

Despite the early recognition of planning and management problems with the layout of the Kwun Tong industrial area in the early 1960s, the lessons learnt took a while to permeate planning practices elsewhere. Thus, in the planning of Kwai Chung Area 29 in 1964, the first major industrial site on the Kwai Chung reclamation, the large square lots set out along continuous road frontages produced a canyon-like townscape with severe servicing problems on the adjacent roadways. For the first major develop-ment at Sha Tin in Fo Tan, planned in mid-1969 (see Fig. 7.12), the same basic layout pattern was followed, even though provision was made for the first time for some open space, cooked-food stalls, a latrine, and some car and lorry parking areas, all as a result of the new planning standards then being introduced.

Thus, in the early years the principles of land allocation for industrial layouts changed little. Initial changes concerned the planning standards applied for land allocations within each town. In the Colony Outline Plan of 1969 an average of 928 workers to the gross industrial hectare was thought appropriate as the basis upon which to allocate industrial sites within each town. For Sha Tin and Tuen Mun (Castle Peak) that figure was reduced to 740. By 1975, a further change had occurred as additional experience was gained. The appropriate section of the then Hong Kong Outline Plan stated:

Surveys show a considerable range of worker densities in existing industrial areas, a significant intensification of worker occupancy rates and increases in industrial building plot ratios. It has been noted that in several industrial areas these trends have produced a poor working environment and an overloading of transporta-tion and access facilities. Whilst in the long term, it is expected that a higher degree of automation will tend to lower occupancy rates, nevertheless there is a need to limit worker density to a level at which industry can function efficiently and a good working environment can be preserved. After considering all these factors it is concluded that a maximum gross density of 800 workers per hectare should be aimed at and this should be the standard to be adopted for planning new in-dustrial areas.[62]

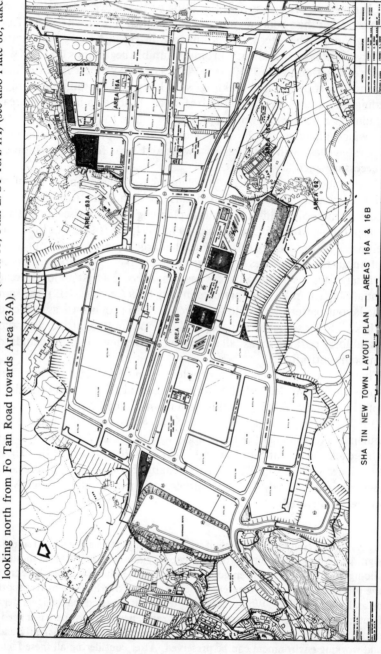

Fig. 7.12　Industrial layout for Fo Tan, Sha Tin new town, 1976 (Area 16, Plan L/ST 16A/1A) (see also Plate 8b, taken looking north from Fo Tan Road towards Area 63A).

Source: Territory Development Department, Hong Kong government.

It was suggested that, depending on the worker occupancy ratios, this could require the building plot ratios to be set as low as 5.0 on some sites. At the same time, new parking, loading, and unloading standards were introduced for application at the individual lot scale.

In terms of any major shift in planning attitude to the conceptual design of industrial areas in Hong Kong, apart from the introduction of traditional Western industrial estate concepts for the two special sites at Tai Po and Yuen Long in 1977 (introduced on industrial diversification rather than planning grounds), significant change did not really come until the late 1970s. Early in 1978, the Secretary for the Environment requested an investigation into the conflicting demands for ground-floorspace in existing industrial buildings between heavy machinery, parking, lorry access, and other uses. This was investigated by a planning team within the Town Planning Office, who recommended that certain uses ought to be provided centrally on industrial sites, rather than by individual factory owners. This suggestion, in turn, following consideration within the Land Development Policy Committee, led to the formation of a working party to devise a suitable pilot scheme for testing such a concept, and they, in turn, reported in November 1979.[63]

They noted that:

in existing industrial areas, such as Kwun Tong and San Po Kong, there are examples of parking and loading/unloading spaces within industrial lots being illegally converted for storage and other industrial purposes. Loading/unloading activities are instead carried out on-street causing considerable traffic congestion problems. All these point to the need for more ground floor accommodation for industrial activities ... and at the same time, more coordinated provision and control of parking and loading/unloading areas in industrial areas.[64]

Despite difficulties over control and implementation, the Land Development Policy Committee agreed in May 1980 that Tuen Mun Area 17 industrial zone should be utilized as a pilot scheme area. The idea was that the whole site would be sold to a single developer for a co-ordinated development, within which he would have to provide two central facilities for parking and commercial services, and for use mainly by the workers in the area: 'e.g. canteens, cooked food stalls, banks, child care centres, games rooms, office spaces, Neighbourhood Police Unit, sitting out areas, local open space, etc'.[65] Special lease conditions for the site were drawn up during 1981, and the site was finally put out to tender early in 1982 for completion by June of that year. It was stated at the time that the developer was required by the lease conditions to develop the whole site in accordance with his master plan, drawn up in agreement with the planners' brief, and was to assume responsibility for the management of the whole scheme on completion. While a buyer was found for the site, property conditions in Hong Kong were not conducive to an early start, but by mid-1988 the Nan Fung Industrial City was being extensively advertised on television by the developer as a new and forward-looking concept in Hong Kong industrial planning.

While site formation was still in progress, the submitted plans showed that additional to the normal multi-storeyed factory buildings around the periphery of the site, the central space was to be taken up by a new six-storey complex containing three floors of car and lorry parking, with the three upper floors being reserved for offices, a restaurant, and shops, together with a nursery, clinic, and varied recreational facilities. It was these that were being heavily promoted in the developer's advertising, and it will be interesting to see how clients react in the fiercely competitive Hong Kong property market.

Even with such innovations the industrial environment in Hong Kong is slow to change. Despite the public outcries that accompany the occasional serious industrial catastrophies, often caused by fires in ill-managed and badly controlled factory buildings, it is the industrial infrastructure itself that has proved the slowest to respond to planning changes. Despite increasing concern in Hong Kong over environmental and safety matters, serious interruption to the Territory's industrial livelihood is taboo. The fact remains that for the foreseeable future improvement in the industrial areas, including those of the new towns, will be slow, and will come about only as industrial processes change and demand new factory conditions, and as workers and owners gradually demand better managed and planned industrial buildings within which to operate. As long as most enterprises in Hong Kong remain small, pressures from those interests will remain weak, especially while demand for existing factory floorspace remains buoyant and competitive. The working environment in the Hong Kong new towns seems destined to be the last to respond to the changing perspectives and expectations that have brought such major revision and improving standards in housing and other community-demanded facilities within Hong Kong's urban areas.

Some Other Problems — a Conclusion

Intervention and Flexibility

In commenting on some aspects of the design of the various elements that make up the Hong Kong new towns it should be readily apparent now that those plans have often had to be changed. Indeed, it is commonly said, almost as a platitude, that 'planning is a continuous process', 'planning is the art of the possible', and so forth. Indeed, it has already been noted here that town-centre development in Tsuen Wan provides but one excellent example of how the overall concept of a town has come to be affected by a whole series of unforeseen outside events and interventions. There are many other examples in all of the new towns.

Perhaps the most fundamental fact that must be grasped as part of the Hong Kong new-town story is the adjustment process that all the towns have had to undertake continually as Territory-wide forecasts and requirements for particular land uses have been demanded and changed. It has been quite properly argued that the Hong Kong new towns have been and are 'public housing led',[66] that is, that they exist, grow, and have their design determined primarily to meet the long-term production targets of the Hong Kong Housing Authority and its predecessors. Other uses are expected to adjust accordingly, whether industrial or private, either by contracting to give extra developable land for housing if annual targets are forecast not to be met, or by expanding to service the increased population targets that each town has from time to time been forced to accept as new intakes of public housing families are programmed to be absorbed, and as Territory-wide population forecasts have been revised.

This remains an on-going process, and it is upon this that the future full development of all eight Hong Kong new towns will depend for the 1990s, whatever the relative strategic arguments over harbour-orientated development versus dispersed development elsewhere.[67] Within that argument, more detailed changes are undoubtedly set to occur as a well-publicized shift takes place within the public housing programme for the 1990s, from straight rental accommodation to an additional emphasis on home-ownership and private-sector partnership schemes within the new estates still planned for new towns like Junk Bay and Tin Shui Wai. Already, in Tuen Mun, 1988 was seeing the last public rental estate under construction for that town — its remaining public sites now being programmed for varied selling schemes.

Sometimes such pressures for change in use allocations can work advantageously. A good example is the opportunity given to replan the industrial zones in Areas 2 and 45 of Tsuen Wan, proposed in 1981–2 as a result of a Territory-wide agreement to reduce the amount of industrial land programmed for development, partly to utilize available resources more effectively and partly to meet pressing housing land requirements. While the Tsuen Wan proposals involved comprehensive private-sector redevelopment, with resultant advantage to the existing factory owners whose sites became much more valuable, western Tsuen Wan will undoubtedly gain a major improvement to its environmental standards when the obsolescent industrial buildings are replaced by modern commercial and residential buildings housing some 50,000 or so people, and traffic can be removed to the new coastal bypass road.[68]

However, such pressures can of course also operate disadvantageously. The increased demands for public housing sites in Kwai Chung in 1968 dealt a serious and permanent blow to the proper development of that part of Tsuen Wan new town as we have already noted. Another case occurred in Sha Tin in 1981, when Stage II of the town's development was under review. At that time, it was suggested that full development of the head-of-the-valley sites for public housing (Area 31) would seriously overstretch the sites' capabilities to provide a living environment up to the then full planning standards and requirements. It was, therefore, suggested that the site should be developed at a reduced scale, and that replacement accommodation should be built in Area 125 to the north-east of Ma On Shan.[69]

Though supported in the Secretariat, the Director of Housing was forthright:

This department finds the suggested deletion of the housing estates in Sha Tin Area 31A and B to be neither necessary nor desirable in the public interest. The change would be quite unacceptable to this Department.[70]

The change was not therefore made, and legitimate planning arguments fell before the all-important priorities of the public housing targets. Nevertheless, the planning objections do not go away, and one wonders just what environmental disadvantages will remain for the inhabitants to bear as they live on in the area into the next century.

Some idea of the ultimate cost sometimes borne is perhaps provided by the case of the inhabitants of Mayfair Gardens, Tsing Yi. There, in the late 1980s, major controversy broke out on safety grounds, because of the close proximity of some of this private residential development to the oil tanks of a storage installation introduced as part of the general policy of concentration of industrial activities on the southern and western shores of the island. Despite the high-profile public debate, well supported in the press, the eventual outcome was only a marginal improvement by the agreed vacation of those residential towers nearest to the storage site. Many, however, wondered how the private development had come to be allowed in the first place. Sometimes the hunger for sites produces strange bedfellows. Clearly, change in the new-town planning process produces its own conflicts and unwanted outcomes, which the Hong Kong planning system is occasionally hard put to to resolve.

Such planning adjustments also come from other causes. Early in 1985, discussion within the Sha Tin Planning Sub-committee was centred upon the finding of infill sites or upgrading existing population intakes in order to bring the forecast population of the town as a whole closer to the overall target allowed for by the committed infrastructure development.[71] In short, changes in occupancy rates and smaller family size were bringing a lower density uptake of housing areas, and hence utilization of resources. In the opposite direction, during the early development of Kwai Chung, the influx of resettlement housing into Area 10 resulted in the population targets for the area being exceeded, with the result that the Director of Water Supplies had to object (since his plans were based on older and smaller population forecasts), with the result that a crash programme of housing readjustments had then to be instituted to reduce the incoming population to acceptable limits.[72]

Such are the perils of population forecasting in new-town planning. Nearly always forecasts are wrong, and the penalties of immutable targets are serious. Perhaps the most notable of recent years concerning the new towns has proved to be the public outcry over the lack of adequate education places in some of the new towns, particularly (initially in Tuen Mun), caused by inadequacies in the monitoring of migration changes and family growth within the towns' populations. The result again had to be a crash programme of adjustments to meet and contain the very real public discontent. One result of this imbalance was that some towns had up to a third of their school populations, in some categories, migrating in the late 1980s, while over sixty new schools were programmed for the new towns for the early 1990s. Thus, robustness, flexibility, and change are crucial elements of new-town planning in Hong Kong as elsewhere, and government has been sharply reminded of the penalties of not complying when such problems have arisen in the planning and provision of new town services.

Environmental Matters

Given the unusual engineering requirements of large-scale excavation and reclamation within the new-town programme, it is not surprising that the constraints imposed by the natural environment have sometimes been rather overlooked in the headlong dash for progress. Sometimes the effects are marginal, but at times the constraints of the environment have unexpectedly intruded.

The stability of slopes is a major factor in Hong Kong, and it was the reassessment of the potentials for disaster that led to the establishment of the Geotechnical Control Office in 1977 following particularly serious landslide disasters in 1972 and 1976. The Office has since became involved in the vetting of all new-town planning from that date on. Sometimes layout modifications are only marginal, as for example, for the slope adjustments required adjacent to the development sites in Areas 4C and 4F at Sha Tin,[73] and usually surmountable, even though there may be a dispute as to who is to pay. For example, there was a dispute between government and the developer over the necessary remedial works on the housing development remedial works site in Area 42, also in Sha Tin, where development was to take place on one of the former racecourse borrow platforms.[74]

Site problems can at times be quite expensive to put right. For example, the reclamation for the original trunk road scheme adjacent to the Sha Tin racecourse site was originally programmed to allow for settlement before the road was to be built. Because it was delayed due to clearance problems in the borrow areas required to provide the fill, and disruption by local fisherman on the reclamation site (initial reaction to the early new-town works was not always favourable), the reclamation work was not so carefully controlled as perhaps it might otherwise have been. The result was that pockets of soft sand were trapped within the fill, resulting in expensive and necessary remedial work and removal when the road was already under construction. There was a cost overrun of some HK$13.5 million in order to complete the scheme.[75] This caused some searching questions to be asked at the time.

By far the best known and major effect of such geotechnical problems affected the planning of Tuen Mun. One of the earliest tasks of the new Control Office when it was set up was to investigate the slope-stability problems then coming to the fore in the eastern foothills of the Castle Peak hill range on the western fringes of the new town, particularly in Areas 8 and 19. Their study recommended in Area 8 that any constructed slopes would need to be as shallow as 1 in 4, and that even then the suitability of developing the planned upper platform for housing was doubtful. Long-term monitoring was also recommended. The outcome was a decision to relocate the housing elsewhere, and the adjacent Area 42 to the north was also changed from medium density housing to public open space.[76]

Similar issues affected the later planning work on Area 19 to the south when the stadium and associated works there were being designed.[77] Serious doubts existed about the slopes formed from earlier borrow activity in the area in 1978, and the result was the imposition of a scheme which severely restricted access to the slopes above and to the west of the planned development.

Environment matters of other kinds have also intruded from time to time in the Hong Kong new-town planning process, and as the government's own activities in the field of environmental protection have increased in the 1980s so the consultative tasks of the new-town planners have also expanded. Sometimes interventions have been unexpected. A recent example of such a case concerned the access road to the east of the new Junk Bay road tunnel, which was objected to on noise grounds at a very late stage by the Commissioner for Environmental Protection.

The details of the proposals in relation to the preferred principal access route have only recently come to my attention and I am most unhappy with what I have seen. According to the Minutes of the Junk Bay Steering Group meeting on 8th December 1981, at which I was not represented, it was reported that . . . because of the better performance on Cost, Land Use, and programming . . . Alignment 1 should be adopted as the principal access. Alignment 1 involves a 1 kilometre stretch of dual 2-lane carriageway climbing steeply along the side of the hills high above the main part of the town . . . The impact of a major road on the environment is always substantial, but the small scale of the setting in Junk Bay, and the elevation of the road will mean that Alignment 1 will dominate a large proportion of the town, and not only from the noise standpoint.[78]

In the end, Alignment 1 prevailed and was endorsed as acceptable by the Land Development Policy Committee in June 1982, even though an attempt was made to reopen the issue before the Development Progress Committee as late as August 1984. In early 1985 it was finally agreed that:

application of the detailed findings and recommendations of the Environmental Assessment Reports to the development of Junk Bay New Town . . . should continue to be considered on a project specific basis by the Project Manager Junk Bay, subject to further detailed investigations and policy approved from the appropriate authority as and when necessary, the availability of funds and compliance with established practice and procedure.[79]

Somehow it reads as a rather less that whole-hearted endorsement of the principles of environmental protection and a willingness to support progress and past practice rather than constraint.

Fung Shui and Geomancy

Before concluding this diverse chapter on new-town design matters, it is perhaps appropriate to end on one topic that is most certainly distinctly Chinese and yet is of continuing importance to all scales of town planning in Hong Kong. It is also a useful reminder of the axiom that all planning remains culture bound. There is not the space here to launch into a full discussion of the meaning and significance of the term *fung shui*; in any case that can be found elsewhere;[80] but suffice to say that it relates to the precise location, orientation, and significance of buildings and other features to the natural landscape, and that ignoring it brings misfortune to those that fail to comply. Such beliefs continue to be widely held: it is well known, for example, that the new Hong Kong Bank headquarters in Hong Kong was influenced by such matters, and means that consideration of them enters into many new-town planning matters in the Territory.

The implications are essentially twofold. Firstly, certain natural features, particularly hills and wooded slopes, are regarded as untouchable, because of *fung-shui* significance, while those features which need to be removed can only be affected at a price — that is, that the hoary spectre of compensation raises its head, and there is nothing like '*fung shui*' significance to raise the stakes in the matter of negotiations between villagers and government. Where possible therefore, attitudes to compensation within government being what they are, interference is avoided if at all feasible on planning grounds. But one example will suffice:

District Office Tuen Mun have indicated that a large proportion of the Tai Lam foothills, which have 'fung shui' significance, would be adversely affected by the original alignment of Distributor Road 9. A memo ... indicated that 'it is expected that very tedious and protracted negotiations will be involved to overcome the fungshui problem and to this end it is best to avoid clearing this area if at all possible'.[81]

Such are some of the specialist problems of Hong Kong new-town planning. As with many things, such problems can be overcome at a price — the spirits may be placated — but not surprisingly that price can be too high and as a result the plan must be changed. Here, for once, in the Tuen Mun case, the road was changed and cultural requirements, expediency, or due regard for traditions, term it as you may, entered another small place in the annals of planning the Hong Kong new towns.

Notes

1. J. Barnett, *An Introduction to Urban Design* (New York, Harper and Row, 1982), p. 7.
2. J. Jacobs, *The Death and Life of Great American Cities* (New York, Random House, 1961).
3. C.S. Chau, 'High Density Development: Hong Kong as an Example' in R.Y.W. Kwok and K.S. Pun, *Planning in Asia — Present and Future: Proceedings from the Asian Regional*

Workshop/Conference of the Commonwealth Association of Planners 1981 (Hong Kong, University of Hong Kong, Centre of Urban Studies and Urban Planning, 1982), pp. 5–6.

4. A. Koerte, 'Confinement versus Liberation — A Cross-Cultural Analysis on High-Rise, High-Density Living' in Y.M. Boey (ed.), *High-Rise, High-Density Living: Singapore Professional Centre Convention 1983 — Selected Papers* (Singapore, Singapore Professional Centre, 1984), p. 176.

5. T.K. Soon, 'Ring: As Answer to Highrise Living' *Singapore Straights Times*, 26 April 1975, p. 11.

6. Y.K. Chan, 'Life in Confined Living Space: With special reference to Housing in Hong Kong' in Y.M. Boey (1984), see note 4 above, p. 188.

7. Y.K. Chan (1984), see note 4 above, p. 188.

8. Y.K. Chan (1984), see note 4 above, p. 190.

9. P.K.W. Fong. 'The Management of High-Rise Residential Development in Hong Kong' in P. Hills (ed.), *State Policy, Urbanization and the Development Process: Proceedings of a Symposium on Social and Environmental Development, University of Hong Kong, October 1984* (Hong Kong, University of Hong Kong, Centre of Urban Studies and Urban Planning, 1985), p. 101.

10. Roger Bristow, *Land-use Planning in Hong Kong: History, Policies and Procedures* (Hong Kong, Oxford University Press, 1984), p. 229.

11. Colony Outline Planning Division. *The Colony Outline Plan: Book 3, Vol. 1 — Concepts and Outline Proposals* (Hong Kong, Crown Lands and Survey Office, 1969), p. 36.

12. Yuncken Freeman Hong Kong, *Sha Tin New Town Master Landscape Plan: Phase One Report — Volume One* (Hong Kong, New Territories Development Department, 1977), p. 1.

13. Yuncken Freeman Hong Kong (1977), see note 12 above, p. 1.

14. Urbis Planning Design Group and Brian Clouston and Partners Hong Kong Limited, *Tai Po Landscape and Recreation Study: Final Report* (Hong Kong, New Territories Development Department, 1979). This report set out what was virtually a new plan for the expanded town, and it formed the basis of what is now regarded as one of the most successful of the new-town designs in landscaping terms.

15. Sha Tin New Town Development Office, *Sha Tin New Town Development Stage II: Master Landscape Plan — Brief* (Hong Kong, New Territories Development Department, 1976), at 24/1 in ENV 70/24/05I, Buildings and Lands Registry, Hong Kong, para.3.3, p. 1.

16. Yuncken Freeman Hong Kong (1977), see note 12 above, p. 16.

17. Yuncken Freeman Hong Kong (1977), see note 12 above, p. 3.

18. D.T. Stewart, *Public Transport for Several New Towns in Hong Kong* (Hong Kong, Maunsell Consultants Asia, 1983), p. 16.

19. P. Addenbrooke, D. Bruce, I. Courtney, S. Helliwell, A. Nisbet, and T. Young, *Urban Planning and Design for Public Transport* (London, Confederation of British Road Passenger Transport, 1981), p. 30.

20. D.T. Stewart (1983), see note 18 above, p. 13.

21. Scott Wilson Kirkpatrick & Partners, *Tuen Mun New Town Transport Study: Final Report, Volume 1* (Hong Kong, New Territories Development Department, 1978), para.5.1, p. xix.

22. The Hong Kong Tramway Company (part of Wharf Holdings) first proposed a simple figure-of-eight system for the town in 1972. Protracted negotiations with the government lasted until June 1983, when the company finally decided to withdraw as the potential operator of the proposed system. The Kowloon–Canton Railway Corporation (a Hong Kong publicly owned corporation) agreed to take on the operation of the system in 1984, with construction commencing in 1986 and the first part of the system becoming operational in September 1988.

23. The legal framework for the operator's franchise was provided by the Kowloon–Canton Railway Corporation (Amendment) Ordinance (No. 56 of 1986), which protected the operator for 20 years by providing an operating monopoly in its area. It aroused considerable argument during its passage through the Legislative Council, see *Hong Kong Hansard* (Hong Kong, Government Printer) 16 July 1986, pp. 1523–7, and 30 July 1986, pp. 1733–51.

24. Sha Tin New Town Development Office in conjunction with Maunsell Consultants Asia, 'Road Planning for Shatin New Town', in Hong Kong Council of Social Service, *Symposium on 'Social Planning in a New Town' — Case Study: Shatin New Town* (Hong Kong, Hong Kong Council of Social Service, 1976), p. 163.

25. Sha Tin New Town Development Office et al. (1976), see note 24 above, p. 162.

26. Scott Wilson Kirkpatrick & Partners (1978), see note 21 above, paras.8.65–6, p. 171.

27. Maunsell Consultants Asia, Shankland Cox, Brian Clouston and Partners Hong Kong Limited, *Junk Bay New Town Study: Draft Final Report, March 1982* (Hong Kong, New Territories Development Department, 1982), p. 73.

28. Land Development Planning Committee Paper No. 43, 28 February 1964, *Kwai Chung Valley Layout Plans: Areas 10 (Part), 17 and 29 (Part)*, at 28 in BL 4/5282/60II, Buildings and Lands Registry, Hong Kong.

29. Land Development Planning Committee Paper No. 43 (1964), see note 28 above, paras.5(ii) and (iii), p. 3.

30. Public Works Department Land Conference, 23 December 1965, *Tsuen Wan District — Kwai Chung Commercial Centre Area 17: High Level Pedestrian Ways*, at 17/3 in BL 4/5282/60IV, Buildings and Lands Registry, Hong Kong.

31. Memorandum from District Commissioner New Territories to Director of Public Works, 17 October 1967, at 41 in BL 4/5282/60V, Buildings and Lands Registry, Hong Kong.

32. Tsuen Wan New Town Development Office, *Town Centre Parking for Kwai Chung: Initial Appraisal* (Hong Kong, New Territories Development Department, 1981), p. 1.

33. Land Development Planning Committee Paper No. 69, 26 February 1965, *Tsuen Wan Area 18 (Part): Town Centre Development Control*, at 4 in BL 4/5282/60IV, Buildings and Lands Registry, Hong Kong. The scheme was shown on Plan LTW 32K.

34. Minutes of the 49th Meeting of the Land Development Planning Committee, 26 February 1965, at 5 in BL 4/5282/60IV, Buildings and Lands Registry, Hong Kong, item 7, para.(d).

35. Memorandum from New Territories District Planning Division to Project Manager Tsuen Wan, 24 November 1977, *Mass Transit Extension to Tsuen Wan: Tsuen Wan Area 6 — Revised Layout Plan TWNT/4*, at 45B in BL 4/5282/60VIII, Buildings and Lands Registry, Hong Kong.

36. Outline Zoning Plan LTW 146A of August 1977 was the last to show Area 6 as the Town Centre zone. Plan LTW 146C of August 1978 replaced the zoning by an ordinary 'Commercial/Residential' classification to allow private development of the podium then planned above the relocated Mass Transit Railway Tsuen Wan Depot, which was then planned to be constructed in most of Area 6 to the north of Castle Peak Road.

37. Hong Kong Society of Architects Planning Commitee, *Report to Government: Town Planning Ordinance, Hong Kong Town Planning Board — Sha Tin and District Outline Development Plan and Explanatory Statement* (Hong Kong, Hong Kong Society of Architects, 1961), para.E5, p. 6.

38. Land Development Planning Committee Paper No. 154, 28 April 1967, *Sha Tin New Town, Phase I (Revised)* and Minutes, at 8 and 22 in BL 8/5282/61II, Buildings and Lands Registry, Hong Kong.

39. Land Development Planning Committee Paper No. 245, 30 May 1969, *Sha Tin New Town — Stage 1, Phase I — Central Area 7 and Industrial Area 16: Layout Plans Nos. LST 49A, LST 53A and Sketch No. TP1/69*, at 46 in BL 8/5282/61II, Buildings and Lands Registry, Hong Kong.

40. Minutes of the 98th Meeting of the Land Development Planning Committee, 30 May 1969, at 47 in BL 8/5282/61II, Buildings and Lands Registry, Hong Kong, para.3.2.

41. Memorandum from Principal Government Town Planner to Project Manager Sha Tin, 1 March 1974, at 67 in BL 8/5282/61III, Buildings and Lands Registry, Hong Kong, para.3, p. 1.

42. Maunsell Consultants Asia and William Holford and Partners, *Planning Report: Sha Tin Areas 7 and 20 — Layout Plan No PST/2: Explanatory Statement* (Hong Kong, New Territories Development Department, 1974).

43. Maunsell Consultants Asia et al. (1974), see note 42 above, para.5.1, p. 2.

44. See memoranda at 67 and 72 from Principal Government Town Planner and Director of Urban Services respectively, in BL 8/5282/61III, Buildings and Lands Registry, Hong Kong.

45. Director of Public Works, *City of Victoria — Central Area Redevelopment: Report by the Director of Public Works Hong Kong* (Hong Kong, Government Printer, 1961), pp. 23–5. A discussion of this problem is given in Bristow (1984), see note 10 above, pp. 234–7.

46. Town Planning Office, *Explanatory Statement: Town Centre Sha Tin New Town — Planning Areas Nos. 7 and 20: Sketch Plan No. C/SCP/10 — Preliminary* (Hong Kong, Public Works Department, 1975), para.9.7, p. 7.

47. Memorandum from Sha Tin New Town Development Office to Government Town Planner, 20 May 1975, at 7 in BL 8/5282/61V, Buildings and Lands Registry, Hong Kong.

48. Sha Tin New Town Development Office, *Sha Tin New Town. Area 7 Town Centre Layout Plan: Levels 1 and 2* (Plans STP 75/014B), Sheets 1 and 2, April 1976; and *Sha Tin New Town Layout Plan — Area 20* (Plan STP 77/005), April 1977, (Hong Kong, New Territories Development Department 1976–7).

49. Yuncken Freeman Hong Kong, *Sha Tin Town Centre Study: 1. Urban Planning Controls* (Hong Kong, New Territories Development Department, 1978), para.10.2.2, p. 166. The whole study was in three volumes.

50. Director of Public Works (1961), see note 45 above, pp. 23–5.

51. Tuen Mun New Town Development Office, *Planning Report: Tuen Mun New Town Planning Areas 11 and 37A — Town Centre: Explanatory Statement — Layout Plans Nos. LTM 2/11/1, LTM 2/11/2* (Hong Kong, New Territories Development Department, 1975), para.4.1, p. 2.

52. Yuncken Freeman Hong Kong, *Tuen Mun Town Centre Study* (Hong Kong, New Territories Development Department, 1978) (3 vols.).

53. Tuen Mun New Town Development Office, *Planning Report: Tuen Mun New Town Planning Areas 11 and 37A — Town Centre: Explanatory Statement to the Layout Plan* (Hong Kong, New Territories Development Department, 1979), Plan LTM 2/11/4, para.9.2, p. 4.

54. Shankland Cox, Binnie and Partners International, and Peat Marwick Mitchell & Co., *Tin Shui Wai Urban Development: Master Plan* (Hong Kong, Mightycity Ltd., 1980).

55. Maunsell Consultants Asia et al. (1982), see note 27 above, pp. 39–49.

56. Excellent summaries are: D.W. Drakakis-Smith, *High Society: Housing Provision in Metropolitan Hong Kong 1954 to 1979 — A Jubilee Critique* (Hong Kong, University of Hong Kong, Centre for Asian Studies, 1979), and E.G. Pryor, *Housing in Hong Kong* (Hong Kong, Oxford University Press, 1983). A useful set of further references is given in A.G.O. Yeh, *Reference Materials on Urban Development and Planning in Hong Kong* (Hong Kong, University of Hong Kong, Centre of Urban Studies and Urban Planning, 1984), pp. 44–61.

57. L.S.K. Wong, *Housing in Hong Kong: A Multi-Disciplinary Study* (Hong Kong, Heinemann Asia, 1978) contains some helpful chapters. Further design critiques can also be found from time to time in the Hong Kong-based professional journals *Asian Architect and Builder* and *Building Journal, Hong Kong*, as well as further information on public housing matters in the annual reports of the Hong Kong Housing Authority.

58. See Plan LTW 32A, circulated by the Superintendent of Crown Lands and Survey on 5 May 1961.

59. 'Multi-Level Town Centre for Hong Kong Estate', *Far East Architect and Builder*, February 1966, pp. 47–51.

60. Bristow (1984), see note 10 above, pp. 85, 87, and 245. See also, J.D.K. Lam, *The New Territories Small House Policy* (Hong Kong, New Territories Administration, 1980).

61. D. Adams, 'Hong Kong Property: The Changing Nature of the Industrial Market', *Estates Gazette*, 31 January 1987, pp. 380–2.

62. Colony Planning Division, *Hong Kong Outline Plan* (Hong Kong, Town Planning Office, 1979), Chapter 5, *Industry*, paras.5.2–3, pp. 5.4–5.

63. Town Planning Office, *Report of the Working Party on New Industrial Layout and Design of Industrial Buildings* (Hong Kong, Town Planning Office, 1979). Copy at 24A in TPO 0/01/51III, Town Planning Registry, Hong Kong.

64. Town Planning Office (1979), see note 63 above, para.3.4, p. 2.

65. Tuen Mun New Town Development Office, *Tuen Mun New Town, Area 17, Explanatory Statement, Layout Plan No. LTM 2/17G* (Hong Kong, New Territories Development Department, 1982).

66. K.S. Pun, 'New Towns and Urban Renewal in Hong Kong', in D.R. Phillips and A.G.O. Yeh, *New Towns in East and South-east Asia: Planning and Development* (Hong Kong, Oxford University Press, 1987), p. 42.

67. M.R. Bristow, 'The Role and Place of Strategic Planning in Hong Kong', *Planning and Development, Journal of the Hong Kong Institute of Planners*, Vol. 4, No. 1, March 1988, pp. 14–20.

68. The proposal became possible by a zoning amendment to the Outline Zoning Plan for Tsuen Wan (Plan LTW/146C), approved by the Town Planning Board in August 1981. The detailed proposals for the redevelopment were set out in Outline Development Plan TWNT/1B, circulated in May 1981.

69. Memorandum from Secretary for the New Territories to Director of New Territories Development, 7 April 1981, at 61 in BL 8/5282/61X, Buildings and Lands Registry, Hong Kong. Further correspondence is at 62, 64, and 65 in the same file.

70. Memorandum from Director of Housing to Director of New Territories Development, 23 April 1981, at 64 in BL 8/5282/61X, Buildings and Lands Registry, Hong Kong.

71. Sha Tin Works Progress Committee, Planning Sub-committee Paper No. 18/85, 30 October 1985, *Infill Sites for Sha Tin Proper*, at 74 in TPD D/ST/200I, Town Planning Registry, Hong Kong.

72. Land Development Planning Committee Paper No. 93, 24 September 1965, *Tsuen Wan and District Outline Development Plan: Area 10 — Residential Layout at Kwai Chung*, at 12 in BL 4/5282/60IV, Buildings and Lands Registry, Hong Kong.

73. See copies at 36/1 and 61 in BL 8/5282/61IX, April 1980, Buildings and Lands Registry, Hong Kong.

74. See copies 124 and 126 in ENV 70/24/05II, May/June 1979, Buildings and Lands Registry, Hong Kong.

75. See copies 100 and 102/1 in ENV 70/24/05II, September 1978, Buildings and Lands Registry, Hong Kong.

76. See 56/1 in ENV 73/05/03II, September 1979, Buildings and Lands Registry, Hong Kong.

77. See copies 11, 11/1 and 11/2 in ENV 73/05/03VI, September 1981, Buildings and Lands Registry, Hong Kong.

78. Memorandum from Commissioner for Environmental Protection to Project Manager Junk Bay, 7 January 1982, at 63 in ENV 70/61/02VIII, Buildings and Lands Registry, Hong Kong, para.3, p. 1.

79. Minutes of the 34th Meeting of the Development Progress Committee, 10 January 1985, at M3 in TPD/D/JB/300(SS)1, Town Planning Registry, Hong Kong.

80. D. Lung, 'Fung Shui: An Intrinsic Way to Environmental Design, with illustration of Kat Hing Wei', *Asian Architect and Builder*, October 1979, pp. 16–23. See also pp. 26–9 of the same issue.

81. Tuen Mun New Town Development Office, *Planning Report: Tuen Mun New Town Planning Area 4A and 4C: Explanatory Statement to the Layout Plan* (Hong Kong, New Territories Development Department, 1981), Plan LTM 7/4/3, October 1981, para.2.1(b), p. 1.

8. An Evaluation

ANY evaluation to be meaningful has to be set against known objectives. Although one of the consistent themes in Hong Kong has been an incremental and pragmatic approach towards new-town policies — 'the new towns policy of Hong Kong does not rest upon a long tradition of planning thought and practice and ... it can be regarded as the outcome of cumulative reactions to events'[1] — there remains a consistent vision that has been restated many times in government publications with regard to policy objectives. These are summed up in the planners' own official summary document about town planning in Hong Kong, last published in 1984:

The new town scheme was established to fulfill several objectives: to solve the housing problem by creating new land to meet the Ten-Year Housing Target Programme; attract industry to new areas; alleviate Hong Kong's problems of urban congestion by decentralizing population to the New Territories while providing a breathing space for the over-crowded urban areas and improving environmental conditions for remaining urban dwellers.

New towns aim to achieve 'self-containment' and 'balanced development'. In order to create a satisfactory living environment and to minimize commuting, each new town aims at providing adequate working opportunities, shopping, recreation and other community facilities for its local residents. By 'self-contained development' the daily needs of the residents can be met within the new town. By 'balanced development' new towns may be able to supply all the necessary employment opportunities, and above all, to provide an optimal housing mix between public/private housing, ownership/rental units and high/low density housing through which a healthy social mix within a community may be achieved. These concepts seem to be very idealistic and may not be achieved fully in reality ... However, the planning of each new town will continue to apply these concepts as they will, hopefully, achieve a balance in the long run. In the physical form of the new town, civic design principles are often applied so as to achieve an aesthetically enjoyable environment for residence, work and recreation.[2]

Such statements are mere echoes of earlier explanations advanced in the 1970s by government planners such as Wigglesworth and Crosby. In papers written by both, the words 'self-contained' and 'balanced' occur again and again as the basic planning concepts then being applied in the designing and construction of the first new towns in Hong Kong.[3] Only Kwun Tong was accepted as being the initial exception.[4] Elsewhere, planning objectives for the new-town developments were specified as:

(a) to create a balanced and vigorous 'self-contained' community to meet the basic needs of all its residents;
(b) to provide new opportunities and freedom of choice for residents in the location, type and standard of housing, education, employment, shopping and recreation;
(c) to create a meaningful community where people can relate healthily with a strong sense of place and where people can develop socially;

(d) to provide ease, safety and convenience of movement for residents to and from their places of work, learning, shopping and recreation;

(e) to use the available resources efficiently, wisely and imaginatively;

(f) to create an attractive and convenient city appropriate to the district.[5]

Self-contained ... means that facilities will be provided within the town itself to enable the basic needs of all its residents to be met to a large extent within their own community.[6]

The acid test, of course remains — how far have such worthy aspirations been achieved, some ten years on since the words were uttered, and nearly three decades after the programme began? The most fundamental concepts still remain those of self-containment and balance, and as we shall see, they have generated considerable discussion over recent decades. But first, we need to reconsider the three aims with which the planners began — for housing, industry, and decongestion. With development programmes well on the way to completion (see Tables 8.1 and 8.2) evidence is already beginning to accumulate, and monitoring and evaluation is now both possible and required in order to plan more effectively for an optimal future for Hong Kong development.

Housing Policies

It has been noted many times by both planners and commentators that the Hong Kong new towns owe their being and detailed form to the vicissitudes of the Hong Kong government's varied policies towards public housing. Relevant comments are numerous,[7] but just a few might usefully be picked out at random:

public housing is the major impetus of new town development in Hong Kong;[8]

The attempt to solve [the housing problem] has now become a major concern of urban planning in Hong Kong and the need to provide land for public housing has become the principal impetus behind many development programmes ... To meet this target, large sites have to be made available quickly for the construction of large, conventional, public housing estates ... The main opportunities exist in the new towns and rural towns in the New Territories.[9]

The development of new towns in Hong Kong has never been and is not likely to be infrastructure-led. It has been dominated and led by public housing development.[10]

The reasons for that dominance lie, of course, in immediate terms in the shortage of easily developable land, set out in some detail in Wigglesworth's early paper of 1971,[11] and developed much more comprehensively in the later annual reports of the Special Committee on Land Production/Supply in the years 1977–85.[12] But there were deeper reasons, of which the most fundamental were the desire to utilize development land productively — suggested by Drakakis-Smith[13] and Keung[14] (reasons which

Table 8.1 Territorial Population Shifts, 1961–2001 (per cent)

	Censuses					
	1961	1971	1976	1981	1986	2001 estimate
Main urban area	82	81	77	73	64	54
New Territories	14	17	22	26	35	46
Marine	4	2	1.3	1	0.7	0.4

Note: 29 is the percentage in the new towns in 1986.

Source: Census and Statistics Department, *Hong Kong 1986 By-Census — Summary Results* (Hong Kong, Census and Statistics Department, 1986).

also motivated the clearance and resettlement of squatters), and the fundamental requirement to avoid social and hence economic disturbances.

As expressed in the 1967 Report on the Kowloon riots:

Overcrowded housing conditions and shortage of open space are two aspects of urban congestion which point to the need for a continuing programme of urban renewal and new town development. These are costly in time as well as money and may, in turn, create new social tensions through the displacement of large numbers of people into a new environment. Nevertheless, we believe that the growing aspirations of the people demand a better social environment and as this can only be achieved to the extent necessary, by a combination of new building and rebuilding we would strongly endorse any proposals, such as the development of new communities, designed to reduce population stress in the central areas of Hong Kong and Kowloon.[15]

The inception of the Ten-year Housing Programme in the 1970s and the major expansions in that decade in education and social welfare provision, which had great impact upon the new-town programme, all grew out of one dominant determinant — the need to maintain Hong Kong as a viable, and above all, stable social community in the face of rapid economic and community change.

The speeding up of public housing development programmes ... could be considered a viable means towards defusing social tension by improving the living environments on the one hand, and by disintegrating the social fabric of the squatters which was thought to be a source of social disturbances on the other ... Housing development ... has therefore been a strategy of welfare redistribution aimed at reducing the pressure of social conflicts and potential political unrest.[16]

The obsession with security even had some direct effects, for as Tsuen Wan expanded, the imposition of a green belt to separate it, albeit narrowly, from the western edge of New Kowloon was demanded in the 1960s on security grounds. Such feelings too underpinned the more idealistic notions of 'balance' that structured new-town planning in Hong Kong for so long. There were good reasons in the early days for wishing the new

Table 8.2 New-town Population Growth, 1960–1986

New Towns	1960	1961	1965	1971	1976	1979	1980	1981	1986	Target
						Populations in Thousands				
Tsuen Wan	80[1]	85		266	460			599	646	817
Sha Tin			24[1]	24	30			109	356	800
Tuen Mun			20[1]	21	34			90	262	530
Tai Po						35[1]		40	120	220
Sheung Shui/Fanling						43[1]		50	87	226
Yuen Long						37[1]		51	76	150
Junk Bay							13[1]	13	14	425
Tin Shui Wai								3[1]	2	135

Note: 1. Populations at dates of designation.

Sources: Principally *Hong Kong 1986 By-Census*, supplemented by Territory Development Department documentation, Hong Kong government.

settlements to be distant and self-contained, and unattached to the older urban core.

Yet, at the same time, the early new-town schemes both in Kwun Tong and Tsuen Wan were anything but balanced, but were, in fact, initially resettlement estates.

However, plans for Tsuen Wan/Kwai Chung are largely based at present on the large government low-cost housing programme, [and] the original decision to proceed with the development of Shatin and Castle Peak as new towns was influenced by the need for sites for government-built high-density housing.[17]

Thus, early criticism of their housing and hence social structures homed in on their potential 'one-class factory town' nature:

One may foresee a continuous redistribution of low income people into new towns, together with the problems of attracting an inflow of sufficient (and suitable) economic activities.[18]

This was a classic chicken-and-egg problem.

For those who move to these new towns, faster allocation of public housing or cheaper rents or lower prices of private accommodation are the main attractions,[19]

which, of course, describes a migration mechanism which reinforced the problem. The result was that even by the end of the 1970s it could be argued that:

new towns are not 'balanced communities' even in [a] demographic sense ... Furthermore, they are quasi-homogenous working class communities ... Besides, there are practical difficulties in making available a whole spectrum of services and jobs for different socio-economic groups, in attracting sufficient amounts of industrial and commercial investment in the new town and in luring individuals of different socio-economic status to live alongside each other.[20]

In Hong Kong,

it is difficult for new towns to achieve ... 'social balance'. Most new towns are planned to have a large proportion of their population living in public housing [see Table 8.3] ... Since there is an income limit for public housing applicants, most new towns are expected to have an overwhelming proportion of low income working class population. The objective of social balance will be defeated as a result.[21]

Yeh notes that in the 1981 Census, while the overall percentage of the population in public housing was only 32 per cent in the urban core, the average for the three large new towns was 62 per cent, which was almost double. The result was that all three had over 50 per cent of their working population classified as production workers, while only Sha Tin had any appreciable number (9 per cent) in the professional and managerial class.

Table 8.3 Public/Private Housing Splits in the New Towns at 1986 and on Completion (per cent)

New Towns	Permanent Public Housing Units[1]		Modern Private Housing Units[2]	
	1986	Target	1986	Target
Tsuen Wan	62 / 1	67[3]	27	33[3]
Sha Tin	56 / 13	63[3]	19	37[3]
Tuen Mun	60 / 18	50[3] / 20[3]	10	30[3]
Tai Po	41 / 14	45[3] / 11[3]	25	44[3]
Sheung Shui/Fanling	37 / 13	45[3] / 10[3]	19	45[3]
Yuen Long	23 / —	38[3]	60	62[3]
Junk Bay	—	48[3] / 15[3]	—	37[3]
Tin Shui Wai	—	41[3] / 6[3]	—	53[3]
Hong Kong average	38 / 4	—	41	—
All New Towns	46 / 10	62[3]	27	38[3]
	(67[3])		(33[3])	

Notes: 1. The percentages show, where possible, public rented (including Housing Society units), followed by Home Ownership Scheme units. Public temporary housing is excluded.

2. The percentages include private flat units and modern houses only. Traditional stone dwellings are excluded, as are all institutional and temporary dwelling units.

3. Percentages are calculated as the crude public/private split of 100 per cent.

Sources: Principally *Hong Kong 1986 By-Census* (Tertiary Planning Unit × Living Quarters), supplemented by Territory Development Department documentation, Hong Kong government.

This was over twice the rate of either of the other two new cities. One important difference which assists in explaining these figures is that housing allocations and jobs are not directly linked in Hong Kong as they were in the early years of some British new towns; in Hong Kong the composition is only affected by the massive 'quasi-voluntary' migration represented by the public housing programme, and inadequate public housing supply in main urban areas.[22]

Reviewing more up-to-date figures from the 1986 By-census, the position had, of course, by then changed (see Table 8.4). Indeed, some idea of the overall magnitude of the change over the five years 1981–6 is given by the percentage shifts in population proportions for the main areas of the Territory due to internal migration. These percentages are shown in Table 8.1. Already, by 1986, approaching one-third of Hong Kong's population was in the first six new towns. Yet, the overall position had not changed greatly in percentage terms (see Table 8.3). Public housing, whether or not temporary housing units were included in the calculation, still predominated. Only in Tsuen Wan was the private sector providing a significant number of dwelling units within the total stock and this was very much a relic of developments earlier than the new town. The position, of course, for the three smaller and newer expanding towns of Tai Po, Sheung Shui/Fanling, and Yuen Long was rather different, due again to the legacy of the private dwelling stock of the original towns around which the new estates were then beginning to be built. Nevertheless, despite the 1986 position, the public/private mix is stated to be on course for the target objectives set in the various Outline Development Plans and programmes for each of the towns.

Yet, there are some doubts, as Leung points out:

The new towns programme has brought about a decentralization of population in Hong Kong and has reduced the population densities of the inner city areas. But this result has been achieved not only through the creation of new towns but also through some large-scale residential development in suburban locations such as North Point, Quarry Bay, Pokfulam, and Kowloon Bay, as well as at more central locations such as Hung Hom and Kowloon City. The latter developments could not have been predicted at the beginning of the 1970s. In fact, however, such development, together with residential developments along the route of the MTR [Mass Transit Railway] in the urban area, have competed with the new towns for middle-income migrant families. They have also adversely affected private residential development in the new towns and thus, in turn, the overall development of the new towns. It is the public housing programme that has 'moved' vast numbers of people to the new towns, those with a lower bargaining power in the public housing allocation exercise and those who cannot improve their housing conditions by their own efforts.[23]

These facts have two important implications for the future of the new towns. Firstly, the private-sector development in them is competing from a generally inferior position within a metropolitan housing market that covers the whole of the Territory and is centred upon Hong Kong Island. In the private sector, distance from the urban core has to be offset by

Table 8.4 Hong Kong New-town Populations at the 1986 By-census

Housing Types	Hong Kong Total	Kwun Tong	Main Urban Area	Tsuen Wan	Tuen Mun	Sha Tin	Tai Po	Sheung Shui /Fanling	Yuen Long	New Towns[1]	New Territories
Housing Authority rental blocks	2,058,091	249,718	1,202,285	388,941	172,207	182,651	54,285	37,324	17,892	853,300	855,806
Housing Society rental blocks	127,608	13,608	90,608	20,755	—	15,232	—	—	—	35,987	36,876
Housing Authority home ownership estates	219,394	19,243	92,407	6,720	44,835	47,012	14,012	10,661	—	123,249	126,987
Private housing blocks	2,086,546	80,115	1,776,803	154,238	20,153	53,340	22,722	9,884	40,558	300,895	309,743
Modern individual homes	164,647	511	13,853	14,987	3,059	11,613	3,346	6,657	4,977	44,639	150,794
Temporary housing	361,634	9,940	157,493	36,743	10,787	24,346	14,133	16,611	4,998	107,618	204,141
Other units	340,921	5,110	141,869	23,219	11,417	21,616	11,172	6,069	7,315	80,808	199,052
Totals (Target populations)	5,358,717	387,245	3,475,318	645,603 (817,000)	262,458 (530,000)	355,810 (800,000)	119,679 (220,000)	87,206 (226,000)	75,740 (150,000)	1,546,496	1,883,399

Note: 1. Junk Bay and Tin Shui Wai were not separately listed, as new-town settlement had not yet begun on either site in 1986. Target populations for these towns at that time were 185,000 and 135,000 respectively. Junk Bay was increased to 420,000 in 1988.

Source: Census and Statistics Department, *Hong Kong 1986 By-census — Tertiary Planning Unit: Living Quarters, Households and Population by Type of Living Quarters* (Hong Kong, Census and Statistics Department, 1986), Census District Tables, pp. 4–11.

Fig. 8.1   The Hong Kong Territorial Development Strategy of 1984 — proposed
initial new reclamations and other schemes for urban growth in the 1990s.
The first schemes begun in the mid-1980s were at Hung Hom Bay,
Kowloon, and the small schemes near to Pokfulam, Hong Kong Island.

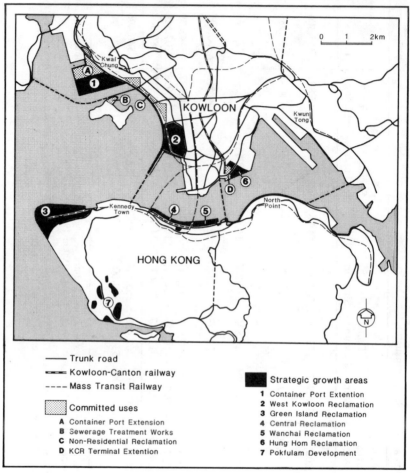

- ——— Trunk road
- ▬▬▬ Kowloon-Canton railway
- ---- Mass Transit Railway

▨ Committed uses

  A Container Port Extension
  B Sewerage Treatment Works
  C Non-Residential Reclamation
  D KCR Terminal Extention

■ Strategic growth areas

  1 Container Port Extention
  2 West Kowloon Reclamation
  3 Green Island Reclamation
  4 Central Reclamation
  5 Wanchai Reclamation
  6 Hung Hom Reclamation
  7 Pokfulam Development

Source: Based on 'Initial Development Strategy' in *Planning for Growth* (Hong Kong, Lands
and Works Branch, 1985), p. 33.

greater amenity, lower price, or sheer lack of opportunity in the main urban
market before developers and purchasers are willing to consider new-town
developments. Should the re-emphasis on the urban core, foreshadowed
in the Territorial Development Strategy of 1984 (see Figs. 8.1 and 8.2)
actually take place, then later phases of private development in the new
towns are likely to face still greater levels of competition from private
schemes in the core area, with increasing likelihood, therefore, of the creation of working class ghettoes in those new towns like Tin Shui Wai which
lie furthest from the metropolitan centre.

Much the greatest influence over the future social structure of the Hong
Kong new towns, however, remains with the Hong Kong Housing Author-

ity and its public housing policies. In the 1990s redevelopment in the oldest areas is likely to become more dominant — it has already taken place in the oldest resettlement estates in both Kwun Tong and Tsuen Wan. But by far the most important areas of influence remain through allocation and building policies.

The late 1980s saw significant alterations to public housing allocation mechanisms following a round of public consultation in 1984–5.

In 1984, for the first time, the Housing Authority officially consulted the public in formulation of its policies ... [and] the Authority subsequently made amendments in the light of these comments to its allocation policy in December ... As a result, two-person households are now eligible for applying for rental and home ownership flats. The housing need of singletons is also taken care of by providing hostel rooms in permanent public housing.[24]

Much more controversial was a second change attempted in 1985.[25] This suggested assessing the joint incomes of tenant households and applying a one hundred per cent rental surcharge to those with more then ten years residence and having aggregate incomes fifty per cent greater than the waiting list income limit (then set at HK$7,500 per month). The result was a well-orchestrated public outcry, rejection in the Hong Kong District Boards, and eventual suspension of the proposals.

The final and perhaps most important phase of revision occurred in 1987 with the release of a further policy document setting out proposals for the 1990s.[26] This suggested that the demand for rental accommodation may well be approaching satisfaction by the mid-1990s (though quantitative satisfaction says nothing about acceptable quality or locations — factors well known in contemporary British housing debates[27]). It was, therefore, suggested that Hong Kong should yet again emulate the Singapore model, with a shift towards greater levels of assisted home ownership.[28] Thus, the new towns are likely to see additional allocations of sites for Home Ownership Schemes or Private Sector Participation Schemes within the public sector (already under way in Tuen Mun in late 1988, for example), while the proposal to grant housing loans for private purchase may well increase the demand for the cheaper private accommodation that Hong Kong's developers prefer to construct in the new towns. The result is a new set of uncertainties in the housing market which are bound in the longer term to affect the communities and social life of today's new towns.

Yet, as to 'solving the housing problem', the first of the new-town programme objectives, one is inclined to agree with Pun that:

The real causes of the housing problem and the best means to deal with them are still subjects of debate ... Given present policies, practices, and attitudes, it is doubtful if the housing problem can ever be solved in Hong Kong ... However, the attempt to solve this problem has now become a major concern of urban planning.[29]

As we have seen, a continuing major part of that effort will remain within the new-town development programme, at least well into the 1990s, and

Fig. 8.2 The Hong Kong Territorial Strategy of 1983.

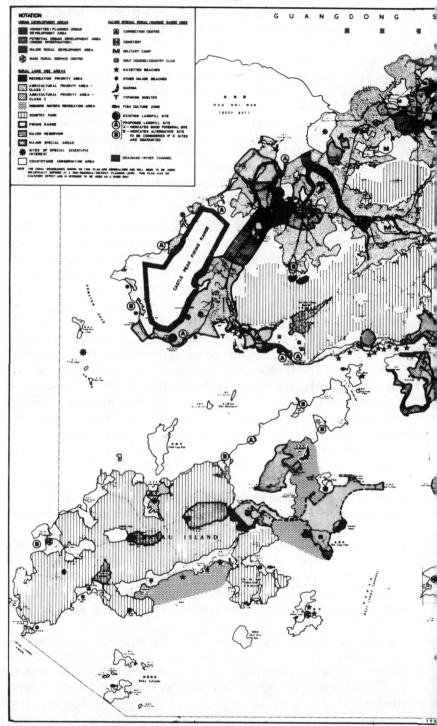

Source: Strategic Planning Unit, Lands and Works Branch, Hong Kong government.

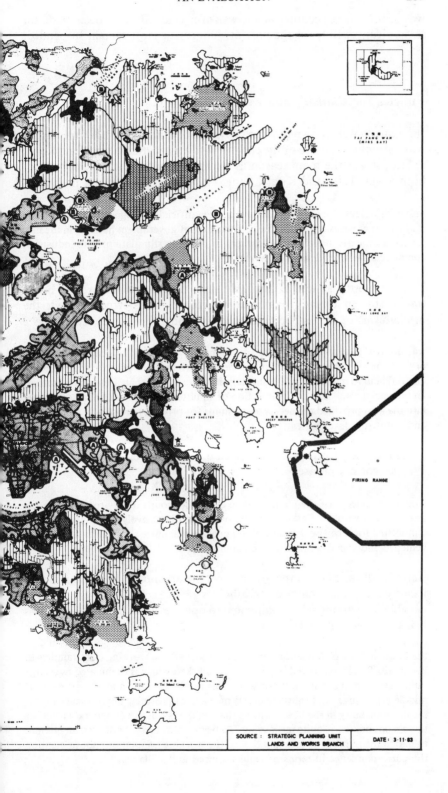

SOURCE :   STRATEGIC PLANNING UNIT
           LANDS AND WORKS BRANCH   DATE : 3·11·83

by the turn of the century an answer of a kind will have been made for this objective. But, for the present, judgement must remain suspended!

Policies for Industry and Employment

It is equally well known that the provision of additional sites for industry was a primary purpose of the early new-town programme in Hong Kong; indeed, it was the main reason as we have seen for the development of both Kwun Tong and Kwai Chung. As Wigglesworth put it in 1971,

unlike situations elsewhere in Asia, it has been officially recognized in Hong Kong that a further necessity will be the construction of government housing in the new towns at an early stage of development in order to stimulate private industrial, commercial and residential development.[30]

In other words, as well as available sites, the industrialist was to be attracted by an already available workforce, transferred through the mechanisms of the public housing programme. For Kwun Tong:

was not designed as a self-contained community because it is located within two or three miles of Kowloon ... It was needed primarily to provide additional industrial land to make up for the shortage in the existing urban areas and is, rather, an industrial satellite ... The injection of squatter resettlement housing schemes into the area provided the necessary stimulus for private, particularly commercial and industrial development.[31]

All later new towns were conceived of as being 'self-sufficient', to use Wigglesworth's phrase.[32]

The basic concept of the plan ... is to establish groups of environmental areas devoted to a variety of uses, each compactly and intensively developed ... It is a modified form of 'Buchananism' designed to maximize the health, safety, convenience and social welfare of the community.[33]

Initially, distance from the urban core, the attempt to build up a strong local identity and the large threshold size of each town were thought capable of enabling self-containment to operate.[34] Yet by the 1970s it was being pointed out that:

the large number of industrial jobs planned will attract working class families to live there. This is reinforced by the housing market, which is dominated by a large public sector and a private sector which has produced units mainly in the lower-middle price range ... [Thus] the proclaimed aim of providing appropriate employment opportunity in the new towns so that residents can live and work within the town's boundaries is quite misleading. To begin with, there is not even an attempt to match the number of jobs and that of the working population, not to mention the correspondence in terms of skills required and skills available.[35]

In the early stages of development therefore the general observation has been that:

The new towns at present have a large number of people living in public housing, but cannot attract industry and private housing development. As a result, there is a general lack of employment opportunities in the new towns and it is necessary for the majority of the residents to commute to the urban areas daily for work through the often congested transportation network ... Moreover, although it may be possible to achieve 'self-containment' at the neighbourhood level in social services and facilities, it is difficult to attain total 'self-containment' in employment in the new towns, especially in white collar jobs.[36]

Various explanations have been put forward for this.

Although new towns are growing rapidly, largely attributable to the efficient public housing programmes, they have been unable to achieve the goal of self-containment. They generally encounter difficulties in attracting industry, especially in the early stages of development, due to their inadequate infrastructure and industrial linkages.[37]

Thus, even for the manufacturing sector, which has always been considered the foundation of the employment provision for the Hong Kong new towns, it has been suggested that:

under normal supply and demand conditions, the new towns cannot attract industrial entrepreneurs. For manufacturing activities already operating in the urban core, decentralisation is most unlikely except in special circumstances ... Under such circumstances, additional incentives are ... necessary, e.g. the reduction of land cost or the provision of extra facilities and services.[38]

This relevance of relative costs is crucial. As Yeh points out:

Hong Kong Government does not have an active policy to promote industrial development and employment in the new towns ... Zoning is a passive control over land use ... for reservation of land cannot ensure industries will move into the new towns ... Although the Government is concerned with industrial diversification, little attention has been paid to industrial decentralisation, which is vital to the viability of new town development in Hong Kong.[39]

The result, as Leung points out, is that:

The *laissez-faire* policy of the Hong Kong government means that there is very little leverage ... on the distribution of population and employment. The new towns, so far, owe their success to a considerable extent to the differential in the cost of land when compared with inner city areas ... This differential is measured in the eyes of industrialists ... in absolute terms, namely, how much in dollars and cents can be saved by decentralising and whether the savings more than compensate for the inconvenience ... [Additionally] the relationship between land cost and labour cost has a considerable bearing on decentralisation. If the labour cost is low relative to land cost, whether because of skill or occupation density, it would make financial sense for the industrialists to decentralize. Unfortunately for town planners, the trend of industrial development in Hong Kong has been in the reverse direction. The end result is that industrial locations in the urban areas are still very much preferred over the new towns.[40]

Thus, 'to most industrial establishments in main urban areas, the perceived disadvantages of locating in new towns prevail over the advantages'.[41] While the low levels of rents and property prices are perceived as the major advantage, they are offset by significant suggested problems concerned with keeping existing staff, the availability of replacement employees from the new towns (particularly at the managerial and supervisory levels), and perceived difficulties over linkages and accessibility of suppliers, sub-contractors, customers, and general transportation issues.[42]

These quoted views emanate from a survey of industrialists initiated by the government in 1983 to assess the relative advantages or otherwise of urban concentration or dispersion, and in part carried out as a result of a gradual realization that the new-town employment strategies were not working as planned. Yet, as we saw in Chapter 2, such an eventuality was foreseen even before the new towns were begun. The Special Committee on Housing in 1958 itself suggested that:

the centre of employment is bound to remain in the city and around the harbour shores. New towns may follow industrial expansion into new areas: industrial expansion may be facilitated but it cannot be created.[43]

Certainly by the early 1980s trends were sufficient to cause concern.

For example, the total number of manufacturing jobs available in [Sha Tin's] two industrial areas of Fo Tan and Tai Wai is about five times below the estimated figure based on its existing planning standards [in 1981] . . . The employment problem is further complicated by the mismatch of jobs and workers in the new towns. For example, less than 50 per cent of the employment opportunities in the new towns of Sha Tin and Tuen Mun were occupied by local workers. Over 20 per cent of their workers were from Kowloon/New Kowloon and the rest from nearby districts.[44]

Yet, dismay over such figures betrayed a fundamental misunderstanding about how labour markets operate. As Wang and Yeh explain:

The mismatch of workers and employment in new towns is mainly related to the recent migration history of both the workers and the firms. Most of the new town residents still retain a strong tie with their existing jobs. Moreover, it is difficult to find a comparable job in the new towns and some of them do not want to lose their seniority in their existing jobs in the main urban area. Some prefer to work in the main urban area because of higher salaries, welfare, fringe benefits, status and security. On the other hand, firms relocated in the new towns from the main urban area often bring along their own workers. For example, 79 per cent of the manufacturing firms that moved to Tuen Mun [up to 1983] retained all or part of their original workers.[45]

Thus, one can sum up the situation of the 1980s with Sit and Wong:

Official statements of the new towns being 'balanced' and 'self-contained' may thus mislead people about the reality of the programme and raise false expectations.[46]

The employment structure in the new towns is quite unbalanced ... thus employment opportunities are only attractive to certain groups of people, while to some other people, residing in the new towns still means commuting to the urban core to work ... If the new towns can fulfil the mission of housing the overspill of urban population and developing as new growth points for manufacturing activities then they can be considered a successful venture. To strictly enforce the concept of self-containment and balanced community is doomed to be a failure.[47]

This seems but an echo of a comment of a decade before:

The area of the territory is such that ... it is inconceivable that any real degree of self-sufficiency could be achieved by the new towns.[48]

So what can one deduce about the reality for the Hong Kong new towns within the contemporary industrial economy.[49] It is gradually becoming clearer that Hong Kong operates as a complex set of overlapping sub-markets at a whole variety of scales — Territory-wide, sub-regional, urban, district, or even local. Particularly with rapidly improving communications, the interaction and expansion of these varied sub-markets is expanding. The new towns, as rapidly growing urban centres and hence employment nodes, are, as would be expected, destined to play an increasing role within the evolving complex, multi-nodal structure. Integration rather than segregation would, therefore, seem to be the appropriate terminology for the processes of the 1990s, and this will require a considerable adjustment to earlier new-town policies.

Yet, some evidence already exists of a shift taking place. Certainly in industrial and employment planning in the late 1980s 'sub-regional balance' replaced the earlier notions of new-town self-containment as the guiding notion of strategic planning in the Territory (see Chapter 3, p. 102). Some credence to this concept is given by the migration statistics reported in the 1986 Hong Kong By-census (see Table 8.5) which emphasizes the development of localized migration patterns for each new town.

The tone of current policy is aptly summarized by the following passage taken from the north-east New Territories Planning Statement of 1986:

At present, this Sub-Region is deficient in terms of employment balance. Research indicates that only 44% of the Sub-Region's resident workforce works locally and therefore a high proportion of the resident workforce commute out of the Sub-Region to other sub-regions to work. Given the predominance of the metropolitan area as a place of work [to be intensified in the 1990s], the short and medium term outlook for employment balance in NENT [North Eastern New Territories] remains uncertain.[50]

Table 8.5 Migration Summary from the 1986 Hong Kong By-census: Internal Migrants, 1981–1986

Areas of Origin	Areas of Destination			Total Internal Migrants
	Main Urban Area	New Towns	Rest of New Territories	
Main urban area	444,731	401,597 (35%)	30,639	876,967
New Towns	62,489 (5%)	118,706 (10%)	15,603 (1%)	196,798 (17%)
Rest of New Territories	18,830	44,030 (4%)	4,102	66,962
Marine	5,768	8,078 (1%)	2,527	16,373
Total internal migrants	531,818	572,411 (49%)	52,871	1,157,100 (21.6% Hong Kong pop.)

Source: Census and Statistics Department, *Hong Kong By-Census — Summary Results* (Hong Kong, Census and Statistics Department, 1986), E. Internal Movement of Population, p.26.

Self-contained labour markets for each of the Hong Kong new towns now seems a policy consigned to the waste-bin.

Decentralization and the relationships between the new towns and the older urban core represented the third part of the Town Planning Office's 1984 objectives with which we began. However, before we consider this strategic question further, there remains a set of matters related to the towns themselves which deserves consideration first. As Chow has put it:

The major area of concern has been the decentralization of population which is the primary objective of the new town development; the adequacy of facilities in the new towns is another subject for intensive investigation. However, few attempts have been made to understand the impact of moving to the towns upon the life-style of these new residents in the New Territories.[51]

However briefly, it is a topic that deserves at least some consideration here.

Social Questions

It has been suggested that:

Any vigorous evaluation of the new town development should . . . take the various aspects of the lives of the new town inhabitants into consideration and should not be content with an assessment of the satisfaction of housing needs. As people are moving into a new environment, adjustments and adaptations are inevitably required and [some] may incur a cost who, in exchange for a better living environment, have found it necessary to make sacrifices in other areas. This cost may be expressed in the form of longer travelling hours to and from work, or a weaker family supportive network as they are further away from their relatives remaining in the urban area.[52]

Chow states that:

more evidences are now available to suggest that, despite the improvements in housing conditions, new town inhabitants are paying a high price in adjusting to the new environment.[53]

However, there is in Hong Kong no central organization for monitoring the social aspects of new-town development. What is known comes largely from small-scale one-off surveys by interested academics,[54] and the casework and reports of the voluntary social services sector.[55]

So far no special social service policies have been designed for the new towns. Government policies regarding the satisfaction of such needs as housing, education, medical care, social welfare and employment apply throughout the whole territory of Hong Kong.[56]

Until very recently that applied to almost all planning standards too.

The new towns therefore were and are not perceived in any way as unique places with special problems, at least in so far as general public policy implementation is concerned. It is only when specific problems require special solutions, such as the shortage of primary education places in Tuen Mun in the early 1980s, that unique policies are introduced on a pragmatic basis as special measures.

Yet, it is no coincidence that Tuen Mun, the most remote of the Hong Kong new towns, has tended to become the case-study town for social investigations into the Hong Kong new towns, just as Kwun Tong before it tended to be investigated in the 1970s, on account of social problems arising from its early inadequate provision of community facilities. For Tuen Mun, problems arose because of relative isolation and the wish of new inhabitants to maintain employment and kinship links with their relatively distant former home areas.

Wang and Yeh assert that:

new towns were initially developed as a quick response to social problems manifested in the form of housing demand. The task was to build as many flats as quickly as possible. As a consequence, public housing estates and new towns developed at the early stages ... reflected a lack of careful planning and design.[57]

This is a statement with which, from Chapter 7, we might well agree. Yet, early surveys of new-town residents in Hong Kong found other areas of concern, rather than detailed planning design matters.

To some,

the new towns give the general impression of being quite inadequate in terms of the provision of facilities and services ... This is partly because the new towns are still in their early stages of development, but such as impression can create a negative image of the new towns and has a deterrent effect on potential movers.[58]

But, because such a large proportion of new inhabitants are public housing migrants, this reluctance comes to be expressed in a perception of being a 'forced mover' as reported in Han.[59]

The findings on Tuen Mun show that Tuen Mun has provided a better housing and living environment to the migrant households relative to their former living conditions ... However, the findings also show that there is a high degree of dissatisfaction with several aspects of Tuen Mun. The two most consistent sources of dissatisfaction are transportation [to the main urban area for work or social links] and medical services. Others are lack of shopping and market facilities, and lack of a variety of goods.[60]

Similar sentiments were reported in another early survey for both Tuen Mun and Tsuen Wan:

There is a high degree of satisfaction among the residents of both Tsuen Wan and Tuen Mun, irrespective of housing type, regarding various aspects of life in the new towns with two notable exceptions. Getting to work and social interaction have a generally lower grading.[61]

Thus, the perceptions of early new-town migrants in Hong Kong related to their expectations, having regard to their earlier living environments, and their wish to maintain past work and social links. Only time weakens the second of these characteristics. Thus, as Chan points out,

both 'balanced community' and 'self-containment' are not feasible town planning concepts in the case of Hong Kong, which is characterized by a high level of interdepenency and interpenetration between the constituent components of the society ... 'Balanced community' even if achieved, may only mean 'balance' in a demographic sense, while socially individuals belonging to the same socio-economic stratum would interact exclusively with each other, and inter-strata relationship[s] would be minimized or even avoided. Similarly 'self-containment', if realized, would be tantamount to segregation between the new towns and other parts of Hong Kong. It is also doubtful whether self-containment would necessarily generate community identification; however, even if it can be generated, it is still arguable whether a high degree of localism or 'parochialism' would really benefit both the new towns and Hong Kong as a whole.[62]

Thus, concern has moved away from the necessary provision of facilities, important though it is to the inhabitants of the new towns, to wider questions to do with the social development of the communities. As Chan puts it:

If too much attention is paid to the physical and quantitative aspects of community services and facilities, it may turn out that some of them are ill-used or under-used while certain other needs remain unsatisfied ... Planned social intervention is particularly necessary in the early stage of the implementation of the new town plan. This planned social intervention should aim at mobilizing the new residents to form informal and semi-formal networks of interpersonal relationships, and at coordinating these networks.[63]

Yet, the failure of the Mutual Aid Committees as social organizations in the new towns[64] is a warning of the problems of such imposition from above.

Community organisation works have been externally initiated and supported, local motivation for organisation has been weak, and the linkages between organisations were also weak or non-existing.[65]

Such comments of the 1980s seem to belie the optimism of the 1970s as reported by Hayes.[66]

We can therefore now suggest an answer to one of the research questions posed by Chow in 1987:

the present social service provisions for the new towns have largely been planned according to experiences gained from the urban areas ... the question remains whether or not social services in the new towns should have functions different from those in the urban areas.[67]

The answer might well be 'yes they should'. As he puts it himself:

the quality of life ... involves the satisfaction of certain basic needs, like those for food, shelter, medical care, work, education, recreation and mobility ... The second level is more complicated and includes such aspects as the ways in which people are relating to each other ... and the level of satisfaction derived from such relationships.[68]

Objectives such as these require the installation of specialized machinery and programmes in the new communities that are required to evolve in new towns.

Concern in Hong Kong amongst professionals is, therefore, currently moving away from the assessment and provision of facilities and community needs to more subtle assessments of the realities of the development of the new communities. Already some evidence of tensions is arising. Despite the support for high-density living reported in Chapter 7,[69]

more evidences are now available to suggest that, despite the improvements in housing conditions, new town inhabitants are paying a high price in adjusting to the new environment.[70]

What may be more difficult to identify and assess are the changes which are occuring in the structure and composition of the families in the new towns, the inhabitants' relationships with one another, and their general mental health situation. Reports are coming out that, despite their improved residential facilities, new towns often have higher delinquency rates, that child abuse and family tragedies are more frequent there than in other areas, and that new town inhabitants seem to be enduring a higher level of stress and strain.[71]

While it would be wrong to over-emphasize the problems, clearly social policy-makers in Hong Kong, despite the major effort of government to introduce special policies for community building in the new towns, are still in a learning mode; at the least as much as the other professional groupings concerned with the development of the new towns of the Territory into the 1990s and beyond.

The Role of the New Towns in Hong Kong

Despite the ongoing commitment to the new town concepts of 'self-containment' and 'balance' reported so frequently in government publications and academic commentaries, the brief reviews of housing, industrial and employment structures, and sociological questions all suggest that reality is rapidly developing differently.

In some ways, it is rather surprising that such ideas were ever expected to hold, for as we have already stated current problems were foreseen from the beginning. We have already reported Prescott's comment of 1971: 'it is inconceivable that any real degree of self-sufficiency could be achieved by the new towns';[72] and Wigglesworth, who was involved in the early planning of Tuen Mun, also wrote in 1971:

although the government is committed to a new town programme and is taking positive steps to deal with the over-concentration apparent in the existing urban areas, there are problems to be overcome. Experience in other parts of the world has indicated that new or satellite towns built to relieve population pressure in mother cities ... have often been only partially successful ... This has happened ... also to some extent in Hong Kong.[73]

Indeed, as we noted in Chapter 3, the Population and Housing Working Group of the Colony Outline Plan exercise had themselves noted in 1969 that balance was not yet working in the new-town areas and that policy revisions were required.

Hence Pun's statement of 1986 seems unduly optimistic:

All new development areas are now planned to ensure a balance between the population and the housing supply, between demand for and provision of infrastructure services, between the workforce and employment opportunities, between people in different income and social groups, and between land use and transportation. These areas, when fully developed as planned, will be largely self-sufficient towns with minimum urban problems.[74]

This is emphasized by the fact that as early as 1981 the Acting Secretary of the New Territories was already publicly implying that self-containment as a planning aim had effectively been abandoned.[75]

While there are indeed special characteristics about new-town planning in Hong Kong, and we have already mentioned the *ad hoc* and incremental nature of the process, as well as noting with C.K. Leung:

thus urban sprawl into the New Territories in Hong Kong either as a process of urbanization or as an expression of core-periphery relationship in the context of metropolitan development is intertwined with the delicate and probably unique issue of organization and administration of the New Territories,[76]

especially with regard to land questions; all this omits one major misconception in the conceptual planning of the Hong Kong new towns. This problem has been admirably put by W.T. Leung, also in 1980. On Kwun Tong:

this proceeded in more or less a policy vacuum, when there did not exist a clearly defined set of planning goals for the overall land-use distribution in Hong Kong;[77]

or on Tsuen Wan:

the emphasis was on the community to be developed and not on the specific roles to be undertaken by the new towns in the national [Territorial] context ... What remains to be resolved is perhaps the right recipe for the programme, such as the planning strategy to be adopted and the nature of communities to be created.[78]

Part of the required thinking has been expressed by Leong:

The establishment of the new towns in the New Territories would constitute decentralisation of a kind ... The expanded urban structure will loosen the compactness of the existing city ... How far this expansion or 'mini-decentralization' will affect the well being of Hong Kong's urban growth, which has been extremely economically healthy so far, will be interesting to watch ... Although the department is satisfied that all the new urban centres will be totally self-contained ... people movement will result and increased distances due to decentralisation will increase mobility.[79]

Hence the transport problems associated with the new towns that other observers have noted:

Major new urban centres were established with little apparent attention being given to their transport linkages with the existing urban areas, in which many new town residents continue to work ... Many would argue, with some justification, that the Government's unwillingness (or inability) to play a more positive role in shaping the development of the territory's transport systems during the 1970s and, in particular, to anticipate the transport consequences of land use planning and housing policy decisions have contributed significantly to the present problem.[80]

In fact, both of these statements point to the same failure, an inability to consider in Hong Kong the role and function of the new towns strategically. This problem deserves some extended discussion, for it is fundamental to the long-term future of the Territory. Some measure of the failure can be made by examining the conceptual nature of such attempts at strategic planning as have been experienced in Hong Kong since Abercrombie's first effort in 1948.[81]

Strategic Issues

As was described in Chapter 2, Abercrombie's outline strategy was rapidly rendered obsolete in terms of its population forecasts and policies by the events surrounding the Chinese Revolution of 1949. Yet, although its population projections proved inaccurate, the integrated planning strategy suggested was followed in many details in the decade following the Second World War. Thus, many of the transport improvements suggested were precisely followed, while in terms of new towns, both Tsuen Wan and Kwun Tong were implemented, though, significantly, Abercrombie referred to them as being 'in and near Kowloon'.[82] He considered them as part of the main urban area, as they ultimately were to become, rather than within his definition of true new towns.

Strategic decision-making then remained effectively in abeyance in Hong Kong until the Colony Outline Plan of 1965–71, despite an attempt in the Planning Memorandum Number 4 of 1960; and, as we know, new-town designations proceeded regardless. This betrays a particular perspective on the concepts behind the new towns. It is well documented that they were public-housing based, and this meant in effect that choosing the sites and implementing construction were essentially land allocation or provision exercises with quite narrowly defined purposes in mind — additional sites for locating public housing or industrial buildings. Only afterwards was the concept of developing these embryonic structures into a 'town' properly considered.

It was this step to introduce the concept of the 'town' that introduced the fatal flaw, for it introduced with it the idea of independence and the planning terms of self-containment and balance that were so enthusiastically embraced by the new-town planners. Almost from the beginning, despite initial thoughts of the development of Sha Tin as a dormitory town, the mistake of thinking of the Hong Kong towns as independent entities rather than satellites was introduced and perpetuated. Hong Kong's policy-makers were unable or unwilling to comply with Sit's admonition:

planners have to admit frankly the nature of the new town to get themselves over the psychological hurdle imposed by the notions of independence and balance connected within the term 'new town'.[83]

This misconception was not eradicated by the Colony Outline Plan of 1971. It is unfair to comment with Chan that:

in planning the development of new towns, the government has apparently not undertaken any serious and comprehensive study and has not given alternative development strategies suitable comparison and evaluation. Some of the objectives of developing new towns have not been clearly defined.[84]

Yet, the final part of the statement hints at an important truth, for while alternative strategies for the growth of the then planned new towns were considered in the late 1960s (see Fig. 3.2), the alternatives were essentially differential population targets developed in 'town' or 'area' terms, rather than the alternative that reality demanded of considering integrated strategies for the Territory as a whole, which joined interlinked urban complexes.

Thus, while internal structure, activity, and movement within each new town was considered and developed for each urban area as its own internal plan evolved, no equivalent model was developed at the time either for the Territory as a whole (the nascent metropolitan region), or for that matter for the main urban area itself, as an overall integrated urban structure. Planning in the 1960s was a disparate set of spatial or sectoral studies (such as those done for Territory-wide transportation[85]), which the Colony Outline Plan and its successor document of the 1970s — the Hong Kong Outline Plan — failed to integrate into a well-considered cohesive overall strategy.

In part, this was due to the way in which the Colony Outline Plan was set up. It was the product of the deliberations of six sectoral committees, as described in Chapter 3, working from the 1968 population projections which suggested that Hong Kong's population would grow from 3.7 to

5.8 million by 1986; and therefrom deriving employment estimates, the structure of the population by broad types of accommodation, and land requirements for the 20-year forecast period. The strength of the plan-making was in the intentions of the six committees — geography, population and housing, commerce and industry with agriculture and fisheries, utilities and services, transportation, and community requirements, of which population and housing was much the most dominant; the weakness was in the subsequent integration, despite the final statement on objectives:

The basic intention is to make the Colony a better place to live in ...

It would be necessary to accommodate about 900,000 people in subsidised housing in the new towns. This would represent about 68% of their combined populations. The population distribution assumed as a basis for the Colony Outline Plan will not evolve unless there are policy decisions concerning the various means by which a strategy of decentralization and new town growth can be achieved.

The scale and disposition of Government and Government-aided Housing will considerably influence the future distribution of population. In order to overcome the reluctance of people to move to new town areas, the aim should be the development of reasonably self-contained communities at each stage of new town growth so as to provide a range of employment and accommodation as well as adequate community facilities and public transportation services.

It will be desirable to encourage the growth of private housing in the new towns so as to broaden the class structure of the population and reduce the burden on public funds. Certain administrative inducements and selective controls may be necessary to achieve this.

Decentralisation to new towns is one of the pre-requisites to the achievement of environmental improvement in the older parts of the main urban areas.[86]

While in general it was stated that:

The planning process requires an approach which progresses from the general to the particular. Accepting this, the delineation of specific areas for residential, industrial and other uses at the district level should initially have regard to the predominent functions for which the district concerned is best suited,[87]

the failure to consider effectively the strategic inter-relationships and interactions *between* districts built in a serious flaw into the land-allocation and zoning processes associated with the district zoning plans. For the new towns this problem was compounded by the excessive concentration on self-containment and an ignoring of the inter-urban or metropolitan-scale relationships which were bound to occur.

In the event, a considered choice between strategies was effectively side-stepped, as the Plan itself made clear, and was pointed out in Chapter 3:

Ideally, the choice of one of these alternatives should be guided by a detailed assessment of the relative economics of each. Whilst it is possible that this could be done after a prolonged study, it is considered that a decision has to be made on the best information now available ... It is therefore considered that Government's basic policy should be decentralisation to new towns and improvement of the environment in the existing urban areas ... This gives positive expression to the strategy which in recent years has been followed but not stated in explicit terms by Government.[88]

This raised three important questions, which remained unanswered. Firstly, it implied that the government felt itself so committed to an already determined course of action, that real alternatives were no longer practicable; secondly, it left a serious conceptual gap between simplistic objectives at the Territory level and detailed operational planning at the district or new-town level; and thirdly, it revealed the government's obsession with costs. The problem for Hong Kong was and is that economically optimal solutions may not always be the best planning solutions, and in 1965–71 not even that sub-optimal route was taken in determining a role for the new towns into the next quarter century.

This initial inability to consider the role of the Hong Kong new towns strategically in functional or activity terms continued. The Hong Kong Outline Plan of 1979, essentially an updating of the earlier 1960s work, was based upon a strategy of meeting theoretical land requirements based on housing, industry, or community facilities' needs.[89] Its strategy for the new towns was short and succinct:

It is assumed in this Plan that the development programmes of the New Towns and new development areas in the New Territories will materialize as now envisaged and their design populations will be as given in Chapter 16 [the chapter setting out the housing targets and policies].[90]

Only with regard to the main urban areas was some doubt now beginning to set in:

The bulk of the population seems to be content to continue to live in these areas ... From the aspect of the provision of community and other facilities ... the Main Urban Areas could accommodate a population of around 5.0 million. The Comprehensive Transport Study has proved that of the three land use alternatives tested, Land Use 3, which envisages further concentration up to 3.8 million within the Main Urban Areas, would be the least costly from the viewpoint of communications. The principal planning target for the Main Urban Areas is to improve the living and working environment as far as possible according to the development standards recommended.[91]

Once again, the planning emphasis had reverted to the detail: the fundamental strategic implications of what was being reported and suggested remained unspoken and unheeded; and the new-town programme went forward as before.

However, the Territorial Development Strategy of 1984 (see Fig. 8.1) has been represented as being a fundamental shift in Hong Kong's planning. As Taylor expresses it:

Much of the government's action until very recently has been piecemeal in nature — *reactive* planning in response to external demands or crises, rather than forward (or *proactive*) planning aimed at implementing a longer-term vision of the territory's future development pattern. Since 1984 this situation has changed, and for the first time a long-term development strategy is in place which is aimed at purposefully reshaping Hong Kong's urban form to facilitate predetermined, and not just *ad hoc*, objectives.[92]

But, as mentioned in Chapter 3, Taylor is critical of the process by which the plan's preferred strategy (see Fig. 8.1) was arrived at:

There are aspects of the TDS [Territorial Development Strategy] which are distinctive to the work of the Strategic Planning Unit, reflecting partly the unique constraints ... which confront planners in Hong Kong, and partly the personal proclivities of the SPU's planning staff ... Of particular importance to LUTO [the Land Use–Transportation Optimization model used by the planners], and to the entire TDS planning process, is the definition of the objectives which form the basis for the model's determination of 'optimal' development strategies. LUTO requires that each planning objective be stated in quantitative terms as an 'objective function' ... In their choice of methodologies the SPU ultimately promoted the view that quantifiable (and particularly financial) criteria are the most significant ones to bear in mind when plans like the TDS are drawn up to reshape the urban environment in Hong Kong.[93]

Taylor's more general criticism of the Territorial Development Strategy methodology is that it is 'primarily based on maximising governmental welfare rather than a more broadly defined community interest'.[94] But what are its implications for the new towns? The preferred strategy for the 1990s of redirecting future major expansion to the new reclamations in the harbour adjacent to the main urban core for future major development in Hong Kong rests only upon the quantified assessment of public land production costs, inter-zonal transport costs in terms of infrastructure and travel time, and land revenues to government. Expressed in these terms (and it is as limited as this, for reasons that Taylor describes), it seems an absurdly narrow set of criteria upon which to determine a long-term planning strategy which might well terminate the Hong Kong new-town programme.

The underlying simplistic objective of the Territorial Development Strategy itself was, in fact, expressed in a 1986 paper by Choi, the government engineer in charge of the optimization studies:

The purpose of [the] development strategy in the present context is to provide guidance for directing investments on land use development and transport infrastructure.[95]

That, regrettably, is not a commonly understood acceptable basis for effective strategic regional or metropolitan planning. The wish to avoid subjective judgement in the planning process seems in Hong Kong to have removed almost all consideration of the necessary social, environmental, and, in effect, integrated strategic planning issues that are required to be examined in order to produce a well-founded plan for the future; even though a need remains, when it is recognized that the effects of implementing such a strategy as the current one into the next century will be profound for the future of the Territory.

Into the Nineties

As Hong Kong approaches the 1990s, and, in 1997, a new future involving an undetermined level of land-use integration into the People's Republic of China, the future of the new-town programme in the Territory seems rather less certain than the production of the Territorial Development Strategy would suggest. In fact, those who have to determine strategic development policies for the 1990s still face a number of important dilemmas, the answers to which the Strategy does not yet provide.

The first of these relates to a question which was raised in Chapter 1. To repeat:

one of the more important questions that has to be answered about any new-town programme is the role that the new settlements are expected to play within the existing or planned settlement network for the area.

Self-containment and balance was an attempted answer to that problem — the dilemma is, that it is not yet working, and seems increasingly recognized as not ever to work as a long-term principle. Where now? The reactive answer, which is currently being implemented, is to improve the inter-urban transport links to meet the current demands being made upon them. Yet that, in itself, further accentuates the advantages of the metropolitan core, accelerates the growth of traffic flows, and diminishes the self-containment which still remains as the long-term, stated, if illusory, aim.

As yet in Hong Kong there is no pronouncement on the type of metropolitan urban structure that is being aimed for and no prescription for the future. The likely outcome seems to be that a metropolis will be produced by the market, to which the planners will then have to react in the time-honoured Hong Kong way. One is, at the least, entitled to ask if the outcome might be more effective, efficient, amenable (use whatever qualifier or value you might wish to apply), were the change to be more purposeful (prescriptive), or at the very least facilitated rather than being tamely followed, should the overall government objective, first expressed some thirty years ago, still remain — 'The basic intention is to make the Colony a better place to live in.'[96]

Such a discussion does, of course, provide a somewhat ambiguous answer for the third government objective concerning the new-town programme that was set out at the beginning of this chapter. As Table 8.1 showed, there is no doubt that a redistribution of population has occurred, and for many a marked improvement in housing conditions; if not always, as has been suggested, in overall quality of life. The doubt, in the long term, lies in the existing urban area. Should major reconcentration adjacent to the urban core occur, as defined in the initial stage of the Territorial Development Strategy (see Fig. 8.1), as well as increasing integration of the new towns with that same urban core, then increasing pressures on both transport networks, employment and retail nodes, and other core area attractions would seem inevitable. Certainly such changes will set difficult and possibly intractable urban planning problems for the core area. These problems as yet, have hardly been addressed in Hong Kong, despite the 1987 announcement of a new harbour area master plan,[97] and the initial proposals for *Metroplan* in April 1988.

A halt to the existing new-town development programme in the mid-1990s also sets up some additional internal problems, thus posing other dilemmas for the government, not yet properly examined. While the earlier new towns will be largely complete, further incremental development opportunities still remain (see Fig. 8.3). Perhaps the most difficult decision originally concerned Junk Bay. Development planning, with the hiccups examined in Chapter 6, proceeded on the basis of full development of the site's potential, yet the Territorial Development Strategy evolved on the basis of Phase I development only. The decision to complete the new twin-tunnel approach road to the town from East Kowloon introduced, however, a dilemma common in Hong Kong planning — existing or prior commitments produce a development momentum which it is hard to stop. It is a philosophy well expressed in Eason's official review of the Territorial Development Strategy:

In line with the principle that the fullest possible benefit should be derived from investment in infrastructure, it has been possible to identify additional development opportunities within existing or already planned development areas which will reduce the need to do so in new areas.[98]

Thus, having already committed investments which carry with them optimal usage or take-up targets, the incentive to make use of that capacity (otherwise they become unused assets) becomes overwhelming.

By the end of 1988, the decision to proceed with first the second and then the third stages of Junk Bay, thereby increasing its target population from 185,000 to 350,000 and then 420,000, represented a major departure from the Strategy. Whatever sense it might have made in terms of local utilization of assets, because of its location adjacent to the eastern end of the harbour area (in effect, like Kwun Tong and Tsuen Wan before it, it is likely to become a mere extension of the main urban area), it will impose major modifications to the activity and function patterns of East Kowloon, Kwun Tong, and adjacent parts of Hong Kong Island (through the new Eastern Harbour Crossing). The result is that important new infrastructure investments will now be utilized to full capacity — mostly on the transportation side — but that important planning impacts will occur elsewhere before they have been properly considered. They will be major constraints upon the options for *Metroplan*, for example. Of course,

Fig. 8.3 Growth areas and potentials identified by the five sub-regional planning studies carried out in Hong Kong in the early 1980s.

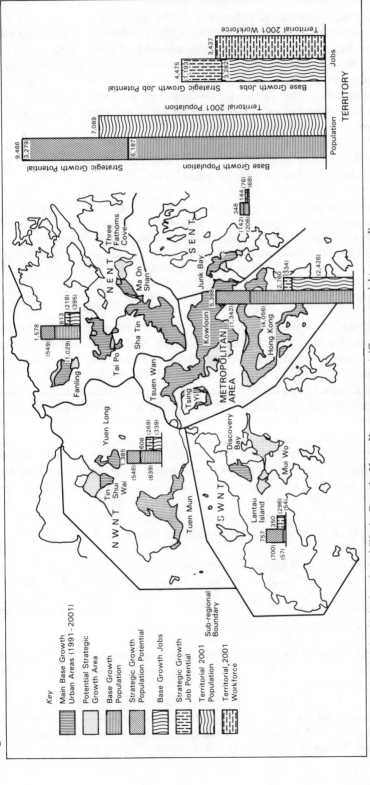

Source: Strategic Planning Unit, Lands and Works Branch, Hong Kong government (Crown copyright reserved).

Note: 1. Population and job totals include those for the marine population. 2. Population and job figures are in thousands.

it also represents a further major evolution of the 1980s new-town programme: a course of action which the acceptance of the Territorial Development Strategy seemed theoretically to foreclose. The example of Junk Bay merely suggests that other areas like Tuen Mun East or further extensions to Ma On Shan or Tin Shui Wai may well give rise to similar arguments at later stages, whatever the results so far from the limited evaluations of the Territorial Development Strategy, its update TDS II or the transportation investigations of the second Comprehensive Transportation Study expected in late 1988.

Just as Junk Bay represented a planning and development dilemma for the Hong Kong government, so too does Tin Shui Wai as a new town in a different way. As Taylor points out:

The 135,000 residents of the first phase of Tin Shui Wai . . . represent one 'fixed' population whose interests are very much affected by the location of new growth. They live far away from the centres of employment and entertainment in the territory and their community is too small to support the large-scale public services . . . found in larger New Towns. If the 'centre of gravity' in Hong Kong shifts back towards the main urban area . . . it would not be surprising to see considerable discontent emerge among Tin Shui Wai residents.[99]

This is, of course a renewal of the viable threshold argument, but there is also another, for Tin Shui Wai also has a major infrastructure investment which works in its favour, just as at Junk Bay. The decision on economic grounds to reclaim the Tin Shui Wai site as one project created a land bank which, on all measures of past performance and asset utilization, will force the government to commit it to development as soon as possible. These later stages of Tin Shui Wai (with Junk Bay) alone more that meet the revised 'mobile' population target of some 0.2 million which is now expected to require development sites by the late 1990s. So much for the likelihood of major new developments in the harbour area, or major strategic shifts in the medium-term development prospects in Hong Kong.

There is, of course, one further long-term dilemma about which no answers are as yet known — the development situation after 1997. Academics are already considering the question:[100]

The rapid growth of Shenzhen has opened up possibilities for collaborative development across the Shenzhen–Hong Kong boundary which were not present before creation of the Special Economic Zone in 1979. Even in the absence of covert collaboration, though, Shenzhen's development will have implications for Hong Kong's territory-wide planning.[101]

Certainly more cognizance of possible integrated planning would seem to be in order, and already to be recognized amongst some in the Hong Kong government:

Finally, the long-term growth of Hong Kong needs to be viewed in a wider regional context in which connection the rapid development occurring in the Shenzhen Special Economic Zone is to be noted.[102]

It would not seem particularly outrageous to suggest that given Shenzhen's present internal 'frontier' with the rest of China, post-1997 may see a greater integration of the Special Economic Zone and the Hong Kong Special Autonomous Region to form a new, expanded and consolidated metropolitan area — a new era in the planning of the whole sub-region.

Some Conclusions

How might one sum up an evaluation of the Hong Kong new-town programme? It was asserted in Chapter 1 that for the British new towns the 'administrative machine needed to be planner, financier, developer, and manager all rolled into one'. The Hong Kong government has never really aspired to that all-embracing, interventionist, paternalistic role, and some of the new-town failings can be placed at its door for just such a reason. As Scott and Cheek-Milby comment in another context:

Government, in short, tends to be reactive rather than proactive, except where it is pursuing an explicitly political objective. And if, as one commentator has pointed out, it cannot be regarded as anti-welfare, its response to social problems is still very conservative.[103]

These are terms that we have seen before, yet reactive planning largely accounts for the fact that the nature and form of the Hong Kong new towns are born out of short-term thinking and policy-making with limited horizons. Even though they are creations with major long-term consequences, formative decisions have proceeded on an incremental, pragmatic basis, as with much else in Hong Kong planning.[104]

Such situations have had important consequences for the future. Notwithstanding the achievement of building eight new cities in what will be about three decades, nagging problems remain, some of which have been suggested in this chapter. Just three more are worth a mention as speculative questions.

Possible relationships with Shenzhen and other parts of southern China were already affecting internal Hong Kong planning by the late 1980s. For example, the expected decision in late 1988 to commit public resources for the construction of Route 'X' (to connect Tsuen Wan under Tai Mo Shan to Yuen Long and the north-west New Territories) would provide a new western north-south corridor across the Territory forming a key link in a new route from Kwai Chung and the harbour to the new western border crossing into China at Lok Ma Chau. This duplication of the eastern route through the new towns of Sha Tin, Tai Po, and Sheung Shui/Fanling would clearly alter the whole strategic balance between the relative advantages of the eastern and western new towns in Hong Kong, and perhaps open up again strategic planning questions about the ultimate levels of growth in the north-west New Territories, in general, and Tin Shui Wai in particular, as well as possible new routes for integration with Shenzhen. Certainly, even this single investment decision in transportation improvement creates new planning dilemmas for the Territory that the original Territorial Development Strategy hardly addressed.

The Hong Kong new towns, by and large, are planned with only marginal shifts in transport modal splits in mind. Yet, with rising incomes and aspirations, how far are such assumptions realistic? If they are, then the outcome is a demand for more mobility and better public transport (a demand that none of the Hong Kong new towns except perhaps Junk Bay or Tin Shui Wai is well suited to meet), or if they are not, then individual car ownership will rise with all that that could mean for the Territory's road system and parking in the new-town residential and employment areas.

The second reverts to the question of management.

In the early days of resettlement it was too readily assumed that once the buildings were up the job was done ... Nobody quarrels with the importance or urgency of the works. I maintain that management — not only of the housing estates but of the whole town — is of as great importance in improving the quality of life — and this is what it is all about.[105]

The issue here is not so much past policies, for at least as far as social concerns and community building are concerned, we have commented on these earlier. The question is more one of adequacy for the future.

It is notable in most of the British new towns, for example, that the Development Corporations set up a detailed monitoring mechanism for understanding the community and economic development of their towns. This enabled them to adjust housing and industrial policies rapidly as circumstances changed and experience grew. Because of the organizational arrangements for the Hong Kong new towns (see Chapter 4), such monitoring is currently largely absent, with the expected result that policy-makers react slowly to problems as they arise, and information about the new towns in terms of social and economic issues is sparse and uncoordinated. Without some improvement problems will not be foreseen and policy will remain reactive. It would seem likely also that as the towns rapidly grow larger, the problems will multiply, thus undermining the government's ultimate objectives of social order in the Territory. Clearly, present evidence is already beginning to suggest deficiencies in information about the towns which require remedying.

The matter of new-town management is worth taking further however, for there are other issues involved. One of the more fascinating in current circumstances is that of overall management responsibility. Leaving aside current debates about the representativeness of the District Boards and their position after 1997,[106] there is little doubt that they are 'flexing their muscles' with regard to intervention in new-town development matters. This is only to be expected as the new-town 'immigrant' populations grow, and they begin to utilize their perceived representation through their local District Boards to affect and modify local new-town policies that directly affect them. As yet District Boards have little impact on new-town policy, except at the margin. But as political awareness increases, demands for local influence are bound to modify current procedures; and it seems likely that the new-town District Boards will be at the vanguard of local administrative change and influence in the Hong Kong of the 1990s.

The third area of comment lies within the whole arena of standards and enforcement, which, in a way, is but a further aspect of new-town management, but largely on the environment side. Enforcement in Hong Kong, particularly within the building control field, remains an endemic problem.[107] For the present, the new towns remain in a privileged position: but one wonders for how long? As the new towns mature and take on more of the ambience of the older main urban area, will social attitudes and environmental responsibilities revert back to older ways, such that the new-town fabric comes to resemble more that of the older city core? Or will the experience of the 'new' environments generate sufficient management and pride to maintain present standards of urban living, design, and space in the new towns into the next century? Perhaps the 1987 decision to revise the Town Planning Ordinance in Hong Kong and to extend existing planning controls, particularly in the New Territories, is a harbinger of better things to come.

The problem of enforcement, of course, goes further. It applies not only within the towns, as a matter of urban design and development control, but even more to containment at the urban fringe. Until recently, most of the Hong Kong new towns have remained 'naturally' contained by their physical settings. The expansions of Yuen Long and Sheung Shui/Fanling first alerted planners to the problems of the urban fringe in Hong Kong, and the incipient urbanization of the north-west New Territories was recognized early on as a major issue during the 1980s sub-regional study. Yet again, present attitudes towards statutory planning controls in the New Territories outside of the urban areas — or rather the lack of them — leads one to believe that this is another managerial problem which is going to intensify rather than go away, whatever the planning ordinance revision may bring for the 1990s. Certainly, the development of Tin Shui Wai and the maintenance of green belt between the major new towns of the north-west and northern New Territories is likely to prove a major land management problem for the 1990s and beyond unless present procedures and enforcement capabilities are tightened up and used.

It would however be churlish to end on a questioning or disparaging note. It is not an understatement to conclude that:

Hong Kong is undergoing a period of dynamic change as far-reaching development programmes forge ahead to create new urban centres that will ultimately accommodate more than two million people ... Thousands of people each month are moving to these centres in one of the biggest social achievements in the history of Hong Kong.[108]

It is not for nothing that the 'Hong Kong solution' is increasingly being examined to provide possible models for Chinese urban expansion, and that the new towns of the Territory have become magnets for professional visitors from all over the world. Even if emulation is rarely possible or even desirable, there is not a little envy as overseas observers look out over the half-million cities that now fill once placid valleys that formerly were the home of paddy fields, traditional Chinese villages, and silted inlets. The urbanization of the Hong Kong New Territories in three decades is the present monument to that past achievement, and the expanded metropolis that awaits 1997 and the twenty-first century is a fit testament to the vision and skills of the Hong Kong government and its planners.

Notes

1. W.T. Leung, 'The New Towns Programme', in T.N. Chiu and C.L. So (eds.), *A Geography of Hong Kong* (Hong Kong, Oxford University Press, 1986), p. 252.

2. Town Planning Division, *Town Planning in Hong Kong* (Hong Kong, Lands Department, 1984), pp. 26–7, republished in revised form in 1988.

3. J.M. Wigglesworth, 'The Development of New Towns', in D.J. Dwyer (ed.), *Asian Urbanisation: A Hong Kong Casebook* (Hong Kong, Hong Kong University Press, 1971), pp. 52, 57, and 63; and A.R. Crosby, 'Physical Planning for the New Town', in Hong Kong Committee of the International Council on Social Welfare, *Symposium on Social Planning in a New Town: Case Study — Shatin New Town* (Hong Kong, Hong Kong Council of Social Service, 1976), pp. 5, 6, 11, and 12.

4. J.M. Wigglesworth (1971), see note 3 above, p. 52.

5. A.R. Crosby (1976), see note 3 above, p. 5.

6. A.R. Crosby (1976), see note 3 above, p. 12.

7. A selection of such citations is:
D.W.T. Han, 'Migration of Residential Satisfaction in a New Town: The Case of Tuen Mun', in C.K. Leung, J.W. Cushman, and C.W. Wang (eds.), *Hong Kong: Dilemmas of Growth* (Hong Kong, University of Hong Kong, Centre of Asian Studies, 1980), p. 341;
'Hong Kong's New Towns', in *Hong Kong Annual Report 1979* (Hong Kong, Government Printer, 1979), p. 2;
M.K. Lee Fong, 'Directions in Urban Growth in Hong Kong', in C.K. Leung et al. (1980), see above, p. 280;
W.T. Leung, 'Hong Kong's New Towns Programme: A Social Perspective', in C.K. Leung et al. (1980), see above, p. 376;
K.S. Pun, 'New Towns and Urban Renewal in Hong Kong', in D.R. Phillips and A.G.O. Yeh (eds.), *New Towns in East and South-east Asia: Planning and Development* (Hong Kong, Oxford University Press, 1987), p. 42;
V.F.S. Sit, 'New Towns for the Future', in V.F.S. Sit (ed.), *Urban Hong Kong* (Hong Kong, Summerson Eastern, 1981), p. 154;
Town Planning Division (1984), see note 2 above, p. 26; and (1988), p. 32.
L.H. Wang and A.G.O. Yeh, 'Public Housing-Led New Town Development: Hong Kong and Singapore', *Third World Planning Review*, Vol. 9, No. 1, February 1987, pp. 41–63;
J.M. Wigglesworth (1971), see note 3 above, p. 50;
K.Y. Wong, 'New Towns — The Hong Kong Experience', in J.Y.S. Cheng (ed.), *Hong Kong in the 1980s* (Hong Kong, Summerson Eastern, 1982), p. 120;
A.G.O. Yeh, 'New Towns in Hong Kong', in P.L.Y. Choi, P.K.W. Fong, and R.Y.W. Kwok (eds.), *Planning and Development of Coastal Open Cities — Part Two: Hong Kong Section* (Hong Kong, University of Hong Kong, Centre of Urban Studies and Urban Planning, 1986), p. 113; and,
A.G.O. Yeh and P.K.W. Fong, 'Public Housing and Urban Development in Hong Kong', *Third World Planning Review*. Vol. 6, No. 1, February 1984, p. 81.

8. A.G.O. Yeh, 'Spatial Impacts of New Town Development in Hong Kong', in D.R. Phillips and A.G.O. Yeh (1987), see note 7 above, p. 60.

9. K.S. Pun, 'Urban Planning', in T.N. Chiu and C.W. So (1986), see note 1 above, p. 237.

10. W.T. Leung (1986), see note 1 above, p. 277.

11. J.M. Wigglesworth (1971), see note 3 above, pp. 49–51.

12. Special Committee on Land Production, *Report of the Special Committee on Land Production* (Hong Kong, Government Printer, 1977); Special Committee on Land Production, *Special Committee on Land Production: Report to His Excellency the Governor* (Hong Kong, Government Printer, 1981); and Special Committee on Land Supply, *Special Committee on Land Supply: Report to His Excellency the Governor* (Hong Kong, Government Printer, 1982–5 annually).

13. D.W. Drakakis-Smith, *High Society: Housing Provision in Metropolitan Hong Kong 1954 to 1979 — A Jubilee Critique* (Hong Kong, University of Hong Kong, Centre of Asian Studies, 1979), pp. 83, 134–5, and 157.

14. J.K. Keung, *Government Intervention and Housing Policy in Hong Kong: A Structural Analysis* (Cardiff, University of Wales Institute of Science and Technology, Department of Town Planning, Planning Research Paper No. 30, 1981); and J.K. Keung, 'Government Intervention and Housing Policy in Hong Kong', *Third World Planning Review*, Vol. 7, No. 1, February 1985, pp. 23–44.

15. Commission of Inquiry, *Kowloon Disturbances 1966 — Report of Commission of Inquiry* (Hong Kong, Government Printer, 1967), paras. 515–6, p. 138.

16. L.H. Wang and A.G.O. Yeh (1987), see note 7 above, p. 44.

17. J.M. Wigglesworth (1971), see note 3 above, pp. 68 and 50.

18. L.H. Wang and A.G.O. Yeh (1987), see note 7 above, p. 55.

19. N.W.S. Chow, *Moving into New Towns — The Costs of Social Adaptation* (Hong Kong, University of Hong Kong, Centre of Urban Studies and Urban Planning, 1987); pp. 3–4. See also, N.W.S. Chow, 'Moving into New Towns: The Costs of Social Adaptation', *The Asian Journal of Public Administration*, Vol. 9, No. 2, December 1987, pp. 132–42.

20. Y.K. Chan, *The Development of New Towns in Hong Kong* (Hong Kong, Chinese University of Hong Kong, Social Research Centre, Occasional Paper No. 67, 1977), p. 17.

21. A.G.O. Yeh (1986), see note 7 above, p. 121.

22. A.G.O. Yeh (1986), see note 7 above, p. 117.

23. W.T. Leung (1986), see note 1 above, p. 274.

24. P.K.W. Fong, 'Public Housing Policies and Programmes in Hong Kong — Past, Present and Future Developments' in Choi, Fong, and Kwok (1986), see note 7 above, pp. 110 and 108–9. The consultative report referred to was: Hong Kong Housing Authority, *A Review of Public Housing Allocation Policies: A Consultative Document* (Hong Kong, Government Printer, 1984).

25. Hong Kong Housing Authority, *Green Paper: Housing Subsidy to Tenants of Public Housing* (Hong Kong, Government Printer, 1985).

26. Hong Kong Housing Authority, *Long-Term Housing Strategy: A Policy Statement* (Hong Kong, Government Printer, 1987).

27. D. Clapham and J. English, *Public Housing: Current Trends and Future Developments* (Beckenham, Croom Helm, 1987).

28. L.H. Wang and A.G.O. Yeh (1987), see note 7 above, p. 60. Only 24 per cent of public housing flats in Singapore were available for rent in 1987.

29. K.S. Pun (1986), see notes 9 and 1 above, p. 236.

30. J.M. Wigglesworth (1971), see note 3 above, p. 50.

31. J.M. Wigglesworth (1971), see note 3 above, pp. 52 and 53.

32. J.M. Wigglesworth (1971), see note 3 above, p. 59.

33. J.M. Wigglesworth (1971), see note 3 above, p. 60.

34. L.H. Wang and A.G.O. Yeh (1987), see note 7 above, pp. 54–5.

35. W.T. Leung (1980), see note 7 above, pp. 382 and 381.

36. A.G.O. Yeh and P.K.W. Fong (1984), see note 7 above, p. 93.

37. P.K.W. Fong (1986), see notes 24 and 7 above, p. 110.

38. K.Y. Wong (1982), see note 7 above, pp. 118–30.

39. A.G.O. Yeh (1986), see note 7 above, p. 123.

40. C.Y. Leung, 'The Land Tenure System', in J.Y.S. Cheng (ed.), *Hong Kong in Transition* (Hong Kong, Oxford University Press, 1986), pp. 230 and 231.

41. A.G.O. Yeh (1986), see note 7 above, p. 118.

42. Hong Kong Productivity Centre, *Industrial Mobility Study: Executive Summary* (Hong Kong: Strategic Planning Unit, 1983), p. 13; reproduced in A.G.O. Yeh (1986), see note 7 above, pp. 118–9.

43. Special Committee on Housing, *Final Report of the Special Committee on Housing 1956–58* (Hong Kong, Government Printer, 1978), para. 42, p. 21.

44. L.H. Wang and A.G.O. Yeh (1987), see note 7 above, p. 58. The statistics quoted were from: Sha Tin New Town Development Office, *Sha Tin New Town Industrial Survey* (Hong Kong, New Territories Development Department, 1981); and Working Group on Promotion of Industrial Investment in Tuen Mun, *Tuen Mun Industrial Survey 1983 — Industries and Workers: Past and Future Outlook* (Hong Kong, Tuen Mun District Board, 1983). See also, Tsuen Wan District Board, *Unemployment/Underemployment Situation in Tsuen Wan: A Report* (Hong Kong, Tsuen Wan District Board, 1983).

45. As note 44 above.

46. V.F.S. Sit (1981), see note 7 above, p. 158.

47. K.Y. Wong (1982), see note 7 above, p. 125.

48. J.A. Prescott, 'Hong Kong: The Form and Significance of a High Density Urban Development', in D.J. Dwyer (1971), see note 3 above, p. 13.

49. A summary is given in A.G.O. Yeh, 'Employment Location and New Town Development in Hong Kong', in P. Hills (ed.), *State Policy, Urbanisation and the Development Process* (Hong Kong, University of Hong Kong, Centre of Urban Studies and Urban Planning, 1985), pp. 60–65.

50. Town Planning Office, *Planning Statement for the Northeastern New Territories Sub-Region* (Hong Kong, Buildings and Lands Department, 1986), paras. 4.7.2–3, p. 21.

51. N.W.S. Chow (1987), see note 19 above, p. 1.

52. N.W.S. Chow (1987), see note 19 above, p. 2.

53. N.W.S. Chow (1987), see note 19 above, p. 5.

54. Some representative academic studies are:

Y.K. Chan (1977), see note 20 above;

Y.K. Chan, *Life Satisfaction in Crowded Urban Environment* (Hong Kong, Chinese University of Hong Kong, Social Research Centre, Occasional Paper No. 75, 1978);

C.Y. Choi and Y.K. Chan, *Housing Policy and Internal Movement of Population: A Study of Kwun Tong — A Chinese New Town in Hong Kong* (Hong Kong, Chinese University of Hong Kong, Social Research Centre, Research Report A62.17.0.1, 1977);

N. Chow, A. Tang, and T.F. Chau, *A Study of the Values, Leisure Behaviour and Misbehaviour of the Youth in Tsuen Wan and Kwai Chung* (Hong Kong, Cosmos Books, 1984);

N.W.S. Chow, 'The Quality of Life of Tuen Mun Inhabitants', *The Asian Journal of Public Administration*, Vol. 10, No. 2, December 1988, pp. 194–206.

M.K. Fong, *Some Observations on the Degree of Satisfaction of the Residents of Tai Po Township on Their Living Environment*, Paper presented at the First Asia-Pacific Conference on Urban Reconstruction, Taipei, 1978;

G. Gilbert, 'Social Problems in the Development of Shatin New Town', in Hong Kong Committee of the International Council on Social Welfare (1976), see note 3 above, pp. 84–8;

D.W.T. Han (1980), see note 7 above;

D.W.T. Han, 'Social Planning for the New Town', in Hong Kong Committee of the International Council on Social Welfare (1976), see note 3 above, pp. 24–38;

J. Hayes, 'Building a Community in a New Town: A Management Relationship with the New Population', in C.K. Leung et al. (1980), see note 7 above, pp. 309–40;

P. Hodge, 'Social Planning for Growing Cities' in International Council on Social Welfare, *Social Planning for Growing Cities: Role of Social Welfare — Proceedings of the International Council on Social Welfare Regional Conference for Asia and Western Pacific 1975* (Hong Kong, Hong Kong Council of Social Service, 1976), pp. 7–29;

J.F. Jones, K.F. Ho, B.L. Chau, M.C. Lam, and B.H. Mok, *Neighbourhood Associations in a New Town: The Mutual Aid Committees in Sha Tin* (Hong Kong, Chinese University of Hong Kong, Social Research Centre, Occasional Paper No. 76, 1978);

H.C. Kuan, S.K. Lau, and K.F. Ho, *Organising Participatory Urban Services: The Mutual Aid Committees in Hong Kong* (Hong Kong, Chinese University of Hong Kong, Institute of Social Studies, Occasional Paper No. 2, 1983); and in Y.M. Yeung and T.G. McGee (eds.), *Community Participation in Delivering Urban Services in Asia* (Ottawa, International Research Centre, 1986), pp. 211–37.

S.K. Lau, 'Comments on the Social Infrastructure of the Shatin New Town', in Hong Kong Committee of the International Council on Social Welfare (1976), see note 3 above, pp. 59–63;

A.L.C. Lu, *Tuen Mun Community Needs Survey* (Hong Kong, Shue Yan College, Faculty of Social Science, 1977);

P. Ng, Y.K. Chan, and S.K. Lau, 'Social Problems and the New Towns', in Hong Kong Committee of the International Council on Social Welfare (1976), see note 3 above, pp. 89–91;

W.T. Leung (1986), see note 1 above, and

S. Vasoo, 'Residents' Organisations in the New Towns of Hong Kong and Singapore: Some Issues and Future Developments', *The Asian Journal of Public Administration*, Vol. 9, No. 2, December 1987, pp. 143–54.

55. Some of the studies published by social welfare organizations in Hong Kong are: Caritas Tuen Mun Family Service Unit, 'Adjustment Problems encountered by Families in Tuen Mun', *Welfare Quarterly of the Hong Kong Council of Social Services*, No. 97, Summer 1986. pp. 31–3;

W.T. Chan, 'Situation of Residents in Tuen Mun New Town' (in Chinese), *Welfare Quarterly of the Hong Kong Council of Social Services*, No. 62, Autumn 1977, pp. 5–12.

W.T. Chau and M.Y. So, *A Study on Tuen Mun's Community Need* (Hong Kong, Young Women's Christian Association [YWCA], 1977);

N.W.S. Chow, 'The Service Gap: Past and Present Problems — Possible Remedial Action', in Hong Kong Council of Social Services, *Proceedings of a Symposium on Social Services in the New Towns* (Hong Kong, Hong Kong Council of Social Services, 1983);

Hong Kong Council of Social Services, 'Role of Government in Community Building', *Welfare Quarterly of the Hong Kong Council of Social Services*, No. 67, Winter 1978, pp. 17–8;

M.Y. So, 'A General Outline for Community Development in Tuen Mun — A Proposal', in Community Development Committee, *Community Development Resource Book 1975–76* (Hong Kong, Hong Kong Council of Social Services, 1977), pp. 67–71; and

M.Y. So, 'The Role of Community Development in a New Town: A Social Worker's Experience' (in Chinese), *Welfare Quarterly of the Hong Kong Council of Social Services*, No. 62, Autumn 1977, pp. 21–5.

56. N.W.S. Chow (1987), see note 19 above, p. 8.

57. L.H. Wang and A.G.O. Yeh (1987), see note 7 above, p. 52.

58. K.Y. Wong (1982), see note 7 above, p. 125.

59. D.W.T. Han (1980), see note 7 above, p. 348.

60. D.W.T. Han (1980), see note 7 above, p. 370.

61. W.T. Leung (1980), see note 7 above, p. 387.

62. Y.K. Chan (1977), see note 20 above, p. 16.

63. Y.K. Chan (1977), see note 20 above, pp. 23–4.

64. H.C. Kuan et al. (1983), see note 54 above, pp. 33–7.

65. Y.K. Chan (1977), see note 20 above, p. 20.

66. J. Hayes (1980), see notes 54 and 7 above, pp. 309–40.

67. N.W.S. Chow (1987), see note 19 above, pp. 9–10.

68. N.W.S. Chow (1987), see note 19 above, p. 7.

69. See also Y.K. Chan, 'Density and Its Implications', in Hong Kong Council of Social Services, *Report of the Symposium on Development within Environmental Constraints* (Hong Kong, Hong Kong Council of Social Services, 1978), p. 128; D.J. Conway, *Human Response to Tall Buildings* (Strondsberg, Penn., Dowden Hutchison & Ross, 1977); and S.E. Millar, *Health and Well-being in relation to High Density Living in Hong Kong* (Canberra, Australian National University, Ph.D. Thesis, 1976).

70. N.W.S. Chow (1987), see note 19 above, p. 4.

71. Caritas Tuen Mun Family Service Unit (1986), see note 55 above, pp. 31–3.

72. J.A. Prescott (1971), see notes 48 and 3 above, p. 33.

73. J.M. Wigglesworth (1971), see note 3 above, pp. 68–9.

74. K.S. Pun (1986), see notes 9 and 1 above, p. 241.

75. Speech by the Acting Secretary of the New Territories, 18 September 1981; reported in K.Y. Wong (1982), see note 7 above, p. 124.

76. C.K. Leung, 'Urbanisation and New Towns Development', in C.K. Leung et al. (1980), see note 7 above, p. 292.

77. W.T. Leung (1980), see note 7 above, p. 376.

78. W.T. Leung (1980), see note 7 above, p. 378.

79. K.C. Leong, 'Housing Technology in relation to Urban Growth', in C.K. Leung et al. (1980), see note 7 above, pp. 435–6.

80. P.K.W. Fong and P. Hills, 'Urban Transport Problems in Hong Kong', in P.L.Y. Choi et al. (1986), see note 7 above, p. 131.

81. A further examination of this question is given in: M.R. Bristow, 'The Role and Place of Strategic Planning in Hong Kong', *Planning and Development: Journal of the*

Hong Kong Institute of Planners, Vol. 4, No. 1, March 1988, pp. 14–20.

82. Sir Patrick Abercrombie, *Hong Kong: Preliminary Planning Report* (Hong Kong, Government Printer, 1948), paras. 17–8, p. 4.

83. V.F.S. Sit, 'Hong Kong's New Towns Programme and Its Regional Implications', in C.K. Leung et al. (1980), see note 7 above, p. 413.

84. Y.K. Chan (1978), see note 69 above, p. 129.

85. Separate studies on various transport problems in Hong Kong proliferated from the 1960s onwards. The first major Territory-wide study to be produced was: Wilbur Smith and Associates, *Hong Kong Comprehensive Transport Study* (Hong Kong, Wilbur Smith and Associates, 1976), 3 vols. The exercise was repeated during the period 1986–8 as the Comprehensive Transportion Study Two, also undertaken by Wilbur Smith for the Hong Kong government.

86. Colony Outline Planning Division, *The Colony Outline Plan: Book 3, Vol. 1 — Concepts and Outline Proposals* (Hong Kong, Crown Lands and Survey Office, 1968), paras. 3.2 and 4.2.6, pp. 2–3.

87. Colony Outline Planning Division (1969), see note 86 above, para. 5.2, p. 3.

88. Colony Outline Planning Division (1969), see note 86 above, paras. 3–4, pp. 23–4.

89. Colony Planning Division, *Hong Kong Outline Plan* (Hong Kong, Town Planning Office, 1979), Chapter 17, pp. 17.1–18.

90. Colony Planning Division (1979), see note 89 above, para. 6.1, p. 17.9.

91. Colony Planning Division (1979), see note 89 above, para. 5.1–3, pp. 17.8–9.

92. B. Taylor, 'Rethinking the Territorial Development Strategy Planning Process in Hong Kong', *The Asian Journal of Public Administration*, Vol. 9, No. 1, June 1987, p. 26.

93. B. Taylor (1987), see note 92 above, pp. 28, 33, and 38.

94. B. Taylor (1987), see note 92 above, p. 40.

95. Y.L. Choi, 'The LUTO Model and Its Applications in Hong Kong', *Planning and Development: Journal of the Hong Kong Institute of Planners*, Vol. 1, No. 1, March 1986, p. 27.

96. Colony Outline Planning Division (1969), see note 86 above, para. 3.1, p. 2.

97. Speech to the Legislative Council by the Governor, Sir David Wilson, 7 October 1987, *Hong Kong Hansard* (Hong Kong, Government Printer), p. 27.

98. A.G. Eason, 'Territorial Development Strategy Studies: A View of the Process', *Planning and Development: Journal of the Hong Kong Institute of Planners*, Vol. 1, No. 1, March 1986, p. 5.

99. B. Taylor (1987), see note 92 above, p. 44.

100. B. Taylor, 'Development by Negotiation: Chinese Territory and the Development of Hong Kong and Macao'. in F.J. Costa, A.K. Dutt, L.J.C. Ma, and A.G. Noble (eds.), *Asian Urbanisation: Problems and Processes* (Berlin, Gebrüder Borntraeger, 1988).

101. B. Taylor (1987), see note 92 above, p. 46.

102. E.G. Pryor, 'An Overview of Territorial Development Strategy Studies in Hong Kong', *Planning and Development: Journal of the Hong Kong Institute of Planners*, Vol. 1, No. 1, March 1986, p. 13; also published in *Australian Planner: Journal of the Royal Australian Planning Institute*, Vol. 24, No. 2, June 1986, p. 9.

103. I. Scott and K. Cheek-Milby, 'An Overview of Hong Kong's Social Policy-Making Process', *The Asian Journal of Public Administration*, Vol. 8, No. 2, December 1986, p. 172.

104. Roger Bristow, *Land-use Planning in Hong Kong: History, Policies and Procedures*. (Hong Kong, Oxford University Press, 1984), pp. 284–90.

105. Memorandum from the District Commissioner New Territories to the Colonial Secretary, 19 April 1973, at 23 in NT 4811:C, City and New Territories Administration Registry, Hong Kong.

106. J.L. Perry and S.Y. Tang, 'Applying Research on Administration Reform to Hong Kong's 1997 Transition', *The Asian Journal of Public Administration*, Vol. 9, No. 2, December 1987, pp. 113–31.

107. Bristow (1984), see note 104 above, p. 160.

108. 'Hong Kong's New Towns', see note 7 above, p. 1.

Appendices

Appendix 1

Chronology of Principal New-town Plans

Year of Approval	Tsuen Wan (incl. Kwai Chung and Tsing Yi)	Sha Tin	Tuen Mun (Castle Peak)
1954	LTW 17C	LST 2	
1955			
1956			
1957			
1958			
1959			
1960			
1961	*LTW 57*	*LST 19*	
1962			
1963	*LTW 63A*		
1964	*LTW 75*		LCP 11A
1965	*LTW 103*	PWD Plan	PWD Plan
1966		*LST 47*	*LCP 32*
1967		PWD Plan	
1968			
1969			
1970			
1971	*LTW 131:2*		LCP 43
1972		LST 59A	
1973			
1974			TM 1C
1975			
1976	*LTW 145:6*		
1977		STP 76/2022	TM 1E
1978	*LTY 24*	*LST 69*	
1979	TWNT 30		

Tai Po	Sheung Shui/ Fanling	Yuen Long	Junk Bay	Tin Shui Wai
			LJB 1/1	
			LJB 10A	
			LM 89A (draft)	

Chronology of Principal New-town Plans *(cont.)*

Year of Approval	Tsuen Wan (incl. Kwai Chung and Tsing Yi)	Sha Tin	Tuen Mun (Castle Peak)
1980			LTM 1/0/1
1981			
1982		STP/OD/1	
1983	{ *S/KC/1* *S/TY/1*		*LTM 2*
1984		D/ST/2/1	
1985	*S/TW/1*	*S/ST/1*	LTM 1/0/4I
1986		D/ST/1/1	
1987			
1988			
(current statutory plan)	*S/TW/2* *S/KC/4* *S/TY/3*	*S/ST/4*	*S/TM/6*
(current departmental plan)	various	D/ST/3/1 (under preparation)	LTM 1/0/1H (under preparation)

Notes: 1. Plan references in italics are statutory Outline Zoning Plans, the remainder refer to departmental plans relating to the whole town, or in a few cases to significant major extensions.
   2. The planning of Tsuen Wan was unique. Because of the original decision to proceed under the Town Planning Ordinance, no departmental plans for the whole town have been produced and, except for Tsing Yi Island, none is shown here. Statutory plans also were divided for the three main parts of the town from 1971.
   3. Not all plan revisions are shown in this table; only those covering major design changes are included, except where reference number changes and current 1988 plans have also been given.
   4. Currently, Outline Zoning Plans are prepared in the Town Planning Office headquarters, while Outline Development Plans are the responsibility of the area offices of the Territory Development Department. All were branches of the Lands and Works Branch of the Hong Kong government, and are expected to form part of the new Environment Department from 1 April 1989.

Tai Po	Sheung Shui/ Fanling	Yuen Long	Junk Bay	Tin Shui Wai
TPF/80/120				
TPF/80/100C				
			JB/82/001D	MDP/TSW/1
TPF/84/143	TPF/84/200	OD/NWNT/3A		OD/TSW/2
TPF/84/100				
	NTNE/86/200		D/JB/1	OD/TSW/3
S/TP/3			D/JB/2	
NTNE/87/100				
S/TP/3	*S/FSS/1*	—	*S/JB/A* *(under preparation)*	—
NTNE/87/100 (under preparation)	NTNE/86/200 (under preparation)	OD/NWNT/3B (under preparation)	D/JB/3 (under preparation)	OD/TSW/3A (under preparation)
NTNE/84/143B	NTNE/83/217			

5. For a number of the new towns significant plans during their planning histories were prepared by consultants. Some of the more important of these are as under:

Scott Wilson Kirkpatrick & Partners	1959 Kwai Chung Sha Tin Tuen Mun (Castle Peak) Tai Po Junk Bay
University of Hong Kong/Gregory and others	1959 Tsuen Wan
Mighty City/Shankland Cox and others	1980 Tin Shui Wai Master Plan
Maunsell Consultants Asia/Yuncken Freeman Hong Kong	1978 Junk Bay
Maunsell Consultants Asia/Shankland Cox and others	1981 Junk Bay
Shankland Cox and others	1983 Tin Shui Wai

Appendix 2

New Towns: Statistical Summaries

Each of the eight Hong Kong new towns is first listed separately. This is followed by a Territory-wide aggregate tabulation of the new towns and the rural townships. These townships are outside the new-town programme, but are regarded by the government as an integral part of the development programme. The statistics have been provided through the courtesy of the Territory Development Department, and are published by permission.

Appendix 2a: Tusen Wan New Town — Designated 1961

New-town Area (hectares)	*31.3.87*	*up to 31.3.97*
Land Area	3,165	3,165
Development Area		
Existing and Committed[1]	2,052	
Potential[2]	130	
Total	2,182	2,182
Serviced Land		
Residential	464	614
Industrial	255	324

	31.3.87	up to 31.3.97
GIC Facilities	232	318
Other	568	853
Total Land Serviced	1,519	2,109
Local Open Space	46	72
District Open Space	17	87
Green Belt	983	983

1. Area with definite development programme.
2. Area with no definite development programme which depends on the optimization of existing and planned infrastructure.

Population

	at designation	*31.3.87*	*up to 31.3.97*	*Current Target*
Total	80,000	678,383	829,484	861,229

Housing

		Population	*31.3.87* *Per cent*	*Living Quarters*
Public Sector	: Total	452,479	67	110,386
	: Rental		65	
	: HOS/PSPS		2	
Private Sector	: Total	225,904	33	70,381
All Accommodation	: Total	678,383	100	180,767

		Population	*up to 31.3.97* *Per cent*	*Living Quarters*
Public Sector	: Total	532,128	64	132,703
	: Rental		61	

Appendix 2a (cont.)

			: HOS/PSPS	Living Quarters
Private Sector	: Total	397,356	3	111,083
All Accommodation	: Total	829,484	36	243,786

		Population	Current Target Per cent	Living Quarters
Public Sector	: Total	532,128	62	132,703
Private Sector	: Total	329,101	38	121,356
All Accommodation	: Total	861,229	100	254,059

Education

	31.3.87	up to 31.3.97
Primary school	70	82
Secondary school	44	54
Post-secondary school (training centre and technical institute)	4	4
Special school	9	14

Community Facilities

	31.3.87	up to 31.3.97
Children's and Youth Centre	23	36
Community Centre	14	20
Fire Station	4	5
Ambulance Depot	2	3
Hospital beds	2,980	4,403
Polyclinic/Specialist Clinic/General Clinic/Health Centre	9	11
Police Station	5	9

	31.3.87	up to 31.3.97
Cultural Complex	1	2
Library	4	6
Magistracy	1	1
Sports Stadium/Complex	3	4
Swimming Pool Complex	2	6
Indoor Recreation Centre	5	21
Hostel for the Elderly	8	16
Post Office	10	15
Market	29	38

Expenditure (in HK$ millions)

	31.3.87	up to 31.3.97
Engineering	3,009	7,739
Community Facilities	601	2,463
Housing Authority Expenditure	1,640	3,935
Total	5,250	14,137

Appendix 2b: Tuen Mun New Town — Designated 1965

New-town Area (hectares)

	31.3.87	up to 31.3.97
Land Area	2,113	2,113
Development Area		
Existing and Committed[1]	1,207	
Potential[2]	219	
Total	1,426	1,426

Appendix 2b (cont.)

Serviced Land	at designation	31.3.87	up to 31.3.97	Current Target
Residential		338	430	
Industrial		144	164	
GIC Facilities		207	299	
Other		248	367	
Total Land Serviced		937	1,250	
Local Open Space		4	14	
District Open Space		14	76	
Green Belt (incl. Non-intensive District Open Space)		687	687	

1. Area with definite development programme.
2. Area with no definite development programme which depends on the optimization of existing and planned infrastructure.

Population	at designation	31.3.87	up to 31.3.97	Current Target
Total	20,000	290,993	534,417	561,854

Housing		Population	Per cent 31.3.87	Living Quarters up to 31.3.97
Public Sector	: Total	238,921	82	62,593
	: Rental		64	
	: HOS/PSPS		18	
Private Sector	: Total	53,072	18	20,655
All Accommodation	: Total	290,993	100	83,248

	Population	up to 31.3.97 Per cent	Living Quarters
Public Sector : Total	341,253	64	92,927
: Rental		44	
: HOS/PSPS		20	
Private Sector : Total	193,164	36	64,930
All Accommodation : Total	534,417	100	157,857

	Population	Current Target Per cent	Living Quarters
Public Sector : Total	341,253	61	92,927
Private Sector : Total	220,601	39	73,298
All Accommodation : Total	561,854	100	166,225

Education

	31.3.87	up to 31.3.97
Primary school	31	38
Secondary school	16	35
Post-secondary school	1	1
Special school	0	0

Community Facilities

	31.3.87	up to 31.3.97
Children's and Youth Centre	13	21
Community Centre	5	9

Appendix 2b (cont.)

	31.3.87	up to 31.3.97
Fire Station	2	5
Ambulance Depot	2	3
Hospital beds	1,943	3,541
Polyclinic/Specialist Clinic/General Clinic/Health Centre	3	5
Police Station	2	4
Cultural Complex	1	1
Library	3	4
Magistracy	0	1
Sports Stadium/Complex	1	3
Swimming Pool Complex	1	2
Indoor Recreation Centre	2	8
Hostel for the Elderly	11	13
Post Office	4	4
Market	13	18

Expenditure (in HK$ millions)

	31.3.87	up to 31.3.97
Engineering	3,215	5,319
Community Facilities	1,278	3,700
Housing Authority Expenditure	3,182	5,189
Total	7,675	14,208

Appendix 2c: Sha Tin New Town (incl. Ma On Shan) — Designated 1965

New-town Area (hectares)

	31.3.87	up to 31.3.97
Land Area	3,606	3,606

	at designation	31.3.87	up to 31.3.97	Current Target
Development Area				
Existing and Committed[1]			1,916	
Potential[2]			169	
Total			2,085	2,085
Serviced Land				
Residential		399	552	
Industrial		54	82	
GIC Facilities		371	489	
Other		367	479	
Total Land Serviced		1,191	1,602	
Local Open Space		38	82	
District Open Space		16	95	
Green Belt		1,521	1,521	

1. Area with definite development programme.
2. Area with no definite development programme which depends on the optimization of existing and planned infrastructure.

Population	*at designation*	*31.3.87*	*up to 31.3.97*	*Current Target*
Total	24,000	426,762	696,618	702,446

Housing	*Population*	*Per cent*	*Living Quarters*
Public Sector : Total	286,131	67	71,166
: Rental		55	
: HOS/PSPS		12	

Appendix 2c (cont.)

	Population	up to 31.3.97 Per cent	Living Quarters
Private Sector : Total	140,631	33	49,596
All Accommodation : Total	426,762	100	120,762

	Population	up to 31.3.97 Per cent	Living Quarters
Public Sector : Total	444,095	63	115,506
: Rental		46	
: HOS/PSPS		17	
Private Sector : Total	252,523	37	90,231
All Accommodation : Total	696,618	100	205,737

	Population	Current Target Per cent	Living Quarters
Public Sector : Total	444,095	63	115,506
Private Sector : Total	258,351	37	92,009
All Accommodation : Total	702,446	100	207,515

Current targets relate to the situation in 1987, and have since been superseded by the decision to proceed with Ma On Shan Stage 2.

Education

	31.3.87	up to 31.3.97
Primary school	28	47
Secondary school	21	53
Post-secondary school	4	5
Special school	2	3

Community Facilities

	31.3.87	up to 31.3.97
Children's and Youth Centre	24	40
Community Centre	7	14
Fire Station	2	5
Ambulance Depot	2	5
Hospital beds	1,454	2,987
Polyclinic/Specialist Clinic/General Clinic/Health Centre	3	9
Police Station	4	7
Cultural Complex	1	2
Library	2	3
Magistracy	1	1
Sports Stadium/Complex	2	4
Swimming Pool Complex	1	3
Indoor Recreation Centre	1	7
Hostel for the Elderly	9	16
Post Office	5	12
Market	16	25

Expenditure (in HK$ millions)

	31.3.87	up to 31.3.97
Engineering	3,648	5,966
Community Facilities	1,809	3,338
Housing Authority Expenditure	2,955	5,307
Total	8,412	14,611

Appendix 2d: Tai Po New Town — Designated 1979

New-town Area (hectares)

	at designation	31.3.87	up to 31.3.97	Current Target
Land Area		3,458	3,458	
Development Area				
Existing and Committed[1]		1,051		
Potential[2]		31		
Total		1,082	1,082	
Serviced Land				
Residential		293	405	
Industrial		60	78	
GIC Facilities		109	187	
Other		181	311	
Total Land Serviced		643	981	
Local Open Space		4	13	
District Open Space		6	59	
Green Belt		2,141	2,141	

1. Area with definite development programme. Excludes Agricultural Priority Areas and Recreation Priority Areas outside Sha Lo Tung.
2. Area with no definite development programme which depends on the optimization of existing and planned infrastructure.

Population

	at designation	31.3.87	up to 31.3.97	Current Target
Total	48,000	155,909	288,957	293,879

Housing

31.3.87

		Population	Per cent	Living Quarters
Public Sector	: Total	97,313	62	26,429
	: Rental		47	
	: HOS/PSPS		15	
Private Sector	: Total	58,596	38	20,431
All Accommodation	: Total	155,909	100	46,860

up to 31.3.97

		Population	Per cent	Living Quarters
Public Sector	: Total	178,412	62	47,934
	: Rental		50	
	: HOS/PSPS		12	
Private Sector	: Total	110,545	38	46,211
All Accommodation	: Total	288,957	100	94,145

Current Target

		Population	Per cent	Living Quarters
Public Sector	: Total	178,412	61	47,934
Private Sector	: Total	115,467	39	47,159
All Accommodation	: Total	293,879	100	95,093

Appendix 2d (cont.)

Education

	31.3.87	up to 31.3.97
Primary school	29	37
Secondary school	10	17
Post-secondary school	0	0
Special school	1	1

Community Facilities

	31.3.87	up to 31.3.97
Children's and Youth Centre	6	10
Community Centre	4	7
Fire Station	1	2
Ambulance Depot	1	1
Hospital beds	0	1,700
Polyclinic/Specialist Clinic/General Clinic/Health Centre	2	3
Police Station	1	1
Cultural Complex	0	1
Library	1	1
Magistracy	0	0
Sports Stadium/Complex	0	1
Swimming Pool Complex	0	1
Indoor Recreation Centre	1	7
Hostel for the Elderly	2	3
Post Office	2	3
Market	5	8

Expenditure (in HK$ millions)

	31.3.87	up to 31.3.97
Engineering	2,591	3,657

	31.3.87	up to 31.3.97
Community Facilities	203	1,360
Housing Authority Expenditure	1,544	3,399
Total	4,338	8,416

Appendix 2e: Sheung Shui/Fanling New Town — Designated 1979

New-town Area (hectares)	31.3.87	up to 31.3.97
Land Area	782	782
Development Area		
Existing and Committed[1]	614	
Potential[2]	100	
Total	714	714
Serviced Land		
Residential	140	215
Industrial	33	63
GIC Facilities	65	145
Other	93	184
Total Land Serviced	331	607
Local Open Space	9	24
District Open Space	3	38
Green Belt	67	67

1. Area with definite development programme. Excludes Agricultural Priority Areas and land committed but not yet programmed.
2. Area with no definite development programme which depends on the optimization of existing and planned infrastructure.

Appendix 2e (cont.)

Population

	at designation	31.3.87	up to 31.3.97	Current Target
Total	44,000	112,601	234,775	245,694

Housing

	Population	31.3.87 Per cent	Living Quarters
Public Sector	: Total	72,181	65	20,711
	: Rental		55	
	: HOS/PSPS		10	
Private Sector	: Total	40,420	35	13,699
All Accommodation	: Total	112,601	100	34,410

	Population	up to 31.3.97 Per cent	Living Quarters
Public Sector	: Total	138,094	59	39,060
	: Rental		47	
	: HOS/PSPS		12	
Private Sector	: Total	96,681	41	35,685
All Accommodation	: Total	234,775	100	74,745

	Population	Current Target Per cent	Living Quarters
Public Sector	: Total	141,693	58	39,804
Private Sector	: Total	104,001	42	36,752
All Accommodation	: Total	245,694	100	76,556

Education

	31.3.87	up to 31.3.97
Primary school	19	28
Secondary school	7	20
Post-secondary school	0	1
Special school	0	0

Community Facilities

	31.3.87	up to 31.3.97
Children's and Youth Centre	4	9
Community Centre	2	4
Fire Station	2	2
Ambulance Depot	1	1
Hospital beds	98	1,298
Polyclinic/Specialist Clinic/General Clinic/Health Centre	2	4
Police Station	1	1
Cultural Complex	0	1
Library	0	1
Magistracy	1	1
Sports Stadium/Complex	0	1
Swimming Pool Complex	1	2
Indoor Recreation Centre	0	6
Hostel for the Elderly	1	3
Post Office	2	3
Market	4	7

Expenditure (in HK$ millions)

	31.3.87	up to 31.3.97
Engineering	1,327	2,312
Community Facilities	137	2,739
Housing Authority Expenditure	1,211	2,529
Total	2,675	7,580

Appendix 2f: Yuen Long New Town — Designated 1978

New-town Area (hectares)

	31.3.87	up to 31.3.97
Land Area	398	398
Development Area		
Existing and Committed[1]	329	
Potential[2]	70	
Total	398	398
Serviced Land		
Residential	98	145
Industrial	14	20
GIC Facilities	38	58
Other	70	106
Total Land Serviced	220	329
Local Open Space	3	12
District Open Space	0	14

Green Belt

	at designation	31.3.87	up to 31.3.97	Current Target
Population				
Total	42,000	111,123	181,182	198,096

1. Area with definite development programme.
2. Area with no definite development programme which depends on the optimization of existing and planned infrastructure.

Housing

	Population	*31.3.87* Per cent	*Living Quarters*
Public Sector : Total	37,793	34	8,991
: Rental		34	
: HOS/PSPS		0	
Private Sector : Total	73,350	66	21,646
All Accommodation : Total	111,123	100	30,637

	Population	*up to 31.3.97* Per cent	*Living Quarters*
Public Sector : Total	76,023	42	21,510
: Rental		42	
: HOS/PSPS		0	
Private Sector : Total	105,159	58	30,731
All Accommodation : Total	181,182	100	52,241

Appendix 2f (cont.)

	Population	Current Target Per cent	Living Quarters
Public Sector : Total	76,023	38	21,510
Private Sector : Total	122,073	62	36,324
All Accommodation : Total	198,096	100	57,834

Education	*31.3.87*	*up to 31.3.97*
Primary school	18	26
Secondary school	14	23
Post-secondary school	0	0
Special school	0	0

Community Facilities	*31.3.87*	*up to 31.3.97*
Children's and Youth Centre	3	5
Community Centre	3	6
Fire Station	1	1
Ambulance Depot	1	1
Hospital beds	0	0
Polyclinic/Specialist Clinic/General Clinic/Health Centre	1	2
Police Station	2	2
Cultural Complex	0	1
Library	1	1
Magistracy	0	1
Sports Stadium/Complex	1	1
Swimming Pool Complex	1	1

	31.3.87	up to 31.3.97
Indoor Recreation Centre	2	5
Hostel for the Elderly	1	0
Post Office	1	3
Market	1	2

Expenditure (in HK$ millions)

	31.3.87	up to 31.3.97
Engineering	465	1,017
Community Facilities	223	920
Housing Authority Expenditure	535	1,230
Total	1,223	3,167

Appendix 2g: Junk Bay New Town — Designated 1982

(Note — all statistics relate to Phases I and II only. Phase III announced in 1988 and currently being planned will increase target population to 420,000 and cover a larger site area.)

New-town Area (hectares)

	31.3.87	up to 31.3.97
Land Area	1,430	1,430
Development Area		
Existing and Committed[1]	485	
Potential[2]	217	
Total	693	693

Appendix 2g (cont.)

Serviced Land	at designation	up to 31.3.97
Residential	51	127
Industrial	10	65
GIC Facilities	38	97
Other	77	284
Total Land Serviced	177	573
Local Open Space	0	27
District Open Space	0	117
Green Belt	737	737

1. Area with definite development programme.
2. Area with no definite development programme which depends on the optimization of existing and planned infrastructure.

Population	at designation	31.3.87	up to 31.3.97	Current Target
Total	7,000	8,657	262,944	420,000

Housing		Population	Per cent 31.3.87	Living Quarters
Public Sector	: Total	5,153	60	3,928
	: Rental		60	
	: HOS/PSPS		0	
Private Sector	: Total	3,504	40	1,473
All Accommodation	: Total	8,657	100	5,401

	Population	up to 31.3.97 Per cent	Living Quarters up to 31.3.97
Public Sector : Total	177,187	63	54,838
: Rental		43	
: HOS/PSPS		20	
Private Sector : Total	85,757	37	35,257
All Accommodation : Total	262,944	100	90,095

	Population	Current Target Per cent	Living Quarters up to 31.3.97
Public Sector : Total	190,452	58	55,527
Private Sector : Total	135,315	42	46,261
All Accommodation : Total	325,767	100	101,788

Education

	31.3.87	up to 31.3.97
Primary school	0	18
Secondary school	0	15
Post-secondary school	0	0
Special school	0	0

Community Facilities

	31.3.87	up to 31.3.97
Children's and Youth Centre	0	6
Community Centre	0	6

Appendix 2g (cont.)

	31.3.87	up to 31.3.97
Fire Station	0	1
Ambulance Depot	0	1
Hospital beds	300	300
Polyclinic/Specialist Clinic/General Clinic/Health Centre	0	3
Police Station	0	2
Cultural Complex	0	0
Library	0	0
Magistracy	0	0
Sports Stadium/Complex	0	0
Swimming Pool Complex	0	1
Indoor Recreation Centre	0	7
Hostel for the Elderly	0	5
Post Office	0	2
Market	0	1

Expenditure (in HK$ millions)

	31.3.87	up to 31.3.97
Engineering	891	6,214
Community Facilities	24	1,328
Housing Authority Expenditure	362	3,724
Total	1,277	11,266

Appendix 2h: Tin Shui Wai New Town — Designated 1982

New-town Area (hectares)

	31.3.87	up to 31.3.97
Land Area	225	225

	at designation	31.3.87	up to 31.3.97	Current Target
Development Area				
Existing and Committed¹			201	
Potential²			24	
Total			225	225
Serviced Land				
Residential			0	53
Industrial			0	0
GIC Facilities			0	33
Other			0	105
Total Land Serviced			0	191
Local Open Space			0	9
District Open Space			0	18
Green Belt			0	0

1. Area with definite development programme.
2. Area with no definite development programme which depends on the optimization of existing and planned infrastructure.

Population

	at designation	31.3.87	up to 31.3.97	Current Target
Total	0	0	131,084	136,905

Housing

	Population	Per cent	Living Quarters
Public Sector : Total	0	0	0
: Rental		0	
: HOS/PSPS		0	

Appendix 2h (cont.)

Private Sector : Total	0	0
All Accommodation : Total	0	0

	Population	*up to 31.3.97* Per cent	*Living Quarters*
Public Sector : Total	69,182	54	21,760
: Rental		50	
: HOS/PSPS		4	
Private Sector : Total	61,902	46	21,572
All Accommodation : Total	131,084	100	43,332

	Population	*Current Target* Per cent	*up to 31.3.97* *Living Quarters*
Public Sector : Total	69,182	51	21,760
Private Sector : Total	67,723	49	23,600
All Accommodation : Total	136,905	100	45,360

Education

	31.3.87	*up to 31.3.97*
Primary school	0	10
Secondary school	0	10
Post-secondary school	0	0
Special school	0	1

Community Facilities

	31.3.87	up to 31.3.97
Children's and Youth Centre	0	7
Community Centre	0	3
Fire Station	0	1
Ambulance Depot	0	1
Hospital beds	0	0
Polyclinic/Specialist Clinic/General Clinic/Health Centre	0	1
Police Station	0	1
Cultural Complex	0	1
Library	0	0
Magistracy	0	0
Sports Stadium/Complex	0	1
Swimming Pool Complex	0	1
Indoor Recreation Centre	0	3
Hostel for the Elderly	0	3
Post Office	0	1
Market	0	3

Expenditure (in HK$ millions)

	31.3.87	up to 31.3.97
Engineering	158	1,998
Community Facilities	0	796
Housing Authority Expenditure	0	1,761
Total	158	4,555

Appendix 2i: New Towns and Rural Townships Development Programme — Aggregate Data

Area (hectares)	New Towns		Other Development Areas	
	31.3.87	up to 31.3.97	31.3.87	up to 31.3.97
Land Area	15,177	15,177	3,019	3,019
Development Area				
Existing and Committed[1]	7,855		1,015	
Potential[2]	960		937	
Total	8,815	8,815	1,952	1,952
Serviced Land				
Residential	1,783	2,541	151	232
Industrial	570	796	9	9
GIC Facilities	1,060	1,626	98	143
Other	1,604	2,689	148	567
Total Land Serviced	5,017	7,652	406	951
Local Open Space	104	253	2	9
District Open Space	56	504	1	11
Green Belt	6,136		1,056	

1. Area with definite development programme.
2. Area with no definite development programme which depends on the optimization of existing and planned infrastructure.

Population

Total	1,784,428	3,159,461	104,195	132,117

New town populations at designation: 631,000; 1988 target: 3,440,103.

Housing

Public Sector Units	304,204	527,671		
Private Sector Units	197,881	476,759		
Population percentages:[1]				
Public Rental	54	48		
HOS/PSPS	11	13		
Private Residential	35	39		

Education

Primary school	195	286	4	31
Secondary school	112	227	9	16
Post-secondary school	9	11	0	1
Special school	12	19	0	0

Community Facilities

Children's and Youth Centre	73	134	1	2
Community Centre	35	69	1	5
Fire Station	12	22	7	7
Ambulance Depot	9	16	0	2
Hospital beds	6,775	14,229	97	97
Polyclinic/Specialist Clinic/General Clinic/Health Centre	20	38	5	7
Police Station	15	27	6	7

1. 1988 targets: Public Rental and HOS/PSPS: 56; Private Residential: 44.

Appendix 2i (cont.)

Cultural Complex	3	9	0	0
Library	11	16	4	4
Magistracy	3	5	0	0
Sports Stadium/Complex	7	15	2	4
Swimming Pool Complex	6	17	1	4
Indoor Recreation Centre	11	64	0	4
Hostel for the Elderly	32	59	0	4
Post Office	24	43	6	0
Market	68	102	3	7

Expenditure (in HK$ millions)

Engineering	15,304	34,222	916	3,134
Community Facilities	4,275	16,644	5	1,187
Housing Authority Expenditure	11,429	27,074	86	429
Total	31,008	77,940	1,007	4,750

Bibliography

Hong Kong

Official Publications

Abercrombie, P., *Hong Kong: Preliminary Planning Report* (Hong Kong, Government Printer, 1949).

Architectural Division, *Ten-Year Housing Programme — Part 1: New Estates, Housing Department* (Hong Kong, Housing Department, 1973).

Building Ordinance Office, *Building (Planning) (Amendment) (No. 2) Regulations 1962* (Hong Kong, Government Printer, 1962).

Clarke, R.C., *Town Planning: Future Policy* (Hong Kong, Town Planning Office, 1960).

Colony Outline Planning Division, *The Colony Outline Plan: Book 1, Working Papers* (Hong Kong, Crown Lands and Survey Office, 1968).

—— *The Colony Outline Plan: Book 2, Vol. II — Report on Population and Housing* (Hong Kong, Crown Lands and Survey Office, 1969).

—— *The Colony Outline Plan: Book 3, Vol. I — Concepts and Outline Proposals* (Hong Kong, Crown Lands and Survey Office, 1969).

—— *The Colony Outline Plan: Book 3, Vol. II — Standards and Locational Factors* (Hong Kong, Crown Lands and Survey Office, 1970).

Colony Outline Planning Team, *Hong Kong: The Colony Outline Plan — Planning Report 1* (Hong Kong, Crown Lands and Survey Office, 1964).

Colony Planning Division, *The Hong Kong Outline Plan* (Hong Kong, Town Planning Office, 1979).

Commission of Inquiry, *Kowloon Disturbances 1966 — Report of Commission of Inquiry* (Hong Kong, Government Printer, 1967).

Commissioner for Resettlement, *Report on Squatters and Resettlement* (Hong Kong, Hong Kong Government, 1955).

Container Committee, *Report of the Container Committee* (Hong Kong, Government Printer, 1966).

—— *Second Report and Recommendations of the Container Committee* (Hong Kong, Government Printer, 1967).

Coopers and Lybrand Associates Limited, *Land Development Corporations Study: Executive Summary* (Hong Kong, Hong Kong Government, 1983).

Director of Public Works, *City of Victoria, Hong Kong — Central Area Redevelopment: Report by the Director of Public Works, Hong Kong* (Hong Kong, Government Printer, 1961).

District Commissioner New Territories, *Urban Expansion into the New Territories: Note by the District Commissioner New Territories* (Hong Kong, New Territories Administration, 1959).

Environment Branch, *Keeping Hong Kong Moving: The White Paper on Internal Transport Policy* (Hong Kong, Government Printer, 1979).

Freeman Fox & Partners (Far East), HFA Hong Kong, EBC Hong Kong, and Watson Hawksley Asia, *North Eastern New Territories Study: Final Report* (Hong Kong, New Territories Development Department, 1982).

Freeman Fox, Wilbur Smith and Associates, *Hong Kong Long Term Road Study* (Hong Kong, Government Printer, 1968).

—— *Hong Kong Mass Transit: Further Studies* (Hong Kong, Government Printer, 1970).

—— *Hong Kong Mass Transport Study* (Hong Kong, Government Printer, 1967).

Giles, A.R., *Visit of A.R. Giles to Crawley, Stevenage and Harlow, August 1953, to study Compulsory Purchase and Betterment* (Hong Kong, Public Works Department, 1953).

Government Information Services, *Planning for Growth* (Hong Kong, Government Printer, 1985).

Hong Kong Government, *Civil and Miscellaneous Lists: Hong Kong Government — 1 January 1975* (Hong Kong, Government Printer, 1975).

—— *Civil and Miscellaneous Lists: Hong Kong Government — 1 July 1977* (Hong Kong, Government Printer, 1977).

—— *Civil and Miscellaneous Lists: Hong Kong Government — 1 July 1985* (Hong Kong, Government Printer, 1985).

—— *Civil and Miscellaneous Lists: Hong Kong Government — 1 July 1986* (Hong Kong, Government Printer, 1986).

—— *District Administration in Hong Kong: White Paper* (Hong Kong, Government Printer, 1981).

—— 'Hong Kong's New Towns', *Hong Kong Annual Report 1979* (Hong Kong, Government Printer, 1979), pp. 1–10.

—— 'Land Development Schemes', *Executive Council Paper No. 156* (Hong Kong, Hong Kong Government, 1959).

—— *A Pattern of District Administration in Hong Kong: Green Paper* (Hong Kong, Government Printer, 1980).

—— *Review of Policies for Squatter Control, Resettlement and Government Low-Cost Housing 1964*, White Paper (Hong Kong, Government Printer, 1964).

—— *Transport in Hong Kong: A Paper for Public Information and Discussion*, Green Paper (Hong Kong, Government Printer, 1974).

Hong Kong Housing Authority, *Green Paper: Housing Subsidy to Tenants of Public Housing* (Hong Kong, Government Printer, 1985).

—— *Long-Term Housing Strategy: A Policy Statement* (Hong Kong, Government Printer, 1987).

—— *Report to Housing Authority on Public Consultation: Green Paper on Housing Subsidy to Tenants of Public Housing* (Hong Kong, Government Printer, 1985).

—— *A Review of Public Housing Allocation Policies: A Consultative Document* (Hong Kong, Government Printer, 1984).

Hong Kong Productivity Centre, *Industrial Mobility Study: Executive Summary* (Hong Kong, Strategic Planning Unit, 1983).

Housing Commision, 'Report of the Housing Commission', *Hong Kong Sessional Papers*, No. 12/38 (Hong Kong, Local Printing Press, 1938).

Interdepartmental Committee on New Industrial Areas, *Report of Interdepartmental Committee, 14 May 1954: New Industrial Areas* (Hong Kong, Hong Kong Government, 1954).

Interdepartmental Committee on the Squatter Problem, 'Report of the Interdepartmental Committee on the Squatter Problem', *Hong Kong Sessional Papers*, No. 4/48 (Hong Kong, Government Printer, 1948).

Kowloon Tong Committee, *Report of the Committee Appointed to Advise the Governor of Hong Kong as to whether Any and if so What Relief or Monet-*

ary Assistance should be granted to the Kowloon Tong and New Territories Development Co. Ltd. or to the Subscribers to the Kowloon Tong Scheme (Hong Kong, Government Printer, 1929).

Lam, J.D.K., *The New Territories Small House Policy* (Hong Kong, New Territories Administration, 1980).

Land Development Planning Committee, *Large Scale Development in the New Territories*, Paper No. 14 (Hong Kong, Hong Kong Government, 1962).

—— *Proposed New Towns at Castle Peak and Sha Tin*, Paper No. 71 (Hong Kong, Hong Kong Government, 1965).

—— *Sites for New Towns and Large Development Schemes*, Paper No. 23A (Hong Kong, Hong Kong Government, 1963).

—— *Urban Development in the New Territories*, Paper No. 36 (Hong Kong, Hong Kong Government, 1963).

Land Development Policy Committee, *Broad Assessment of Future Demand for and Supply of Housing*, Paper No. 23/78 (Hong Kong, Hong Kong Government, 1978).

—— *Demand for Public Housing*, Paper No. 24/78 (Hong Kong, Hong Kong Government, 1978).

—— *Land Production*, Paper No. 29/78 (Hong Kong, Hong Kong Government, 1978).

—— *Long Term Land Requirements for Housing*, Paper No. 32/78 (Hong Kong, Hong Kong Government, 1978).

—— *Main Urban Areas Design Population*, Paper No. 19/77 (Hong Kong, Hong Kong Government, 1977).

McKinsey and Company Incorporated, *The Machinery of Government: A New Framework for Expanding Services* (Hong Kong, Government Printer, 1973).

New Territories Development Consultants, *Development Investigation of the North Western New Territories*, (4 vols.) (Hong Kong, New Territories Development Department, 1981).

New Territories Development Department, *Development Investigation of North Western New Territories — Phases I–III* (Hong Kong, New Territories Development Department, 1979).

Nicol, A., *Report of 18 September 1945* (into conditions in Hong Kong) (Hong Kong, Public Works Development, 1945).

Owen, D., *Future Control and Development of the Port of Hong Kong: Report* (Hong Kong, Government Printer, 1941).

Owen, W.H., *Report on Town Planning and Housing* (Hong Kong, Public Works Department, 1940).

Planning Division, *Planning Memorandum No. 5: The Application of Population Density Control to Outline Zoning and Outline Development Plans and Related to Building Heights and Coverage* (Hong Kong, Crown Lands and Survey Office, 1962).

Rouse, H.S., *Report on the Conditions in Hong Kong at 27 November 1945* (Hong Kong, Hong Kong Government, 1945).

Scott Wilson Kirkpatrick & Partners, Robert Matthew Johnson-Marshall and Partners, Coopers and Lybrand Associates Ltd., and Collier Petty Ltd., *Harbour Reclamations and Urban Growth Study: Final Report* (Hong Kong, Lands Department, 1983).

Special Committee on Housing, *First Interim Report of the Special Committee on Housing* (Hong Kong, Government Printer, 1956).

—— *Second Interim Report of the Special Committee on Housing* (Hong Kong, Government Printer, 1957).

—— *Final Report of the Special Committee on Housing 1956–58* (Hong Kong, Government Printer, 1958).

Special Committee on Land Production, *Report of the Special Committee on Land Production* (Hong Kong, Government Printer, 1977).

—— *Special Committee on Land Production: Report to His Excellency the Governor* (Hong Kong, Government Printer, 1981).

Special Committee on Land Supply, *Special Committee on Land Supply: Report to His Excellency the Governor, March 1982* (Hong Kong, Government Printer, 1982).

—— *Special Committee on Land Supply: Report to His Excellency the Governor, March 1983* (Hong Kong, Government Printer, 1983).

—— *Special Committee on Land Supply: Report to His Excellency the Governor, March 1984* (Hong Kong, Government Printer, 1984).

—— *Special Committee on Land Supply: Report to His Excellency the Governor, March 1985* (Hong Kong, Government Printer, 1985).

Strategic Planning Unit, *Hong Kong Territorial Development Strategy: Vol. I — Introductory Statement* (Hong Kong, Strategic Planning Unit, 1982).

—— *Hong Kong Territorial Development Strategy: Vol. II — Broad Methods and Policy Assumptions* (Hong Kong, Strategic Planning Unit, 1982).

—— *Hong Kong Territorial Development Strategy: Vol. III — Demographic Inputs* (Hong Kong, Strategic Planning Unit, 1982).

—— *Hong Kong Territorial Development Strategy: Vol. IV — Review of Current Development Programmes* (Hong Kong, Strategic Planning Unit, 1983).

—— *Hong Kong Territorial Development Strategy: Vol. V — Alternative Strategies and Evaluation* (Hong Kong, Strategic Planning Unit, 1984).

—— *Hong Kong Territorial Development Strategy: Vol. VI — Territorial Development Strategy — Initial Results* (Hong Kong, Strategic Planning Unit, 1984).

—— *Hong Kong Territorial Development Strategy: Vol. VII — Initial Development Strategy* (Hong Kong, Strategic Planning Unit, 1984).

—— *An Outline of Strategic Planning in Hong Kong: A Positional Statement* (Hong Kong, Strategic Planning Unit, 1982).

Tang, B., *Port Development Strategy Study: Final Report* (Hong Kong, Marine Department, 1986).

Town Planning Division, *North Lantau Development Study*, (Hong Kong, Lands Department, 1981).

—— *Town Planning in Hong Kong* (Hong Kong, Lands Department, 1984).

Town Planning Office, *Information Pamphlet: Hong Kong Planning Standards and Guidelines* (Hong Kong, Buildings and Lands Department, 1987).

—— *Metroplan* (Hong Kong, Buildings and Lands Department, 1988).

—— *Planning Memorandum No. 1: Proposed Measures for the Accommodation of Surplus Population* (Hong Kong, Crown Lands and Survey Department, 1956).

—— *Planning Memorandum No. 4: Ten Year Development Programme* (Hong Kong, Crown Lands and Survey Department, 1960).

—— *Planning Statement for the Northeastern New Territories Sub-Region* (Hong Kong, Buildings and Lands Department, 1986).

—— *Report of the Working Party on New Industrial Layout and Design of*

Industrial Buildings (Hong Kong, Town Planning Office, 1979).

Urban Services Department, *Recreation and Civic Facilities for New Towns*, in Hong Kong Committee of the International Council on Social Welfare (1976), pp. 117–32 (see under *Other Publications* section).

Wakefield, J.T., *An Outline of the Activities of the Singapore Improvement Trust and Recommendations for the Constitution of an Improvement Trust (to be called a Housing Council) in Hong Kong* (Hong Kong, Hong Kong Government, 1952).

—— *Report on Squatters, Simple-Type Housing for Squatters and Permanent Housing for Employees of Government and Utility Companies* (Hong Kong, Social Welfare Office, 1951).

Wilbur Smith and Associates, *Hong Kong Comprehensive Transport Study* (3 vols.) (Hong Kong, Government Printer, 1976).

—— *Hong Kong Comprehensive Transport Study Two* (Hong Kong, Government Printer, 1988).

—— *New Territories Transport Requirements* (Hong Kong, Government Printer, 1973).

Working Group on New Territories Urban Land Acquisitions, *Report of the Working Group on New Territories Urban Land Acquisitions* (Hong Kong, Government Printer, 1979).

Working Group on Private Sector Participation, *Report of the Working Group on Private Sector Participation in Land Production*, in Special Committee on Land Supply (1982), Appendix II.

Working Party on Slum Clearance, *Report of the Working Party on Slum Clearance and the Effects on Urban Redevelopment of the Buildings (Amendment) (No. 2) Ordinance 1964* (Hong Kong, Government, Printer, 1985).

Working Party on Squatters, *Report to the 1963 Working Party on Government Policies and Practices with regard to Squatters, Resettlement and Government Low Cost Housing* (Hong Kong, Government Printer, 1964).

New Towns*

Kwun Tong

City District Officer Kwun Tong, *Report on the Provision of Community Requirements in Kowloon Planning Area 14* (Hong Kong, Department of Chinese Affairs, Kwun Tong District Office, 1970).

Secretary for Chinese Affairs, *Planning and Development of the Kwun Tong Industrial Area* (Hong Kong, Hong Kong Government, 1969).

—— *Development in the Ngau Tau Kok, Kun Tong Area* (Hong Kong, Department of Chinese Affairs, 1958).

Working Committee on the New Industrial Area at Kun Tong, *Report of the*

---

*For each of the Hong Kong new towns detailed planning information about the stages of development of the whole town, and for detailed parts of each town can be found in the annual Development Programmes produced by the Territory Development Department and its predecessor, the New Territories Development Department, as well as the Explanatory Statements attached to each Outline Zoning or Development Plan, and Layout Plans and Planning Briefs. The listing hereunder is not exhaustive.

Working Committee on the New Industrial Area at Kun Tong (Hong Kong, Hong Kong Government, 1956).

Tsuen Wan/Kwai Chung/Tsing Yi

Development and Airport Division, *Further Report on Development at Tsing Yi* (Hong Kong, Public Works Department, 1973).

Gregory, W.G., Mackey, S., Firth, J.R., Wong, C.H., and Leung, K.W., *Tsuen Wan Development — A Feasibility Report* (Hong Kong, Cathay Press, 1959).

Land Development Planning Committee, *Kwai Chung Valley Layout Plans*: *Areas 10* (Part), *17 and 29* (Part), Paper No. 43 (Hong Kong, Hong Kong Government, 1964).

—— *Tsuen Wan Area 18 (Part): Town Centre Development Control*, Paper No. 69 (Hong Kong, Hong Kong Government, 1965).

—— *Tsuen Wan and District Outline Development Plan: Area 10 — Residential Layout at Kwai Chung*, Paper No. 93 (Hong Kong, Hong Kong Government, 1965).

New Territories Development Department, *Hong Kong's New Towns — Tsuen Wan* (Hong Kong, Public Works Department, 1976).

—— *Hong Kong's New Towns — Tsuen Wan* (Hong Kong, Public Works Department, 1979).

Public Works Department Land Conference, *Tsuen Wan District: Kwai Chung Commercial Centre Area 17 — High Level Pedestrian Ways* (Hong Kong, Public Works Department, 1965).

Scott Wilson Kirkpatrick & Partners, *Report on Reclamation at Gin Drinkers Bay* (Hong Kong, Government Printer, 1959).

Tsuen Wan Development Office, *Tsuen Wan* (folder and pamphlets) (Hong Kong, New Territories Development Department, 1985 onwards).

Tsuen Wan District Board, *Unemployment/Underemployment Situation in Tsuen Wan: A Report* (Hong Kong, Tsuen Wan District Board, 1983).

Tsuen Wan New Town Development Office, *Town Centre Policy for Kwai Chung: Initial Appraisal* (Hong Kong, New Territories Development Department, 1981).

—— *Tsuen Wan New Town Development Programme: Forecast of Expenditure, Aug. 1974* (Hong Kong, New Territories Development Department, 1974 and annually thereafter).

Yuncken Freeman Hong Kong, *Tsuen Wan New Town: Landscape and Recreation Study* (3 vols.) (Hong Kong, New Territories Development Department, 1978).

Sha Tin

Development Division, *Report on Development at Sha Tin* (Hong Kong, Public Works Department, 1965).

—— *Report on the Development of Sha Tin New Town, Stage I (Revised)* (Hong Kong, Public Works Department, 1967).

Land Development Planning Committee, *Proposed New Towns at Castle Peak and Sha Tin*, Paper No. 71 (Hong Kong, Hong Kong Government, 1965).

—— *Sha Tin New Town: Stage 1, Phase I; Central Area 7 and Industrial Area 16 — Layout Plans Nos. LST 49A, LST 53A, and Sketch No. TP1/69*, Paper No. 245 (Hong Kong, Hong Kong Government, 1969).

—— *Sha Tin New Town: Phase I (Revised)*, Paper No. 154 (Hong Kong, Hong Kong Government, 1967).

Land Development Policy Committee, *New Development Areas for Public Housing — An Appraisal of Junk Bay, Sha Tin Area B, and Tuen Mun Eastern Extension*, Paper No. 25/79 (Hong Kong, Hong Kong Government, 1979).

Maunsell Consultants Asia, *Sha Tin Stage II Engineering Feasibility Study* (Hong Kong, New Territories Development Department, 1977).

Maunsell Consultants Asia and William Holford and Partners, *Planning Report, Sha Tin Areas 7 and 20: Layout Plan No. PST/2 — Explanatory Statement* (Hong Kong, New Territories Development Department, 1974).

New Territories Development Department, *Hong Kong's New Towns — Sha Tin* (Hong Kong, Public Works Department, 1976).

—— *Hong Kong's New Towns — Sha Tin* (Hong Kong, Public Works Department, 1979).

Public Works Department, *Agreement No. CE 10/76: Sha Tin New Town Stage II — Engineering Feasibility Study — Brief* (Hong Kong, Public Works Department, 1976).

Scott Wilson Kirkpatrick & Partners, *Report on Reclamation at Sha Tin* (Hong Kong, Government Printer, 1959).

Sha Tin Development Office, *Sha Tin* (folder and pamphlets) (Hong Kong, Territory Development Department, 1987 and onwards).

Sha Tin New Town Development Office, *Administration Planning and Development for Shatin New Town*, in Hong Kong Committee of the International Council on Social Welfare (1976), pp. 104–16 (see under *Other Publications* section).

—— *Draft Landscape Brief: Brief for a Study and Preparation of a Master Landscape Plan for Sha Tin New Town* (Hong Kong, New Territories Development Department, 1976).

—— *Sha Tin* (folder and pamphlets) (Hong Kong, New Territories Development Department, 1982).

—— *Sha Tin New Town Development Programme: Forecast of Expenditure — August 1974* (Hong Kong, New Territories Development Department, 1974 and annually thereafter).

—— *Sha Tin New Town Development Stage II: Master Landscape Plan — Brief* (Hong Kong, New Territories Development Department, 1976).

—— *Sha Tin New Town Industrial Survey* (Hong Kong, New Territories Development Department, 1981).

—— *Sha Tin New Town Industrial Survey* (Hong Kong, New Territories Development Department, 1986).

Sha Tin New Town Development Office in conjunction with Maunsell Consultants Asia, *Environmental Considerations in relation to Shatin*, in Hong Kong Committee of the International Council on Social Welfare (1976), pp. 151–8 (see under *Other Publications* section).

—— *Road Planning for Shatin New Town*, in Hong Kong Committee of the International Council on Social Welfare (1976), pp. 159–63 (see under *Other Publications* section).

Sha Tin Works Progress Committee, Planning Sub-committee, *Infill Sites for Sha Tin Proper*, Paper No. 18/85 (Hong Kong, New Territories Development Department, 1985).

Town Planning Board, *Castle Peak and Shatin Outline Zoning Plans Nos. LCP/*

31A and LST/46A, Paper No. 100 (Hong Kong, Town Planning Board, 1966).

—— *Sha Tin Outline Development Plan LST 42*, Paper No. 70 (Hong Kong, Town Planning Board, 1964).

Yuncken Freeman Hong Kong, *Sha Tin New Town Master Landscape Plan: Phase One Report* (2 vols.) (Hong Kong, New Territories Development Department, 1977).

—— *Sha Tin Town Centre Study* (4 vols.) (Hong Kong, New Territories Development Department, 1978).

Tuen Mun (Castle Peak)

Development Division, *Report on Development at Castle Peak* (Hong Kong, Public Works Department, 1965).

Land Development Planning Committee, *Proposed New Towns at Castle Peak and Sha Tin*, Paper No. 71 (Hong Kong, Hong Kong Government, 1965).

Land Development Policy Committee, *New Development Areas for Public Housing — An Appraisal of Junk Bay, Sha Tin Area B, and Tuen Mun Eastern Extension*, Paper No. 25/79 (Hong Kong, Hong Kong Government, 1979).

National Hydraulics Research Station, *Tuen Mun New Town: Physical Model Studies of Proposed Harbour Development* (Hong Kong, New Territories Development Department, 1978).

New Territories Development Department, *Hong Kong's New Towns — Tuen Mun* (Hong Kong, Public Works Department, 1976).

North Western Development Office, *Tuen Mun* (folder and pamphlets) (Hong Kong, Territory Development Department, 1986 and onwards).

Scott Wilson Kirkpatrick & Partners, *Report on Reclamation at Castle Peak* (Hong Kong, Government Printer, 1959).

—— *Tuen Mun New Town Stage II Engineering Feasibility Study* (Hong Kong, New Territories Development Department, 1976).

—— *Tuen Mun New Town Transport Study: Final Report* (2 vols.) (Hong Kong, New Territories Development Department, 1978).

—— *Tuen Mun Stage II Extension Study* (Hong Kong, New Territories Development Department, 1978).

Town Planning Board, *Castle Peak and Shatin Outline Zoning Plans Nos. LCP/ 31A and LST/46A*, Paper No. 100 (Hong Kong, Town Planning Board, 1966).

Tuen Mun District Advisory Board, *Industrial Sub-Committee's Report on Tuen Mun New Town Industrial Survey* (Hong Kong, Tuen Mun District Advisory Board, 1978).

Tuen Mun New Town Development Office, *Tuen Mun New Town: Eastern Extension Area Planning Statement* (Hong Kong, New Territories Development Department, 1985).

Working Group on Promotion of Industrial Investment in Tuen Mun, *Tuen Mun Industrial Survey 1983: Industries and Workers — Past and Future Outlook* (Hong Kong, Tuen Mun District Board, 1983).

Yuncken Freeman Hong Kong, *Tuen Mun New Town Landscape Master Plan* (Hong Kong, New Territories Development Department, 1978).

Yuncken Freeman Hong Kong, Scott Wilson Kirkpatrick & Partners, Jones Lang Wootton, and Levett & Bailey, *Tuen Mun Town Centre Study* (3 vols.) (Hong Kong, New Territories Development Department, 1979).

Junk Bay

Civil Engineering Office, *Agreement No. CEI/75, Item NDE 18(1): Junk Bay Development — Revised Brief and Schedule of Fees, November 1976* (Hong Kong, Public Works Department, 1976).

Environment Branch, *Junk Bay Development: Environment Branch Points of View* (Hong Kong, Hong Kong Government Secretariat, Environment Branch, 1980).

Development Progress Committee, *1985 Junk Bay Development Review*, Paper No. 41/85 (Hong Kong, Hong Kong Government, 1985).

—— *1985 Junk Bay Review: Background Report* (Hong Kong, Hong Kong Government, 1985).

Hong Kong Productivity Centre, *Junk Bay Survey* (Hong Kong, New Territories Development Department, 1981).

Industrial Land Sub-committee, *Junk Bay New Town: Provision of Industrial Land Therein and Relationship to other Industrial Areas* (Hong Kong, Hong Kong Government, Land Development Policy Committee, 1981).

Junk Bay Development Office, *Situation Report* (Hong Kong, New Territories Development Department, 1980).

Junk Bay Development Office and Junk Bay Consultants, *Existing Industries in Junk Bay* (Hong Kong, New Territories Development Department, 1981).

Junk Bay Development Steering Group, *Recommendations on Junk Bay Development Stage I — Engineering and Environmental Study: for Industrial Land Sub-Committee of Land Development Policy Committee* (Hong Kong, Hong Kong Government, 1975).

Land Development Policy Committee, *Development of Junk Bay New Town and Contingent Issues*, Paper No. 10/82 (Hong Kong, Hong Kong Government, 1982).

—— *Development of Junk Bay New Town: Outline Development Plan and Development Programme Review — Draft Paper* (Hong Kong, Hong Kong Government, 1983).

—— *Development of Junk Bay New Town: Outline Development Plan and Development Programme Review*, Paper No. 18/83 (Hong Kong, Hong Kong Government, 1983).

—— *Junk Bay*, Paper No. 29/76, (Hong Kong, Hong Kong Government, 1976).

—— *Junk Bay New Town Phase I Outline Development Plan — Plan No. JB/83/001D*, Paper No. 4/86, (Hong Kong, Hong Kong Government, 1986).

—— *New Development Areas for Public Housing: An Appraisal of Junk Bay, Sha Tin Area B, and Tuen Mun Eastern Extension*, Paper No. 25/79 (Hong Kong, Hong Kong Government, 1979).

—— *The Potential Industrial Use of Junk Bay*, Paper No. 399 (Hong Kong, Hong Kong Government, 1974).

Maunsell Consultants Asia, *Junk Bay Urban Development — Feasibility Study* (Hong Kong, New Territories Development Department, 1978).

Maunsell Consultants Asia, Shankland Cox, and Brian Clouston and Partners Hong Kong Limited, *Junk Bay Development Study: Draft Final Report — March 1982* (Hong Kong, New Territories Development Department, 1982).

—— *Junk Bay Development Study: Final Report* (Hong Kong, New Territories Development Department, 1982).

—— *Junk Bay Development Study: Interim Report — August 1981* (Hong Kong, New Territories Development Department, 1981).

—— *Junk Bay Development Study: Junk Bay Town — Alternative Development*

Concepts, Initial Evaluation (Technical Note No. 2) (Hong Kong, New Territories Development Department, 1981).

—— *Junk Bay Development Study: Junk Bay Town — Goals and Objectives, Initial Evaluation* (Technical Note No. 1) (Hong Kong, New Territories Development Department, 1981).

New Territories Development Department, *Junk Bay* (pamphlet) (Hong Kong, New Territories Development Department, 1983).

Scott Wilson Kirkpatrick & Partners, *Report on Reclamation at Junk Bay* (Hong Kong, Government Printer, 1959).

Shankland Cox, Binnie and Partners, and Maunsell Consultants Asia, *Junk Bay East Coast Study: Final Report* (Hong Kong, New Territories Development Department, 1983).

Other New Towns

New Territories Development Department, *Fanling* (pamphlet) (Hong Kong, New Territories Development Department, 1983).

—— *Fan Ling–Sheung Shui* (folder and pamphlet) (Hong Kong, Territory Development Department, 1987 onwards).

—— *Islands* (pamphlet) (Hong Kong, New Territories Development Department, 1983).

—— *Market Towns* (Hong Kong, New Territories Development Department, 1978).

—— *North-Western New Territories* (pamphlet) (Hong Kong, New Territories Development Department, 1982).

—— *Sai Kung* (folder and pamphlets) (Hong Kong, Territory Development Department, 1987 and onwards).

—— *Tai Po* (pamphlet) (Hong Kong, New Territories Development Department, 1982).

—— *Tai Po* (folder and pamphlets) (Hong Kong, Territory Development Department, 1987 and onwards).

Shankland Cox and Binnie and Partners, *Tin Shui Wai Urban Development: Interim Report* (Hong Kong, New Territories Development Department, 1983).

—— *Tin Shui Wai Urban Development: Master Development Plan* (2 vols.) (Hong Kong, New Territories Development Department, 1983).

Urbis Planning Design Group and Brian Clouston and Partners Hong Kong Limited, *Tai Po Landscape and Recreation Study: Final Report* (Hong Kong, New Territories Development Department, 1979).

Other Publications

Adams, C.D., 'Hong Kong Property: The Changing Nature of the Industrial Market', *Estates Gazette*, 31 January 1987, pp. 380–2.

—— 'Recent Trends in the Supply of Land for Industrial Development in Hong Kong: A Case Study in Planned Decentralization', *Land Development Studies*, Vol. 4, No. 3, September 1987, pp. 173–91.

Akers-Jones, D., 'The Basis of Planning for Social and Community Facilities in the New Towns — A Historical Perspective', in Hong Kong Council of Social Service (1983), Opening Speech.

Asian Architect and Contractor, 'Junk Bay — Town of the Future', *Asian Architect and Contractor*, Vol. 17, No. 3, March 1988, pp. 19–21.

Birch, A. (ed.), *The New Territories and Its Future: Proceedings of a Symposium of the Royal Asiatic Society, Hong Kong Branch* (Hong Kong, Royal Asiatic Society, Hong Kong Branch, 1982).

Birch, A., Yao, Y.C., and Sinn, E. (eds.), *Research Materials for Hong Kong Studies* (Hong Kong, University of Hong Kong, Centre of Asian Studies, 1985).

Boey, Y.M. (ed.), *High-Rise, High-Density Living: Singapore Professional Centre Convention 1983 — Selected Papers* (Singapore, Singapore Professional Centre, 1984).

Boxer, B., 'Space, Change and Feng Shui in Tsuen Wan's Urbanisation', *Journal of Asian and African Studies*, Vol. 3, No. 1, 1970, p. 34.

Brandon, W.P.J. (ed.), *Architecture, Building, Urban Design and Urban Planning in Hong Kong, 1983: A Collection of Articles constituting the Special Report 1983 of the Appointments Board, University of Hong Kong* (Hong Kong, University of Hong Kong, Appointments Board, 1983).

Bristow, M.R., 'Planning by Demand: A Possible Hypothesis about Town Planning in Hong Kong', *Hong Kong Journal of Public Administration* (now *The Asian Journal of Public Administration*), Vol. 3, No. 2, December 1981, pp. 199–223.

—— 'The Role and Place of Strategic Planning in Hong Kong', *Planning and Development: Journal of the Hong Kong Institute of Planners*, Vol. 4, No. 1, March 1988, pp. 14–20.

Bristow, Roger, *Land-use Planning in Hong Kong: History, Policies and Procedures* (Hong Kong, Oxford University Press, 1984).

Caritas Tuen Mun Family Service Unit, 'Adjustment Problems encountered by Families in Tuen Mun', *Welfare Quarterly of the Hong Kong Council of Social Service*, No. 97, Summer 1986, pp. 31–3.

Castells, M., *The Shek Kip Mei Syndrome: Public Housing and Economic Development in Hong Kong* (Hong Kong, University of Hong Kong, Centre of Urban Studies and Urban Planning, Working Paper No. 15, 1986).

Chan, K., *Industrial Development in New Towns: The Case of Hong Kong* (London, University of London, University College, M. Phil. Dissertation, 1985).

Chan, R., *An Anatomy of the Failure of the Hong Kong Government's Announced 10 Years Public Housing Plan in 1972* (Hong Kong, Research and Resource, 1982).

Chan, W.T., 'Situation of Residents in Tuen Mun New Town' (in Chinese), *Welfare Quarterly of the Hong Kong Council of Social Service*, No. 62, Autumn 1977, pp. 5–12.

Chan, Y.K., 'Density and Its Implications', in Hong Kong Council of Social Service (1978), pp. 126–9.

—— 'The Development of New Towns', in King and Lee (1981), pp. 37–50.

—— *The Development of New Towns in Hong Kong* (Hong Kong, Chinese University of Hong Kong, Social Research Centre, Occasional Paper No. 67, 1977).

—— 'Life in Confined Living Space: With Special Reference to Housing in Hong Kong', in Boey (ed.) (1984), pp. 188–91.

—— *Life Satisfaction in Crowded Urban Environment* (Hong Kong, Chinese University of Hong Kong, Social Research Centre, Occasional Paper No. 75, 1978).

—— *The Rise and Growth of Kwun Tong: A Study of Planned Urban Development* (Hong Kong, Chinese University of Hong Kong, Social Research Centre, Occasional Paper, 1973).

—— 'Urban Density and Social Relations', *Journal of the Chinese University of Hong Kong*, Vol. 5, No. 1, 1979, pp. 315–22.

Chan, Y.K., and Choi, C.Y., 'Hong Kong's Industrial New Towns', *Ekistics*, Vol. 46, No. 277, 1979, pp. 239–42.

Chau, C.S., 'High Density Development: Hong Kong as an Example', in Kwok and Pun (eds.) (1982), pp. 1–14.

Chau, W.T., and So, M.Y., *A Study on Tuen Mun's Community Need* (Hong Kong, Young Women's Christian Association [YWCA], 1977).

Cheng, J.Y.S. (ed.), *Hong Kong in the 1980s* (Hong Kong, Summerson Eastern, 1982).

—— *Hong Kong in Transition* (Hong Kong, Oxford University Press, 1986).

Cheung, R., *Tsuen-Wan: A Brief History of Its Development* (Hong Kong, University of Hong Kong, BA Dissertation, 1954).

China Mail, 5 October 1920, 10 August 1921, 12 September 1921, and 27 October 1921.

Chiu, T.N., 'Urban Structure and Technological Innovation: Policy Implications of the Hong Kong Experience', in Leung, Cushman, and Wang (eds.) (1980), pp. 439–54.

Chiu, T.N., and So, C.L. (eds.), *A Geography of Hong Kong* (Hong Kong, Oxford University Press, second edition, 1986).

Choi, C.Y., *Housing Policy and Internal Movement of Population: A Study of Kwun Tong, A Chinese New Town in Hong Kong* (Hong Kong, Chinese University of Hong Kong, Social Research Centre, Research Report A62.17.0.1, 1977).

—— 'Urbanisation and Redistribution of Population in Hong Kong — A Case Study', in Goldstein, S. (ed.), *Patterns of Urbanisation: Comparative Country Studies* (Liege, International Union for the Scientific Study of Population, 1975).

Choi, C.Y., and Chan, Y.K., *Public Housing Development and Population Movement: A Study of Kwun Tong, Hong Kong* (Hong Kong, Chinese University of Hong Kong, Social Research Centre, Occasional Paper, 1978).

Choi, P.L.Y., Fong, P.K.W., and Kwok, R.Y.W. (eds.), *Planning and Development of Coastal Open Cities — Part Two: Hong Kong Section* (Hong Kong, University of Hong Kong, Centre of Urban Studies and Urban Planning, 1986).

Choi, Y.L., 'The LUTO Model and Its Applications in Hong Kong', *Planning and Development: Journal of the Hong Kong Institute of Planners*, Vol. 1, No. 1, March 1986, pp. 21–31.

Chow, N., Tang, A., and Chau, T.F., *A Study of the Values, Leisure Behaviour and Misbehaviour of the Youth in Tsuen Wan and Kwai Chung* (Hong Kong, Tsuen Wan District Board, 1985).

Chow, N.W.S., *A Critical Analysis of the Social Welfare Policy in Hong Kong* (Hong Kong, Cosmos Books, 1984).

—— *Moving into New Towns — The Costs of Social Adaptation*, (Hong Kong, University of Hong Kong, Centre of Urban Studies and Urban Planning, 1987).

—— 'Moving into New Towns: The Costs of Social Adaptation', *The Asian Journal of Public Administration*, Vol. 9, No. 2, December 1987, pp. 132–42.

—— 'The Quality of Life of Tuen Mun Inhabitants', *The Asian Journal of Public Administration*, Vol. 10, No. 2, Dec. 1988, pp. 194–206.

—— 'The Service Gap: Past and Present Problems — Possible Remedial Action', in Hong Kong Council of Social Service (1983).

Community Development Committee, *Community Development Resource Book 1975–76* (Hong Kong, Hong Kong Council of Social Service, 1977).

Costa, F.J., Dutt, A.K., Ma, L.J.C., and Noble, A.G. (eds.), *Asian Urbanisation: Problems and Processes* (Berlin, Gebrüder Borntraeger, 1988).

Crosby, A.R., 'Physical Planning for the New Towns', in Hong Kong Committee of the International Council on Social Welfare (1976), pp. 2–14.

Cruden, G.N., *Land Compensation and Valuation Law in Hong Kong* (Singapore, Butterworths, 1986).

Cuthbert, A.R., 'Architecture, Society and Space — The High-Density Question Re-examined', *Progress in Planning*, Vol. 24, 1985, pp. 71–160.

—— *Hong Kong: Ideology, Space and Power — Fundamental Economic Imperatives and the Devolution of Urban Form* (Hong Kong, University of Hong Kong, Centre of Urban Studies and Urban Planning, Working Paper, 1985).

Davis, S.G., *Land Use Problems in Hong Kong* (Hong Kong, University of Hong Kong Press, 1964).

—— 'The Rural-Urban Migration in Hong Kong and Its New Territories', *The Geographical Journal*, Vol. 128, No. 3, May 1962, pp. 328–33.

—— *Symposium on Land Use and Mineral Deposition in Hong Kong and South China* (Hong Kong, University of Hong Kong Press, 1964).

Don, J.S., 'Organisation for Development of the New Towns in Hong Kong', in Hong Kong Committee of the International Council on Social Welfare (1976), pp. 92–103.

Drakakis-Smith, D.W., *High Society: Housing Provision in Metropolitan Hong Kong 1954 to 1979 — A Jubilee Critique* (Hong Kong, University of Hong Kong, Centre of Asian Studies, 1979).

—— 'The Hinterlands of Towns in the New Territories', in Dwyer (1971), pp. 167–81.

—— 'Housing Needs and Planning Policies for the Asian City — The Lessons from Hong Kong', *International Journal of Environmental Studies*, Vol. 1, No. 2, 1971, pp. 115–28.

—— 'Traditional and Modern Aspects of Urban Systems in the Third World: A Case Study in Hong Kong', *Pacific Viewpoint*, Vol. 12, No. 1, May 1971, pp. 21–40.

Dwyer, D.J., 'The Urbanisation of the New Territories', in Royal Society (1968), pp. 75–89.

Dwyer, D.J., (ed.), *Asian Urbanisation: A Hong Kong Casebook* (Hong Kong, Hong Kong University Press, 1971).

—— *The City as a Centre of Change in Asia* (Hong Kong, Hong Kong University Press, 1972).

Eason, A.C., 'Territorial Development Strategy Studies: A View of the Process', *Planning and Development: Journal of the Hong Kong Institute of Planners*, Vol. 1, No. 1, March 1986, pp. 4–7.

EBC Hong Kong, 'Tuen Mun Town Park', *Asian Architect and Contractor*, Vol. 14, No. 11, November 1985, pp. 30–3.

Endacott, G.B., *Government and People in Hong Kong 1841–1962: A Constitutional History* (Hong Kong, University of Hong Kong Press, 1964).

Far East Architect and Builder, 'Multi-Level Town Centre for Hong Kong Estate', (Wah Fu), *Far East Architect and Builder*, February 1966, pp. 47–51.

Fong, M.K., *Some Observations on the Degree of Satisfaction of the Residents of Tai Po Township on their Living Environment*, Paper presented at the First Asia-Pacific Conference on Urban Reconstruction, Taipeh, 1978.

Fong, P.K.W., 'The Management of High-Rise Residential Development in Hong Kong', in Hills (ed.) (1985).

—— 'Public Housing Policies and Programmes in Hong Kong — Past, Present and Future Developments', in Choi, Fong, and Kwok (eds.) (1986), pp. 97–112.

Fong, P.K.W., and Hills, P., 'Urban Transport Problems in Hong Kong', in Choi, Fong, and Kwok (eds.) (1986), pp. 127–44.

French, B., 'Educational Consideration in relation to the New Towns', in Hong Kong Committee of the International Council on Social Welfare (1976), pp. 141–8.

Fung, B.C.K., 'Squatter Relocation and the Problem of Home-work Separation', in Wong (ed.) (1978), pp. 233–65.

Fung, K.Y., *Development of Tsuen Wan* (Hong Kong, University of Hong Kong, BA Dissertation, 1959).

Fung, T., 'Public Housing Management in Hong Kong's New Towns', in Yeung (ed.) (1983), pp. 199–214.

Ganesan, S., 'The Property Sector of Hong Kong before and after 1997', in Jao, Leung, Wesley-Smith, and Wong (eds.) (1985), pp. 445–68.

Gilbert, G., 'Social Problems in the Development of Shatin New Town', in Hong Kong Committee of the International Council on Social Welfare (1976), pp. 84–8.

Goodstadt, L.F., 'Urban Housing in Hong Kong 1945–63', in Jarvie and Agassi (1969), pp. 257–98.

Gregory, W.G., 'An Architect's Comments on Land Use in Hong Kong', in Davis (ed.) (1964), pp. 20–39.

Hackett, N., 'Landscape Impact on Tai Po New Town', *Asian Architect and Contractor*, Vol. 14, No. 11, November 1985, pp. 44–9.

Hadland, B.J., 'Land Policies in Hong Kong', in Wong (ed.) (1978), pp. 72–90.

Han, D.W.T., 'Migration and Residential Satisfaction in a New Town: The Case of Tuen Mun', in Leung, Cushman, and Wang (eds.) (1980), pp. 341–74.

—— 'Social Background of Housing in Hong Kong', in Wong (ed.) (1978), pp. 1–22.

—— 'Social Planning for the New Town', in Hong Kong Committee of the International Council on Social Welfare (1976), pp. 24–38.

Harris, P.B., 'Policy Process and Policy Formulation in Hong Kong', in Leung, Cushman, and Wang (eds.) (1980), pp. 31–48.

Hayes, J.W., 'Building a Community in a New Town: A Management Relationship with the New Population', in Leung, Cushman, and Wang (eds.) (1980), pp. 308–40.

—— 'The Impact of the City on the Environment: Squatters before and after Development — The Case of Tsuen Wan, Hong Kong', in Hill and Bray (eds.) (1978), pp. 69–78.

Hill, R.D., and Bray, J.M. (eds.), *Geography and the Environment in Southeast Asia* (Hong Kong, University of Hong Kong Press, 1978).

Hills, P.R., *Environment Assessment and the New Town Planning Process in*

Hong Kong, Paper at the World Health Organisation Training Course on Environmental Impact Assessment, University of Aberdeen, July 1985.

Hills, P.R. (ed.), *State Policy, Urbanization and the Development Process: Proceedings of a Symposium on Social and Environmental Development, University of Hong Kong, October 1984* (Hong Kong, University of Hong Kong, Centre of Urban Studies and Urban Planning, 1985).

Hills, P.R., and Yeh, A.G.O., 'New Town Developments in Hong Kong', *Built Environment*, Vol. 9, Nos. 3/4, 1983, pp. 266–77.

Hoadley, J.S., *Planned Development and Political Adaptability in Rural Hong Kong* (Hong Kong, Chinese University of Hong Kong, Social Research Centre, Occasional Paper, 1980).

Hodge, P., 'Social Planning for Growing Cities', in International Council on Social Welfare (1976), pp. 7–29.

Hong Kong Committee of the International Council on Social Welfare, *Symposium on Social Planning in a New Town: Case Study — Shatin New Town, April 30 — May 1, 1976* (Hong Kong, Hong Kong Council of Social Service, 1976).

Hong Kong Council of Social Service, *Proceedings of a Symposium on Social Services in the New Towns* (Hong Kong, Hong Kong Council of Social Service, 1983).

—— *Report of the Symposium on Development within Environmental Constraints* (Hong Kong, Hong Kong Council of Social Service, 1978).

—— 'Role of Government in Community Building', *Welfare Quarterly of the Hong Kong Council of Social Service*, No. 67, Winter 1978, pp. 17–18.

—— 'Social Services provided by Voluntary Organisations in Tsuen Wan' (in Chinese), *Welfare Quarterly of the Hong Kong Council of Social Service*, No. 62, Autumn 1977, pp. 16–26.

—— *Symposium on Social Services in New Towns* (Hong Kong, Hong Kong Council of Social Service, 1983).

Hong Kong and Far East Builder, 'Sha Tin Plan', *The Hong Kong and Far East Builder*, Vol. 16, No. 1, 1961, pp. 50–1.

Hong Kong Society of Architects' Planning Committee, *Report to Government: Town Planning Ordinance, Hong Kong Planning Board — Sha Tin and District Outline Development Plan and Explanatory Statement* (Hong Kong, Hong Kong Society of Architects, 1961).

Hopkins, K., 'Public and Private Housing in Hong Kong', in Dwyer (1972), pp. 200–15.

Hopkins, K. (ed.), *Hong Kong: The Industrial Colony — A Political, Social and Economic Survey* (Hong Kong, Oxford University Press, 1971).

International Council on Social Welfare, *Social Planning for Growing Cities: Role of Social Welfare — Proceedings of the International Council on Social Welfare Regional Conference for Asia and Western Pacific, 1975* (Hong Kong, Hong Kong Council of Social Service, 1976).

Jarvie, I.C., and Agassi, J. (eds.), *Hong Kong: A Society in Transition* (London, Routledge and Kegan Paul, 1969).

Jao, Y.C., Leung, C.K., Wesley-Smith, P., and Wong, S.L. (eds.), *Hong Kong and 1997: Strategies for the Future* (Hong Kong, University of Hong Kong, Centre of Asian Studies, 1985).

Johnson, G.E., 'From Rural Committee to Spirit Medium Cult: Voluntary Association in the Development of a Chinese Town', *Contributions to Asian Studies*, Vol. 1, 1971, pp. 123–43.

—— 'Leaders and Leadership in an Expanding New Territories Town', *The China Quarterly*, No. 69, 1977, pp. 109–25.

Jones, D., 'Development Scenario — Pint Pot or Widow's Cruse', *South China Morning Post*, 5 November 1980, p. 2.

Jones, J.F., Ho, K.F., Lo Chau, B., Lam, M.C., and Mok, B.H., *Neighbourhood Associations in a New Town: The Mutual Aid Committee in Shatin* (Hong Kong, Chinese University of Hong Kong, Social Research Centre, Occasional Paper No. 76, 1978).

Ip, D.F., Leung C.K., and Wu, C.T., *Hong Kong: A Social Sciences Bibliography* (Hong Kong, University of Hong Kong, Centre of Asian Studies, 1974).

Kan, A.W.S., 'Implications of Concentrated Utilization of Local Facilities and Services in Public Housing Estates', in King and Lee (1981), pp. 51–80.

Keung, J.K., 'Government Intervention and Housing Policy in Hong Kong', *Third World Planning Review*, Vol. 7, No. 1, February 1985, pp. 23–44.

—— *Government Intervention and Housing Policy in Hong Kong: A Structural Analysis* (Cardiff, University of Wales Institute of Science and Technology, Department of Town Planning, Planning Research Paper No. 30, 1981).

King, A.Y.C., 'The Political Culture of Kwun Tong: A Chinese Community in Hong Kong', in King and Lee (eds.) (1981), pp. 147–68.

King, A.Y.C., and Lee, R.P.L. (eds.), *Social Life and Development in Hong Kong* (Hong Kong, Chinese University of Hong Kong Press, 1981).

Koerte, A., 'Confinement versus Liberation: A Cross-cultural Analysis on High-Rise, High-Density Living', in Boey (ed.) (1984), pp. 175–87.

Kong, C.C., 'Citizen's Participation in the Planning and Management of Tsuen Wan New Town' (in Chinese), *Welfare Quarterly of the Hong Kong Council of Social Service*, No. 62, Autumn 1977, pp. 26–9.

Kuan, H.C., Lau, S.K., and Ho, K.F., *Organising Participatory Urban Services: The Mutual Aid Committees in Hong Kong* (Hong Kong, Chinese University of Hong Kong, Institute of Social Studies, Occasional Paper No. 2, 1983).

Kwan, A.H.S., *Social Planning in New Communities: A Comprehensive Study of Britain and Hong Kong* (Birmingham, University of Birmingham, M.Soc.Sc. Dissertation, 1979).

Kwok, R.Y.W., and Pun, K.S. (eds.), *Planning in Asia — Present and Future: Proceedings from the Asian Regional Workshop/Conference of the Commonwealth Association of Planners 1981* (Hong Kong, University of Hong Kong, Centre of Urban Studies and Urban Planning, 1982).

Lai, D.C.Y., and Dwyer, D.J., 'Kwun Tong, Hong Kong: A Study of Industrial Planning', *Town Planning Review*, Vol. 35, No. 4, December 1965, pp. 299–310.

—— 'A New Industrial Town in Hong Kong', *Ekistics*, Vol. 18, No. 108, 1964, pp. 340–5.

—— 'Tsuen Wan: A New Industrial Town in Hong Kong', *Geographical Review*, Vol. 54, No. 2, March 1964, pp. 151–69.

Lai, L.W.C., 'The Formation of Squatters and Slums in Hong Kong: From Slump Market to Boom Market', *Ekistics*, Vol. 39, No. 312, May 1985, pp. 231–8.

Lau, S.K., 'Comments on the Social Infrastructure of the Shatin New Town', in Hong Kong Committee of the International Council on Social Welfare (1976), pp. 59–63.

Lau, S.K., Kuan, H.C., and Ho, K.F., 'Leaders, Officials, and Citizens in

Urban Service Delivery: A Comparative Study of Four Localities in Hong Kong', in Yeung, Y.M., and McGee, T.G., (eds.), *Community Participation in Delivering Urban Services in Asia* (Ottawa, International Development Research Centre, 1986), pp. 211–37.

Lee, R.P.L., 'High-Density Effects in Urban Areas: What do we know and What should we do?', in King and Lee (eds.) (1981), pp. 3–20.

—— 'The State of Affairs in a Chinese Satellite Town: The Case of Kwun Tong', *Chung Chi Bulletin*, No. 57, pp. 17–20.

Lee Fong, M.K., 'Directions in Urban Growth in Hong Kong', in Leung, Cushman, and Wang (eds.) (1980), pp. 267–88.

Lee, R.P.L., Cheung, T.S., and Wong, O.P., 'Sociological and Related Studies in Hong Kong: A Selected Bibliography', in King and Lee (eds.) (1981), pp. 325–66.

Leong, K.C., 'Housing Technology in relation to Urban Growth: The Case of Hong Kong', in Leung, Cushman, and Wang (eds.) (1980), pp. 419–38.

Leung, C.K., 'Some Aspects of Industrial Freight Transport in the New Towns: with special reference to Tsuen Wan', in Birch (ed.) (1982), pp. 61–7.

—— 'Urbanization and New Towns Development', in Leung, Cushman, and Wang (eds.) (1980), pp. 289–308.

Leung, C.K., Cushman, J.W., and Wang G.W., (eds.), *Hong Kong: Dilemmas of Growth* (Hong Kong, University of Hong Kong, Centre of Asian Studies, 1980).

Leung, C.Y., 'The Land Tenure System', in Cheng (ed.) (1986), pp. 208–34.

Leung, W.T., 'Hong Kong's New Towns Programme: A Social Perspective', in Leung, Cushman, and Wang (eds.) (1980), pp. 375–96.

—— 'The New Towns Programme', in Chiu and So (eds.) (1986), pp. 251–78.

—— *Tsuen Wan Town: A Study of a New Town in Hong Kong* (Hong Kong, University of Hong Kong, M.Phil Dissertation, 1972).

Liang, C.S., 'Growth of Satellite Towns in Hong Kong', in *Chung Chi Journal*, Vol. 1, No. 2, 1962, pp. 200–41.

—— 'Overcrowding and Environmental Deterioration: The Case of Hong Kong', *Journal of the Chinese University of Hong Kong*, Vol. 3, No. 1, 1975, pp. 219–53.

Lin, T.B., Lee, R.P.L., and Simonis, V.E. (eds.), *Hong Kong — Economic, Social and Political Studies in Development* (White Plains, New York, M.E. Sharpe, 1979).

Lo, C.P., 'Changing Population Distribution in the Hong Kong New Territories', *Annals of the Association of American Geographers*, Vol. 58, No. 2, March 1968, pp. 273–84.

Lowe, C.J.G., 'How the Government in Hong Kong Makes Policy', *The Hong Kong Journal of Public Administration* (now *The Asian Journal of Public Administration*), Vol. 2, No. 2, December 1980, pp. 63–70.

Lu, A.L.C., *Tuen Mun Community Needs Survey* (Hong Kong, Shue Yan College, Faculty of Social Science, 1977).

Lui, A.S.Y., *A Comparative Study of the Transport Strategies for Two New Towns* (Hong Kong, University of Hong Kong, M.Soc.Sc. Dissertation, 1982).

Ma, W.Y., 'The Development of Kwun Tong', in Davis (1964), pp. 40–2.

Millar, S.E., *Health and Well-being in relation to High Density Living in Hong Kong* (Canberra, Australian National University, Ph.D. Thesis, 1976).

Miners, N.J., *The Government and Politics of Hong Kong* (Oxford University Press, fourth edition, 1986).

Mo-Kwan, L.F., 'Directions in Urban Growth in Hong Kong', in Leung, Cushman, and Wang (eds.) (1980), pp. 267–87.

Mok, V., *The Nature of Kwun Tong as an Industrial Community: An Analysis of Economic Organisations* (Hong Kong, Chinese University of Hong Kong, Social Research Centre, Occasional Paper, 1972).

—— 'Small Factories in Kwun Tong: Problems and Strategies for Development', in King and Lee (eds.) (1981), pp. 81–104.

Moore, G., *Tsuen Wan Township: A Study Group Report on its Development* (Hong Kong, University of Hong Kong Press, 1959).

Mountjoy, A.B., 'Housing and New Towns in Hong Kong', *Geography*, Vol. 65, No. 1, January 1980, pp. 53–7.

Myers, J.T., 'Residents' Images of a Hong Kong Resettlement Estate: A View from the Chicken Coop', in King and Lee (eds.) (1981), pp. 21–36.

Ng, P., Chan, Y.K., and Lau, S.K., 'Social Problems and the New Towns', in Hong Kong Committee of the International Council on Social Welfare (1976), pp. 89–91.

Ng, W.B., 'Hong Kong: New Towns on Land from the Sea', *Town and Country Planning*, Vol. 30, No. 4, April 1962, pp. 173–5.

Owen, N.C., 'Economic Policy', in Hopkins (ed.) (1971), pp. 141–206.

Perry, J.L., and Tang, S.Y., 'Applying Research on Administrative Reform to Hong Kong's 1997 Transition', *The Asian Journal of Public Administration*, Vol. 9, No. 2, December 1987, pp. 113–31.

Phillips, D.R., 'New Towns bring New Hope for Expanding Hong Kong', *Geographical Magazine*, Vol. 52, No. 3, March 1980, pp. 180–7.

—— 'The Planning of Social Service Provision in the New Towns of Hong Kong', *Planning and Administration*, Vol. 8, No. 1, March 1981, pp. 8–23.

—— 'Service Provision in New Towns: The Hong Kong Example', *Geografische Tijdschrift*, Vol. 17, No. 5, September 1983, pp. 326–36.

—— 'Social Services and Community Facilities in the Hong Kong New Towns', in Phillips and Yeh (eds.) (1987), pp. 82–108.

Phillips, D.R., and Yeh, A.G.O. (eds.), *New Towns in East and South-east Asia: Planning and Development* (Hong Kong, Oxford University Press, 1987).

Pope, R.D., 'A History of Letter A/B Land Exchange Policy', *The Hong Kong Surveyor*, Vol. 1, No. 1, 1985, pp. 7–9.

Prescott, J.A., 'Hong Kong: The Form and Significance of a High-Density Urban Development', in Dwyer (1971), pp. 11–9.

Pryor, E.G., *Housing in Hong Kong* (Hong Kong, Oxford University Press, second edition, 1983).

—— 'An Overview of Territorial Development Strategy Studies in Hong Kong', *Australian Planner: Journal of the Royal Australian Planning Institute*, Vol. 24, No. 2, June 1986, pp. 5–14.

—— 'An Overview of Territorial Development Strategy Studies in Hong Kong', *Planning and Development, Journal of the Hong Kong Institute of Planners*, Vol. 1, No. 1, March 1986, pp. 8–20.

—— 'Project Management for Hong Kong's New Towns', *The Asian Architect and Contractor*, Vol. 20, No. 2, January 1986, pp. 48–53.

—— 'Redevelopment and New Towns in Hong Kong', in Wong (1978), pp. 266–86.

—— 'Squatting, Land Clearance and Urban Development in Hong Kong', *Land Use Policy*, Vol. 1, No. 1, July 1984, pp. 225–42.

—— '"Supplementary Notes" to Y.C., Jao, "Land Use Policy and Land Taxation in Hong Kong"', in Wong (1976), pp. 308–13.

Pun, C.H., *Industrial Decentralisation in Hong Kong* (Hong Kong, University of Hong Kong, M.Soc.Sc. Dissertation, 1984).

Pun, K.S., *Decentralization versus Resource-Conserving Development: A Study of their relevance in the Formulation of a Development Policy in Hong Kong* (Hong Kong, University of Hong Kong, Ph.D. Thesis, 1979).

—— 'New Towns and Urban Renewal in Hong Kong', in Phillips and Yeh (eds.) (1987), pp. 41–58.

—— 'Planning for Environmental Balance: A Theoretical Study of the Hong Kong Situation', in Hill and Bray (eds.) (1978), pp. 323–44.

—— 'Urban Planning', in Chiu and So (eds.) (1986), pp. 223–50.

—— 'Urban Planning in Hong Kong — Concepts and Approaches', *The Asian Architect and Builder*, Vol. 9, No. 12, December 1980, pp. 48–56.

—— 'Urban Planning in Hong Kong: Its Evolution since 1948', *Third World Planning Review*, Vol. 6, No. 1, Feb. 1984, pp. 61–78.

Richmond, G.M., *Urban Housing in Hong Kong* (Toronto, York University, M.Phil. Thesis, 1971).

Royal Asiatic Society, *The Changing Face of Hong Kong: Royal Asiatic Society Hong Kong Branch Symposium, November 2–3rd, 1968* (Hong Kong, Ye Olde Printerie, 1971).

Royal Town Planning Institute Hong Kong Branch, *The Law in relation to Town Planning: Report of the Proceedings of a Seminar held at the University of Hong Kong on 23rd June 1973*, (Hong Kong, Royal Town Planning Institute, 1973).

Schmitt, R.C., 'Implications of Density in Hong Kong', *Journal of the American Institute of Planners*, Vol. 29, No. 3, August 1963, pp. 210–7.

Scott, I., 'Administering the New Towns of Hong Kong', *Asian Survey*, Vol. 22, No. 7, July 1982, pp. 659–75.

—— 'Administrative Growth and Change in the New Territories', in Leung, Cushman, and Wang (eds.) (1980), pp. 95–114.

Scott, I., and Cheek-Milby, K., 'An Overview of Hong Kong's Social Policy-Making Process', *The Asian Journal of Public Administration*, Vol. 8, No. 2, December 1986, pp. 166–76.

Shankland Cox, Binnie and Partners International, and Peat Marwick Mitchell & Co., *Tin Shui Wai Urban Development Master Plan* (Hong Kong, Mightycity Co. Ltd., 1980).

Sin, K.F., *Building Project Finance in Hong Kong: Law and Practice* (Singapore, Butterworths, 1987).

Sit, V.F.S., 'Hong Kong's New Towns Programme and Its Regional Implications', in Leung, Cushman, and Wang (eds.) (1980), pp. 397–418.

—— 'New Territories: Site for Hong Kong's Second Industrialization', in Sit (1981), pp. 238–49.

—— 'New Towns for the Future', in Sit (1981), pp. 142–59.

—— *Urban Hong Kong* (Hong Kong, Summerson Eastern, 1981).

Sit, V.F.S., and Birch, A., *Tuen Mun: From Ancient Port to City of The Future* (Hong Kong, Hong Kong Geographical Association and Tuen Mun Rural Committee, 1982).

Smart, A., 'The Development of Diamond Hill from Village to Squatter Area: A Perspective on Public Housing', *The Asian Journal of Public Administration*, Vol. 8, No. 1, June 1986, pp. 43–63.

Smith, I., *Administrative Adaptation and the New Towns Policy in Hong Kong*, Paper at Waigani Seminar on Urbanization, University of Papua New Guinea, Port Moresby, 1979.

Smyly, W.J., 'Tsuen Wan Township', *Far Eastern Economic Review*, Vol. 33, No. 9, 31 August 1961, pp. 395–421.

So, M.Y., 'A General Outline for Community Development in Tuen Mun', in Community Development Committee (1977), pp. 67–71.

—— 'The Role of Community Development in a New Town: A Social Worker's Experience' (in Chinese), *Welfare Quarterly of the Hong Kong Council of Social Service*, No. 62, Autumn 1977, pp. 21–5.

Stewart, D.T., *Public Transport for Several New Towns in Hong Kong* (Hong Kong, Maunsell Consultants Asia, 1983).

Szeto, W., 'The Work of the Town Planning Board', in Royal Town Planning Institute (1973), pp. 7–15.

Tang, R.C.P., 'Health and Medical Consideration in relation to the New Towns', in Hong Kong Committee of the International Council on Social Welfare (1976), pp. 133–5.

Tang, S.H., 'The Role of the Government in the Future Industrial Development of Hong Kong', in Jao, Leung, Wesley-Smith, and Wong (eds.) (1985), pp. 405–40.

Taylor, B., 'Development by Negotiation: Chinese Territory and the Development of Hong Kong and Macao', in Costa, Dutt, Ma, and Noble (eds.), (1988), pp. 103–15.

—— 'Rethinking the Territorial Development Strategy Planning Process in Hong Kong', *The Asian Journal of Public Administration*, Vol. 9, No. 1, June 1987, pp. 25–55.

—— *Rethinking the Territorial Development Strategy Planning Process* (Hong Kong, University of Hong Kong, Centre of Urban Studies and Urban Planning, Seminar Paper, 1986).

Vasoo, S., 'Residents' Organisations in the New Towns of Hong Kong and Singapore: Some Issues and Future Developments', *The Asian Journal of Public Administration*, Vol. 9, No. 2, December 1987, pp. 143–54.

Vigers, S., *New Town Planning in Sha Tin, Hong Kong — 1972–1982* (Edinburgh, University of Edinburgh, M.Phil. Thesis, 1982).

Wang, L.H., and Yeh, A.G.O., 'Public Housing-Led New Town Development: Hong Kong and Singapore', *Third World Planning Review*, Vol. 9, No. 1, February 1987, pp. 41–63.

Wiggham, E.B., 'Management for the New Town', in Hong Kong Committee of the International Council on Social Welfare (1976), pp. 15–23.

Wigglesworth, J.M., 'The Development of New Towns', in Dwyer (ed.) (1971), pp. 48–69.

—— 'Hong Kong's Approach to Planning for Major Urban Growth', *Habitat International*, Vol. 10, Nos. 1 and 2, 1986, pp. 93–102.

—— 'Planning in Hong Kong', *Journal of the Town Planning Institute*, Vol. 51, No. 7, July 1965, pp. 283–9.

—— *Planning Law and Administration in Hong Kong, with Particular Reference to the Position of the United Kingdom* (Hong Kong, University of Hong Kong, Ph.D. Thesis, 1986).

Will, B.F., 'Housing Design and Construction Methods', in Wong (ed.) (1978), pp. 91–127.

—— 'A Selected Bibliography on Housing in Hong Kong', in Wong (ed.) (1978), pp. 325–34.

Wong, A.K., *The Kaifong Associations and the Society of Hong Kong* (Taipei, Orient Cultural Service, 1972).

Wong, F.M., *Family Structure and Processes in a New Industrial Town* (Hong Kong, Chinese University of Hong Kong, Social Research Centre, Occasional Paper, 1977).

Wong, J., *The Cities of Asia: A Study of Urban Solutions and Urban Finance* (Singapore, University of Singapore/Economic Society of Singapore, 1976).

Wong, K.Y., 'New Towns: The Hong Kong Experience', in Cheng (ed.) (1982), pp. 118–30.

Wong, L.S.K., 'An Overview of Housing Provision and Housing Needs in Hong Kong', in Wong (ed.) (1978), pp. 23–54.

—— 'Socio-Economic Characteristics of Public Housing Provision', in Wong (ed.) (1978), pp. 128–59.

—— 'Squatters in Pre-War Hong Kong', *Journal of Oriental Studies,* Vol. 8, No. 1, January 1970, pp. 189–205.

—— 'The Squatter Problem', in Wong (ed.) (1978), pp. 204–32.

Wong, L.S.K. (ed.), *Housing in Hong Kong: A Multidisciplinary Study* (Hong Kong, Heinemann Asia, 1978).

Wu, C.T., *Development of Kwun Tong Industrial Area* (Los Angeles, University of California Los Angeles, School of Architecture and Planning, Working Paper No. 4, 1972).

Yeh, A.G.O., 'Employment Location and New Town Development in Hong Kong', in Hills (ed.) (1985), pp. 60–85.

—— 'New Towns in Hong Kong', in Choi, Fong, and Kwok (eds.) (1986), pp. 113–26.

—— 'Planning for Uncertainty: Hong Kong's Urban Development in the 1990s', *Built Environment*, Vol. 11, No. 4, 1985, pp. 252–67.

—— *Reference Materials on Urban Development and Planning in Hong Kong* (Hong Kong, University of Hong Kong, Centre of Urban Studies and Urban Planning, Working Paper, 1984).

—— 'Spatial Impacts of New Town Development in Hong Kong', in Phillips and Yeh (eds.) (1987), pp. 59–81.

—— *Urban Development and Planning in Hong Kong: A Research Guide* (Hong Kong, University of Hong Kong, Centre of Asian Studies, 1987).

Yeh, A.G.O., and Fong, P.K.W., 'Public Housing and Urban Development in Hong Kong', *Third World Planning Review*, Vol. 6, No. 1, February 1984, pp. 79–84.

Yeung, Y.M., and Drakakis-Smith, D.W., 'Comparative Perspective on Public Housing in Singapore and Hong Kong', *Asian Survey*, Vol. 14, No. 8, 1974, pp. 763–75.

—— 'Planning for High-Density Urban Centres: Lessons from Hong Kong and Singapore', in Leung, Cushman, and Wang (eds.) (1980), pp. 455–70.

—— 'Public Housing in the City States of Hong Kong and Singapore', in Taylor and Williams (1982), pp. 217–38 (see next section).

Other General References

Abercrombie, P., *Greater London Plan 1944* (London, His Majesty's Stationery Office, 1945).

Abrams, C., Kobe, S., and Koenigsberger, O., *Growth and Urban Renewal in Singapore: Report prepared for the Government of Singapore* (New York, United Nations Technical Assistance Programme, 1963).

Ackernecht, D., and Assaf, S., *Tall Buildings in Urban Context* (Dhahran, University of Petroleum and Minerals, College of Environmental Design, 1986).

Addenbrooke, P., Bruce, D., Courtney, I., Helliwell, S., Nisbet, A., and Young, T., *Urban Planning and Design for Public Transport* (London, Confederation of British Road Passenger Transport, 1981).

Ashworth, W., *The Genesis of Modern British Town Planning: A Study in Economic and Social History of the Nineteenth and Twentieth Centuries* (London, Routledge and Kegan Paul, 1954).

Bailey, J. (ed.), *New Towns in America: The Design and Development Process* (New York, Wiley, 1973).

Barlow, M., *Report of the Royal Commission on the Distribution of the Industrial Population*, Command 6153, (London, His Majesty's Stationery Office, 1940).

Barnett, J., *An Introduction to Urban Design* (New York, Harper and Row, 1982).

Bayley, S., *The Garden City: Unit 23*, Course A305, *1-2PRG — History of Architecture and Design 1890 — 1939* (*Arts: A Third Level Course*) (Milton Keynes, Open University Press, 1975).

Blumenfeld, H., 'Transportation in the Modern Metropolis', in Spreiringen (ed.) (1971), pp. 122–38.

Buchanan, C., and Partners, *South Hamsphire Study: Report on the Feasibility of Major Urban Growth* (London, Her Majesty's Stationery Office, 1966).

Buchanan, C.D., and others, *Traffic in Towns: A Study of the Long Term Problems of Traffic in Urban Areas — Report of the Working Group* (The Buchanan Report) (London, Her Majesty's Stationery Office, 1963).

Building Journal Forum, 'Fung Shui and Architecture: Star-Crossed Reality or Organised Superstition?', *Building Journal Hong Kong*, February 1986, pp. 70–3.

Burnley, I., and Forrest, J. (eds.), *Living in Cities: Urbanism and Society in Metropolitan Australia* (Sydney, Allen and Unwin, 1986).

Cherry, G.E. (ed.), *Shaping an Urban World: Planning in the Twentieth Century* (London, Mansell, 1980).

Cherry, G.E., *Cities and Plans: The Shaping of Urban Britain in the Nineteenth and Twentieth Centuries* (London, Arnold, 1988).

Chiang, M., 'Fung Shui and Its Application in City Planning', *Asian Architect and Contractor*, Vol. 15, No. 5, May 1986, pp. 19–22.

—— 'Fung Shui in the Design of Regions and Cities: Part 1 — The Theory and Numbers of Fung Shui in the Design of Regions and Cities', *Asian Architect and Contractor*, Vol. 15, No. 9, September 1986, pp. 26–8.

Chung, W.N., 'Classical Chinese Architecture and Landscape Design — I. The Rise and Fall of Empires, the Fortunes of Families', *Building Journal Hong Kong*, February 1986, pp. 76–7.

—— 'Classical Chinese Architecture and Landscape Design — II. Contrast and Neutral: the Modern Interpretation of Yin and Yang', *Building Journal Hong Kong*, March 1986, pp. 78–9.

Cities Commission, *Report to the Australian Government: A Recommended New Cities Programme for the Period 1973-1978* (Canberra, Australian Government Publishing Services, 1973).

Clapham, D., and English, J., *Public Housing: Current Trends and Future Developments* (Beckenham, Croom Helm, 1987).

Colonial Office, *Colonial Development and Welfare Advisory Committee Notes, No. 953* (London, Colonial Office, 1947).

Committee on the Regional Plan of New York and Its Environs, *Regional Plan of New York and Its Environs: Vol. III, Neighborhood and Community Planning — Regional Survey* (New York, Committee on the Regional Plan of New York and Its Environs, 1929).

Concannon, T.A.L., 'A New Town in Malaya: Petaling Jaya, Kuala Lumpur', *Malayan Journal of Tropical Geography*, Vol. 5, No. 1, 1955, pp. 39–43.

Conway, D.J., *Human Response to Tall Buildings* (Stroudsberg, Penn., Dowden Hutchison & Ross, 1977).

Cookson-Smith, P., 'A Celestial Planning Guide, Part I', *Building Journal Hong Kong*, February 1986, 73–5.

—— 'A Celestial Planning Guide, Part II', *Building Journal Hong Kong*, March 1986, pp. 70–5.

Creese, W.L., *Search for Environment: The Garden City, Before and After* (New Haven, Yale University Press, 1966).

Cullingworth, J.B., *Environmental Planning 1939–1969: Volume III, New Towns Policy* (London, Her Majesty's Stationery Office, 1979).

Dupree, H., *Urban Transportation: The New Town Solution* (Aldershot, Gower, 1987).

Edwards, H.M., *The Design of Suburbia: A Critical Study in Environmental History* (London, Pembridge Press, 1981).

Fraser, J.M., 'Planning and Housing at High Densities in Two Crowded Tropical Cities', *Town and Country Planning Summer School: Report of Proceedings, St. Andrews, 1960* (London, Town Planning Institute, 1960), pp. 104–16.

Freestone, R., 'The Conditions of the Cities and the Response: Early Garden City Concepts and Practice', in Burnley and Forrest (eds.) (1986), pp. 13–27.

Galantay, E.Y., *New Towns: Antiquity to the Present* (New York, George Braziller, 1975).

Gamer, R.E., *The Politics of Urban Development in Singapore* (Ithaca, Cornell University Press, 1972).

Golany, G., *New Town Planning: Principles and Practice* (New York, Wiley, 1976).

—— (ed.), *International Urban Growth Policies: New Town Contributions* (New York, Wiley, 1978).

Goldstein, S. (ed.), *Patterns of Urbanisation: Comparative Country Studies* (Liege, International Union for the Scientific Study of Population, 1975).

Hillman, M., and Potter, S., 'Movement Systems for New Towns', in Golany (ed.) (1978), pp. 37–52.

Houghton-Evans, W., 'Schemata in British New Town Planning', in Cherry (1980), pp. 101–28.

Housing Committee, *Housing Committee Report: Singapore* (Singapore, Government Printer, 1947).

Howard, E., *Tomorrow: A Peaceful Path to Real Reform* (London, Swan Sonnarschein, 1898). Currently reprinted as Howard, E., *Garden Cities of Tomorrow* (Eastbourne, Attic Books, 1985).

Jacobs, J., *The Death and Life of Great American Cities* (New York, Random House, 1961).

Johnson-Marshall, P., 'Residential Areas with Special Reference to High Density', in Kwok and Pun (eds.) (1982), pp. 60–6.

Le Corbusier, C.E., *The City of Tomorrow* (London, Architectural Press, 1929).

—— *The Radiant City* (trans.) (New York, Orion Press, 1964).

Koenigsberger, O.H., and Safie, M., *Urban Growth and Planning the Developing Countries of the Commonwealth — A Review of Experience from the Past 25 Years* (London, United Nations Interregional Seminar on New Towns, June 1973).

Lee, B.T., 'New Towns in Malaysia', in Phillips and Yeh (eds.) (1987), pp. 153–69.

Lim, H.K., *The Evolution of the Urban System in Malaya* (Kuala Lumpur, Penerbit Universiti Malaya, 1978).

Ling, A., *Runcorn New Town: Master Plan* (Runcorn, Runcorn Development Corporation, 1967).

Liu, T.K., 'Design for Better Living Conditions', in Yeh (ed.) (1975), pp. 126–9.

Livingston Development Corporation, *Livingston Plan* (Livingston, Livingston Development Corporation, 1979).

Llewellyn-Davies, R., Weeks, J., and Partners, *Washington New Town Master Plan* (Washington, County Durham, Washington Development Corporation, 1966).

Local Government Board, *Housing Manual on the Preparation of State-Aided Housing Schemes* (London, His Majesty's Stationery Office, 1919).

Lung, D., 'Fung Shui: An Intrinsic Way to Environmental Design, with illustration of Kai Hing Wei', *Asian Architect and Builder*, Vol. 8, No. 10, October 1979, pp. 16–23.

Merlin, P., *New Towns* (London, Methuen, 1971). Originally published as Merlin, P., *Les Villes Nouvelles* (Paris, Presses Universitaires de France, 1969).

Ministry of Housing and Local Government, *Northampton, Bedford and North Buckinghamshire Study* (London, Her Majesty's Stationery Office, 1965).

Ministry of Town and Country Planning Technical Team, *1946 Technical Report, Stevenage New Town — Provisional Development Proposals* (London, Ministry of Town and Country Planning, 1946).

Minoprio, A., 'Some Design Problems and Trends in the Planning of Towns', *Town and Country Planning Summer School: Report of Proceedings, Oxford University, 1951* (London, Town Planning Institute, 1951), pp. 21–42.

Mitchell, R.E., 'Some Social Implications of High Density Housing', *American Sociological Review*, Vol. 36, No. 1, February 1971, pp. 18–29.

New Towns Committee, *Interim Report*, Command 6759, (London, His Majesty's Stationery Office, 1946).

—— *Second Interim Report*, Command 6794, (London, His Majesty's Stationery Office, 1946).

—— *Final Report*, Command 6876, (London, His Majesty's Stationery Office, 1946).

Osborn, F.J., and Whittick, A., *New Towns: Their Origins, Achievements and Progress* (London, Leonard Hill, 1977).

Pacione, M. (ed.), *Problems and Planning in Third World Cities* (Beckenham, Croom Helm, 1981).

Pepler, G.L., *Report of the Interdepartmental Group on Administrative and*

Legislative Arrangements needed for the Development of Satellite or New Towns (London, Ministry of Town and Country Planning, 1944).

Perry, C., 'The Neighborhood Unit', in Committee on the Regional Plan of New York (1929), pp. 34–5.

Peterborough Development Corporation, *Greater Peterborough Master Plan* (Peterborough, Peterborough Development Corporation, 1970).

Purdom, C.B., *The Building of Satellite Towns* (London, Dent, 1925).

Rodwin, L., *The British New Towns Policy: Problems and Implications* (Cambridge, Massachussets, Harvard University Press, 1956).

Rubenstein, J., 'French New-Town Policy', in Golany (ed.) (1978), pp. 75–103.

Schaffer, F., 'The New-Town Movement in Britain', in Golany (ed.) (1978), pp. 13–22.

Scott, L.F., *Report of the Committee on Land Utilisation in Rural Areas*, Command 6378, (London, His Majesty's Stationery Office, 1942).

Singapore Improvement Trust, *Master Plan: Report of Survey* (Singapore, Government Printing Office, 1955).

Singapore State and City Planning Office, *Singapore Long Range Concept Plan* (Singapore, Government Publication Office, 1970).

Soon, T.K., 'Ring: As an Answer to Highrise Living', *Singapore Straits Times*, 26 April 1975, p. 11.

Spreiringen, P.D.I. (ed.), *The Modern Metropolis — Its Origins, Growth, Characteristics, and Planning: Selected Essays by Hans Blumenfeld* (Cambridge, Massachussets, MIT Press, 1971).

Stern, R.A.M. (ed.), with Messenga, J.M., *The Anglo-American Suburb* (London, Architectural Design, 1981).

Tan, K.J., Loh, C.T., Tan, S.A., Lau, W.C., and Kwok, K., 'Physical Planning and Design', in Wong and Yeh (eds.) (1985), pp. 56–112.

Taylor, J.L., and Williams, D.G. (eds.), *Urban Planning Practice in Developing Countries* (Oxford, Pergamon, 1982).

Thomas, R., 'Britain's New-Town Demonstration Project', in Golany (ed.) (1978), pp. 23–35.

Unwin, R., *Town Planning in Practice* (London, T. Fisher Unwin, 1909).

Wang, L.H., 'Residential New Town Development in Singapore: Background, Planning and Design', in Phillips and Yeh (eds.) (1987), pp. 23–40.

Wang, L.H., and Tan, T.H., 'Singapore', in Pacione (ed.) (1981), pp. 218–49.

Watanabe, S.J., 'Garden City Japanese Style: The Case of Den-en Toshi Company Ltd., 1918–28', in Cherry (ed.) (1980), pp. 129–43.

Wilson, L.H., 'Cumbernauld: The Design of a High Density New Town', *Town and Country Planning Summer School: Report of Proceedings, St. Andrews, 1960* (London, Town Planning Institute, 1960), pp. 57–74.

Wilson, L.H., and Wolmersley, L., *Irvine New Town Planning Proposals* (London, Her Majesty's Stationery Office, 1967).

—— *Redditch New Town: Report on Planning Proposals* (Redditch, Redditch Development Corporation, 1966).

Wong, A.K., and Yeh, S.H.K. (eds.), *Housing a Nation: Twenty Five Years of Public Housing in Singapore* (Singapore, Maruzen Asia, 1985).

Yeh, S.H.K. (ed.), *Public Housing in Singapore: A Multi-Disciplinary Study* (Singapore, Singapore University Press, 1975).

Yeung, Y.M. (ed.), *A Place to Live: More Effective Low-Cost Housing in Asia* (Ottawa, International Development Research Centre, 1983).

Index